WE THE PEOPLE – GET TRUMP

Because They Want to Get America & Us
- Trump's just standing in their Way

By Gus George Mollasis
With a foreword by the Forgotten Men, Women &
Children of America

PAGE LEFT BLANK INTENTIONALLY

Copyright © Year 2024

All Rights Reserved by **Gus George Mollasis.**

No part of this publication may be reproduced in any form, or by any means, electronic or mechanical, including photocopying, recording, or any information browsing, storage, or retrieval system, without permission in writing from Gus George Mollasis.

ISBN

Hardcover: 978-1-965134-76-4

Paperback: 978-1-965134-77-1

A NEW TESTAMENT FOR FREEDOM

What follows is the follow-up to my book Get Trump. Within the following pages are many events I witnessed as our country experienced one of the most challenging times in our history. Like the Good Lord who had to come back to make right a world that had gone so terribly wrong, so too did a man named Donald J. Trump have to come back to right the many wrongs in a noble fight between good and evil to restore and save our republic.

Contents

Dedication --

Prologue America – A Republic Rises and is Made Great Again -- 1

Foreword by the Forgotten Men, Women & Children in America --- 6

I. The 2020 Election – Rigged or the Safest Ever? -------- 7

II. January 6, 2021 -- 30

III. Covid-19: The Gift that Keeps Giving---------------- 86

IV. Lessons, Flashbacks, Love of Movies & Getting Canceled-- 116

V. Joe Biden – A Presidential Puppet Like No Other -- 167

VI. Out to *Get Trump, America, and You* ------------------ 189

VII. We the People and Our American Dreams -------- 205

VIII. Time for a Rewrite and New Leading Man or Woman? 254

IX. Usual Suspects Act Out Their Narrative ---------------- 274

X. Orwellian Ministry of Lies ------------------------------ 287

XI. Only One Man Can Save The Republic ------------ 308

XII. America – A Republic Rises and Is Made Great Again -- 333

XIII. Good vs Evil & the Only Vote That Counts --------- 347

Epilogue: Not So Great Debate Awakens Nation As to what's at stake--- 451

Afterword: A Cry for Transparency & Fair Elections ----- 459

Acknowledgements and One very special number --------- 460

Dedication

For Mom and Dad who made our home great and helped make America greater every day

Prologue
America – A Republic Rises and is Made Great Again

The Trump MAGA Movement is a story they can't bury. No matter how hard they try.

On the day that they tried to kill the MAGA movement with a bullet, Donald J. Trump rose bloodied and determined not to stay on the ground – but instead, rise to his feet and hurl three fist pumps into the air while yelling...*Fight...Fight...Fight!*

It is a moment in American history that they don't want you to see, remember, and revere like so many proud days in our past. These vignettes of heroism and bravery make the idea of America into something more than an idea and into actual reality in real time of a man facing death and taking a bullet for liberty.

Those heroic moments of patriots like the founders sacrificing everything to form the union. Men like *Thomas Jefferson, James Madison, John Adams* and Ben Franklin envisioned, penned, and edited their vision of America. They are sometimes remembered in history books. The stories of *George Washington, Patrick Henry,* and *Paul Revere* fighting for freedom and liberty come alive in the telling of their stories. And finally, the goodness and wisdom of Abraham Lincoln, who healed our nation when it needed it most.

I have seen, all too often, their stories glossed over, written with a woke revisionist pen, as idiots, traitors, and America haters who lack sense and common sense, period, pushed to have their statues torn down and their stories erased and forgotten.

Most shockingly, within days of a seminal moment in American history taking place live and in living color for all of our eyes to see, almost immediately, the press started shaping the narrative of what took place - as an assassin's bullet came with centimeters of changing American history forever – and not for the better.

It started with the coverage on CNN who uncharacteristically were carrying the event live. The initial headlines from the founders of HEADLINE NEWS. "*Secret Service rushes Trump off stage after he falls at rally,*" CNN's headline read shortly after news broke that there was possible gunfire at a Pennsylvania Trump rally.

We have been told that the first draft of history is made by our so-called journalists. Yet just as the assassin thankfully missed killing the president by mere centimeters, CNN, The name you can trust in the *news*, initially missed the story and blew the headline. Lawmakers noticed and were outraged at the downplaying of such a historic event. "*Falls at rally'? Is this a real headline? This is disgraceful,*" Sen. Josh Hawley, R-Mo., posted to X on Friday evening. "*Even in a horrifying moment such as this, they just can't help themselves,*" Sen. Marco Rubio, R-Fla., posted. Other commenters and media critics also slammed the Washington Post for a headline stating: "*Trump escorted away after loud noises at Pa. rally.*" [1]

In the moments that followed this historic, tragic, and nearly catastrophic event that took the life of one American hero, they could not help themselves. The former president's oldest son took notice.

"Someone attempted to assassinate my father tonight, and this is what CNN is focused on. These people are vile. CNN's Jamie Gangel attacks Trump for saying, "*Fight! Fight! Fight!*" after someone tried to murder him. Literally, she complains about what he did five seconds after he was shot: "That's not the message that we want to be *sending right now. We want to tamp it down.*"

Tamp it down. And tamp it up. All in the service of *Getting TRUMP* and writing their first draft of history. A history that they have been trying to write, re-write, and grotesquely edit ever since Donald J. Trump made his way down the escalator.

They have lied about Trump's successes as a president while ignoring the incompetence and inability of his successor to not only do the job – but even show up for the job. And in doing so they white-washed, in black and white print and with the streak of yellow journalism that would have made *William Randolph Hearst* blush. The coverage of the Biden coup in the days following the ultra-successful and unifying RNC convention and just days after a real live former American President and probable future president was almost taken from us because they want to push his heroic story to the back pages of the news and history.

That is why it is up to us, as eyewitnesses of history – to make sure that not only they get the story right but that the story continues to be told. It is up to us to remember, report and document all we can from this time as history was being made before us.

It is up to us to remember that they first stole, yes, I said, stole an election from the 45th President. This after savaging many of his noble efforts to make America great in his first term with spying, impeachments and a China Virus, whose origins they will not investigate. Thankfully, they mostly failed and he mostly succeeded. He was more right than not. And they were more wrong. History will show they were, more times than not, on the wrong side of it. History will and must record that, as the 45th president attempted to run to become the 47th president, the full force of a deep state establishment government came at him with everything that their legal arsenal could muster, not as warfare but as lawfare. In bringing four preposterous indictments in courts all across the land their goal was easy to read. They would Get Trump by bankrupting him financially, if not spiritually, in the greatest display of election interference ever seen.

Now, after lying to the American public for years about President Biden's condition, they want you to believe their story and lies. As President Trump visited families whose lives were shattered by illegal aliens who took the lives of their loved ones, the story about a woman that they want to make a little history with, Kamala Harris, is being rewritten –just in time they hope for her coronation. Obsessed with breaking glass ceilings but caring not a thing about getting the story right and telling the truth, they are trying to scrub the title of BORDER CZAR from the Harris narrative. But they can scrub all they want; that was her biggest and most important job, and in true Harris form - she BLEW IT!

That brings us to one of the most iconic images ever seen in the long and great history of our republic. It is akin to the image of the soldiers raising the flag at Iwo Jima. The shot of former president Trump raising his fist while mouthing fight, fight, fight, just minutes after a bullet glances his ear and his life is spared. It is a moment and image that shall live on in the hearts and minds of those who witnessed it. It is a moment of history. Our American history. A moment that someday will be captured in stone for all to see and remember and be inspired by, a moment that is carved into our collective conscience as a people.

And it is a moment that some sadly don't want us to remember, and it is the moment that they want us to quickly forget. Because it happened, and it is history. And of course, it shows the former president in a light that is, at the very least – courageous and at most, heroic.

And that is why they want to bury the story, the president, and the whole movement.

As the story played out and the investigation as to why a 20-year-old loner and loser was able to outfox law enforcement, the FBI, and the Secret Service, some of those in hearings reluctantly asked questions, knowing that the longer this went on, the more focus and light it would shine on the brave man who took the bullets and then raised his hand to encourage a nation to fight for its freedom and liberty. Patrick Henry would be damn proud of not only President Trump but also the MAGA nation as a whole.

Yet it is the cowards, traitors, and the despicable who hide with not a pen in hand and not from a rooftop with a gun, but instead with a modern keyboard in a darkened room where they can spew their hateful theories.

"Trump planned it."

"Trump wasn't shot by a bullet it was shrapnel."

"Damn it. The kid missed his shot to make a little history and America great again."

It was their first shot at re-writing this chapter of American history. And because of the sickness inside them- they missed their mark and failed to see what we saw on that day.

Even Google tried to get in on the act, appearing to hamper searches for the event on its search engine. In response to reports that Google blocked the Trump assassination attempt from appearing in autocomplete search results, The Washington Stand found that a Google search for "assassination attempt" yields autocomplete results such as "on Hitler" and "on Ronald Reagan" but no mention is made of Trump. Likewise, a search for "assassination attempt on" returns autocomplete results for such figures as Adolf Hitler, Ronald Reagan, Vladimir Lenin, Bob Marley, Harry Truman, Prince Charles, Gerald Ford, and Pope John Paul II. Again, no mention is made of Trump. A search for "assassination attempt on tru" yields autocomplete results such as "assassination attempt on Truman," "how many presidents had an assassination attempt," and "assassination attempt meaning." A search for "assassination attempt on Trump" is met with no autocomplete results or suggestions.[2]

No amount of revisionist history will change what happened on July 13th, 2024. It was a fateful day when a former president of the United States faced an assassin's bullets. He took a bullet and a shot that nearly killed him and in the moments after, he raised his hands defiantly as he professed to fight, fight, for the country he so loved.

It was a moment that will live on in our memory. It is destined to become a vital, inspirational, and hopeful day that has become a part of our history and will live on throughout history. And shame on us, if we, as patriotic witnesses of history, allow anyone to bury this story and retell our history and lie about what really happened on that day. It's up to us to tell the story accurately and bravely to future generations of proud Americans so that they will always remember the day when history was made and written. A time when a president named Trump, after being shot and hit, rose up with clenched fists, defiantly vowing to - FIGHT, FIGHT, FIGHT for his country. A day that will always be remembered. A day in American history when a man named Donald J. Trump and a movement named MAGA refused to die.

Foreword by the Forgotten Men, Women & Children in America

We had been forgotten for too long. Then he came along. The Outsider. The Real estate guy. The TV star with the funny hair and the never-die attitude. He never gave up on us, and that's why we can never give up on him and America. We are forgotten no more. The hardworking Americans who want a piece of the American dream as long as we are willing to work hard for it. The immigrants who wait in line and come through the front door and do not take the easy, sneaky, and illegal way into the country over the border. The soldiers who proudly fight for our country. This man supported us through thick and thin- tried to avoid wars, and when some of us died, he remembered our names and honored our memories to our families. The children taken into trafficking and slavery and the kids not born yet- he didn't forget us, and he fought to give us a voice. The American family who struggles to make ends meet, he hears us and wants to lower our burden. For those of us who are very sick – he fought to give us a right to try medicines that might help. And when a virus was released as a weapon, he fought to give us options and never forced the shot on us. He is a man who believes in America first. And he is a man who has not forgotten any one of us. It does not matter where we live, how we live and or who we live with, nor does it matter if we are black, white, or brown, a male or a female; he is fighting for all of us and our chance at our American Dream.

He hasn't forgotten us, and that's why we can never forget him. He will make America Great Again - because, let's face it, he's already done it once. He gets us. He gets America. That is Why We, the People, Get Trump and why, on Election Day, we won't forget Donald J. Trump.

With gratitude,

The once-forgotten men, women, and children of America, remembered by the 45th President of the United States and, God willing, the 47th President of the United States

I. The 2020 Election – Rigged or the Safest Ever?

Holy Spirit visits me at foot of Statue on Election Eve, -2020

Out In public On Election Day –then back home to watch Horror story Unfold

A Pause that doesn't refresh – but steals

Trump won and you know it

Where's the Proof that Trump won? Where's the Proof that Biden won?

Liars figure and Figures Lie

Flag waving with Fellow Patriots protesting a crooked Election

Holy Spirit visits me at foot of Statue on Election Eve -2020

I had stared at this statue that adorned our waterfront in Sarasota, Florida for many years. A statue depicting the iconic kiss planted by one happy sailor to an unsuspecting nurse in Times Square on VJ day back in August of 1945.

The kiss – and the statue that depicted it here were named *Unconditional Surrender*. A statue that signified the ending of a war. And a statue that strangely and sadly had turned into a lightning rod of political controversy.

To me, it was a place I would go occasionally for inspiration and, dare I say, to feel a sense of PRIDE.

Pride in what? In America -and for a time in America when *we the people, united to fight the real forces of evil, fascists,* and tyrants in World War II.

This statue, to me, at least represented VJ-Day and an end to World War II. A time for celebration – that "WAR IS OVER" – and a time for Americans, all Americans, to be grateful and happy for the peace. A time when a sailor kissing a nurse in Times Square was captured on the cover of Life Magazine and the iconic image was to be forever remembered and frozen in our memory of a time when the fighting stopped and our boys were coming home. A time when good beat evil celebrated with a kiss.

Looking up at the statue, I thought of all those who fought in that World War. Thought of those who never came back, those who came back wounded, and those who came back to their homeland after fighting on foreign soil to keep America and the world free from tyranny.

As I pondered – I thought of my own personal fight and take on this statue. How I captured what it meant in a PBS documentary titled *"Unconditional Surrender."* I thought about how most of the people I talked to about the statue reacted to it in a favorable way as they imitated the kiss and posed with a loved one. I thought about the detractors who wanted it moved because they felt it *wasn't good art*. Was it great art? Probably not. That wasn't the point to me, and I found it to most people. Most people who visited the statue told me that it made them feel good either about themselves or their country.

And that's why – on Election Eve 2020, I went to this spot to do a little soul searching, some pondering, and maybe even a little praying for what was to be over the next 24 hours or so. As I prayed, pondered and pontificated – I kept seeing the number 316. Now, 316 was a good number scripturally. John 3:16 to Christians means one thing –in fact, it means everything - to those who profess to have faith in Jesus Christ.

"For God so loved the world: That he gave his only begotten Son, that whosoever believeth in him should not perish, but have everlasting life."

A verse about sacrifice, for sure. About faith – absolutely. But a proclamation much bigger than that. A passage about *"Everlasting life."* Forever. Free to live forever if you believe in the Lord. Seemingly an easy deal for some to make. Not so easy for others. For the man running for reelection, it was a deal that he had already made. And why, as I stood here looking at this statue titled *"Unconditional Surrender,"* I saw and even heard those numbers 3:16. And why, as I said a quiet prayer at the feet of the sailor and the nurse on Sarasota's Bayfront, I felt confident and calm as the sun was setting on the evening before Election night, 2020.

Out In public On Election Day –then back home to watch Horror story Unfold

Two rules on how I watch my *MUST See TV*.

When my beloved Detroit Red Wings are in the Stanley Cup Playoffs, and I'm not there to cheer them on in person, I can't watch them on TV in public for a variety of reasons. I can't watch multiple screens with strangers who more or less have a varied understanding of the game and a stake in the outcome. And to be completely honest, if someone on my team *F-ups* on the ice –there's a great chance the F-bombs will be unleashed, sadly, by me. And because of that, I spare those out in public –both my excess passion for my team in Red and my lack of control in pulling for them.

I feel the same way about *Presidential Election Night*.

Too many people. Too many distractions. An inability to focus and an inability to be calm.

I know and get who I am. Still against my better judgment, I ventured out to a big Election Night gathering held at a Hotel replete with food, beverages, and plenty of MAGA-hatted supporters of President Trump.

Saw many familiar faces there. Gentlemen in jackets. Attractive ladies on their arms. A plethora of smart, well-dressed, and groomed folks donning their Trump buttons or caps with the appropriate "Make America Great Again" messaging.

I joined them, attired in my black jacket, white shirt, Casablanca tie, and, of course, my red MAGA hat, feeling that this was one of the few places I felt safe enough to come out and wear my Trump attire. I had kept much of *my Trump stuff* - hats, shirts, mugs, etc. in the closet over the years, choosing not to wear them out, not because I wasn't proud of our President, but because I didn't want to face the wrath of those who hated, and got red when they saw the red of our official uniform. So I chose to wear my Red to Trump rallies and meetings where like-minded people met, and the threat of my tires being slashed or my car being keyed was at a minimum.

With me on this night, I brought a few copies of my book, *Get Trump*. I planned on giving away my book as a goodwill gesture on this special night that I, and many others, had hoped would be a victory party for not only our candidate – but also for our country.

After hanging out for a bit with some friends and making my rounds around the crowded and friendly venue, I found a spot near the bar and watched as the results began to come in. It was hard hearing the pundits on TV with crowd noise, so after a short while I decided to say my goodbyes and head home to watch the results come in. Before I did, I noticed that the vote in Georgia was extremely close. That wasn't a good sign. Something seemed weird. I headed home a little shaken and not sure what the night would bring.

A Pause that doesn't refresh – but steals

Coca-Cola. Love it. The taste. The fizz. The bottle. The old ads. I am a collector of Coca-Cola memorabilia. Not so much anymore. No room. And who is going to want this stuff when I die? Anyway, I have this classic cardboard ad in mint condition with *two wholesome, beautiful American girls* pointing to a globe and saying – *"Here's to our G.I. Joes."*

The date is 1944. The location they're pointing to is Europe. The D-Day invasion. The message is clean, clear, and made with a united purpose that's easy to understand. Coca-Cola also had another slogan that they used over the years. *"The pause that refreshes"* Great campaign. Great message. I thought about that as I looked at the two gals featured on my Coca-Cola collectible on Election Night 2020, as those counting the votes over the airwaves suddenly paused.

Needless to say, I wasn't *toasting this Joe* running for President, and this pause was anything but refreshing. All of a sudden with Trump holding big leads in battleground races, THEY STOPPED COUNTING VOTES!

What? Why? Where?

As much of *America Slept* -something foul-smelling was being uncorked on Election Night. I recognized it right away, *this lack of fizz* that they were imposing, not on our taste buds, but on the power of our votes. A pause that refreshes? Hardly. More appropriately, a pause that steals.

But credit must be given to those who created this story just in time for Election Night, 2020. The scriptwriters, those responsible for concocting this improbable narrative about the possibility of a *Red Wave Mirage –on Election Night 2020*, had forewarned and foreshadowed the plot twist to anyone in Camp Blue or Camp Red who was listening and paying the least bit of attention.

To those in the Blue Biden camp – the not-so-subliminal message was clear, *"Don't worry if Joe is down early; it's just a mirage, and he will ultimately WIN."* And the message to those in Trump's Red camp, *"Not so fast, your MAGA boy may be winning early, but this thing isn't even close to being over."*

Would you like a Coke while we wait for the results? A Red Mirage – & The Pause that doesn't refresh.

As I mentioned, I have always been a fan of Coca-Cola, and I love its unique taste. The signature and trademark bottle. The slogans and jingles. *"It's the real Thing."* "I'd like to teach the world to sing..." Coca-Cola, as much as any product, represented Madison Avenue branding at its best.

And now one of their slogans or phrases that I liked best was, *"Coca-Cola, the pause that refreshes,"* threatened to give me indigestion. I don't think I was the only one feeling that way.

With roots in Atlanta, Georgia, The Coca-Cola Company had become iconic and synonymous with America in the way that *Elvis, Levi's, and Mickey Mouse* were symbols for the good old USA. But on this night, as he sat in the White House awaiting results, the man who knew a little bit about branding himself, the 45th President of the United States, was sure about one thing. He, like the drink that he loved, was the "the real thing," and not the fake thing or fake candidate. Years ago, he coined the term fake news. And years before that touted himself as "The Donald." On this night, the man who was his own man and his own brand felt it in his heart, head, and gut that he would be reelected President of the United States. Then he took another sip of his Coke and, after a brief pause, looked quizzically at the TV Screen.

Still, the 45th President felt decent. Confident. Then he took another sip and gazed at the screen. Something was starting to bother him and hit him in his gut, but he couldn't put his finger on it- at least not yet.

Well ahead in the key swing states, like in 2016, The President had one of those Yogi Berra moments, "Déjà vu All over again." And while he was ahead, he knew what the great Yankee catcher knew and professed, *"It ain't over till it's over."*

Then, all of a sudden, it hit him. A pop. But not a soda pop. The sound of the fizz being taken out of the election. A paused vote count that was far from refreshing.

Someone named JAMES Bradley from California, of all places, tweeted on TWITTER, the social media platform that The President was banned from, recently reminding us all where Trump stood when they stopped counting on ELECTION NIGHT.

James Bradley (@JamesBradleyCA) tweeted at 3:04 PM on Mon, Aug 14, 2023:

On November 3rd, 2020, when the vote count was halted that night:

Trump held PA by 682,000 votes (15.2%)
Trump held GA by 311,000 votes (7.5%)
Trump held MI by 307,000votes (9.8%)
Trump held WI by 128,000 votes (4.9%)
Trump held NC by   77,000 votes   (1.4%)

In the morning when the counting resumed, miraculously, Joe Biden was ahead in all the counts.

And all over the White House, all that remained were dashed hopes, lost votes, and many empty bottles and cans of Coca-Cola scattered about, a symbol of a time when many American people all woke up the day after the Presidential Election with a bad taste in their mouths.

Trump won, and you know it

Do you think still think that Biden won in 2020? Really? Come on, man. He. Him. Her. Or She.

Or if you are curious, have a pulse, and at least have a brain and maybe think Trump won in 2020.

Come on, man, you can tell me. After all, you've seen, do you still believe *Sleepy Joe* cobbled together 81 million votes to win the last election?

After what I've seen, I'm more convinced than ever he didn't win, but it's more because of what I haven't seen over the last nearly four years. That's why they are trying to *GET TRUMP* so badly.

They know what happened last time. What really happened?

They cheated. In many ways and forms. They know their candidate is not only up to the task, but their narrative of being compassionate and humble went out the window as he attacked half of the country, calling them extremists.

But it is he and his policies that are extreme. An Invaded border. High Inflation. Wars all over the planet. Rising crime rates. And on and on. If you still think he won, well, that's your opinion. But where is your proof? Where are his supporters? Have they all abandoned him? Where are all those 81 million voters?

You'd think you'd see a few t-shirts, bumper stickers or yard signs. I have seen none. Because they don't exist. They never did. They were made up. Like the Joe Biden narrative itself. Phony. Fake.

And if you really press them, really get into their face, they will blink and admit that he didn't get all those votes. But you know what? They don't care. All that they care about is that they beat Trump and want to beat him again.

No cost is too high. And that disturbs me as much as anything. Trump won and they know it. And they know that he will win again. What they will do to try and stop him should scare everyone.

Where's the Proof that Trump won? Where's the Proof that Biden won?

It depends on your level of curiosity and of course, your ability to seek and find the proof.

PROOF. Where is the proof that there was fraud in the 2020 Election- to the point that it made a difference in the outcome? *Where is the proof that the Election was stolen?*

They all want proof. The media. The swampy establishment types. All those who reside in cushy government jobs in DC which includes senators, congressmen, their entourages, and anyone who makes a living by constantly being re-elected and keeping their jobs and thus maintaining their influence over and not serving in the best interests of the American people.

They all want proof now. These folks who are not the least bit curious in investigating any evidence that the 2020 Presidential Election could have been and most likely was stolen. Just saying that invites a look of disdain from the types in power —who at one time were eager to chase any lead down any rabbit hole if it led to one place — *Getting Donald Trump*. Forever, their goal, Getting Trump and stopping the movement to wake up America and the American electorate. That's why they tried as hard as they could to fabricate the lie and build upon it that supposedly had them catching the orange man red-handed as he, with the help of the once great red power Russia – colluded and fixed the 2016 Election. With zeal, they chased any preposterous tale – if it meant getting him and stopping his effort to make America Great Again. Stories of golden showers and whispers in the dark were proof enough to provoke wall-to-wall coverage and investigation after investigation —that led to not one —but two specious impeachments of the president and a waste of time and taxpayer money.

They accused with no proof. Savagely attacked a man, and his supporters with not a scintilla of believable evidence – and now they demanded unshakeable proof that the election was stolen while stating there is no time to investigate any claims that 2020 was rigged, stolen, or at the least suspicious.

Still they have time and taxpayer money to go after and Get Trump for, in essence – a third impeachment with their less than curious and partisan show trial – ala the Soviets – that is, their January 6th Insurrection trials.

Their curiosity to investigate is always at a fever pitch. Like the judges in Salem, Massachusetts from darker days in our history, they know where there is smoke, there is fire, and they know how to tell a good witch from a bad witch. But most importantly, they knew which witch to bring into the People's House and question.

Nancy Pelosi? Not the least bit curious to ask her a question.

Some lower-level woman who worked with the president's chief of staff allegedly heard his security detail talking about Trump's temperament and rage- to the point that he grabbed the wheel of his Presidential Limo demanding he be driven down to the Capitol so that he could – what? Take his part in storming the Capitol?

So the witch trial continued with one goal- to get Trump and prevent him from ever becoming President again. Two show animals were brought in to give the trial an air of legitimacy – two supposed Republicans – Liz Cheney and Adam Kinzinger – two extraordinary creatures –their scientific name *Rhinocerotidae* – better known as pure RINOS – Republicans in name only, who were only there because they hated Donald J. Trump.

They were eager to highlight anything that hurt Trump and hide anything that helped him. The perfect foils to the former president and a talking point that the left loved citing, the fact that they were Republicans. But like all true RINOS, they would turn on a dime if it benefited them and moved their agenda along. And the agenda was clear – regarding the J-6 witch trials, implicate the former president as being the instigator of an insurrection to overthrow the government and stop a peaceful transfer of power. That they fail to mention that of the hundreds of thousands of Trump supporters who gathered on that day to peacefully protest, only a relative handful of patriots from all over America acted violently, and there is more than growing evidence that they were coerced and coaxed into entering the Capitol-by-capitol police and potentially Federal agents. They want you to believe that this was a pre-planned, orchestrated coup by all the president's men and women to take over the government and pull it off without any real weapons. Finally, the glaring storyline that they never mention concerns *Ashli Babbit*, a Trump supporter through and through and the only person to die that day as a direct result of the protest at the hands of an incredibly dubious capitol police officer who had a sketchy history of acting irresponsibly with a firearm.

Those were the shots being fired from both sides.

Trump and the MAGA nation had gathered on January 6, 2021, utilizing their constitutional right to peacefully protest an election that they felt was stolen. The J-6 committee was there to find Trump guilty of instigating an insurrection and yet one more impeachable act to add to their Get Trump laundry list. But the list that remains the longest is the one providing questions and acknowledges all the evidence *regarding potential cheating* that was either ignored, downplayed or dismissed because it didn't have standing and didn't fit with their narrative.

From common sense to *mathematical anomalies.* To a *pause in the vote* count on election night. To *unprecedented bell-weather indicators* being turned upside down. To *votes being discovered under tables and run through machines in Georgia after officials were told to go home, after a break in a water main* that never happened. To the dropping off a votes in the middle of the night to pinging sounds and *mules taking selfies as proof they made their deliveries* in the landmark film *2000 Mules.* From *pizza boxes covering windows in Detroit* so that the vote counting could not be viewed by the public to the biggest evidence of all - The *Media Suppression of Hunter Biden's Story with the help of TWITTER & FBI to kill the story* and help Biden win.

It's been reported that had they known about the story – 17% of the electorate *would not have voted for BIDEN.* That's not an insignificant amount (17 %). That's enough to swing the election taking it from a close nail-biter win for Biden to a Trump landslide. *And in a recent poll 79% of all Americans believe that Trump would have won if they had known about Hunter's laptop.*[3]

It's been echoed by some, as if to be some kind of consolation prize or a disqualifier, that *"there's always cheating and fraud–* but is there enough to change the election results?"

If you're that laissez-faire about fraud, what is the number that gets you angry or concerned?

But the real proof that Trump won last time, is what they are doing to him this time around as the 2024 election approaches.

The *election interference.* The *trials.* The *indictments.* The *conviction.* The deep state digging in. The Elites smearing. The Establishment swearing to destroy Trump at all costs. All the insiders get together and collaborate to make sure that the one true outsider who serves the people and not them doesn't get the keys to the kingdom again. The Watergate-like cover-up regarding the puppet in the white house with an all-out and coordinated effort to cover for the cognitive shortcomings of Joe Biden by large portions of the government, including Kamala Harris and the Biden Administration, the media, academia, and Hollywood. This interference already apparent in the 2024 election, suppressing vital information on candidate Joe Biden while blocking other potential candidates who could have secured the nomination. And finally bullets rang out in the direction of Trump at one of his rallies. *The ultimate election interference was miraculously prevented* by either fate or luck by a turn of a head in a field in rural Pennsylvania.

Election Interference. Cheating. Whatever you call it. And the reasons they do it is simple.

One: They believe they can get away with it as they continue to get Trump and get you.

Two. They know Trump won in 2020 and they have no reason to believe a lower energy, less sharp, and less popular Biden than even before, has a snowball's chance in hell of defeating Trump.

Number one proof to me that there was cheating in the election relies on evidence but is also made from the gut and from anecdotal information that I see and don't see every day.

Do you really think that Joe Biden garnered all that excitement and motivated 81 million people to vote for him with the campaign he ran from his basement? Please.

Having been to a number of Trump rallies, I know the energy there is measurable, real, passionate, and reliable. These events are filled with loyal Trump supporters who love their country and their candidate – a man fighting for them and their rights to life, liberty, and the pursuit of happiness.

Fast forward to the cusp of the 2024 election, and all the signs that were there in 2020 are once again there today. Energy and Enthusiasm from Trump while Biden stumbles like a zombie through his campaign and eventually his Waterloo on a June night at a debate in Georgia.

The polls are pointing to a Trump landslide. That is why they are scrambling to remove and replace him with anybody- Hell, it's been rumored that Jimmy Carter has been contacted. He'd be the perfect choice. Good man. Bad President. One with a short time to live. Jimmy and Hillary. Jimmy and Michelle, what the hell. That could be the bumper sticker.

But seriously, what if Biden survives, secures the nomination, continues to run, and somehow gets the votes to win? *Not the people who voted - but the votes to win.* What would you say then if by some chance, this corpse cobbles together enough votes from dead people voting Chicago-style and illegals voting from around the world to WIN the election again?

What would you say?

You'd say something was wrong, and it was rigged. And you would not be wrong.

Finally, do you know the biggest evidence that Biden did not win the election in 2020 and was merely installed? The fact that they lied about what we could all plainly see in front of us for four years. The decaying of an old frail man came into focus on a debate stage. If they can lie about that, they can surely lie about what is much harder to see- the votes stolen, created, and jammed through the system in the middle of the night while America slept.

Michael Charles, author of *Save America Now, Rules for Conservatives, and the Birth Famine* has some thoughts of who won the election in 2020.[4]

Charles points out that: *"At about midnight on the East Coast, Trump led in all the battleground states by large margins. The betting odds were more than 75% for Trump to win. Then for some unexplainable reason WISCONSIN, MICHIGAN, PENNSYLVANIA, NORTH CAROLINA and NEVADA all stopped counting votes simultaneously…in unison…took a "pause" at around 1 AM. None of those states counted any additional votes for the next three hours. So what did they do for those 3 hours?"*

Charles points out a couple of things:

1. *"All of those 5 states have Democrat governors".*

2. *Suddenly during the three-hour shutdown, in the dead of night when most people were sleeping, all those states found enough votes for Biden to catch Trump. Five for five. At midnight in Michigan, Trump was ahead by 5% (400 thousand votes), with 80% of the votes already counted. When the next 10% of votes of about 400,000 were counted from Wayne County (Detroit), then suddenly Biden caught Trump with 90% of the votes in. Biden made up 5% with 10% of the total vote. That means that all the votes (close to 100%) from Wayne went to Biden. That also means*

that practically all registered voters voted in Wayne County. Does anyone believe any of that is possible? The same thing happened in Madison, Wisconsin, in Raleigh, NC, in Las Vegas, NV, and could be happening in Phil, PA, by Friday. So why did all those Democrat stronghold cities take a "pause" to report their votes?

3. Not one pundit questioned why a shutdown in counting votes happened in all those states simultaneously. Not one. Not even on FOX. Not one questioned how almost all of the newly counted votes in those battleground states went to Biden. Only News Max pointed out the coincidence of it happening in those five states with Democrat governors with Trump ahead before the "pauses."

4. Wisconsin is now reporting 3,239,920 votes cast when there are only 3,129,000 registered voters on record. More people voted than actually registered. When questioned, the Democrat Sec of State says there are 3.6 million registered voters from late registrations. Even if there are 3.6 million registered voters, that means that 90% of them voted when the average was 55 to 60% across the USA. How did almost all votes from Madison go for Biden? Almost 100% of registered voters, not just votes? Did ballot harvesting happen? How about in those other battleground states?

5. "CNN, FOX, NBC, ABC, CBS all refused to call the elections in Texas and Florida until almost all votes were counted, yet FOX called Arizona only 30 minutes after the polls closed with less than 50% of the votes. Arizona had a million outstanding votes in Republican Maricopa County with Biden ahead in the state by only 100,000 when Arizona was called for Biden."

If you think that the media cartel was hard at work demonizing Trump for the last 4 years ... 94% negative Trump reports.... then it was in full swing last night at protecting those Democrat governors in the battleground states.

Think about this for a moment: "resist" by Democrats from the first day that Trump was elected, recounts, no peaceful transition of power, impeachment, three years of false accusations about Trump colluding with Russia to affect the 2016 election, Mueller, Comey/ Clapper/Brennan with the FISA requests and the Steele Dossier paid by Hillary Clinton, 22 FBI agents lost their jobs because of spying on Trump, riots/looting/violence, continued polls that proved to be wrong, $400 billion by Soros and Bloomberg for Biden, Wall Street 4 to 1 in donations to Biden, lack of coverage about the Bidens' relationships with China/Russia/Ukraine/Burisma, and then Covid-19, Covid-19, Covid-19, Covid-19 around the clock by the media ...with little mention of the record economic and international results by Trump.

Covid-19 became the reason for the unsolicited mail-out of ballots by Democrat governors. Covid-19 was used to scare voters and to distract them from Trump's accomplishments. Covid-19 was used as the reason to shut down economies in Democrat-run states. Let's see what happens with Covid-19 now that Democrats and the media no longer need it.

So, did those battleground states run by Democrats use ballot harvesting or any other types of election fraud? How did the vote tallies change so dramatically after those Democrat governors "paused" in their election counts in the dead of night? In all five Democrat-controlled battleground states? If the media, Democrats, and deep state could be in such collusion against Trump for four years, then how hard is it to question collusion in ballot counting last night by those Democrat governors?

What gets lost with a Biden election? For starters, any investigation of Biden with Burisma and China, the Barr investigations, the Durham investigations, the investigations of deep state players, and Constitution integrity with DC as a state and with packing the Supreme Court. Democrats had lots on the line, so they practiced "the end justifies the means," just as Alinsky instructed. They cheated, and the media helped.

Who won the election? Average working Americans lost. Election integrity lost. No matter who won, America got less great.

How many Biden t-shirts do you see? Hats. Signs. People excited. Where have all the 81 million voters gone?"

That last point really hit home with me in my gut.

Do you know how many BIDEN T-shirts I've seen people wearing in the last four years?

Yes, exactly. None. Even with the abuse that wearing MAGA attracts- I see an array of Trump bumper stickers, MAGA cap-wearing Americans, youth in Trump T-shirts, and signs on the lawns touting Trump. And of course, I see many people still excited about their man and candidate who loves America just as they do.

With Biden, not so much. Biden is a show even when he shows up, just as he did on debate night and has been for four years. That's why they hid him in the basement back in 2020 and have been covering up for the frailty of their ghost-like leader ever since.

Still we must not take the next election for granted and why it is imperative to make the margin of victory so big that it's *"too big to rig."*

If President Trump picks up an additional 10% of votes (7.5 million votes) on top of his nearly 75 million votes from last time would give him an unbeatable 82.5 million votes in November 2024. Even if Biden maintained his made-up total of 81 million votes from last time –Trump still won the popular vote outright and a comfortable electoral landslide victory.

Surely no one believes that this version of Biden will increase his fake total of 81 million votes from 2020, and most see him losing at least 10% of his total – (8.1 Million votes), giving him a total of approximately 73 million votes. If that prognosis is true – Trump will win in landslide proportions in the popular vote 82.5million to 73 million votes for Biden, as well as the more important Electoral College with close to 400 electoral votes.

One other thing will be put to rest along with the myth of Joe Biden being an effective and powerful president – and that is that Donald Trump won a presidential election for the third time while only getting credit twice.

And those are numbers we can live with as we put the rigged election, election interference Manchurian candidates, and the deep state in our rearview, and get on the road to making America great again by taking the reins from the 46th president and handing them back to the 45th president and the 47th president of the United States.

Liars figure and Figures Lie

That's an old saying about math. Liars figure and figures lie. But a zero is always a zero. And a circle is always a circle.

One thing that can be said that's true about the man from Scranton is that Biden drew perfect ones, circles that are, and his handlers placed his sparse crowds if we could call them that - of media and supporters in them- as he ran what he called a campaign in summer of 2020. All the while – the man from Queens filled huge rectangular, oval and square-shaped arenas – to capacity with both media and supporters who had an infinite amount of enthusiasm for their candidate. An arena filled to the corners with loving supporters and media types who loathed him. And for those of you who don't know- infinite is immeasurable and never-ending. A number that goes on forever - whereas a circle is finite and does what a circle does best- contains itself within itself.

And that was the whole point of the circles.

Joe stayed within the circle and in the basement of his mind – a place where a brain like his can hide from the public – so they don't see the wear on the man and so that they couldn't get an accurate reading or rating on his current cognitive condition. So they hid the below-average former VP…senator…lawyer…student, and master liar in the bowels of dark rooms – far away from the bright lights of the campaign. Had there been a fair and balanced media, who would have been taking copious notes on this guy- many would have been scratching their heads no doubt as to his ability to do the job of being President of The United States in any decent matter.

And if they were honest, an obvious stretch in this story problem of sorts …no doubt…a given would be that they would have come to the same mathematical answer.

Any way you look at this guy in the circle – you can only come to one conclusion – He's not a straight shooter, and the numbers simply don't add up for this guy. His handlers surely knew the problem with Joe and for that reason, didn't want to box him into any situation where he had to take questions at length from even a friendly press, walk across long distances or short distances, or speak extemporaneously off the top of his head or off the cuff.

The problem with the old Joe, was that the number associated with his IQ, while he boasted that it was very high - to anyone looking at the eye, smell, *and feel test*, it was no doubt, not the stuff that geniuses were made of.

Yet even putting aside all the comments from colleagues who were Joe's friends and foes alike in the Washington swamp, which has no real shape but has more of a smell and blob-like consistency, they all pretty much came to the same conclusion about Joe. Joe Biden was far from the brightest bulb and if they had to sum him up in a few words, dim, dull, *and dumb* would work.

And it is this same guy who, when the numbers started coming in after the unprecedented pause in the counting of votes on election night when Donald Trump was way ahead in many key swing states like Michigan and Pennsylvania, swallowed the probability and possibility that he got that BIG NUMBER, 81 Million Votes from a public who hardly saw him campaign, but loved him from here to eternity. Per the smell test – it didn't make sense, and when played out like a movie scene – The 2020 Numbers & Narrative simply didn't add up. And when they are confronted with the possibility that somehow the numbers may have been wrong and that this story problem and math problem should be checked until it was 100% accurate somehow, they shrug their shoulders and utter some concise sound bite like this one from the BRENNAN CENTER for JUSTICE, *"By all measures, the 2020 general election was one of the **most secure** elections in our history."* [5]

These folks seemed to have it all figured out and refused to consider the possibility and great probability that the 2020 Election was not only stolen by Joe Biden and his gang of handlers, it was rigged replete with the most preposterous notion and narrative ever produced and projected onto the American people.

For the following scene or scenario, one must simply use your imagination and pretend you are looking at a large movie screen, like the one at the big Cineplex where Marvel movies are screened. And if you're a little older, *picture yourself at one of those Drive-In Movie Theatres*, where you would go with your best dates, your best friends or family.

On those big screens, those magnificent wide screens are where epics like The *Ten Commandments* were taken to new heights and where films like *Jaws* got that extra bite. Nothing like seeing a great, unforgettable film or movie on the big screen.

The same can be said for the movie that was projected on us all –in *the Projection Election of 2020*.

To get the impact of that movie in particular that was at the same time a drama, comedy, and a farce, one need look at only one *SCENE* from that moment in which three scenarios from three separate elections starring three leading men with five similar plot points was flashed on the screen.

The working title of the said film is *"Joe's Numbers Don't Add Up."* The film stars OBAMA's NUMBERS, TRUMP'S NUMBERS and BIDEN'S NUMBERS. **Once again, picture yourself looking at one of those magnificent big movie screens. Big enough to tell three very different stories all at the same time.**

Three separate stories with three very different outcomes.

Now, let's take a look at the money shot. The climax. And the shot that ties the movie in a bow.

In 2008, Barack Hussein Obama won the Presidential election with over 69 million votes while helping his party with his coattails win the House of Representatives. In the historic election, America rallied and came together to elect the first-ever African-American President. In doing so, Obama captured 873 counties while winning 18 of 19 key Bellwether indicators and the must-win battleground states of Florida,

25

Ohio, and Iowa. Those states are particularly telling because no candidate who has run for president and who won those three states has ever lost a Presidential Election.

Fast forward to the 2020 election and to an elderly candidate named Joe Biden, who for a good part of his campaign, stayed out of the eyesight of the public and the press, opting out of any chance for bad optics and instead deciding to remain in those circles of hardened supporters and just plain circles.

In 2020, the writers of this script, the directors of this movie and the producers of this latest production want you to believe that Joe Biden garnered more votes than his old boss in that historic landmark election. They want you to believe that an elderly white man who hardly campaigned and who had to drop out of two previous Presidential elections, once because he was found to have been a plagiarist and the other time because of a lack of enthusiasm for his candidacy, *got 81 million votes, over 12 million more than the first ever black president!* In looking at the numbers and the twist in the story, Biden, in winning the election, managed somehow to lose House seats while capturing only 477 counties in the United States, compared to Obama's 873. Further, in an unprecedented sleight of hand, Joe Biden, the man from one the smallest states (3) electorally speaking, managed to pull a rabbit out the his hat by managing to lose those three key battleground states of Iowa, Ohio and Florida and still win the election. And as if to follow up that magic trick with something even more hard to believe that had people scratching their heads with a "HOW HE DO THAT?" look - reserved for the likes of David Copperfield or Harry Houdini, Old sleepy Joe won just 1of 19 bellwether indicators while his old boss won 18 of 19 and still managed to pull a presidential win out of his hat!

When we focus on the third protagonist, Donald Trump and his performance in 2020 and in this three-person scene – The Biden 81 Million Vote charade becomes even more unbelievable.

Donald Trump in receiving nearly 75 Million votes, did something rare for an incumbent – he got more votes, a lot more, nearly 12 million more than the first time he ran, and he lost. Or did he? In regards to painting the country red, if you judged it by county, Trump won a staggering 2497 counties in the 2020 election! That's more by far more than Biden, who captured a mere 477 counties. Trump won nearly five times the amount of counties Biden won. When compared to Obama's 873 counties – Trump still won nearly three times the amount of counties. And Trump won more counties than Biden and Obama combined. Trump picked up seats in the house for his colleagues even while losing the election. Finally, Trump matched Obama by winning the key swing states of Iowa, Ohio, and Florida, while Biden lost them all. Again rare to the point that it never happens – except for the election of 2020. Finally, Trump matched Obama's winning formula of taking 18 of 19 key bellwether indicators, while Biden won 1 of 19.

Something did not add up if you looked at this telling scene with three distinct stories playing out comparing exact data points in three Presidential elections and getting highly improbable, if not impossible, results. Something that did not fit. Something that did not figure. Something that raised more questions than it gave solid, believable answers.

Numbers that didn't look right.

Numbers that didn't make sense.

And finally numbers that didn't add up.

When I think of 81 million votes for Biden. I not only don't see it. I don't believe it. Sure they may have tabulated 81 million votes for the man in the plastic bubble and the candidate who stayed in those perfect circles…but there is *NO WAY in hell that 81 million people actually voted for this man.*

And that's why I doubt any and all numbers these establishment types try to feed to us regarding the latest polls, inflation or job numbers or, more importantly, the effectiveness of their latest vaccine.

I can't help get the picture of those three elections compared side by side out of my mind. The numbers don't make sense to me. Go figure- but the numbers don't add up.

Flag waving with Fellow Patriots protesting a crooked Election

I never felt so helpless yet I had to do something. Flag waving was a good way I thought, to show my support for our president at what we presumed to be a stolen or rigged election. So that's what we did in the weeks after the presidential election of 2020. With complete strangers on a busy street - *Tamiami Trail* in South Sarasota County, it afforded me, if nothing else, at least a chance to blow off some steam and connect with fellow patriots.

Deep down, I knew it wouldn't change the outcome. It was a therapy session of sorts. Consisting of many loyal and frustrated Trump supporters doing their best to put a good face on a sad and pretty hopeless situation.

For the most part we were met with enthusiastic honks from fellow supporters who saw the election as we did and occasional cuss words and insults hurled at us from detractors who didn't agree with us.

It was our way of peacefully protesting and exercising our First Amendment rights of free speech. Our signs were handmade from faded markers. Crude and not highly sophisticated. They expressed sentiments like these.

"Trump won!" "The Election was rigged!" "Make America Great Again!"

It wasn't poetry. Just patriotic rants on large post-it notes put into the universe.

Beep! Beep! Beep! Beep!

The positive horns honking gave us energy. As did the thumbs up and shouts of fellow patriots who yelled their support. As for the people who didn't honk but instead flipped us off or yelled some obscenity or some angry rant like "Trump is Fascist."

We took it. Smiled. Occasionally laughed at them or yelled back. We knew it was part of the process. Part of our way to peacefully protest.

And it was on the streets while flag waving for our president and country and against a rigged election – someone brought up the fact that many patriots were heading to Washington on January 6th to protest the election on Capitol Hill.

That sounded interesting I thought, as we waved our flags and signs protesting an election.

Patriots gathering. Taking it to the streets and doing our part to let our voices be heard as horns honked, flags and signs waved under the setting sun over many November and December 2020 nights in Florida.

II.   January 6, 2021

Re-visiting The DC of my youth?

Had to be There / Our Drive to DC to Witness History

D-Day in DC - January 6, 2021

Standing at the Edge of a Crumbling Republic

You Say Insurrection, I say Protest- Let's call the whole thing off

Seeking Justice as God laughs at our Plans

Looking Back on Washington

Face in the Crowd & Our Time of Truth

A Stop In a Richmond Tavern – The Narrative is unmasked

Once Back from January 6, I played Yankee Doodle Dandy

Re-visiting The DC of my youth?

As a child I visited Washington DC many times. It was so much brighter then. It often is in our memory. Reflections of people or places we loved. I loved Washington, D.C. It's majesty. It's pomp and circumstance. The monuments and memorials. *The Washington Monument. The Jefferson Memorial. And of course, the Lincoln Memorial.* Back then to me, Washington DC, was alive. It was bright. Cherry blossoms filled the air. It was not a cliché or postcard to me. Just a place that did something to me – that awakened something deep in my soul and caused something inside of me to swell with pride.

Washington DC, was, after all, a place of heroes. American heroes. American Patriots filled with stories of men and women who battled to make it so. Americans worthy of a sculptor's gaze – but most importantly, a place where "We the People" were invited and welcomed to visit so that we could see our government in action.

A government that worked for us, represented us and was hopefully looking out for each and every one of us.

As I little boy – I remember asking my dad, *"Why were there so many statues in Washington of great heroes and patriots?"*

He said something like, *"So that they could keep an eye on America and make sure we were all on the right road."*

On the right road?

I nodded – kind of getting what my father meant- but not totally grasping the weight of the words.

I do now. The right road ahead. Are we on it? It's a question I've pondered often in my own life and in the life of my country. Now, I was on the road again. No longer a child –once again, I was heading to Washington, D.C.

The date was January 5, 2021.

I had to be there on January 6, 2021- because my President asked me to be there. He'd asked all of us Patriots to be there to see what was going on in the nation's Capital on this day.

As I made my way down the road that was the 14-hour journey from Florida- my head was filled with many thoughts, images, and questions. What would we find there? Were we on the right road as a country? What would the men and women who represented us do in Congress on this day? Would they do the right thing? Would they do the brave thing? That's what I pondered as the miles piled up.

I closed my eyes, and I began to dream. As it became later in the night, I checked my phone as we drove through Georgia. The fate of the special Senate run-off election lay in the balance. Grabbed a few moments of sleep before we landed in DC. It was going to be a long day – but what I didn't know is that it would be the longest day.

Had to be There / Our Drive to DC to Witness History

The day played out in slow motion, and the ride to DC was tiresome for a van filled with five patriots of varied backgrounds. A bubbly British expatriate mother and grandmother and bonafide *Jesus freak* went along with her daughter equally as bubbly and bright and both *filled with the Holy and American spirit*. A younger man – who I had just met and would take some of the pressure of driving the 14 hours to DC and finally, a new friend I knew as a great defender of the 2nd Amendment who taught people the proper ways to defend themselves and use firearms safely as was our right given in the constitution.

Collectively – one may call us the *Sarasota Five* – not *The Five* as seen on Fox News- just five Americans with different backgrounds who actually didn't know each other all that well but knew one thing as our historic trip to the nation's capital unfolded. The day was an important marker in our nation's history. It would tell a lot about the direction in which we were heading as both a country and a people.

Armed with only the spirit of our founding fathers, but with no guns or weapons of any sort- unless you considered a love of country, freedom, and the truth as an *AR something*. *We* were merely armed with our passion to be a witness and voice our displeasure and right to protest. What many of us felt? The 2020 was an election that not only went the wrong way- but one that seemed unfair. Many signs pointed to forces undermining a process that didn't want -*We the People t*o decide who our President would be, but instead concocted a scheme so that their candidate would be chosen and installed by THEM- my pronoun of choice, for all swamp creatures who threatened the future of our Republic.

The night was filled with anticipation and trepidation as we kept our devices tuned to the Senate run-off races in Georgia. While hopeful – we knew that the odds were stacked against the Senate remaining in control of the Republicans. In this van, driving to Washington DC, because we felt in our gut that something nefarious had happened with the 2020 Presidential election. Call it rigged. Fixed. A setup. In my mind –it was a coup to take over power from a sitting president, who the swamp creatures worldwide could not tolerate, not because of his brash personality and mean tweets, but because of what he had threatened to do to them.

And that was simply this: *Donald J. Trump had to go because he threatened their power.*

He threatened to expose and challenge their power even more so than he had done in his first term. That was something that swamp creatures, big and small, with D's, R's, or I's next to their name were in agreement.

He had to go by any means possible. They had to *GET TRUMP*.

As we made our journey toward DC – the results came in in dribs and drabs.

David Perdue was up, as was Kelly Loeffler at different times during the ride –but we knew in our bones that the forces in power could not and would not let them win.

So it was not a shock when both the Democratic challengers defeated both Republican incumbents and allowed the installed resident in the White House, Joseph Biden, to seize power with complete control of the Senate and House.

The updates came in as we drove into the night.

This just in: We can call the winners in the 2021 Georgia runoff elections:

> *"Democrat Jon Ossoff defeated Republican incumbent David Perdue"*

"Democrat Raphael Warnock defeated Republican incumbent Kelly Loeffler"

After the long ride from Sarasota, we approached the cold gray city of Washington DC. We were all exhausted but excited about playing our part as patriots and being a witness to history.

That may be the greatest understatement I've ever uttered – *"being a witness to history."*

D-Day in DC - January 6, 2021

We arrived around 11 am in DC. The streets were eerily quiet. Sure there were occasional police cars with lights flashing and the expected cars, trucks, and Trump supporters sporting their red MAGA-ware.

But for the most part, the District of Columbia seemed quiet. I googled my mind's memory to picture the last time I was in Washington, DC. I had visited many times – as a child, teenager, and young adult. But it had been years since I'd actually been in the nation's capital.

Almost immediately, something seemed different. As a child, I remembered it as much brighter, sharper, and lighter. The buildings of government popped with dare I say, a majesty or light that took me back to my Greek roots.

As I child – Washington, DC, had the look and feel of Ancient Greece. I pictured my ancestors here – making laws and a living and breathing life into this thing they invented called –Democracy. A sense of pride filled my young spirit as I looked at the "Parthenon-like buildings," and I remembered something my mother always taught me – "Kostaki. *The Greeks started everything."*

Of course, she was not totally right about that – but she was right about many of their contributions. "Theatre, The Olympics and Democracy," she told me, gushing with pride. "Our people started them all."

That's what I thought as our van finished the final leg of our Marathon trip to DC to see Democracy and our Constitutional Republic in action.

Three great pillars. Three enormous contributions.

Theater, Olympics, and Democracy.

And three things that would continue to play out on this day.

Strangely as we got into Washington DC around 11 am, the streets were pretty vacant with hardly any traffic. It was cold. Dreary. We decided to leave our van at the Mandarin Washington DC hotel, hailing a cab to the event at the Ellipse near the White House, where the President would soon be speaking to throngs of his supporters who had come from all over the nation to be here on this Day – D-Day in DC.

Squeezing into the cab tightly, we overheard the voice of America's Mayor Rudy Giuliani, speaking on behalf of President Trump over the radio.

As Rudy spoke, my eyes locked with the man, a foreigner who was driving the cab in America's capital.

"Please take us to the Ellipse, near the White House."

"We're going to hear the President speak."

As I surveyed the empty streets, I asked, "Where is everybody."

"They're already there," he shot back.

I looked at the police cars that lined the streets and the temporary barricades that dressed up Washington DC and then engaged in some conversation with the cabbie.

"So, where are you from?"

"*Ethiopia,*" he shot back. *"I've been here over 20 years."*

I looked out the window and back at the rest of the *Sarasota Five*, then back at the driver who was handling the cab with the skills of a veteran New York City cabbie.

"So what do you think?" I asked.

"It's a very sad and bad day," he stated.

"Why?"

"What they are doing to President Trump is not right," he shot back assuredly.

"Everyone with eyes can see what happened," he continued.

"You like President Trump?" I asked.

"Yes. He's my President."

"I respect him and what he did for America."

"Rudy, too."

And with that - a short cab ride from an Ethiopian Cab driver and Trump Supporter we were ready to play our roles and peacefully protest the results of the Election of 2020, on a very cold day in DC, January 6, 2021.

Standing at the Edge of a Crumbling Republic

I was cold. All of Washington was on this day. It usually is in January. It is what one comes to expect with the coming bitterness of winter. But today I felt an especially deep chill that cut through to my bones. Something that left me nervous. Anxious. Distracted. And feeling a sense of hopelessness.

Something felt strange as I made my way out of the warm taxi cab and well wishes from my new friend and fellow Trump supporter and toward the Ellipse, where the President was speaking.

The crowd was huge. It always is at a Trump rally. And this was no different. A lot bigger. A lot colder. The crowd was a little more somber. Yet hopeful, but still with concern in their eyes as they must have felt what I was feeling on this day- *Our Republic slipping away—crumbling before our eyes* on a cold day in DC.

Still, as we made our way toward where the President was speaking, I was optimistic.

Thankfully, I had abandoned my knucklehead idea of bringing a lot of my "GET TRUMP" books down to the rally to do a makeshift book signing. I had visions of setting up a rudimentary book signing that, in actuality, would've played out like a skit out of a Monty Python.

I could just see it now. Unruly crowds tipping over tables of books, sending them tumbling to the ground as I saw myself calmly asking:

"Who should I make it out to?"

"MAGA 2020"

With a few books shoved in my backpack, we made our way slowly toward the festivities and where the President was speaking.

The crowds were huge. Spread out. The closer we got to the Ellipse, the denser the crowds became. We moved slowly through a crowd filled with many patriots, many carrying crude signs that stated what state they were from while other sentiments denounced the results of the 2020 Election.

"Iowans for Trump," "California is with you, Mr. President." "2020 Rigged," "Stop the Steal."

And we weren't even that close - maybe a couple of football fields away. People were packed in tightly. Some had climbed trees to get a better look at the President as he spoke.

As part of The *Sarasota Five*, we gathered in an area not too far from the Washington Monument. Here, we had a little room to move around and breathe and mix with fellow patriots from all over the country who had gathered here in a sign of unity to protest what many felt was a rigged election.

Standing at the foot of the Washington Monument and listening to the President's speech from the Ellipse near the White House, as he spoke I took in the enormous crowd, and I looked up at the Monument that celebrated our first President.

As President Trump spoke, the crowds warmly greeted him and his words on this cold day in DC.

Well, thank you very much. This is incredible.

Media will not show the magnitude of this crowd. Even I, when I turned on today, I looked, and I saw thousands of people here. But you don't see hundreds of thousands of people behind you because they don't want to show that. We have hundreds of thousands of people here and I just want them to be recognized by the fake news media. Turn your cameras please and show what's really happening out here because these people are not going to take it any longer. They're not going to take it any longer. Go ahead. Turn your cameras, please. Would you show? They came from all over the world, actually, but they came from all over our country.

I just really want to see what they do. I just want to see how they covered. I've never seen anything like it. But it would be really great if we could be covered fairly by the media. The media is the biggest problem we have as far as I'm concerned, single biggest problem. The fake news and the Big Tech. Big tech is now coming into their own. We beat them four years ago. We surprised them. We took them by surprise and this year they rigged an election. They rigged it like they've never rigged an election before. And by the way, last night they didn't do a bad job either if you notice.

I'm honest. And I just, again, I want to thank you. It's just a great honor to have this kind of crowd and to be before you and hundreds of thousands of American patriots who are committed to the honesty of our elections and the integrity of our glorious republic. All of us here today do not want to see our election victory stolen by emboldened radical-left Democrats, which is what they're doing. And stolen by the fake news media. That's what they've done and what they're doing. We will never give up, we will never concede. It doesn't happen. You don't concede when there's theft involved.

Our country has had enough. We will not take it anymore and that's what this is all about. And to use a favorite term that all of you people really came up with: We will stop the steal. Today I will lay out just some of the evidence proving that we won this election and we won it by a landslide. This was not a close election.

You know, I say, sometimes jokingly, but there's no joke about it: I've been in two elections. I won them both and the second one, I won much bigger than the first. OK. Almost 75 million people voted for our campaign, the most of any incumbent president by far in the history of our country, 12 million more people than four years ago. And I was told by the real pollsters — we do have real pollsters — they know that we were going to do well and we were going to win. What I was told, if I went from 63 million, which we had four years ago, to 66 million, there was no chance of losing. Well, we didn't go to 66, we went to 75 million, and they say we lost. We didn't lose.

And by the way, does anybody believe that Joe had 80 million votes? Does anybody believe that? He had 80 million computer votes. It's a disgrace. There's never been anything like that. You could take third-world countries. Just take a look. Take third-world countries. Their elections are more honest than what we've been going through in this country. It's a disgrace. It's a disgrace.

Even when you look at last night. They're all running around like chickens with their heads cut off with boxes. Nobody knows what the hell is going on. There's never been anything like this. We will not let them silence your voices. We're not going to let it happen, I'm not going to let it happen.

(Audience chants: "Fight for Trump.")

Thank you.

And I'd love to have if those tens of thousands of people would be allowed. The military, the secret service. And we want to thank you and the police law enforcement. Great. You're doing a great job. But I'd love it if they could be allowed to come up here with us. Is that possible? Can you just let him come up, please?

And Rudy, you did a great job. He's got guts. You know what? He's got guts, unlike a lot of people in the Republican Party. He's got guts. He fights, he fights.

And I'll tell you. Thank you very much, John. Fantastic job. I watched. That's a tough act to follow, those two. John is one of the most brilliant lawyers in the country, and he looked at this and he said, "What an absolute disgrace that this can be happening to our Constitution." And he looked at Mike Pence, and I hope Mike is going to do the right thing. I hope so. I hope so. Because if Mike Pence does the right thing, we win the election. All he has to do, all this is, this is from the number one, or certainly one of the top, Constitutional lawyers in our country. He has the absolute right to do it. We're supposed to protect our country, support our country, support our Constitution, and protect our constitution.

States want to revote. The states got defrauded. They were given false information. They voted on it. Now they want to recertify. They want it back. All Vice President Pence has to do is send it back to the states to recertify and we become president and you are the happiest people. And I actually, I just spoke to Mike. I said: "Mike, that doesn't take courage. What takes courage is to do nothing. That takes courage." And then we're stuck with a president who lost the election by a lot and we have to live with that for four more years. We're just not going to let that happen.

Many of you have traveled from all across the nation to be here, and I want to thank you for the extraordinary love. That's what it is. There's never been a movement like this, ever, ever. For the extraordinary love for this amazing country, and this amazing movement, thank you.

(Audience chants: "We love Trump.")

By the way, this goes all the way back past the Washington Monument. You believe this? Look at this. That is. Unfortunately gave, they gave the press the prime seats. I can't stand that. No. But you look at that behind. I wish they'd flip those cameras and look behind you. That is the most amazing sight. When they make a mistake, you get to see it on television. Amazing. Amazing. All the way back.

As I listened to the President speak, I thought of the first rally I ever attended, on the eve of the 2020 Election in Sarasota, Florida. That seemed like a thousand years ago. I felt a little sad as I thought about that, and then I was taken out of my thoughts by the President.

And don't worry, we will not take the name off the Washington Monument. We will not cancel culture. You know they wanted to get rid of the Jefferson Memorial. Either take it down or just put somebody else in there. I don't think that's going to happen. It damn well better not. Although, with this administration, if this happens, it could happen. You'll see some really bad things happen. They'll knock out Lincoln too, by the way. They've been taking his statue down. But then we signed a little law. You hurt our monuments, you hurt our heroes, you go to jail for 10 years, and everything stopped. You notice that? It stopped. It all stopped.

And they could use Rudy back in New York City. Rudy. They could use you. Your city's going to hell. They want Rudy Giuliani back in New York. We'll get a little younger version of Rudy. Is that OK, Rudy? We're gathered together in the heart of our nation's capital for one very, very basic and simple reason: To save our democracy. You know most candidates on election evening and, of course, this thing goes on so long. They still don't have any idea what the votes are. We still have congressional seats under review. They have no idea. They've totally lost control. They've used the pandemic as a way of defrauding the people in a proper election.

But you know, you know, when you see this and when you see what's happening. Number one, they all say, "Sir, we'll never let it happen again." I said, "That's good. But what about eight weeks ago?" You know they try and get you to go. They said, "Sir, in four years, you're guaranteed." I said: "I'm not interested right now. Do me a favor, go back eight weeks. I want to go back eight weeks. Let's go back eight weeks."

We want to go back and we want to get this right because we're going to have somebody in there that should not be in there and our country will be destroyed and we're not going to stand for that. For years, Democrats have gotten away with election fraud and weak Republicans. And that's what they are. There's so many weak Republicans. And we have great ones. Jim Jordan and some of these guys, they're out there fighting. The House guys are fighting. But it's, it's incredible.

Many of the Republicans, I helped them get in, I helped them get elected. I helped Mitch get elected. I helped. I could name 24 of them, let's say, I won't bore you with it. And then all of a sudden you have something like this. It's like, "Oh gee, maybe I'll talk to the president sometime later." No, it's amazing.

They're weak Republicans, they're pathetic Republicans and that's what happens. If this happened to the Democrats, there'd be hell all over the country going on. There'd be hell all over the country. But just remember this: You're stronger, you're smarter, you've got more going than anybody. And they try and demean everybody having to do with us. And you're the real people, you're the people that built this nation. You're not the people that tore down our nation.

The weak Republicans, and that's it. I really believe it. I think I'm going to use the term, the weak Republicans. You've got a lot of them. And you got a lot of great ones. But you got a lot of weak ones. They've turned a blind eye, even as Democrats enacted policies that chipped away our jobs, weakened our military, threw open our borders and put America last. Did you see the other day where Joe Biden said, I want to get rid of the America First policy? What's that all about? Get rid of. How do you say I want to get rid of America First? Even if you're going to do it, don't talk about it, right? Unbelievable what we have to go through. What we have to go through.

And you have to get your people to fight. And if they don't fight, we have to primary the hell out of the ones that don't fight. You primary them. We're going to. We're going to let you know who they are. I can already tell you, frankly. But this year, using the pretext of the China virus and the scam of mail-in ballots, Democrats attempted the most brazen and outrageous election theft and there's never been anything like this. So pure theft in American history. Everybody knows it.

That election, our election was over at 10 o'clock in the evening. We're leading Pennsylvania, Michigan, Georgia, by hundreds of thousands of votes. And then late in the evening, or early in the morning, boom, these explosions of bullshit.

And all of a sudden. All of a sudden it started to happen.

(Audience chants: "Bullshit.")

Don't forget when Romney got beat. Romney, hey. Did you see his? I wonder if he enjoyed his flight in last night. But when Romney got beaten, you know, he stands up like you're more typical, "Well, I'd like to congratulate the victor." The victor? Who is the victor, Mitt? "I'd like to congratulate." They don't go and look at the facts. No, I don't know. He got, he got slaughtered. Probably, maybe it was OK, maybe it was. But that's what happened. But we look at the facts and our election was so corrupt that in the history of this country we've never seen anything like it. You can go all the way back.

You know, America is blessed with elections. All over the world they talk about our elections. You know what the world says about us now? They said, we don't have free and fair elections. And you know what else? We don't have a free and fair press. Our media is not free, it's not fair. It suppresses thought, it suppresses speech and it's become the enemy of the people. It's become the enemy of the people. It's the biggest problem we have in this country.

No third-world countries would even attempt to do what we caught them doing. And you'll hear about that in just a few minutes. Republicans are, Republicans are constantly fighting like a boxer with his hands tied behind his back. It's like a boxer. And we want to be so nice. We want to be so respectful of everybody, including bad people. And we're going to have to fight much harder. And Mike Pence is going to have to come through for us, and if he doesn't, that will be a, a sad day for our country because you're sworn to uphold our Constitution. Now, it is up to Congress to confront this egregious assault on our democracy. And after this, we're going to walk down, and I'll be there with you, we're going to walk down, we're going to walk down.

Anyone you want, but I think right here, we're going to walk down to the Capitol, and we're going to cheer on our brave senators and congressmen and women, and we're probably not going to be cheering so much for some of them. Because you'll never take back our country with weakness. You have to show strength and you have to be strong. We have come to demand that Congress do the right thing and only count the electors who have been lawfully slated, lawfully slated.

I know that everyone here will soon be marching over to the Capitol building to peacefully and patriotically make your voices heard.

I looked in the direction of the Capitol building as I took in the President's hopeful words. And I must say it left me a bit sad. Was this the end? Of our country and republic? The President and the sold temps snapped me back to the reality of the moment.

Today we will see whether Republicans stand strong for integrity of our elections. But whether or not they stand strong for our country, our country. Our country has been under siege for a long time. Far longer than this four-year period. We've set it on a much greater course. So much, and we, I thought, you know, four more years. I thought it would be easy.

We've created the greatest economy in history. We rebuilt our military. We get you the biggest tax cuts in history. Right? We got you the biggest regulation cuts. There's no president, whether it's four years, eight years or in one case more, got anywhere near the regulation cuts.

Used to take 20 years to get a highway approved, now we're down to two. I want to get it down to one, but we're down to two. And it may get rejected for environmental or safety reasons, but we got it down to safety. We created Space Force, We, we, we. Look at what we did. Our military has been totally rebuilt. So we create Space Force which, by and of itself, is a major achievement for an administration. And with us it's one of so many different things.

Right to Try. Everybody know about Right to Try. We did things that nobody ever thought possible. We took care of our vets, our vets. The VA now has the highest rating, 91%. The highest rating that it's had from the beginning, 91% approval rating. Always, you watch the VA, it was on television every night, people living in a horrible, horrible manner. We got that done. We got accountability done. We got it so that now in the VA, you don't have to wait for four weeks, six weeks, eight weeks, four months to see a doctor. If you can't get a doctor, you go outside, you get the doctor. You have it taken care of and we pay the doctor.

And we've not only made life wonderful for so many people, we've saved tremendous amounts of money, far secondarily, but we've saved a lot of money. And now we have the right to fire bad people in the VA. We had 9,000 people that treated our veterans horribly. In primetime, they would not have treated our veterans badly. But they treated our veterans horribly.

And we have what's called the account, VA Accountability Act. And the accountability says if we see somebody in there that doesn't treat our vets well or they steal, they rob, they do things badly, we say: "Joe you're fired. Get out of here." Before you couldn't do that. You couldn't do that before. So we've taken care of things, we've done things like nobody's ever thought possible. And that's part of the reason that many people don't like us, because we've done too much.

But we've done it quickly and we were going to sit home and watch a big victory and everybody had us down for a victory. It was going to be great and now we're out here fighting. I said to somebody, I was going to take a few days and relax after our big electoral victory. 10 o'clock it was over. But I was going to take a few days.

And I can say this. Since our election, I believe, which was such a catastrophe, when I watch. And even these guys knew what happened. They know what happened. They're saying: "Wow, Pennsylvania's insurmountable. Wow, Wisconsin." Look at the big leads we had, right. Even though the press said we would lose Wisconsin by 17 points. Even though the press said, Ohio's going to be close, we set a record; Florida's going to be close, we set a record; Texas is going to be close, Texas is going to be close, we set a record.

And we set a record with Hispanic, with the Black community, we set a record with everybody.

Today we see a very important event though. Because right over there, right there, we see the event going to take place. And I'm going to be watching. Because history is going to be made. We're going to see whether or not we have great and courageous leaders, or whether or not we have leaders that should be ashamed of themselves throughout history, throughout eternity they'll be ashamed.

And you know what? If they do the wrong thing, we should never, ever forget that they did. Never forget. We should never ever forget. With only three of the seven states in question, we win the presidency of the United States. And by the way, it's much more important today than it was 24 hours ago, because I don't. I spoke to David Perdue, what a great person, and Kelly Loeffler, two great people, but it was a setup.

And you know, I said, "We have no backline anymore." The only backline, the only line of demarcation, the only line that we have is the veto of the president of the United States. So this is now, what we're doing, a far more important election than it was two days ago. I want to thank the more than 140 members of the House. Those are warriors. They're over there working like you've never seen before. Studying, talking, actually going all the way back, studying the roots of the Constitution, because they know we have the right to send a bad vote that was illegally gotten.

They gave these people bad things to vote for and they voted because what did they know? And then when they found out a few weeks later, again, it took them four years to devise this screen. And the only unhappy person in the United States, single most unhappy, is Hillary Clinton. Because she said: "Why didn't you do this for me four years ago? Why didn't you do this for me four years ago? Change the votes, 10,000 in Michigan. You could have changed the whole thing." But she's not too happy. You know, you don't see her anymore. What happened? Where's Hillary? Where is she?

But I want to thank all of those congressmen and women. I also want to thank our 13, most courageous members of the U.S. Senate. Senator Ted Cruz, Senator Ron Johnson, Senator Josh Hawley, Kelly Loeffler. And Kelly Loeffler, I'll tell you, she has been, she's been so great. She worked so hard. So let's give her and David a little special hand because it was rigged against them. Let's give her and David.

Kelly Loeffler, David Purdue. They fought a good race. They never had a shot. That equipment should never have been allowed to be used, and I was telling these people don't let him use this stuff. Marsha Blackburn, terrific person. Mike Braun, Indiana. Steve Daines, great guy. Bill Hagerty, John Kennedy, James Lankford, Cynthia Lummis, Tommy Tuberville, the coach, and Roger

Marshall. We want to thank them. Senators that stepped up, we want to thank them.

I actually think though, it takes, again, more courage not to step up, and I think a lot of those people are going to find that out and you better start looking at your leadership, because your leadership has led you down the tubes.. You know, we don't want to give $2,000 to people. We want to give them $600. Oh, great. How does that play politically? Pretty good? And this has nothing to do with politics, but how does it play politically? China destroyed these people. We didn't destroy. China destroy them, totally destroyed them. We want to give them $600 and they just wouldn't change. I said give them $2,000, we'll pay it back. We'll pay it back fast. You already owe 26 trillion, give them a couple of bucks. Let them live. Give them a couple of bucks. And some of the people here disagree with me on that, but I just say, "Look, you've got to let people live." And how does that play though? OK. Number one, it's the right thing to do. But how does that play politically? I think it's the primary reason, one of the primary reasons, the other was just pure cheating. That was the primary, super primary reason. But you can't do that, you got to use your head.

As you know, the media has constantly asserted the outrageous lie that there was no evidence of widespread fraud. Have you ever seen these people? While there is no evidence of fraud. Oh, really? Well, I'm going to read you pages. I hope you don't get bored listening to it. Promise? Don't get bored listening to it, all those hundreds of thousands of people back there. Move them up, please, yeah.

All they, all these people, don't get bored, don't get angry at me because you're going to get bored because it's so much. The American people do not believe the corrupt, fake news anymore. They have ruined their reputation. But you know, it used to be that they'd argue with me. I'd fight. So I'd fight, they'd fight, I'd fight, they'd fight. Pop pop. You'd believe me, you'd believe them. Somebody comes out. You know, they had their point of view, I had my point of view, but you'd have an argument.

Now what they do is they go silent. It's called suppression and that's what happens in a communist country. That's what they do, they suppress. You don't fight with them anymore. Unless it's a bad story. They have a little bad story about me, they make it 10 times worse and it's a major headline. But Hunter Biden, they don't talk about him. What happened to Hunter? Where's Hunter? Where's Hunter? They don't talk about him. They'll watch, all the sets will go off. Well, they can't do that because they get good ratings. Their ratings are too good. Now, where's Hunter? You know.

And how come Joe is allowed to give a billion dollars of money to get rid of the prosecutor in Ukraine? How does that happen? I'd ask you that question. How does that happen? Can you imagine if I said that? If I said that it would be a whole different ballgame. And how come Hunter gets three and a half million dollars from the mayor of Moscow's wife, and gets hundreds of thousands of dollars to sit on an energy board, even though he admits he has no knowledge of energy? And millions of dollars up front.

And how come they go into China and they leave with billions of dollars to manage. "Have you managed money before?" "No, I haven't." "Oh, that's good. Here's about 3 billion." No, they don't talk about that. No, we have a corrupt media. They've gone silent. They've gone dead. I now realize how good it was if you go back 10 years, I realized how good, even though I didn't necessarily love them, I realized how good. It was like a cleansing motion, right?

But we don't have that anymore. We don't have a fair media anymore. It's suppression. And you have to be very careful with that and they've lost all credibility in this country. We will not be intimidated into accepting the hoaxes and the lies that we've been forced to believe.

Over the past several weeks, we've amassed overwhelming evidence about a fake election. This is the presidential election. Last night was a little bit better because of the fact that we had a lot of eyes watching one specific state, but they cheated like hell anyway.

You have one of the dumbest governors in the United States. And you know when I endorsed him, and I didn't know this guy, at the request of David Perdue, he said, "Friend of mine's running for governor." "What's his name?" And you know the rest. He was in fourth place, fifth place. I don't know, he was, he was doing poorly. I endorse him, he went like a rocket ship and he won. And then I had to beat Stacey Abrams with this guy, Brian Kemp. I had to beat Stacey Abrams. And I had to beat Oprah, used to be a friend of mine. You know, I was on her last show, her last week, she picked the five outstanding people. I don't think she thinks that any more. Once I ran for president, I didn't notice there were too many calls coming in from Oprah. Believe it or not, she used to like me. But I was one of the five outstanding people.

And I had a campaign against Michelle Obama and Barack Hussein Obama, against Stacey. And I had Brian Kemp, who weighs 130 pounds. He said he played offensive line in football. I'm trying to figure that out. I'm still trying to figure that out. He said that the other night, "I was an offensive lineman." I'm saying: "Really? That must have been a very small team." But I look at that and I look at what's happened and he turned out to be a disaster. This stuff happens.

You know, look, I'm not happy with the Supreme Court. They love to rule against me. I picked three people. I fought like hell for them. One in particular, I fought. They all said, "Sir, cut him loose." He's killing the senators. You know, very loyal senators, they're very loyal people, "Sir, cut him loose, he's killing us, sir, cut him loose." I must have gotten half of the senators. I said: "No, I can't do that, it's unfair to him and it's unfair to the family. He didn't do anything wrong." They made up stories, they're all made-up stories. He didn't do anything wrong. "Cut him loose, sir." I said, "No, I won't do that. We got him through." And you know what, they couldn't give a damn. They couldn't give a damn. Let him rule the right way.

But it almost seems that they're all going out of their way to hurt all of us and to hurt our country. To hurt our country. You know, I read a story in one of the newspapers recently how I control the three Supreme Court justices. I control them. They're puppets.

I read it about Bill Barr, that he's my personal attorney. That he'll do anything for me. And I said, "You know, it really is genius." Because what they do is that, and it makes it really impossible for them to ever give you a victory, because all of a sudden Bill Barr changed. If you hadn't noticed. I like Bill Barr, but he changed, because he didn't want to be considered my personal attorney.

And the Supreme Court, they rule against me so much. You know why? Because the story is — I haven't spoken to any of them, any of them, since virtually they got in — but the story is that they're my puppets. Right? That they're puppets. And now the only way they can get out of that because they hate that it's not good in the social circuit. And the only way they get out is to rule against

48

Trump. So let's rule against Trump. And they do that. So I want to congratulate them.

But it shows you the media's genius. In fact, probably if I was the media, I'd do it the same way. I hate to say it. But we got to get them straightened out. Today, for the sake of our democracy, for the sake of our Constitution, and for the sake of our children, we lay out the case for the entire world to hear. You want to hear it?

Audience responds: "Yeah"

In every single swing state, local officials, state officials, almost all Democrats, made illegal and unconstitutional changes to election procedures without the mandated approvals by the state legislatures. That these changes paved a way for fraud on a scale never seen before. I think we go a long way outside of our country when I say that. So, just in a nutshell, you can't make a change or voting for a federal election unless the state legislature approves it. No judge can do it. Nobody can do it. Only a legislature.

So as an example, in Pennsylvania, or whatever, you have a Republican legislature, you have a Democrat mayor, and you have a lot of Democrats all over the place. They go to the legislature. The legislature laughs at them, says we're not going to do that. They say, thank you very much and they go and make the changes themselves, they do it anyway. And that's totally illegal. That's totally illegal. You can't do that.

In Pennsylvania, the Democrat secretary of state and the Democrat state Supreme Court justices illegally abolished the signature verification requirements just 11 days prior to the election. So think of what they did. No longer is there signature verification. Oh, that's OK. We want voter ID by the way. But no longer is there a signature verification. Eleven days before the election they say we don't want it. You know why they don't want to? Because they want to cheat. That's the only reason.

Who would even think of that? We don't want to verify a signature? There were over 205,000 more ballots counted in Pennsylvania. Think of this, you had 205,000 more ballots than you had voters. That means you had two. Where did they come from? You know where they came from? Somebody's imagination, whatever they needed.

So in Pennsylvania, you had 205,000 more votes than you had voters. And the number is actually much greater than that now. That was as of a week ago. And this is a mathematical impossibility unless you want to say it's a total fraud. So Pennsylvania was defrauded. Over 8,000 ballots in Pennsylvania were cast by people whose names and dates of birth match individuals who died in 2020 and prior to the election. Think of that. Dead people, lots of dead people, thousands. And some dead people actually requested an application. That bothers me even more.

Not only are they voting, they want an application to vote. One of them was 29 years ago, died. It's incredible. Over 14,000 ballots were cast by out-of-state voters, so these are voters that don't live in this state. And by the way, these numbers are what they call outcome-determinative, meaning these numbers far surpass. I lost by a very little bit. These numbers are massive, massive. More than 10,000 votes in Pennsylvania were illegally counted, even though they were received after Election Day. In other words, they were received after Election Day. Let's count them anyway.

And what they did in many cases is, they did fraud. They took the date and they moved it back so that it no longer is after Election Day. And more than 60,000 ballots in Pennsylvania were reported received back. They got back before they were ever supposedly mailed out. In other words, you got the ballot back before you mailed it, which is also logically and logistically impossible, right?

Think of that one. You got the ballot back. Let's send the ballots. Oh, they've already been sent. But we got the ballot back before they were sent. I don't think that's too good, right? Twenty-five thousand ballots in Pennsylvania were requested by nursing home residents, all in a single giant batch, not legal, indicating an enormous, illegal ballot harvesting operation. You're not allowed to do it, it's against the law.

The day before the election, the state of Pennsylvania reported the number of absentee ballots that had been sent out. Yet this number was suddenly and drastically increased by 400,000 people. It was increased, nobody knows where it came from, by 400,000 ballots, one day after the election. It remains totally unexplained. They said, "Well, ah, we can't figure that." Now, that's many, many times what it would take to overthrow the state. Just that one element. Four hundred thousand ballots appeared from nowhere right after the election. By the way, Pennsylvania has now seen all of this. They didn't know because it was so quick. They had a vote. They voted. But now they see all this stuff, it's all come to light. Doesn't happen that fast. And they want to recertify their votes. They want to recertify. But the only way that can happen is if Mike Pence agrees to send it back. Mike Pence has to agree to send it back.

(Audience chants: "Send it back.")

And many people in Congress want it sent back. And think of what you're doing. Let's say you don't do it. Somebody says, "Well, we have to obey the Constitution." And you are, because you're protecting our country and you're protecting the Constitution. So you are.

But think of what happens. Let's say they're stiffs and they're stupid people, and they say, well, we really have no choice. Even though Pennsylvania and other states want to redo their votes. They want to see the numbers. They already have the numbers. Go very quickly. And they want to redo their legislature because many of these votes were taken, as I said, because it wasn't approved by their legislature. You know, that, in itself, is legal. And then you have the scam, and that's all of the things that we're talking about.

But think of this. If you don't do that, that means you will have a president of the United States for four years, with his wonderful son. You will have a president who lost all of these states. Or you will have a president, to put it another way, who was voted on by a bunch of stupid people who lost all of these states.

You will have an illegitimate president. That's what you'll have. And we can't let that happen. These are the facts that you won't hear from the fake news media. It's all part of the suppression effort. They don't want to talk about it. They don't want to talk about it. In fact, when I started talking about that, I guarantee you, a lot of the television sets and a lot of those cameras went off. And that's a lot of cameras back there. But a lot of them went off. But these are the things you don't hear about. You don't hear what you just heard. I'm going to go over a few more states. But you don't hear it by the people who want to deceive you and demoralize you and control you. Big tech, media. Just like the suppression polls that said we're going lose Wisconsin by 17 points. Well, we won Wisconsin. They don't have it that way because they lost just by a little sliver. But they had me down the day before, Washington Post/ABC poll, down 17 points.

I called up a real pollster. I said, "What is that?" "Sir, that's called a suppression poll. I think you're going to win Wisconsin, sir." I said, "But why don't they make it four or five points?" Because then people vote. But when you're down 17, they say, "Hey, I'm not going to waste my time. I love the president, but there's no way."

Despite that, despite that, we won Wisconsin. It's going to see. I mean, you'll see. But that's called suppression because a lot of people when they see that. It's very interesting. This pollster said, "Sir, if you're down three, four, or five people vote. When you go down 17, they say, 'Let's save. Let's go and have dinner and let's watch the presidential defeat tonight on television, darling.'"

And just like the radical left tries to blacklist you on social media. Every time I put out a tweet, that's, even if it's totally correct, totally correct, I get a flag. I get a flag. And they also don't let you get out. You know, on Twitter, it's very hard to come onto my account. It's very hard to get out a message. They don't let the message get out nearly like they should. But I've had many people say, "I can't get on your Twitter." I don't care about Twitter. Twitter's bad news. They're all bad news.

But you know what, if you want to, if you want to get out a message and if you want to go through Big tech, social media, they are really, if you're a conservative, if you're a Republican, if you have a big voice, I guess they call it shadow banned, right? Shadow banned. They shadow ban you, and it should be illegal. I've been telling these Republicans, get rid of Section 230. And for some reason, Mitch and the group, they don't want to put it in there and they don't realize that that's going to be the end of the Republican Party as we know it, but it's never going to be the end of us. Never. Let them get out. Let, let the weak ones get out. This is a time for strength.

They also want to indoctrinate your children in school by teaching them things that aren't so. They want to indoctrinate your children. It's all part of the comprehensive assault on our democracy, and the American people are finally standing up and saying no. This crowd is, again, a testament to it. I did no advertising, I did nothing. You do have some groups that are big supporters. I want to thank that, Amy, and everybody. We have some incredible supporters, incredible. But we didn't do anything. This just happened. Two months ago, we had a massive crowd come down to Washington. I said, "What are they there for?" "Sir, they're there for you."

We have nothing to do with it. These groups are for, they're forming all over the United States. And we got to remember, in a year from now, you're going to start working on Congress and we got to get rid of the weak Congress, people, the ones that aren't any good, the Liz Cheneys of the world. We got to get rid of them. We got to get rid.

You know, she never wants a soldier brought home — I brought a lot of our soldiers home. I don't know, somewhat like it. They're in countries that nobody even knows the name, nobody knows where they are. They're dying. They're great, but they're dying. They're losing their arms, their legs, their face. I brought them back home, largely back home. Afghanistan, Iraq. Remember, I used to say in the old days: "Don't go in Iraq. But if you go in, keep the oil." We didn't keep the oil. So stupid. So stupid these people. And Iraq has billions and billions of dollars now in the bank. And what did we do? We got nothing. We never get. But we do actually, we kept the oil here or we get, we did good.

We got rid of the ISIS caliphate. We got rid of plenty of different things that everybody knows and the rebuilding of our military in three years. People said it couldn't be done. And it was all made in the USA, all made in the USA, best equipment in the world.

In Wisconsin, corrupt Democrat-run cities deployed more than 500 illegal, unmanned, unsecured drop boxes, which collected a minimum of 91,000 unlawful votes. It was razor-thin, the loss. This one thing alone is much more than we would need. But there are many things.

They have these lockboxes. And, you know, they'd pick them up and they disappear for two days. People would say where's that box? They disappeared. Nobody even knew where the hell it was.

In addition, over 170,000 absentee votes were counted in Wisconsin without a valid absentee ballot application. So they had a vote, but they had no application, and that's illegal in Wisconsin. Meaning those votes were blatantly done in opposition to state law and they *came 100% from Democrat areas such as Milwaukee and Madison, 100%.*

In Madison, 17,000 votes were deposited in so-called human drop boxes. You know what that is, right? Where operatives stuff thousands of unsecured ballots into duffle bags on park benches across the city, in complete defiance of cease-and-desist letters from state legislature. Your state legislatures said don't do it. They're the only ones that can approve it. They gave tens of thousands of votes. They came in in duffle bags. Where the hell did they come from?

According to eyewitness testimony, Postal Service workers in Wisconsin were also instructed to illegally backdate approximately 100,000 ballots. The margin of difference in Wisconsin was less than 20,000 votes. Each one of these things alone wins us the state. Great state. We love the state. We won the state. In Georgia, your secretary of state who, I can't believe this guy's a Republican. He loves recording telephone conversations. You know, that was? I thought it was a great conversation personally. So did a lot of other. People love that conversation because it says what's going on.

These people are crooked. They're 100%, in my opinion, one of the most corrupt, between your governor and your secretary of state. And now you have it again last night. Just take a look at what happened. What a mess.

And the Democrat Party operatives entered into an illegal and unconstitution — unconstitutional settlement agreement that drastically weakened signature verification and other election security procedures.

Stacey Abrams. She took them to lunch. And I beat her two years ago with a bad candidate, Brian Kemp. But they took, the Democrats took the Republicans to lunch because the secretary of state had no clue what the hell was happening. Unless he did have a clue. That's interesting. Maybe he was with the other side.

But we've been trying to get verifications of signatures in Fulton County, they won't let us do it. The only reason they won't is because we'll find things in the hundreds of thousands. Why wouldn't they let us verify signatures in Fulton County, which is known for being very corrupt. They won't do it. They go to some other county where you would live.

I said, "That's not the problem." The problem is Fulton County, home of Stacey Abrams. She did a good job, I congratulate her. But it was done in such a way that we can't let this stuff happen. We won't have a country if it happens. As a result, Georgia's absentee ballot rejection rate was more than 10 times lower than previous levels because the criteria was so off.

Forty-eight counties in Georgia, with thousands and thousands of votes, rejected zero ballots. There wasn't one ballot. In other words, in a year in which more mail-in ballots were sent than ever before, and more people were voting by mail for the first time, the rejection rate was drastically lower than it had ever been before.

The only way this can be explained is if tens of thousands of illegitimate votes were added to the tally. That's the only way you could explain it. By the way, you're talking about tens of thousands. If Georgia had merely rejected the same number of unlawful ballots as in other years, they should have been approximately 45,000 ballots rejected. Far more than what we needed to win, just over 11,000. They should find those votes. They should absolutely find that. Just over 11,000 votes, that's all we need. They defrauded us out of a win in Georgia, and we're not going to forget it.

There's only one reason the Democrats could possibly want to eliminate signature matching, opposed voter ID, and stop citizenship confirmation. "Are you a citizenship?" You're not allowed to ask that question, because they want to steal the election.

The radical left knows exactly what they're doing. They're ruthless and it's time that somebody did something about it. And Mike Pence, I hope you're going to stand up for the good of our Constitution and for the good of our country. And if you're not, I'm going to be very disappointed in you. I will tell you right now. I'm not hearing good stories.

In Fulton County, Republican poll watchers were ejected, in some cases, physically from the room under the false pretense of a pipe burst. Water main burst, everybody leave. Which we now know was a total lie.

Then election officials pull boxes, Democrats, and suitcases of ballots out from under a table. You all saw it on television, totally fraudulent. And illegally scanned them for nearly two hours, totally unsupervised. Tens of thousands of votes. This act coincided with a mysterious vote dump of up to 100,000 votes for Joe Biden, almost none for Trump. Oh, that sounds fair. That was at 1:34 a.m.

The Georgia secretary of state and pathetic governor of Georgia, have reached, although he says I'm a great president. You know, I sort of maybe have to change. He said the other day, "Yes, I do. I disagree with president, but he's been a great president." Good, thanks. Thank you very much.

Because of him and others, you have Brian Kemp. Vote him the hell out of office, please. Well, his rates are so low. You know, his approval rating now, I think it just reached a record low. They've rejected five separate appeals for an independent and comprehensive audit of signatures in Fulton County. Even without an audit, the number of fraudulent ballots that we've identified across the state is staggering.

Over 10,300 ballots in Georgia were cast by individuals whose names and dates of birth match Georgia residents who died in 2020 and prior to the election. More than 2,500 ballots were cast by individuals whose names and dates of birth match incarcerated felons in Georgia prison. People who are not allowed to vote.

More than 4,500 illegal ballots were cast by individuals who do not appear on the state's own voter rolls. Over 18,000 illegal ballots were cast by individuals who registered to vote using an address listed as vacant, according to the Postal Service.

At least 88,000 ballots in Georgia were cast by people whose registrations were illegally backdated. Sixty-six thousand votes, each one of these is far more than we need. Sixty-six thousand votes in Georgia were cast by individuals under the legal voting age. And at least 15,000 ballots were cast by individuals who moved out of the state prior to November 3 election. They say they moved right back. They moved right back. Oh, they moved out, they moved right back. OK. They missed Georgia that much. I do. I love Georgia, but it's a corrupt system. Despite all of this, the margin in Georgia is only 11,779 votes.

Each and every one of these issues is enough to give us a victory in Georgia, a big beautiful victory. Make no mistake, this election was stolen from you, from me and from the country. And not a single swing state has conducted a comprehensive audit to remove the illegal ballots. This should absolutely occur in every single contested state before the election is certified. In the state of Arizona, over

36,000 ballots were illegally cast by non-citizens. Two thousand ballots were returned with no address. More than 22,000 ballots were returned before they were ever supposedly mailed out. They returned, but we haven't mailed them yet. Eleven thousand six hundred more ballots and votes were counted, more than there were actual voters. You see that? So you have more votes again than you have voters. One hundred and fifty thousand people registered in Maricopa County after the registration deadline. One hundred and three thousand ballots in the county were sent for electronic adjudication with no Republican observers. In Clark County, Nevada, the accuracy settings on signature verification machines were purposely lowered before they were used to count over 130,000 ballots.

If you signed your name as Santa Claus, it would go through. There were also more than 42,000 double votes in Nevada. Over 150,000 people were hurt so badly by what took place. And 1,500 ballots were cast by individuals whose names and dates of birth match Nevada residents who died in 2020 prior to November 3 election. More than 8,000 votes were cast by individuals who had no address and probably didn't live there. The margin in Nevada is down at a very low number, any of these things would have taken care of the situation. We would have won Nevada, also. Every one of these we're going over, we win.

In Michigan, quickly, the secretary of state, a real great one, flooded the state with unsolicited mail-in ballot applications sent to every person on the rolls in direct violation of state law. More than 17,000 Michigan ballots were cast by individuals whose names and dates of birth match people who were deceased. In Wayne County, that's a great one. That's Detroit. One hundred and seventy-four thousand ballots were counted without being tied to an actual registered voter. Nobody knows where they came from. Also, in Wayne County, poll watchers observed canvassers rescanning batches of ballots over and over again, up to three or four or five times. In Detroit, turnout was 139% of registered voters. Think of that. So you had 139% of the people in Detroit voting. This is in Michigan. Detroit, Michigan. A career employee of the Detroit, City of Detroit, testified under penalty of perjury that she witnessed city workers coaching voters to vote straight Democrat while accompanying them to watch who they voted for. When a

Republican came in, they wouldn't talk to him. The same worker was instructed not to ask for any voter ID and not to attempt to validate any signatures if they were Democrats. She also told to illegally, and was told, backdate ballots received after the deadline and reports that thousands and thousands of ballots were improperly backdated. That's Michigan.

Four witnesses have testified under penalty of perjury that after officials in Detroit announced the last votes had been counted, tens of thousands of additional ballots arrived without required envelopes. Every single one was for a Democrat. I got no votes. At 6:31 a.m. in the early morning hours after voting had ended, Michigan suddenly reported 147,000 votes. An astounding 94% went to Joe Biden, who campaigned brilliantly from his basement. Only a couple of percentage points went to Trump.

Such gigantic and one-sided vote dumps were only observed in a few swing states and they were observed in the states where it was necessary. You know what's interesting? President Obama beat Biden in every state other than the swing states where Biden killed them, but the swing states were the ones that mattered. They're always just enough to push Joe Biden barely into the lead. We were ahead by a lot and within a number of hours we were losing by a little. In addition, there is the highly troubling matter of Dominion Voting Systems. In one Michigan County alone, 6,000 votes were switched from Trump to Biden and the same systems are used in the majority of states in our country.

Senator William Ligon, a great gentleman, chairman of Georgia's senate judiciary subcommittee. Senator Ligon, highly respected, on elections has written a letter describing his concerns with Dominion in Georgia. He wrote, and I quote, The Dominion Voting Machines employed in Fulton County had an astronomical and astounding 93.67% error rate. It's only wrong 93% of the time in the scanning of ballots requiring a review panel to adjudicate or determine the voter's interest in over 106,000 ballots out of a total of 113,000. Think of it. You go in and you vote and then they tell people who you supposed to be voting for. They make up whatever they want. Nobody's ever even heard.

They adjudicate your vote. They say, Well, we don't think Trump wants to vote for Trump. We think he wants to vote for Biden. Put it down for Biden. The national average for such an error rate is far less than 1% and yet you're at 93%. The source of this astronomical error rate must be identified to determine if these machines were set up or destroyed to allow for a third party to disregard the actual ballot cast by the registered voter. The letter continues. There is clear evidence that tens of thousands of votes were switched from President Trump to former Vice President Biden in several counties in Georgia.

For example, in Bibb County, President Trump was reported to have 29,391 votes at 9:11 p.m. Eastern time, while simultaneously Vice President Joe Biden was reported to have 17,213. Minutes later, just minutes, at the next update, these vote numbers switched with President Trump going way down to 17,000 and Biden going way up to 29,391. And that was very quick, a 12,000 vote switch all in Mr. Biden's favor. So, I mean, I could go on and on about this fraud that took place in every state, and all of these legislatures want this back. I don't want to do it to you because I love you and it's freezing out here. But I could just go on forever. I can tell you this.

(Audience chants: "We love you.")

So when you hear, when you hear, while there is no evidence to prove any wrongdoing, this is the most fraudulent thing anybody has, this is a criminal enterprise. This is a criminal enterprise. And the press will say, and I'm sure they won't put any of that on there, because that's no good. And you ever see, while there is no evidence to back President Trump's assertion.

I could go on for another hour reading this stuff to you and telling you about it. There's never been anything like it. Think about it. Detroit had more votes than it had voters. Pennsylvania had 205,000 more votes than it had more. But you don't have to go any. Between that, I think that's almost better than dead people if you think, right? More votes than they had voters. And many other states also.

It's a disgrace that the United States of America, tens of millions of people, are allowed to go vote without so much as even showing identification. In no state is there any question or effort made to verify the identity, citizenship, residency or eligibility of the votes cast.

The Republicans have to get tougher. You're not going to have a Republican Party if you don't get tougher. They want to play so straight. They want to play so, sir, yes, the United States. The Constitution doesn't allow me to send them back to the States. Well, I say, yes it does, because the Constitution says you have to protect our country and you have to protect our Constitution, and you can't vote on fraud. And fraud breaks up everything, doesn't it? When you catch somebody in a fraud, you're allowed to go by very different rules.

So I hope Mike has the courage to do what he has to do. And I hope he doesn't listen to the RINOs and the stupid people that he's listening to. It is also widely understood that the voter rolls are crammed full of non-citizens, felons and people who have moved out of state and individuals who are otherwise ineligible to vote. Yet Democrats oppose every effort to clean up their voter rolls. They don't want to clean them up. They're loaded. And how many people here know other people, that when there are hundreds of thousands and then millions of ballots got sent out, got three, four, five, six, and I heard one, who got seven ballots. And then they say you didn't quite make it, sir.

We won in a landslide. This was a landslide. They said it's not American to challenge the election. This the most corrupt election in the history, maybe of the world. You know, you could go third-world countries, but I don't think they had hundreds of thousands of votes and they don't have voters for them. I mean no matter where you go, nobody would think this.

In fact, it's so egregious, it's so bad that a lot of people don't even believe it. It's so crazy that people don't even believe it. It can't be true. So they don't believe it. This is not just a matter of domestic politics — this is a matter of national security.

So today, in addition to challenging the certification of the election, I'm calling on Congress and the state legislatures to quickly pass sweeping election reforms, and you better do it before we have no country left.

Today is not the end, it's just the beginning. With your help over the last four years, we built the greatest political movement in the history of our country and nobody even challenges that.

I say that over and over, and I never get challenged by the fakeness, and they challenge almost everything we say. But our fight against the big donors, big media, big tech, and others is just getting started. This is the greatest in history. There's never been a movement like that.

You look back there all the way to the Washington Monument. It's hard to believe.

This is where I was standing. I felt like President Trump was giving me a shout-out. I saluted in his direction, looked up at the Washington Monument and then went back to listening to the man.

We must stop the steal and then we must ensure that such outrageous election fraud never happens again, can never be allowed to happen again. But we're going forward. We'll take care of going forward. We've got to take care of going back. Don't let them talk. OK, well, we promised. I've had a lot of people. Sir, you're at 96% for four years. I said I'm not interested right now. I'm interested in right there.

With your help, we will finally pass powerful requirements for voter ID. You need an ID to cash a check. You need an ID to go to a bank, to buy alcohol, to drive a car. Every person should need to show an ID in order to cast your most important thing, a vote. We will also require proof of American citizenship in order to vote in American elections. We just had a good victory in court on that one, actually.

We will ban ballot harvesting and prohibit the use of unsecured drop boxes to commit rampant fraud. These drop boxes are fraudulent. Therefore, they get disapp — they disappear, and then all of a sudden they show up. It's fraudulent. We will stop the practice of universal unsolicited mail-in balloting. We will clean up the voter rolls that ensure that every single person who casts a vote is a citizen of our country, a resident of the state in which they vote and their vote is cast in a lawful and honest manner. We will restore the vital civic tradition of in-person voting on Election Day so that voters can be fully informed when they make their choice. We will finally hold big tech accountable. And if these people had courage and guts, they would get rid of Section 230, something that no other company, no other person in America, in the world has. All of these tech monopolies are going to abuse their power and interfere in our elections, and it has to be stopped. And the Republicans have to get a lot tougher, and so should the Democrats.

They should be regulated, investigated, and brought to justice under the fullest extent of the law. They're totally breaking the law. Together, we will drain the Washington swamp and we will clean up the corruption in our nation's capital. We have done a big job on it, but you think it's easy. It's a dirty business. It's a dirty business. You have a lot of bad people out there.

Despite everything we've been through, looking out all over this country and seeing fantastic crowds. Although this, I think, is our all-time record. I think you have 250,000 people. 250,000. Looking out at all the amazing patriots here today, I have never been more confident in our nation's future. Well, I have to say, we have to be a little bit careful. That's a nice statement, but we have to be a little careful with that statement.

If we allow this group of people to illegally take over our country because it's illegal when the votes are illegal when the way they got there is illegal when the states that vote are given false and fraudulent information.

We are the greatest country on Earth and we are headed and were headed in the right direction. You know, the wall is built. We're doing record numbers at the wall. Now, they want to take down the wall. Let's let everyone flow in. Let's let everybody flow in. We did a great job in the wall. Remember, the wall, they said it could never be done. One of the largest infrastructure projects we've ever had in this country, and it's had a tremendous impact, that we got rid of catch and release. We got rid of all of this stuff that we had to live with.

But now, the caravans, I think Biden's getting in, the caravans are forming again. They want to come in again and rip off our country. Can't let it happen. As this enormous crowd shows, we have truth and justice on our side. We have a deep and enduring love for America in our hearts. We love our country.

We have overwhelming pride in this great country and we have it deep in our souls. Together, we are determined to defend and preserve government of the people, by the people and for the people. Our brightest days are before us. Our greatest achievements, still away. I think one of our great achievements will be election security. Because nobody until I came along had any idea how corrupt our elections were.

And again, most people would stand there at 9 o'clock in the evening and say I want to thank you very much, and they go off to some other life. But I said something's wrong here, something is really wrong, can have happened.

And we fight. We fight like hell. And if you don't fight like hell, you're not going to have a country anymore.

Our exciting adventures and boldest endeavors have not yet begun. My fellow Americans, for our movement, for our children, and for our beloved country. And I say this despite all that's happened. The best is yet to come. So we're going to, we're going to walk down Pennsylvania Avenue. I love Pennsylvania Avenue. And we're going to the Capitol, and we're going to try and give.

The Democrats are hopeless — they never vote for anything. Not even one vote. But we're going to try and give our Republicans, the weak ones because the strong ones don't need any of our help. We're going to try and give them the kind of pride and boldness that they need to take back our country.

So let's walk down Pennsylvania Avenue. I want to thank you all. God bless you, and God Bless America.

Thank you all for being here. This is incredible. Thank you very much. Thank you.[6]

With his words still hanging in the cold Washington air, I made my way down toward the Capitol. While walking with fellow patriots, I noticed the beautiful mammoth Washington government buildings that adorned my path. When I looked at them – they, too, seemed cold. Distant. Dead. Soulless.

And it gave me the opposite feeling I experienced as a child visiting Washington with my family.

Back then, DC was hopeful. In those days –when I looked at these buildings and monuments, they glistened. Shined. Reflected light. And in me conjured up warm feelings of hope and, dare I say, pride in this place called America. Seeing Jefferson in his Memorial and walking up those stairs to greet Abraham Lincoln was akin to going to a Greek Orthodox Easter Church service with my beloved parents and sister. It was something close to being holy and we all knew it was something that was good.

Good. Warm. Proud of my country.

Yet on this day, January 6th, 2021, I had a dilemma and a hard choice to make. Should I travel to Washington DC, and peacefully protest what I thought was a stolen election or should I venture to Tarpon Springs, Florida, to partake in the annual Epiphany celebration?

The Epiphany celebration, for those who don't know, culminates with young Greek boys diving into the murky and chilly waters of the Spring Bayou for a cross, whereupon the diver who retrieves the cross is said to have a blessed year of good fortune.

I had made my choice and decided to go to Washington. It was a cross I had to bear. So I went on my odyssey with hundreds of thousands of faithful patriots- some seeking blessings, others fortune, while most would settle for the truth as we navigated the murky and chilly waters of the place that we knew as the *SWAMP.*

As I became part of an enormous, moving yet orderly group of folks making our way down toward the capital, it's what I didn't notice - that got my attention

And then it hit me – all at once. Something was missing.

Then a *"Eureka"* moment or perhaps more appropriately, dare I say - a moment of epiphany.

It came to me all at once as my friend, who I'll call *J* because of her love of Jesus, asked me in her deliberate and beautiful English accent:

"I have to go to the bathroom. Where are the bathrooms?"

Her words stung me – as I combed my surroundings for any sign of relief that a portable toilet would provide.

As we walked – I asked other patriots, *"Where are the bathrooms?"*

"Didn't see any" and *"I don't know"* were the common retorts.

Our *peaceful protest* had turned into *pee-full request.*

"Where were the bathrooms?"

There were hundreds of thousands of people gathered outside.

"Where were the bathrooms?"

The thought dominated and commanded my immediate attention.

"Where were the bathrooms?" "Surely they had bathrooms, right?"

That was strange. We looked and looked as we walked toward the Capitol building.

Maybe they forgot?

Or maybe they never planned installing the *Johnnies on the Spot* as they were sometimes called.

So as we searched for a place to relieve ourselves –the thought occurred to me with a twist of fate in the cold DC air on this fateful day – January 6th 2021.

Many of us had traveled from all over the world to be here on this important day in our republic's history, believing in our hearts and minds that the election was stolen. The irony was not lost on me as it cut through me like the cold winds of Washington on this very significant and strange day in our capitol.

We were looking for toilets. We were looking for toilets for Pete's sake!

In a lot of ways, perhaps it made perfect sense.

THE SWAMP WAS IN NEED OF TOILETS!

Because Let's Face It – Washington is Full of Shit

That was one headline that made sense for all the obvious reasons and one that surely wouldn't be seen in the New York Times or Washington Post.

Only two conclusions could be made. Either those in charge forgot or deliberately didn't install them on purpose for the many hundreds of thousands of patriots who needed them and gathered in DC on this day to peacefully protest. Whatever the reason, they were so unlike some good reliable plumbers who didn't forget on a fall election night back in November to answer their service call and install, like a toilet, a man named Joe, into the White House – and into his new residence. Incidentally, in case you're wondering, the White House, as far as sightseeing is a place not to miss in Washington, and it's a place where there are 32 bathrooms, but be forewarned, it is place where at least right now *"Deplorables"* are not welcome and not encouraged to go.

And that was bad news for everyone who gathered in DC on January 6, 2021 and looked to Washington for answers, because the shit was truly about to hit the fan.

You Say Insurrection, I say Protest- Let's call the whole thing off

There's an old song by Cole Porter or is it Gershwin?

Doesn't really matter who wrote it – just that it's a great song.

Incidentally it was the brothers Gershwin, George and Ira who penned this classic.

And no matter who is singing it from the iconic Ella Fitzgerald to the kid from Hoboken, named Francis Albert Sinatra, the song plays and works.

It works. Makes sense. And connects to all those who hear it.

Things have come to a pretty pass
Our romance is growing flat
For you like this and the other
While I go for this and that
Goodness knows what the end will be
Oh, I don't know where I'm at
It looks as if we two will never be one
Something must be done
… You say either, I say either
You say neither and I say neither
Either, either, neither, neither
Let's call the whole thing off, yes [7]

Got me thinking of that American classic song as I heard those in much of the media singing from what appeared to be the same song sheets. In regards to what happened on January 6, 2021, was this an insurrection or merely just one of those riots that they labeled peaceful protests as cities all across America burned in the summer of 2020, when the property was damaged, neighborhoods were destroyed, and many lives that mattered were lost?

"You say insurrection. I say peacefully and patriotically protest."

"Let's call the whole thing off."

Before we get too deep into the deep state tune that many seemed to want everybody to sing, we must first examine what an insurrection is and isn't and what a riot is and isn't…and yes, what a peaceful protest is and isn't.

Being there that day on January 6, I was washed in a mix of emotions as many tunes played and danced in my red-capped MAGA head.

I heard and hummed to myself – *The Battle Hymn of The Republic*.

Then a little George M. Cohen, *Yankee Doodle Dandy* and that flag-waving music that I so loved and related to.

And of course – I heard the tune associated with all of President Trump's rallies- The Lee Greenwood anthem, *"I'm proud to be an American."*

We were all there in mass.

From different parts of the country, each with a pained pride in our hearts – all wanting to do something, perhaps change the tune and tone in Washington – and make sure that those in power heard us – The WE THE PEOPLE band, playing America's music written by the people and for the people.

That was me on this cold day in Washington …an unarmed man, unless you count the GET TRUMP books I brought with me as weapons. And to some, they are. But to me, they were the reason I was there. Peacefully protesting- a suspicious election, yes, to say the least. But also to connect with other like-minded patriots. Like minded in the way that they loved this country, loved this President, and knew in their heart of hearts that something was not only rotten in DENMARK. Echoing the officer of the palace guard in Hamlet after the ghost of the dead King appears, walking over the palace walls - sending a wake-up call to the people that there was something rotten in Washington DC.

And in this play, if you will, portrayed on January 6, 2021, the palace walls that shielded those who ruled over the people were breached by *"we the people,"* already being labeled an angry mob by those penning this tale of insurrection, as the ghost of not a betrayed king, but a banished president hovered in the cold Washington air.

But for most of the hundreds of thousands who gathered on this fateful day, and for me in particular, that's not how it was. With broken hearts yet with determined spirits we gathered to support our collective cause. And that collective cause was simply this:

Get to the truth and to the bottom of the SWAMP and what really happened on Election Day, 2020.

We had questions. And we wanted those in DC representing us to ask these questions in the people's house. We wanted inquiries and arguments to be made legally, orderly, and, yes, peacefully. But make no mistake we wanted answers, not talking points and propaganda that *"This was the most secure and fair election ever conducted."*

We were cold. But we weren't stupid. Some of us we old but still had energy. Some of us were young and had never experienced anything like this. Some of us were white. Some of us were black. And most of us wanted to do what was right. Some of us were men. Some of us were women. But almost all of us wanted to do what was fair. Some of us were born in the United States. Some of us had come from other countries. But most of us were proud of this place called America and loved it enough to fight for it …by protesting peacefully, to right what we all felt was a great wrong.

And that's all 99.9% of all we wanted to do on this day. Incidentally, that number is the same percentage of survival rate from COVID-19 had we done nothing. But more on Covid-19 a little bit later, which was part of the master plan to steal the election in the first place.

But first a little about this place called Washington DC.

A place where those who govern us sit as kings and queens and not as our representatives. A place where a small town mayor, turned down the President's offer to provide protection, just in case the crowd got out of control. Yes, the day before the so-called insurrection, Trump – offered to send thousands of National Guard members to the capitol.

In the same manner that most conductors of major Orchestras are willing to chime in and send some of the best players to a concert, The President offered to send his best equipped and trained major free-lance players- THE NATIONAL Guard – to DC so that the music being played on this day wouldn't turn violent.

And no matter how outraged the conductor named Trump was about the Election results, he still wanted the tune being hummed that day to be a peaceful and patriotic one.

He wanted the music that played that day to be more Debussy than Wagner. More *Gershwin* than *Gangsta-Rap*. More peaceful. Less mob-like. Yes, a protest song…but definitely not an *Insurrection Anthem*.

The kid from Queens, after all, was *on the record as being against America's Endless Wars and he was always on the side of law enforcement.*

On this day – when he was humming his tune about a lost election, a rigged election, and our right to protest, all of us in the choir he was preaching to – heard him loud and clear.

We, the hundreds of thousands who had gathered here on this cold day in Washington – who represented the millions who had supported him over his golden halcyon days of a successful reign, a time period when w*e, the people-* got him loud and clear.

We were all cold. We were all pissed. We were all concerned for the Republic. And all of us, every single one of us, who comprised this MAGA movement, were there to do some good! And most of us, as in 99.9% of us were there to peacefully and patriotically protest.

And finally, we, the people who comprised MAGA nation, had come from all over the nation to let our voices be heard in support of a man who traveled the long and unlikely road from Mar-a-Lago to DC to drain a swamp and to, yes, start a political movement, and in the end do much more than that.

This conductor and maestro represented a movement whose time had come. A movement that consisted of forgotten men and women of all races, creeds, and colors singing the praises of a land they loved called America. All singing in different keys but humming the same tune and reading off the same song sheet with their fellow Americans on a cold day in January in DC.

"You say extremist... We say Patriot."

"You say most secure election ever...We say rigged."

"You say tomato. We say ta-mah-to."

"You say America was never great. We say we want to make it America Great again."

"You say insurrection. We say patriotically and peacefully protest."

"Hey let's call the whole thing off."

Seeking Justice as God laughs at our Plans

Above all, January 6, 2021, was a sad day for America.

Was I angry? Hell yes. Many of us were. But above all – the day left me sad.

That's the overall feeling I had as I walked like a disciple of Christ, a soldier in Washington's Army and a zombie in one of those zombie movies around Washington DC, on that fateful day.

Was I delusional? Maybe a little. I actually thought I could set up a makeshift book signing like I was in one of those Barnes and Noble bookstores that thankfully still exist- and sell my *Get Trump* book. I laugh now at the thought - likening it to a potential scene and skit out of MONTY PYTHON.

"Who do I sign to?"

"To Jack, A great patriot..." as protesters marched toward the Capitol building, to some looking like a dangerous mob, while to others looking like a group of minutemen we hoped would save the republic.

Was I hurt? Physically no. Spiritually. Yes. I was drained. It wasn't till later, when I started watching the shaping of the narrative in the mainstream media that I became frustrated with the whole story that they all wanted to tell and sell about January 6th.

Back then, the cold day served as a "slap in the face" and a metaphor for me, waking me up to the plight of what was going on in this place called Washington. It was a place that I adored and revered as a child, but now it was feeling different in my bones and my soul as I walked from the ellipse toward the capitol dome. As a child, I became excited, as Jimmy Stewart's Jefferson Smith in *Mr. Smith Goes to Washington*, when I saw any sight of any monument representing any American hero from the past. In seeing them, the adrenaline rushed to my head and heart. When I thought of these founders, represented in marble and bronze in these places, it was reminiscent of the feeling I had when I walked into my Greek Orthodox Church during Easter services with my loving parents and little sister.

It was a holy place to us. A place to be treated with respect. A good place where good men and women governed and kept our country on the right track.

Now, today, it felt different. Didn't know what it was yet. But something was amiss.

I promised myself on this day to make a journey to the Lincoln Memorial and have that walk up and talk with Abe to see what he was thinking. I wanted to become inspired by him, in the way Jefferson Smith was in the Frank Capra classic from 1939. And of course, I wanted to go to old Abe for answers on what was ailing me and so many in America.

In fact, the Lincoln Memorial was the go-to place to go and meet if we, the Sarasota Five, got separated or lost from each other. That was the only thing that we really planned. A contingency if we got lost or separated from each other.

Made me think about that thing that is attributed to John Lennon, "*Life is what happens when you're busy making plans.*"

And that other phrase, "*If you want to make God laugh, tell Him your plans.*"

Well, aside from being there to protest what we felt was a stolen election – we didn't really have any plans, but one thing was sure – and I didn't know if this was God laughing or not- we surely didn't know how the day would turn out, and it's safe to say it turned out a lot different than what we expected.

Looking Back on Washington

The day played out almost in slow motion. Meandering down toward the capital, it was never my intention to journey the steps that led me here. Nor was it my intention to climb up the scaffolding to a higher perch, where hopefully, I could get a different view of the scene below.

Amidst the apparent chaos that was taking place, I listened to and joined in patriotic chants and cries of *"USA, USA!"* and *"WE LOVE Trump."* The emotion was mesmerizing. A mix of feelings and colors as I looked at the mosaic of my fellow Americans who had made the journey to this hill to do what was guaranteed and promised to all of us in the Constitution- that our voices be heard.

This was ground zero for the MAGA movement that had started up as a man from Queens who sought not to be a King but instead a man of the people, by the people, *and for the people.*

To say that I was caught up in commotion would be an understatement. To say that I was out of control would be inaccurate. To say that some acted badly is also true. But it's also true that there were members of our government who did not do all they could to fend off the violence. In fact, in time, there would be some evidence pointing to the great possibility that our own government contributed to and was part of a more sinister plan.

Needless to say, it was an emotional day for all of America. And for the most part, I remained relatively calm. Talking to patriots of all creeds and colors from all over America who had one thing in common- make those two things in common. In some way, they felt that the 2020 election not only didn't go the way they wanted it to go- but that it was, in fact, rigged or fixed to install the hapless Biden into office. The other given was that most of the people who gathered here loved, truly loved America, and as far as the people I spoke with, THEY ALL LOVED a man named President Trump.

I looked on at fellow Americans draped in various forms of Trump MAGA regalia – from *Keep America Great* to *Make America Great Again* and other shirts that seemed to plead and even pray to higher sources above – even higher than the hill where we had gathered to SAVE AMERICA.

And that's the sentiment I had as I climbed up, snapped photos, and conducted impromptu interviews with the brethren who had gathered here on this cold day in January in the nation's capital.

As I climbed higher and higher, my intentions were not sinister. I was not armed unless you consider a smartphone, video camera, and my books to be weapons. The higher I got, the more mixed my emotions became as the questions persisted.

How did we get here?

What was going to happen?

What happened to the DC I knew in my youth?

What would our founding fathers think?

Would they join in the protest or be ashamed of the proceedings?

And finally - *Were we enlightened and courageous Patriots or merely fools on the hill?*

Finally making it to the top, I looked directly ahead at the Washington Monument in the distance.

It represented a place where I stood just minutes ago as I listened to President Trump's speech in which he implored fellow patriots to march down to the capitol and peacefully and patriotically protest. And that's what I was doing as I stood there *looking back on Washington.*

As I looked out, I thought of my hero, the great actor and American Jimmy Stewart, and how much he loved America, and how much you felt his pain and pride in this place called America as he portrayed a young Jefferson Smith seeking answers in the DC swamp in Capra's classic Mr. Smith Goes to Washington.

I also thought of the Ethiopian cab driver and his words of support for President Trump and Rudy Giuliani as he dropped us off near the ellipse.

I thought of all the folks from all over the country adorned in the MAGA red caps and some in blue all proclaiming with banners from where they came from and their support of Donald J. Trump. *Iowans for Trump. Californians for Trump. New*

Yorkers for Trump. A variety of signs dotted the landscape. As did the *Blacks for Trump* and *Latinos for Trump* signs —and even signs from large *Chinese contingencies waving anti-CCP signs* with notes of support for the 45th President.

A mixed bag, for sure of Patriots. Mainly white. Mainly older. Some young. Some blacks. Yet all wearing red white, and blue as they gathered in this place where history would be made on this day.

And that is what I was thinking about as I took in these scenes from a riot —excuse me, a peaceful protest - as I looked down towards the monument that was erected in honor of our first President George Washington, in a place that was named after him and perhaps had forgotten about him.

I flashed back to the summer and the riots that took place all over America following the George Floyd incident. I thought of all those *peaceful protests* where many people's lives were turned upside down with destruction and death as statues and our history were destroyed, and our history was in danger of being erased.

As history – this Trump Rally would be different from the other three Trump rallies I had attended in tone, temperament, and even temperature.

When I attended the first Trump rally in Sarasota, Florida, the night before Election Day 2016, in front of a packed Robarts Arena of over five thousand people, back then, the MAGA movement was just taking shape and the reality of Trump's presidency was an unlikely dream. The second Trump rally was once again in Florida but this time in Tampa and just before the 2020 election. More than 25,000 people gathered on hot autumn day in October, and MAGA nation was a real viable and recognizable thing now. I recall Governor DeSantis throwing T-shirts into a frenzied crowd as the hope and confidence of a Trump reelection was on the horizon. And the other Trump rally was on July 4th weekend in 2021, in a sweltering Sarasota, Florida, before some 45,000 people and post the 2020 upset and J-6.

This gathering in Washington on January 6th was different. Sadness, madness, and a prevailing sorrow cut through brisk Washington as hundreds of thousands of Trump enthusiasts and MAGA nation descended on the Capitol to peacefully protest and show their support for a man and a movement.

A crowd made up - mainly of a mass of pure patriots and of course, a few assholes.

While listening to the president and stretching to see him from a spot I had gathered near the Washington Monument, most of my fellow protesters and patriots were polite even while being pissed off underneath. Some were watching from trees they had climbed up to get a better look at the man named Trump.

After some time and as the speech finished, many of us made our way toward the capital in an orderly fashion. Once on the capitol grounds, I snapped footage and pictures of an eclectic group of patriots expressing their support of a man while protesting the result.

Climbing up for a Different View and Open Doorway In.

Before I had climbed up to my perch on the Capital building and with chants from my fellow patriots providing the soundtrack, I had noticed an opening on the lower level that led into the capital. Faced with a dilemma, should I go inside or remain outside?

Something was calling me inside. And something was telling me not to go inside.

Was it a voice? No, not really. It was more like a spirit, who I will call the Holy Spirit —who nudged me, warning me to NOT go in.

I listened to the voice. I did not, *Thank God,* go inside the Capital building on the 6th of January. Instead, I remained true to *my creed of being an outsider and not a Washington insider.*

Gathering there in another bubble of sorts, a MAGA cocoon, between the loud chants *of USA, USA, USA and We love Trump. I felt the warmth, passion and* desperation of the day. And I felt something else. The peace. The resolve. The quiet. And in a moment of sublime silence, I looked out at the scene below and off into the direction of where I had come and the Washington Monument.

Looking back at the monument, I thought of the man it honored. Our first president. He was not a king. Just a courageous man. One who shunned power and fought for our country. Not a perfect man. But a man who was perfect for his times. A man, who without his presence, it's hard to imagine America forming into prominence and a historical power.

A sadness and uncertainty about America's future came over me as I stared at the monument and thought of a man named Trump. Once again, like Washington, a man with flaws, not a perfect man, yet a man perfect for his time, a natural leader who had come to this place to fight for the people and against all enemies, foreign and domestic.

In that moment, as I looked back at the Washington Monument with the echoing choruses of USA, USA ringing in my ears, I paused and put my head down in prayer and prayed for America. This day January 6th, after all, also represented *The Epiphany* in my Greek Orthodox faith. As I crossed myself I thought for a moment of all those young boys diving in Tarpon Springs, in the murky Spring Bayou waters, for a cross, their cross and our cross.

A cross to bear. We all had our own crosses to bear in our lives. Today, this was mine and ours as we negotiated the murky waters of the DC swamp.

It was time to leave Washington behind. A curfew called for all those in Washington to exit the district. And that included all of us. Finding my other fellow patriots after losing contact with them for much of the day, we started to make our way out of Washington. As we did, we wished good luck to some of the police who had gathered and were now equipped with battle armor. Tire spike barriers kicked into gear, showing their ominous intentions. Things were getting serious.

On our long walk back to the Mandarin Oriental parking garage, a *man dressed like George Washington* crossing the Delaware caught my attention. When I offered him a copy of my book, Get Trump, tears of gratitude filled his eyes. Meeting this man I would come to call General George Washington gave me hope and served as a good sign on the day that seemed bleak and filled with so many mixed signals.

My phone, which was on life support, even with all the prep to have extra juice and batteries for the day that lay ahead –

had finally gone dead. Metaphorically, it perfectly matched our exhausted and overwhelmed spirits that the day brought. Drained by the encounter with the swamp, we were ready to go home.

Safely in the van, as we were making our way out of the swamp, I sought a charge for my dead smartphone. With my phone charging –a flurry of texts from well-wishers concerned for my safety lit up my screen from people who knew I had made my way to DC.

"Gus, you Okay?" "Are you safe?" "Please call to let me know you are not in danger."

Then just as we were driving past the beautiful Lincoln Memorial glistening in a golden and almost holy light, my smartphone rang. It was my mother. She was crying.

"Are you okay?"

"I'm okay, my country is not," I answered, borrowing a line from Dennis Prager, one of my heroes. While hanging up the phone with my mom, I caught the last glimpse of the Lincoln Memorial.

I smiled. A tired, hopeful smile. Two masterpieces. Two miracles. Two Coincidences? Two acts of collaboration, all conspiring to lift my spirit on a day that seemed hopeless and when many of us seemed helpless.

Hearing my mother's voice as I looked at the Lincoln Memorial was the only sign I needed to know that we were on the right road.

Looking back on Washington and the glorious Lincoln Memorial from the road, I could still hear my mother's righteous, soothing, and kind voice playing in my head and giving me hope for brighter days ahead. I also heard another voice. It was Mr. Lincoln's. His words from his Gettysburg Address echoed in my soul as we drove out of a place called Washington on the 6th of January 2021.

"…this nation, under God, shall have a new birth of freedom and that government of the people, by the people, for the people, shall not perish from the earth"

A Face in the Crowd & Our Time of Truth

There are allegedly over 14,000 Hours of video from January 6, 2021 that much of the public was prevented from seeing.

I was there. And I hope I can find myself – *A Face in the Crowd*…not for ego…but just to show you the setting. What I did. What most Patriots did and didn't do on that day. What the truth is shown from the camera in the sky. For those things that I did on that day, not ashamed in the least. Actually proud.

I was there for mainly one reason. To let my voice be heard in support of a president and protest against the insurrection that took place not on January 6, 2021, but the one that took place on November 3rd 2020. What did I do on that day? I watched and listened to my president make a speech as hundreds of thousands of people looked on with pride and a little hope.

I spoke with fellow patriots from all around the United States.

I interviewed some. I helped others who were hit with tear gas and rubber bullets. I consoled some. Some I was consoled by. I listened. And I heard their fears and hopes.

I took in all their beautiful faces. White retirees from the Midwest. Black urban youths with an edge who were there listening to the man from Queens. Brown people from Mexico. Chinese contingencies protesting the CCP. Hindus for Trump. Arabs for Trump. Jews for Trump. Gays and LBGTQ for Trump. Atheists for Trump. Christians for Trump. All there. All there for the movement and the man.

A mosaic of the American face. I took it all in. A face in the crowd.

Looking, searching, and seeking for my fellow brothers and sisters.

To look them in the eye. To tell them that it was okay.

To have them tell me it was going to be okay.

A face in the crowd of patriots who had come to Washington to protest.

Peacefully and Patriotically. A face in the crowd of faithful Americans who had come seeking the rule of law and the blindness of justice.

A face in the crowd of fellow Americans who loved their country and their president.

Finally, a face in the crowd of Americans who is still filled with hope that our best days are ahead of us because of all the faces in the crowd that I saw on that cold January day in the swamp when we stood with our president and up for our country.

A Stop In a Richmond Tavern – The Narrative is unmasked

Weary from the road, we were getting reports from those we loved and trusted on what was being reported, from many, who many of us now never trusted- the mainstream media. Their take on this historic day in Washington was predictable. *A day that would live in infamy.* In time, many "who were given the huge responsibility of reporting fairly and with balance" – the facts to America and Americans, echoing the talking points of Washington insiders and political operatives, likened the day to be eerily equivalent to 9/11 and as bad as Pearl Harbor.

For a respite, we stopped in a dark Richmond bar as versions of the "truth" were starting to come to light. We watched the transmitted images over the small TV screen in the bar with the sound off, and as a congressional vote to certify the election of 2020 was taking place inside of a chamber from a place called Washington, we had just exited.

For a moment, I let my mind wander to another place in time, as the setting, this darkened pub or tavern if you will, felt like a place out of synch with the rest of our world. Richmond. A place with so much history. A place where one could see the ghosts of a young Patrick Henry delivering his famous *" Give Me Liberty or Give Me Death"* speech in what is now known as St. John's Church. A place that was the first municipal burial ground dedicated expressly for Negroes (enslaved) and free people of color by the city of Richmond was the Shockoe Bottom African Burial Ground, as noted on the 1809 Plan of Richmond as the "Burial Ground for Negroes."

And finally, a place where on April 4, 1865, President Abraham Lincoln toured a fallen city on foot with his young son Tad while visiting the former White House of the Confederacy and the Virginia State Capitol.

History notes that as fires set by the retreating Confederates still smoldered, Lincoln went to the White House of the Confederacy, expecting a communication from the retreating forces. Many wanted Lincoln to make a public gesture of sitting at Jefferson Davis's own desk, symbolically saying to the nation that the President of the United States held authority over the entire land. And as citizens and freed slaves greeted Lincoln as a conquering hero, one admirer reportedly said, "*I know I am free, for I have seen the face of Father Abraham and have felt him.*"[7] When a general asked Lincoln how the defeated Confederates should be treated, Lincoln replied, "Let 'em up easy."[8]

And now I was here on the evening of January 6, 2021, in Richmond, Virginia, inside a small, darkened tavern, straining to see a light that flickered from a TV screen as some more American History was being made. I was hoping and praying that the Almighty would "let us all up easy" to deal with the crisis of confidence that existed in our land.

As I watched Vice-President Pence embrace Nancy Pelosi, seemingly with glee and approval ...a cold, evil chill ran down my spine.

Maybe it was just the sight of seeing the two adversaries together that stunned me. But perhaps it was more than that. My thoughts kept playing back in my mind, and I kept hearing the words of a gentle black lady from Georgia who spoke to me from her heart and with tears in her eyes at the foot of the capitol just hours ago.

I kept hearing her voice play on and on and on as I watched the silent picture in front of me.

"The Vice President has sold out our president Trump."

"He's a traitor." "This is so bad for America."

"They shut down the discussion." "The whole thing is rigged."

That's what I saw as I sat in the dark Richmond Tavern. I kept hearing her voice as I watched the scene play out on the small TV screen sans sound. I was shaken by the images and the comradery of the two people in the chamber- The Speaker of the House, Nancy Pelosi, and the Vice President of the United States – Mike Pence.

Regarding Pelosi, I found her to be the devil incarnate, an opportunist who worked the system that she had come to know and embody as a card-carrying member and royal member of the swamp, a place that she personified.

Mike Pence, while initially confident in his loyalty to both our president and the Constitution, I felt a particular comfort and confidence in the man because of his professed and profound faith.

Still, as I watched the picture play out in front of me, something bothered me. It didn't add up. The glee. The sudden closeness of the two. The coolness. The smugness. The self-righteous tone and vibe that I could feel even with the sound off.

As we huddled, gathering our bearings to place our order – the orders from on high from DC and beyond - were being placed to certify an election that many of us felt was STOLEN...RIGGED and part of A REAL INSURRECTION to overthrow a PRESIDENT and GOVERNMENT, not on January 6, 2021, but on November 3rd, 2020.

This final act of a real insurrection was being acted out in the dark of night –while much of AMERICA slept. Much like it had on Election night when the vote was paused to conduct a re-write to the voting narrative that would miraculously place Biden ahead of Trump and on his way to stealing the keys to the White House. On this night, they had gathered after a rough day in the swamp and did their bidding in the dark of night to certify an election without a proper debate. And as the evil acts that that I felt were being conducted in the name of democracy and on behalf of our now shaky, crumbling Republic, the hypocrisy of it all made me a little sick.

As the workers in the Tavern, posing as *mask Nazis,* made sure that our masks were on tightly between bites of our burgers and the fish and chips we chowed down, the irony was at first lost on me. Here I was in this darkened bar, watching masked politicians close down debate as the brown shirts enforced their draconian mask laws. Then it hit me. Had it not been for *the Chinese Virus* unleashed on us, with the *1984-like* demands to shelter in place and wear those damn masks unless you are buying something on a plane or in a tavern, the excess of mail-in ballots that created the opportunity to vote early and often for Biden – even if you were dead, weren't registered, didn't live in that state or weren't of age. All that mattered was that you hated Trump and in essence, all those who were in his MAGA movement.

And eureka, just like that, the masks were off all of us.

I'm just glad I got to finish my burger before I hit the road and left Richmond for the free state of Florida.

Once Back from January 6, I played Yankee Doodle Dandy

I'm a Yankee Doodle Dandy. The best and most sure way to get me to have a patriotic moment and heartfelt swell of pride in my heart is to play Jimmy Cagney's 1942 Oscar-winning performance in *Yankee Doodle Dandy*.

There is something, actually many things that touch me about this classic American film. Easily my favorite James Cagney performance, just as Bogie's portrayal of Rick in Casablanca is the quintessential Humphrey Bogart performance. That they were both directed by *the greatest director who most people have never heard of*, Michael Curtiz, is an interesting coincidence.

Yankee Doodle Dandy is special to me. Perhaps it's because the first time I encountered the beloved film, I was much younger and my dad was still alive, and Cagney was from his generation. I remember fondly him peeking through my cracked bedroom door to ask me what I was watching and the smile on his face when I told him, *"Yankee Doodle Dandy."* I can still see that warm proud look he flashed in my direction today as if to say, "You're okay, kid; you're discovering one of the gods, one of the best who makes us who we are today."

He loved Cagney, and he loved this country – and he imparted his love of both to both my sister and me. He did it with Baseball too. And, of course, with our church and our faith. He provided building blocks that would help us withstand a world of storms with a home built on principles, morals and, dare I say, goodness.

Whenever I see the scene with Cagney as George M. Cohan, saying, *"My Mother thanks you, my father thanks you, my sister thanks you, and I thank you,"* I get a lump in my throat and cry every time.

Can't help it. And I don't want to help it either. I always want to feel that raw and vulnerable and, dare I say, a little innocent and moved to tears when I see this beloved film. It's the same feeling I get when I hear Ray Charles sing *"America the Beautiful."* Proud. In touch with something deep inside that genuinely moves me. Another moment also from the movies and one I share with my father is watching *"The Pride of The Yankees"* with Gary Cooper portraying the Iron man Lou Gehrig. When he gives the "I consider myself the luckiest man..." speech in the face of his deadly diagnosis with a disease that will take his life, I'm not ashamed to say I lose it with tears that could fill Yankee Stadium.

Yet watching Jimmy Cagney play the old song and dance man, George M. Cohan connects me in another way with my father, George, who was a singing and writing sensation who never got the acclaim for the gifts in his lifetime.

Just one more reason why the film is so special to me and why I'm a Yankee Doodle Dandy.

And why the film was like a warm blanket and cup of hot chocolate and such a welcomed friend to come home to when I returned to teach my class on January 7th after driving home through the night from our nation's Capital after the happenings on the 6th of January.

Having scheduled the film before the trip, I took that as some kind of providence.

I was emotionally spent and exhausted from the previous day. It was like medicine to sit back and watch the film and let it wash over me.

Yet, as the film came to an end and shots of the Capitol dome were flashed on the screen, I could see that the narrative already taking shape by the mainstream media had started to take hold.

A comment that came from one person in the class who reflected with sadness as the film finished, "It's too bad it's not like that today," was not shocking or surprising. The comment, in some ways, was understandable. Yet it still got under my skin to the point that I could not remain under cover and in the closet as to my participation in having gone to Washington.

"What do you mean?" I asked.

"It's too bad America has changed so much, and it wasn't like that yesterday."

"Well, I was there, and in many ways, it was like that yesterday," I shot back.

Shockingly he responded, "You were there at the Capitol yesterday in Washington."

"Yes, I was there. Hundreds of thousands of us were there exercising our constitutional right and expressing our patriotic duty to protest an election that we think wasn't on the level."

The look on his face told it all. He was already starting to paint me with one brush that the media was adept at using to support their narrative.

In time, the term January 6th would come to be an opportunity to paint all those who supported Trump as extremists and election deniers or, worse yet, insurrectionists.

On this day, I was just an American returning home from a long drive and long day in Washington where I went to support - not the overthrow of our government but instead see that our government was working for all the people and it would do the right thing.

In between, surely some people acted out of hand, some who may have even been working for the government, and no doubt some were not acting in the best interest of our country. But most people that day were there to peacefully and patriotically protest an election and show support for a president who we all thought was a Yankee Doodle Dandy.

Looking back on that day – while a lot of how I see Washington changed on that day - I can still see the nation's capital in the same light I did while viewing it in a James

Cagney movie. And for that I'm still thankful. In fact, my mother thanks you, my father thanks you, my sister thanks you and…I thank you for allowing me to still be grateful and continue to let my heart swell with pride as I watch our American movie play out.

III. Covid-19: The Gift that Keeps Giving

A life Flashes Before Me at an undug grave

Who Are The Real Conspiracy Theorists?

Sean Penn, Coward Stern and other fascists on Unvaccinated – "Put them in Prison"

A prescription For Disaster…And Why I didn't *Get the Shot*

A life Flashes Before Me at an undug grave

Bazar doesn't quite describe it.

The funeral for my beloved Aunt Toni that was taking place during *life during Covid-19 time.*

It reminded me of that classic *"Talking Heads"* song *"Life during Wartime."*

As I stared at the undug grave I started to hear the words.

> *"...Heard of some gravesites, out by the highway*
> *...A place where nobody knows...*
> *...Lived in a brownstone, lived in a ghetto*
> *I've lived all over this town...*
> *This ain't no party, this ain't no disco*
> *This ain't no fooling around*
> *No time for dancing, or lovey-dovey*
> *I ain't got time for that now"*

No, there wasn't time for any of that now.

There was only time for a funeral and for *Life during War time.*

And that's what this was. Make no mistake about that.

This was Life during Covid-19.

> *"Heard about Houston? Heard about Detroit?*
> *Heard about Pittsburgh, PA?*
> *You oughta know not to stand by the window*
> *Somebody see you up there*
> *I got some groceries, some peanut butter*
> *To last a couple of days*
> *But I ain't got no speakers, ain't got no headphones*
> *Ain't got no records to play*
> *Why stay in college? Why go to night school?*
> *Gonna be different this time*
> *Can't write a letter, can't send no postcard*
> *I ain't got time for that now."*

As cars full of mourners –many of whom were Greeks, all dressed in their best black arrived to pay their respects- I noticed they were all told to stay in their cars. Social distancing had reached epic proportions. "PLEASE STAY IN YOUR OWN CARS," I was ordered. It was ludicrous. Were we really all doing this —social distancing ourselves into a state of safety at all costs? Were we, sadly turning into a band of fearful soulless zombies?

Zombies. A good word for it. We were after all in a cemetery. My clouded mind and broken heart turned to George Romero's film – *Night of The Living Dead*...a classic film about zombies with scenes so powerful that it's still the only film I won't watch alone at home.

And while I wasn't alone in the cemetery – I felt that way.

They had separated us. First in our home and even now here at our final earthly home.

I waved to friends and family through windshields as protocol dictated life during Covid-19 as the *Cemetery Enforcers* warned us to stay in our cars and not gather too close together.

All the while - the whole affair was unfolding but unlike any funeral I was accustomed to ever attending. Those funerals were usually colored with their delicate amounts of whaling, sobbing, and blurred moments filled with regret, occasional doses of dignified acts- and of course clichés echoed by well-meaning souls —directed at the deceased – *"They are in a better place."*

But the place, this place where we all were - "*Life and now Death during Covid*" was indeed a strange place.

Because of the pandemic we were spared much of the *mourning fare* and what was intended as a quaint sending off of our beloved Antonia that usually accompanied a traditional Greek Orthodox funeral, was instead slowly turning into a *Chinese Fire Drill*. I can still say that can't I?

The funeral for our beloved Aunt Toni was turning into an absurdist comedy. And it was starting to make me sick. Yet we were all trying to do the best we could under the circumstances for my aunt. She was the after all the woman who had encouraged me to *write what I know*, and who insisted when we journeyed to the island of Crete —we pay our respects and visit the grave of the great Greek writer Nikos Kazantzakis - who had penned *Zorba the Greek* amongst his many classics.

As the funeral for our Antonia played out, my own personal Report to Greco, so to speak, I would think of the great Greek writer and the character that he created named Zorba, And of course I would think of my beloved Aunt- who taught me the importance, meaning and weight of words.

My Aunt Antonia's Funeral would have been a story that Nikos Kazantzakis would have appreciated.

Then I thought of his character, Zorba. What would *Zorba the Greek* do during Covid-19?

The answer screamed at me. Dance!

Zorba would dance. Most certainly, he would dance. Even in a cemetery, he would go on living. Zorba wouldn't take this sitting down and he wouldn't tolerate being separated from his fellow human beings. This was even too much madness for Zorba.

Still there we were – lined up in cars at the cemetery-isolated and waiting for instructions from the "*Covid-19 Police.*" As I watched the scene play out – I noticed Father Nick traversing the grounds with fellow Greeks who wanted him to do a quick blessing for their loved ones who had passed and were buried nearby.

As they made their arrangements- I looked around the cemetery –where my father was buried. His brothers, sisters and mother kept him company here in this, his final earthly resting place. Next to my father's stone –was the headstone of my mother, one I prayed would go unused for many years to come.

As the scene continued to play out – I pondered a natural, sad, and unsettling thought. Where was Aunt Toni going to be buried? My eyes surveyed the land and plots that marked the graveyard. I was told that my Uncle Steve had recently purchased three plots near the road – one for my Aunt Antonia and two more. One for him and his twin – Aunt Mary –who sadly was not at the funeral because it was determined that it would be too much for her to take.

I disagreed. And the reason was simple. *My Aunt Mary was a professional mourner.* Tears came to her easily and in buckets. Real tears. Heartfelt tears. Tears that made an impression –that the person leaving would be missed. Now Aunt Mary was missing —with all her tears on demand that she would share willingly with the Covid-19 crowd.

Missing, also apparently, was my Aunt Antonia's grave. Had this really happened? Had they forgotten to dig the grave? I asked the *Covid-19 Police* —who were barking social distancing orders and reasons for the delay. He looked at me with a dumbfounded look that I could even detect through his blue mask he so obediently wore.

"I don't know."

Soon he would scramble and get another enforcer from the cemetery police and get to the bottom of this. *Not the six feet under bottom, but* an excuse masked as an answer as to where my aunt would be buried and why the hole wasn't dug yet.

As Greeks lined up in their cars – the gossip and absurdity of it all, too good not to share with neighbors on their smartphones who were not there, Father Nick scrambled across the cemetery grounds, and that's when I saw it.

A small *Tonka-like truck appeared*. It looked ridiculous under the circumstances. With mourners waiting to mourn it was just getting to the business of digging the grave, the machine scurrying quickly almost in a panic to get to the spot near the road where my Aunt would be buried. It had arrived late. And appropriately so - *Greek Time, f*or this final event that celebrated my aunt's life.

I smiled as my eyes made their way toward the heavens. It was so embarrassing yet so appropriate. And it felt right in so many ways. After all - my aunt loved Kazantzakis and his GREEK take on life and death. And here we were. Living. Breathing. Mourning. All playing in the final act as if we were in a scene from Zorba the Greek.

Aside from the grave-what was missing most was my Aunt Mary (Thea Maria).

I would have welcomed her and her bucket full of tears meandering uncontrollably and zig-zagging (ala the Cretan mourners in Zorba) across the cemetery. My Aunt Antonia would probably have appreciated it as well.

In time -the Covid-19 police assured us that soon the grave would be dug. Father Nick approached from a distance and informed us that soon we could start. As he did, I glanced through windshields and Greeks snickering in their black cars.

It was all so strange. So chaotic. So *Kazantzakis like*. And in so many ways —so perfect.

A great send-off for our beloved Aunt who, as a school teacher in life, taught us all so many things. The importance of Literature. Religion. Science. Art. Drama. History. Politics. Things that the ancient Greeks had pondered for centuries. And of course, the fine art of living. Even on a crazy day in a cemetery. Not so strangely —and as Zorba had instructed – my mind began to dance.

I could see my dad, cigarette in hand – smirking, smiling, and welcoming Antonia - to the cemetery and to the neighborhood.

"Tony- they forgot to dig the grave? The Greeks are going to love that one."

Through the sadness, I smiled at the madness.

"This ain't no party, this ain't no disco
This ain't no fooling around
No time for dancing, or lovey-dovey
I ain't got time for that now."

Who Are The Real Conspiracy Theorists?

It's a term that's akin to being called a racist. When someone wants to marginalize you or diminish your argument or standing, they throw in the ad hominem attack that you are a purveyor of conspiracy theories and that you are, in fact, a *Conspiracy Theorist*.

But what if over time, those Conspiracy theories that you perpetuated to the rolled eyed looks of friends and foes alike - turned out to be true?

What then? What if the CIA was involved in killing JFK?

What if the whole Russian Collusion thing was made up to Get TRUMP?

What if the FBI and Justice department colluded and swayed the election for Biden over Trump?

What if the *Hydroxychloroquine* and *Ivermectin* were effective in fighting Covid-19 all along and big Pharma with some government insiders conspired to demonize those drugs so that the path for the emergency vaccine could be left wide open and greenlighted?

What if masks, lockdowns and the vaccine were ineffective but the government told you they worked? Some of these claims sound preposterous to some of you, and not so outlandish to others. And that leaves one important question that must be asked.

What do you call those conspiracy theories that turn into facts?

The Truth.

I used to be leery of so-called conspiracies and those who traded in them.

I too turned a deaf ear and rolled my eyes a bit when I heard theories from friends who told me about their theories on *Chemtrails*, the *Illuminati*, *Pizza Gate* and hell even whether we *landed on the moon or not?*

The thing is – the more I dug, and the more my government or those in charge of investigating stories fairly – namely the media, suppressed or put their thumb on the scale to promote or kill a story –the more I was curious about *these so-called Conspiracy theories.*

When they outright halted debate on the effectiveness of the COVID-19 vaccine and ostracized many good and qualified people who even so much as raised questions, pointed out flaws, or merely asked – is there another way or a better, *safer way to treat this outbreak?* -I became more open to the possibility that maybe what these conspiracy theorists were selling – wasn't farfetched or due to something wacky that they were smoking.

The more the establishment pushed back on good people like Dr. Peter McCullough, Dr. Robert Malone and Dr. Bhattacharya - to name a few brave souls who dared go against those in our *"Unbrave New World,"* where civil debate was attacked and where the principles of a doctor named *Hippocrates* were buried deep beneath the surface like the ruins of Ancient Greece- the more my eyes were opened to the possibility of all these conspiracies being true.

My eyes opened. My ears listened closer to the rhetoric spoon-fed to us – like good medicine with a little sugar. I became more cynical. More suspect. More suspicious. Not Jaded. Just awake. My eyes opened to the possibility that some people were lying to all of us. And had been for years. I wasn't taking it anymore - hook, line, and sinker from those in power.

I watched and scratched my head a bit as a President who worked for no salary was ridiculed by a diminutive doctor who was, and had been, for years, the highest-paid government employee and was lauded in god-like terms by a press core who took his word as the gospel. All the while the slings and arrows were shot early, often and constantly at a man named Trump for simply placing some hope in two drugs - *Hydroxychloroquine* and *Ivermectin* that may help fight off this terrible plague called Covid-19.

When Trump was banned from Twitter while *Terrorists were allowed to Tweet* – I was all in.

When Russia gate was exposed to be completely false – I placed an order to Amazon for my tin foil hat. When the media killed the Hunter Biden story just days before the election as being Russian Disinformation or some nonsense – I was ready to go to the dark side, the conspiracy side of the moon – hell, I was willing to question if we'd even gone to the moon. I was a film guy and while watching the shots of the men landing on the moon – I always looked at those shots with a little head scratching and with some curiosity. When I discovered a pretty interesting interview with the film master Stanley Kubrick, who stated that he was responsible for shooting and creating his greatest masterwork – the faking of "our landing on the Moon," I was intrigued and curious. Once I found myself scratching my head and, if I could see myself in a mirror- rolling my eyes a bit at my preposterous notions. What were they going to postulate next? That the moon was made out of Cheese? Jeez- what was I thinking? I also knew something else. If I went down this rabbit hole that was the size of those craters on the moon, it would render my very cool interview I did with astronaut Edgar Mitchell, one of only *13 men to have landed on the moon* – meaningless. I would have to throw away all my great reportage and that audacious moment when I asked the famous astronaut who graciously obliged - to sing "*Fly Me to The Moon*" with me in a gorgeous setting that was the Ringling Museum Courtyard as an oversized statue of David watched in the moonlight at a Sarasota Film Festival event. A moment that seemed like a Hollywood set and a production that was out of this world.

As a journalist, and that's what I consider myself, I try to see things straight down the middle. I try to seek the truth at all costs. Search out and expose lies, all for the greater good. Even more so, as an American and under our wonderful constitution, seek my first amendment God Given rights and my freedom of speech, to just, damn it, be curious and question anything and everything without being punished, persecuted, or worse yet - crucified. For those of you non-believers out there, with all due respect, get over it. Crucifixion. Not just one but many crucifixions that have taken place to we the people who dare question those running our 2024 version of Orwell's 1984 ministry of truth.

I'm not overstating what's at stake here.

Finally as a human being and someone who believes in a higher power, namely Jesus Christ, as a Greek Orthodox Christian steeped in knowing right from wrong, I was curious about why we are here, where we came from, and what we should do while we inhabit this marble called earth. Throughout my whole life, I have been aware of the struggle that takes place on this planet, in this country, in our communities and in our hearts – between the two forces pitted against each other – GOOD vs EVIL.

The reason why we do anything – often based on good or bad intentions.

It applies to all people and all governments throughout the history of time.

Now, when someone comes up with a new theory, conspiracy or otherwise – I take it with a respectful grain of salt. I try not to roll my eyes while I try to keep my mind, eyes, ears, and heart open. Yet I question. Always question. In person. On the Internet. At a lecture. At the church coffee hour. Does it pass the smell test? Is it too preposterous to be true? Can it be true? Who benefits if it's true? Who benefits if it's false? Where does the money go? Who benefits?

Questions. Questions. Questions. And our God-given right to ask them.

It's the life blood and something in our blood as good Americans – and it's our duty as human beings to question anything and everything.

There are no sacred cows.

You don't believe in Jesus?

Good for you. Actually bad for you

Seek and you shall find.

I did. I believe in him. Yes - because of the grace and gift of faith. But also because I've done the research. And finally, because of the luck of the draw, to have been born to two incredible human beings – my mother and father who were born of this world but made specifically for the next one. Humble servants and believers who taught us our faith and to have faith in our faith.

Two people who taught us that important thing - to always be open to those with questions.

My faith is a gift. It's not because I was brainwashed, waterboarded, or because I belong to some cult. A faith built often upon my questioning.

This Jesus thing, if it's not true is the greatest hoax of all time and will make the "faked moon landing," "The JFK Single Bullet Theory," and "Trump's Russia Gate" seem like child's play.

Because if Jesus is not the Lord, then a lot of people will have been duped, with me humbly putting my name at the top of that list.

And because I have pondered, wondered, and even questioned God's existence and sometimes his motivation and involvement in the grand design and scheme of things – that doesn't make me a non-believer or someone without faith and with doubts- it makes me someone who is curious to the mystery of it all.

C.S. Lewis – the great writer, former atheist and Christian apologist, said it perhaps better than anyone, and he offered it up to everyone, believers and non-believers alike, as to Who JESUS Was and did it in the form of a multiple-choice question.

Lewis offers three choices, cited by critics as his Trilemma – offering an apologetic theory sometimes described as the "Lunatic, Liar, or Lord", or "Mad, Bad, or God" argument.

Still, like the Lord, who designed us with free will and an ability to make a choice and question whether something is good or evil, the truth or a lie – we are left to question which road we are to travel down or up. And ultimately what answers we will find to be true as to the mysteries of life. C.S Lewis said, *"A man who was merely a man and said the sort of things Jesus said would not be a great moral teacher. He would either be a lunatic — on the level with the man who says he is a poached egg — or else he would be the Devil of Hell. You must make your choice."* [10]

Choice. It is there and essential in all the questions we ask and seek to resolve in life and in death.

Former atheist, journalist and Christian apologist Lee Strobel went on a similar journey as he tried to prove or disprove the divinity of Jesus in his series of books that includes - *"A Case for Faith," "A Case for Christ," and "A Case for the Creator."* In his books, Strobel started off as a hardened big-city news reporter and non-believing atheist seeking to find out who this JESUS was while deep down wanting to believe that he was a fraud all along. The rationale for Strobel's non –belief was simple.

Says Strobel, *"To be honest, I didn't want to believe that Christianity could radically transform someone's character and values. It was much easier to raise doubts and manufacture outrageous objections that to consider the possibility that God actually could trigger a revolutionary turn-around in such a depraved and degenerate life."* [11] Strobel states, *"If I had stopped asking questions, that's where I would have remained."* [12] The depraved life, of which he speaks openly, is his own. And it's clear that without a belief in the Lord, and his ability to question – Strobel's life story and his after–life story would be much different.

For Strobel...C.S. Lewis, myself and others, a choice is made, and a path is carved out to follow. Sometimes we think alone, on the road like *Kerouac*, but more likely with the help of a greater mapmaker, whose GPS system provides us with all the roads and choices that we can and may take along the way.

Politically speaking, Reagan said, "Trust but verify."

That was the former president's way of dealing with strong Soviet Union in regards to their missile escalation. The Hollywood Cowboy was shrewd. Sharper than many people on the left can ever give him credit for and is definitely a real leader.

His, "Trust but verify" mantra is a principle I try to live by.

Something I apply as a test when practicing my faith as a Christian, but most importantly as I navigate my way through the polarizing political landscape that suppresses questions and those asking them in today's America. Frightful, fearful times indeed –yet times we shall overcome. And for this one crystal clear reason. *We are not the ones who pretend to have all the answers - we are merely the ones with questions and the belief that we have the right to ask them.*

As JFK once proudly asked Americans everywhere, *"Ask not what your country can do for you, ask what you can do for your country."* And one of the greatest things you can do for your country is to keep asking questions of your government while seeking the truth.

Ask. Seek. And you shall find. We are the seekers. Seeking freedom and liberty – a given. But most crucially seeking not only the truth but the lies that seek to smother all those seeking the truth and the liars who created them.

A mosaic of patriots – some call us conspiracy theorists, others a cult of mindless MAGA followers or worse yet, white supremacists who trade in Q Anon.

Yet we are not that at all. We are merely Americans who quite frankly have some questions because as that great Cuban band leader, Desi Arnaz as Ricky Ricardo said to his zany red-haired spouse Lucy played by Lucille Ball - All you experts, elites and establishment types: *"You got some splaining to do."* Because you guessed it – we got questions.

During the rebellious 1960's, those at least who protested seemed authentic in their convictions and in their questioning of the government establishment. Today, the world is turned upside down to the point where many on the left not only placate those in the past they despised they respect them. Where before they pleaded for *"bread and not bombs,"* today they break bread with bomb throwers and bomb makers. Where in the revolutionary and riot-filled 60s, the left almost demanded that anyone over 30 not only be questioned – but never be trusted, today they share the same air space over the boob tube that is now social media as their views toward war the poor and free speech have become increasingly blurred.

Can you imagine those in the war movement of the 1960s sitting down with Secretary of Defense Robert McNamara and taking his word as gospel as to how the mission was going in South Vietnam?

Today that's the norm at places like MSNBC, CNN, network News, and Mainstream Media. The establishment and the protesters speak in one voice. Now the pundits, former warmongers once hated and at least mistrusted in places like Haight Ashbury and Berkley, replete with peace signs and the smell of pot in the air as the backdrop – are celebrated in shiny studios and are paid to be talking heads by the mainstream media who use them as modes of propaganda and to legitimize their evil deeds. They now proudly stand on their hind legs and in their thousand-dollar suits and proclaim warnings at the top of their lungs to a cheering crowd who once jeered them that:

- *Trump will end our Democracy as our border lays wide open to invasion by illegal immigrants.*
- *Trump will get us into wars all the while under their watch the world has slipped into many wars that didn't exist during Trump's first peaceful four year term*
- *Trump will destroy our economy when in fact they are ones who destroyed it with record high inflation, gas prices doubling and home ownership out of reach for most Americans.*

But don't worry, the government will tell you otherwise. These are, but a few of the examples of doublespeak make outright lying - that the brilliant Orwell warned us about in his landmark book *1984*.

Truth is - we are at a point where the Ministry of Truth is no longer a work of scary, masterful fiction. Sadly and frightfully, its story is being played out today in real-time.

This is no conspiracy theory.

They lie to us as often as physically possible.

They lie to us because they know they can get away with it.

They lie to us because they don't care about us or the truth.

They lie to us because if they told us the real truth there would be a real insurrection.

How else could you explain the war against President Trump, not only today in 2024 but as far back as 2015 when he first announced his candidacy for president?

They fear him and they fear us.

The main reasons.

We ask questions, seek the truth and will do something to make America Great Again.

When Trump first mentioned that the news media was FAKE NEWS, I initially thought it to be a little harsh. Turns out he was right all along. His conspiracy theories on what they, the deep state and establishment Washington were doing was spot on – and turned out to be the truth. In the end, it truly was a plot of hoaxes and witch hunts gone wrong, with rants of "*Russia, Russia, Russia*" falling on many deaf ears as much of America wakes up.

Many years from now, when many of the conspiracy theories- such as *the sudden deaths from an unproven vaccine* forced on us by big Pharma for profit and the power-hungry elites hopefully, it will be noted that President Trump first pushed for the use of Hydroxychloroquine and Ivermectin to fight Covid-19 at a time when it could have made a big difference in saving perhaps millions of lives.

It will be noted that while he pushed for *Operation Warp speed* and the development of a vaccine, it was, in fact, his own government doctors and so-called experts who misled, fought, and even lied to him *when he questioned* the use of and efficacy of those non-evasive protocols that could have made a big difference to the many countless souls who perished.

There's that word again. Question. Because Trump asked questions, they persecuted him. Because his questions got close to what they were doing – he was crucified. Those are not theories. Just facts. Hopefully, the more one digs for the truth, the more we shall continue to see just how right Trump was all along in revealing what really happened and what really worked pertaining to COVID-19. And in the end, we shall get an account of all the lies that they told us about the efficacy of vaccines, masks, social distancing, and the effect of lockdowns as Trump's conspiracy theories are proven to be the truth.

Now, when I think of that, I continue to question everything. Especially everything our government does to and supposedly for us.

- *The election of 2020. I have many questions. And yes, I think it was rigged.*
  (More on that in other parts of the book).
- *COVID-19 was formed purposely in a lab, not in a wet market, to hurt some people, make some people rich, and impact the 2020 election.*
- *Covid-19 Vaccine did more harm than good. Lots of questions. But so many people, especially young people, were destroyed and died at the hands of power-hungry globalists like Dr. Fauci, the WEF, WTO, WHO, CDC, Big Pharma, Bill Gates, and a cabal of establishment types who all think they know what's better for us- like in not living at all.*
- *January 6th was a peaceful protest by hundreds of thousands of patriotic Americans, myself included, in support of President Trump protesting a rigged election infiltrated by many deep state insiders working against the President as the final act of a Coup d'etat which took place on November 3, Election Day 2020. The supposed insurrection as labeled by deep-state actors and mind-numb media types, was an inside job by our government. By the way, Ray Epps – is the only one who is completely innocent.*
  (I'm being sarcastic)

I was full of questions. So I did what many of us do when we have questions - I made my way to *my dumb daily smartphone addiction* of scrolling down rabbit holes I pondered whether or not *"we really landed on the moon, or if 9/11, God forbid, was an inside job or partially an inside job, or even whether or not the Titanic actually hit an iceberg, or if there was anything to that bit that many of the world's biggest bankers were on that doomed ship."*

Off one rabbit hole and onto another.

I had questions for Google on Hydroxychloroquine, Ivermectin, *and the Covid-19 Vaccine.*

I wondered what I would get when I did a search on those three treatments for Covid-19.

When I typed the first four letters **Hydr**...Google prompted me directly to:

Hydroxychloroquine Side Effects. That was strange. Or was it?

Once there, *I could go to* - What are the side effects of hydroxychloroquine?

This medicine may cause muscle and nerve problems. Check with your doctor right away if you have muscle weakness, pain, or tenderness while using this medicine. Hydroxychloroquine may cause some people to be agitated, irritable, or display other abnormal behaviors within the first month after the start of treatment.

Now, to get to what hydroxychloroquine actually was and how it was used, I had to type the whole name.

Hydroxychloroquine is used to treat discoid lupus erythematosus (DLE) or systemic lupus erythematosus (SLE or lupus). It is also used to treat acute and chronic rheumatoid arthritis. This medicine is available only with your doctor's prescription.

It was obvious that those running the show wanted me or whoever had questions to see what the side effects were first- not that it was a safe and effective drug and had been for years and for many uses in fighting many illnesses.

Now I plugged in **IVERM** – this time the first five letters of the drug Ivermectin.

What do you think came up? You guessed it.

Ivermectin Side Effects

Adverse side effects from taking Ivermectin, which occur 1-10% of the time with standard doses, include rapid heart rate, swelling of face, swelling of feet, low blood pressure, dizziness, diarrhea, nausea, decreased white blood cell counts, and hepatitis.

Once again, the actual entry for Ivermectin was the second entry in my Google search, and this was the definition it gave as far as use.

Clinical Data. Last Updated: December 20, 2023. Ivermectin is a Food and Drug Administration (FDA)-approved antiparasitic drug used to treat several neglected tropical diseases, including onchocerciasis, helminthiases, and scabies.[1]**. For these indications, ivermectin has been widely used and is generally well...**

But what if you stopped each of your searches at SIDE EFFECTS.

I had more questions and as a wondered what they would say about COVID-19. I was starting to develop a theory- actually a conspiracy theory of my own,

I typed in the entry COVID-19 – kind of knowing what I would find.

When I typed in Covid-19 it went directly to Covid-19 Vaccines.

And from the CDC.Gov page this is what I read.

COVID-19 Vaccines Are Safe, Effective, and Free

Everyone 6 months and older should get an updated COVID-19 vaccine.

People aged 65 years and older who received 1 dose of any updated COVID-19 vaccine (Moderna, Pfizer-BioNTech or Novavax) should receive 1 additional dose of an updated COVID-19 vaccine at least 4 months after the previous updated dose. For more Novavax information, click or tap here.

Now for the second entry: *covid 19 vaccine side effects long term*

Vaccines rarely cause any long-term side effects. If you're concerned about side effects, safety data on COVID-19 vaccines is reported to a national program

called the Vaccine Adverse Event Reporting System in the U.S. This data is available to the public.

Funny thing I noticed when researching this section- when I plugged in Hydroxychloroquine and Ivermectin and Covid-19 in GOOGLE – you would think that all three would tell you what they were first then address the side effects.

I was not shocked. It's quite frankly what I expected from those in big tech, big government, and big pharma. I had to work to get the information. It's there if you dig and aren't discouraged in digging for the truth. The truth is, most people won't do the work, ask the questions, or question authority. For some, that's because they want to believe that they, once again, are not a pronoun choice in an LBGTQ alphabet soup. This THEY is the government. To some –the government is those in power who want to rule over us, the people, but to others, they represent the good guys who want what's good for us.

But when pondering that, ask yourself these questions.

What were THEY thinking as they demanded that we stay in lockdown, wear useless masks, walk one way down grocery aisles, and prevent us from gathering in public at weddings, graduations, and funerals while fearmongering us all into to taking an unproven jab when there were protocols available that were potentially more effective and less dangerous?

As we were stifled, they continued to pitch at a feverish pace, their unproven and unsafe snake oil as being good and safe for you, your friends, family, and neighbors.

It was just their first shot at keeping us obedient.

Through fear-mongering, it was a concerted effort that they hoped would prevent us –the curious and disobedient soldiers of liberty from digging for answers, asking questions, and seeking the Truth.

Regarding but not limited to COVID-19 - We, the People, should not take the word of the government, and we should be able to question everything. They should have to prove everything with peer-reviewed documentation. Scientists who don't agree should be able to question everything from the CDC to the FDA. But they don't want these scientists asking questions – that's why they censored them during Covid-19.

It has been said that the Deep State's motto or mantra is simple: *"Don't question COVID-19, our science, climate change, if the elections were rigged, or the conviction of Trump. Don't you ever question us! If you do, you're an extremist."* They're telling the American people, "Don't you ever question us!" and the American people are seeing who the real dictators are.

They silenced some, but not all of us. Sadly some were forced or coerced into taking their medicine, and the results from these "forced vaccinations" are just beginning to come to light.

Just how many individuals were negatively affected by taking the shot – time will tell, but it will be difficult, if not impossible, to get to the bottom of the whole story. Still, as we see the data on sudden deaths rising over a time when the shot was given and supposedly working to those of us who were low risk, young, athletic, and with no comorbidities - we must continue to ask those questions with the ferocity of a patriot and a seeker of truth.

Because it's not the last shot that they will make us take or the last effort they will take to force the shot into arms. It's not the last Faustian bargain that will be offered.

The good news – is thankfully we all have one shot left in us to get this right.

One shot heard round the world – to be heard and not be part of the herd.

To question and seek answers. To seek and find the truth.

Because the answers to all your questions are there.

My conspiracy theory: *Jesus is real and He's revealing all these evil deeds so that we can get closer to Him and the truth. He knows who shot JFK; and if we landed on the moon. He knows if 9/11 was an inside job. He knows who, how and why Covid-19 was created. He knows if the 2020 election was rigged and even knows who will win the*

2024 election. Finally, He knows all those who are conspiring to do good or bad and what direction America will turn- toward Him or away from Him.

But that's just my theory, and I'm sticking to it before they try to stick it to me and the rest of us. Come to think of it- it makes a heck of a lot more sense than being stuck with an untested jab and with all those side effects -yet to be revealed, that they conspire to hide, like the truth, from us in plain sight.

Sean Penn, Coward Stern and other fascists on Unvaccinated – "Put them in Prison"

I shall never forget them. All of them. And I'm not sure I could ever forgive them. But I must admit I want to give each and every one of them a shot, no not the vaccine, but the kind made with a clenched fist. That's how vile they all are, these celebrities, one worse than the other sharing a common theme – they all wanted to jab us all with the unproven mystery vaccine, and we were supposed to have no say in the matter.

From their lofty elite nests, the media elites and personalities preached to us during the time of COVID-19 the right way to act. All of a sudden, these deviants had ethics and morals. They were telling us, all of us, struggling to make it in middle America, the gulf coast of Florida, and in cities and towns all across this magnificent land, that we should do this and do that regarding this mysterious pandemic.

They did their preaching from places on high, like their penthouses in the big city of New York, their townhouses in Georgetown, and their beach houses in Malibu, mocking all those who didn't agree with them, scolding us all in the process and leaving us ultimatums that we must man up and adhere to their mandates.

The two-time Oscar winner Sean Penn took the role of a Pro-Vax General with gusto and passion, making it a personal cause and, in the end, proving that this Penn is, albeit mightier and dumber than the sword, by believing that the COVID-19 vaccine should be mandatory for all.

"I am so grateful that audiences — and yes, we'll come around to that, I would request only vaccinated audiences — have an opportunity to see this theatrically," the actor told CNN in an interview about his film "Flag Day." *"It's rare these days to have something that is exclusively theatrical. Eventually, it will stream, and that's a better time for the unvaccinated to see it, though I think I'll probably offend them out of that choice."*

"And I do believe that everyone should get vaccinated. I believe it should be mandatory, like turning your headlights on in the car at night."

"The entire history of successful things in this country. And if we're gonna continue with successful things — if we're gonna take some of the great lessons that have been learned in the last year, some of the extraordinary movements, George Floyd, all of what's happening societally — if we're gonna take the good parts of that and move it forward, we're gonna do it interdependently. And I think vaccination is the beginning of that, given that it's such a threat now to business, to lifestyle, to life here and around the world."[13]

A threat to life here and around the world? What the Oscar-winning actor didn't know at the time were the ramifications from the shot. He wasn't aware of the side effects that would make many who took the shot part of a group of people they didn't want to belong in, many dead women, dead children, and *Dead Men Walking*.

While the dead man can't talk, the shock jock named Howard Stern always could, and naturally, he had an opinion on the subject from the safety and comfort of his radio booth.

Enter Howard Stern. He'd ridden his own unique radio signal to stardom by being what they now call a "shock jock." Where Rush Limbaugh is lauded as the undisputed King of conservative talk radio, Howard Stern can surely be anointed the "crowned Prince" of "rebellious rock radio." On his air, you could always count on Howard being controversial, shocking and unafraid to go where no man on radio had ever gone before, mastering both the long-form interview and the tasteless bits that pushed his show to and beyond the edge of good taste but never to a place to be censored. Howard said what he wanted to say, anything he wanted, anytime he wanted, and he was rewarded for doing so. He was, above all

- a pretty damn good interviewer doing his talks in his own eminent style. Stretching his First Amendment rights into superstardom and an enormous kingdom of fame and wealth, Howard used his throne to claim his rightful place at the top of the list of the most famous radio personalities of all time. Howard had become part of the American lexicon and zeitgeist. Howard had found a home and place on the radio where people accepted him, listened to him and invited him into their most personal spaces, their cars, and their homes.

And that is the rub, as a man named Shakespeare used to say.

As people were struggling to deal with the pandemic called Covid-19 and what others called the *Plandemic, a man named Howard Stern, all the while,* stood, sat, but mostly lived in the comfort of his wealth and lofty position that being the prince of Shock jock radio had brought him. Naturally he opened up his big mouth, hell, that's what he was paid to do, and cast his bigger opinions, beaming them across the country and world and into homes, apartments, cars, and struggling businesses.

During a broadcast January 19th on Sirius XM radio show "The Howard Stern Show," he said that hospitals across the U.S. should not admit patients who are unvaccinated against COVID. Always on his to-do list to speak out against anti-vaxxers, the always blunt DJ doubled down on his view, telling listeners, *"If it was up to me, anyone unvaccinated would not be admitted to a hospital. At this point, they have been given plenty of opportunity to get the vaccine."*

"[People] have been told you will die if you get the vaccine. Some of you will live, but most of you will die. [These people] don't trust our government. They think that there's some conspiracy to turn them into a magnet or something like this," Stern said. *"They think they are going to become magnetized if they take the vaccine. I've taken this vaccine three times, and the worst side effect is for a day, I had a little bit of a headache."*

Stern downplayed the conspiracy theorists, saying: *"No one's sitting there conspiring against you,"* Stern continued, *"Americans don't want to create a vaccine that's going to turn you into a robot or magnetize you. There's enough Americans now who have taken it. Look at us as a sampling where nothing has happened to us. It's time for you to get it. Now, if you don't get it, in my America, all hospitals would be closed to you. You're going to go home and die. That is what you should get. Absolutely."*

Howard's position on all things Covid-19 was always stern, as he previously called anti-vaxxers *"imbeciles" and to "go fuck yourself."* The radio host, with no filter and apparently a short supply of actual facts but a complete lacking of empathy, said at the time, *"When are we gonna stop putting up with the idiots in this country and just say it's mandatory to get vaccinated? Fuck 'em. Fuck their freedom. I want my freedom to live. I want to get out of the house already. I want to go next door and play chess. I want to go take some pictures."*[14]

Hey Howard, while you're on the radio and have the face to prove it, we get the picture of who you truly are now. A fascist with big hair, a big mouth, and a big microphone.

Sure for Howard Stern, things changed in a small way. But surely for those who had the courage to listen to him as they made sense of this virus, things changed even more drastically for them, and the ultimate change was in the voice of someone they saw and heard daily, a man who was changing and transforming right in front of them. In front of their own eyes and ears. The man with a coat of armor and a radio sword that he would gladly use on anyone- well he was no longer unafraid or fearless and while it may be a little shocking to some, the relentless mouth that always roared had turned into the *Cowardly Lion*, because well, he had been lying all along about his courage. And that's when Howard Stern had transitioned into COWARD STERN.

But there were still others who could stake their claim of being the most repulsive during these dark and fascist times in America.

A rocker used to hiding behind a mask of sorts, founding member of the band *Kiss*, Gene Simmons, who paraded around the stage in heavy black and white make-up, sees the issue clearly contrasted in black and white.

Gene Simmons blasted COVID-19 deniers and unvaccinated Americans; "If you're willing to walk among us unvaccinated, you are an enemy." "I don't care about your political beliefs. "You are not allowed to infect anybody just because you think you've got rights that are delusional,"

Simmons, 72, said. "You don't have the right to go through a red light — actually the government has the right to tell you to stop." t's because the rest of us hate it. We don't want to smell your smoke."

"I don't want to catch your disease," Simmons added. "I don't want to risk my life just because you want to go through a red light. This whole idea, this delusional, evil idea that you get to do whatever you want and the rest of the world be damned is really terrible."[15]

Terrible begins to describe Late Night Talk Show host Jimmy Kimmel's remedy for people who chose not to get vaccinated. *Kimmel took a shot at Ivermectin*, a Nobel Prize-winning and lifesaving drug that has been used for people with parasitic infections.

Kimmel referenced a statement from Dr. Anthony Fauci, the director of the National Institute of Allergy and Infectious Diseases, in which he said hospitals have begun to run out of intensive care unit beds and will soon be forced to make "tough choices." "That choice doesn't seem so tough to me," Kimmel said. "Vaccinated person having a heart attack? Yes, come right in. We'll take care of you. Unvaccinated guy who gobbled horse goo? Rest in peace, wheezy."[16]

Steve Colbert, who came on the late-night scene and represents a new breed of talk show hosts who consider their platform to be more political and less about appealing to the mass audience. For the new era of late-night hosts that include Jimmy Fallon and Jimmy Kimmel, their target audience is left-leaning, in many cases very left-leaning, and each one of them gives their best shot to capture their share of ratings and the demographic prize-filled time slot. During COVID-19, Stephen Colbert seemed to stand apart from his colleagues, who sat behind a desk late at night and on TV, as he was all in, producing a supposed educational segment, *The Vax–Scene* dedicated to educating everyone through music and many cheesy, tasteless and sickening parodies from different musical genres designed with only one thing in mind. Get everyone to get the shot!

Seeing thelate-night show host dancing around to La Bamba as dancers dressed as COVID-19 shots made light of getting the shot; well, to be honest, the side effect of watching it made me sick. Think I threw up in my mouth a bit for this tasteless bit of strong-arming and propaganda designed to make everyone get the shot. Obviously, celebrity shilling at its best or worst, depending on what you think of the vaccine, but Colbert's staff billed it this way. *From humble beginnings on "A" Late Show to a glorious conclusion on "The" Late Show, we hope you will enjoy this romp through every single frame of Stephen Colbert's long running educational segment, "The Vax-Scene."*[17]

And one thing is sure: you have to see this entire box set just to see how tasteless and disgusting and in the tank Colbert was in supporting and convincing many different types of people with many different types of music to get the shot.

In the end Colbert gets the award for "Our Favorite Famous Fascist during Covid-19" and is the most likely to turn you over to authorities for not adhering to mandates. And finally, the one celebrity I would most like to give a shot to…in the chops.

A Prescription For Disaster…And Why I didn't get *the Shot*

Why I didn't *Get the Shot* EVEN though "my boy" greenlit Operation Warp Speed.

My very conservative Uncle Steve said in his Gregory Peck like monotone voice, "*Your boy said to get the shot…why aren't you getting it?*"

The Boy he was referring to was of course, Donald J. Trump.

"Well…because frankly, that's my choice…and my constitutional right," I shot back.

And that's how it went with my Uncle Steve, who was a man I loved but a man nevertheless who didn't get me. Well, not completely. While he was a conservative and I had gradually moved closer to his way of thinking over the years, he still didn't really get me.

Regarding the shot, we went over and over this many times.

I was not a conspiracy theorist. And I had nothing against taking shots in my life. In fact, I was quite open and used to it. As a child, I suffered from allergies and asthma, getting my share of allergy shots on a regular basis to fight my affliction known as Asthma. Asthma was the disease that would keep me out of major league baseball and, quite honestly, a lack of talent and desire also contributed. But Asthma did in fact, cut my enjoyment as I participated in sports growing up. I would play to the point of exhaustion and to the point of bringing on an attack.

Back then, I don't know, I guess we were tougher. We had less options and perhaps less sense, but I think we played harder and longer than the kids of this generation.

Right about the time I was reluctantly getting into the fascinating and disturbing book, *"Cause Unknown" The Epidemic of Sudden Deaths in 2021 and 2022 by Edward Dowd,* I was in need of my Asthma medication that I relied on to get not only breathe but to get through life day by day.

It's no big deal, but this Greek's *Achilles Heel* has always been my breathing or my inability to catch a good breath. Not complaining- many things are worse to deal with in life, but as a kid, I felt it held me back at times in sports – and while I know it probably didn't cause me my shot at playing right field for my beloved Detroit Tigers as the heir apparent to my hero Al Kaline, my lack of talent did that. Still strangely – it was in fact, a St. Louis Cardinal Pitcher named Bob Gibson who gave me hope that I could accomplish many of my athletic dreams- or at least catch my breath long enough to enjoy all the games of my youth. You see, Mr. Gibson was one of the meanest and most effective pitchers to ever play the game. And I witnessed that first hand as I watched him mow down Al Kaline, Willie Horton and, Norm Cash and all my Detroit Tigers to the tune of 16 strikeouts in a 1968 World Series game —when the world was a lot simpler yet not any less dangerous. In that year, I remember my mom and dad trying to explain to me how and why two great leaders, Robert F. Kennedy and Martin Luther King Jr. were cut down in the prime of their lives. Didn't make any sense then. Still doesn't make sense today.

As I played the games of my youth, baseball, football, and street hockey to the point of bringing on my asthma attacks – there was this St. Louis Pitcher who I could look to for a little hope and relief. Why Bob Gibson? Well he was not only a great pitcher, but he had asthma – just like me. Every time I saw him pitching *Primatene Mist* on his TV commercials – I felt a little tinge of hope. I trusted Bob Gibson- and what he was pitching. I figured if it was good enough for Mr. Gibson –well, it was good enough for me.

As I grew older, my hope of outgrowing Asthma faded as quickly as did my dream of playing pro baseball. Over the years, I would get weekly allergy shots – to keep my Asthma in check.

One thing we didn't have to succumb to ever was wearing a mask.

Can't picture us wearing masks, or social distancing, or being in lock down.

We played. That's what we did. And we did it well.

And we all took our shots. Reluctantly we took our shots for Measles. Mumps. Polio. Whatever was considered safe and would make us safer and shots that were tested over time.

But we took other shots too. These we enjoyed. Shots on the basketball court. On the football field and the baseball diamond. But especially shots we took playing floor hockey or street hockey. I played to the point of exhaustion and right up to the point when I would have an Asthma attack.

For years, I would get allergy shots to control my disease or sickness and keep it check.

It was always a part of my life, this thing called Asthma. As I child, I got my early shots from Dr. Ira Leventer, a nice *Marcus Welby*-like Pediatrician with an excellent bedside manner. As I got older, Dr. Paris, a Greek Doctor and friend, took his best shots to treat my affliction.

I was used to getting shots and taking shots. Probably got close to 1000 allergy shots in my life.

Yet when it came time to get the Covid-19 shot, I passed.

Why? Well, for a variety of reasons. Actually maybe not 19 reasons, but quite a few.

Number One: It was my right not to get the shot. Number Two. I didn't believe the science.

Number Three. Most of the media was pressuring people to get the shot, and I don't believe most of the media.

Number Four. Most of the government was doing the same. And once again, I don't believe or trust most of those in power in our government.

Number Five. Big Pharma was telling us we had to get the shot. Enough said.

Number Six. Doctor Fauci was, is, and should be named Dr. *Fugazi* because he is a fake and a fraud. And in time, way before he meets His maker should be prosecuted to the fullest extent of the law for the crimes he brought on humanity for pushing COVID-19 vaccine shots like a street hustler and drug dealer only with less integrity.

Well, I'll end there, but you get my point. Not the point of the shot, but you get my drift.

Countless times I was coerced to get the shot, shamed to wear a mask, pressured to take a COVID-19 test, or persuaded simply to stay safely socially distanced by paranoid neighbors.

And I for one, was sick of it. All of it. And while I was given more advice than a lonely drunk at the end of a dive bar on the night his old lady flew the coop, I, for the most part, was tolerant and polite to those who disagreed with me.

Then, the straw that broke my back happened strangely enough in a doctor's office.

Out of my Albuterol ventilator, a medicine that I've relied on to combat my asthma and allergies for years, even decades, I asked the Doctor for a refill. The fact that she would not fill it until I was further tested infuriated me. While it was something I didn't want to do, most importantly, it was something I was incapable of doing because of the added cost.

Needless to say I was pissed, which by the way, is not good when it comes to Asthma.

But the straw that broke my back and my patience is what she said next.

"Have you gotten your Covid-19 shot?"

The look on my face must have given away my answer, and my true feelings were not hard to read.

"No. I don't believe in this shot. I don't trust it."

She looked away, and on her way out of the office, she said, "I would seriously consider getting the shot."

I looked at her with a blank look and said, "Not getting it. But I am getting a new doctor."

They were unwilling to fill my prescription for an asthma medicine I've relied on all my life- but they were willing to try and force an unproven vaccine on me.

And as I drove home irate from not only her lack of professionalism but her sorely lacking bedside manner. I thought of Dr. Leventer and Dr. Paris. And I thought of a Doc named Hippocrates.

"First, do no harm," something this old Greek doctor once said.

Wondered what he would have thought about my doctor's visit and how he would have handled it? I'd like to think that he would have refilled my prescription and that he would have taken a shot at listening to my anxieties about a shot that was not tested and that in time, would prove to do more harm than good for many who got the shot.

Anyway all my old doctors are gone now. And sadly taking with them, their gentle bedside manner and ways of treating a patient the right way, *the Hippocratic way,* by first doing no harm.

IV. Lessons, Flashbacks, Love of Movies & Getting Canceled

Do you see what I See? Living in a parallel universe

Boys will be Boys... *Until they become girls*

Counting all the VOTES in my film Class

How I See Films & How I teach my students to See and Love Them

Loyalty – Means Same Thing to Most People including President Trump

Babylon- Not just a raunchy Film of Yesteryear but The State of Film Industry Today

DEI - DIDN'T EARN IT

Everything Everywhere All at Once (AKA) Nothing, Nowhere All at the same time

Mock election back when I was a Kid -Now mocking us and our elections

Poor Things: They just can't help themselves & can't help but F-up OSCARS

VICE- Film and *Proof* Vice President who wasn't a straight cat

What About-ISMS – and ISMS period?

Investigating the Investigators

Conservative Liberal Independent Patriot

My Next Book is a T-Shirt

Where are the Jews?

Do you see what I See? Living in a parallel universe

Part of my job as a filmmaker, film teacher and reviewer is to enlighten others to see - not necessarily what I see- but to look at films and, in essence, art with an open mind and heart. It is not meant to convince those that my opinion of a certain film is right and theirs is wrong- but instead, to examine the film and see what they get from it. Do they get it all – or is it a film they will never get?

In terms of film – and teaching my film students in my classes there is a process. No reviews. A Discussion. Then A vote. And my review.

I wish I could do the same with politics. And discuss the film being made in America today. But sadly, it's impossible. Because – we're all watching different movies.

Some people like the *BIDEN horror flick*. Some people disdain the *Capra-like Trump Movie*.

Yes – I put Capra and Trump in the same sentence. And I will tell you why. Both Capra and Trump want to create similar narratives. For Capra, his films represent a place and narrative that *isn't how the world is - but how it ought to be*. For Trump, an America that isn't living up to its standards of being great but one that should try at least to be great again. Now I know there are folks out there who don't like Trump and, in fact, hate Trump, but that's my point because, hell, there are people out there – who have actually told me that they don't like the Capra's classic –*It's A Wonderful Life*. They don't get – *IT'S A WONDERFUL LIFE*. Imagine that. And Jimmy Stewart's George Baily character –last time I looked –had not been guilty of firing off any volatile, controversial, mean tweets. That would be Mr. Potter.

And let's be frank – as in Capra. For many during Trump's Presidency – It *was a Wonderful Life* under President Trump, who directed his picture of America with great love, care, and competence and, like Capra – did so in a Truman-like fashion.

With President Truman – the buck stopped with him. And with Capra- whose autobiography THE NAME ABOVE THE TITLE- describes how he made films. Not by committee. But with a bold captain commandeering the responsibility of when to yell CUT or Print.

The same was true for Trump. He was in charge of this production called America and he was playing to the same populist audiences that Capra played to back in the 1930s and 1940s. The forgotten men and women who were left behind and voiceless. Both men gave them hope and something to believe in.

One man. One Film. That was Capra's mantra.

America First - That is Trump's MAGA philosophy.

Both men have made a difference. One in Hollywood, the other in a place called America.

And both men whose vision is sorely needed to today to not only make America Great again but also to make American films great again.

Boys will be Boys…Until they become girls

They want us to embrace our differences but they discount the old Boys will be Boys adage …while pushing a Boys being Girls option with fervor and purpose.

If I said this once, I've said it 10,000 times. I'm glad I grew up when I did. You too? And just by saying that, please don't call me a racist or white supremacist. That's ludicrous. Like the argument for so many augmentations to the human body on so many young children and teens. Allegedly, this is a confused demographic and psychographic that the Democrat party loves to focus on, regarding young people and their rights to switch genders as easily as they would change a class that they didn't like in Junior High. Actually, it's probably harder to change your schedule in school than it is to book a gender reassignment.

Back then, we had just assignments. Some I nailed with an A. Some I struggled with to pull a C out of my ass. Now we have gender reassignments, where they are literally cutting, moving, and pulling parts out of your…well, you get the idea.

Here's an idea. *Let kids be kids*. Simplify. Take a couple of steps back. Rewind a bit. Ease back on the sexualizing of children. All children. Everywhere. And let's take it back a bit to another time.

Our time wasn't completely innocent, but it was an age of innocence. Our time wasn't completely simple but it was simpler. The Three R's meant *Reading, Writing and Arithmetic.*

Now we have Drag Queen Story Hour. That's not progress. That's insanity. And it truly does sound like a drag. The Boys Scouts admit girls. And the Girl Scouts admit boys. Which I have to admit – I don't get. Boys competing against girls for medals. Championships are won – but they are tarnished.

As are our wonder years. Boy, I'm glad I grew up when I did. You too, Girl?

That's what I thought. I long for that time when you could say, "Boys will be boys."

Now, boys will be boys until they become girls.

From the department of "How Weird and Wacky Have Things Gotten?" comes this from recent actions by health officials in the Biden administration who have pressed an international group of medical experts to remove age limits for adolescent surgeries from guidelines for the care of transgender minors, according to newly unsealed court documents.

Their fear or rationale? *Age minimums, officials feared, could fuel growing political opposition to such treatments.* Well, yes, that would be the point and the objection from parents who don't want their children mutilating their bodies and changing their identities without deep conversations and counseling.

The latest radical was brainstormed by Rachel Levine, assistant secretary for health at the Department of Health and Human Services, and herself, a transgender woman. Levine urged them to drop the proposed limits from the group's guidelines and apparently succeeded.

The topic is heated and complicated. Funny, but I don't remember ever hearing about one case when I was growing up. The issue today is this. If and when teenagers should be allowed to undergo transgender treatments and surgeries has become a raging debate within the political world.

Opponents say teenagers are too young to make such decisions. Supporters including an array of medical experts, say that young people with gender dysphoria face depression and worsening distress if their issues go unaddressed.

In the United States, setting age limits was controversial from the start. Is the age controversial? Not the procedure? The draft guidelines, released in late 2021, recommended lowering the age minimum to 14 for hormonal treatments, 15 for mastectomies, 16 for breast augmentation or facial surgeries, and 17 for genital surgeries or hysterectomies. Proposed age limits were eliminated in the final guidelines outlining standards of care, spurring concerns within the international group and with outside experts as to why the age proposals had vanished.

In an email, it stated that Admiral Levine *"was very concerned that having ages (mainly for surgery) will affect access to care for Trans-youth and maybe adults, too. Apparently the situation in the U.S.A. is terrible and she and the Biden administration worried that having ages in the document will make matters worse. She asked us to remove them."*[18]

Sadly, the guidelines and age limits weren't the only thing that will be removed if the current push for radical gender reassignment continues at this pace.

Boys will be boys until they become girls.

Anything is possible today. It becomes a question where all things are possible.

How do you feel today is not answered with, "I have a slight headache or stomachache." Now it's "I feel like a girl. I feel like a boy." It's akin to asking someone when they are younger what they want to be when they grow up. Just because they say Astronaut or Fireman doesn't mean we should buy them a spacesuit and fast-track them to NASA or take them to the local firehouse to see if they can make chili.

It's like asking someone what kind of ice cream they want. Chocolate or Vanilla? Hell when you ask that question before dinner, the adult in the room will say, after dinner or let's see if it's okay with your dad. We don't want to spoil your appetite.

But today that same child wanders in a bit dazed and confused into their junior high or high school counselor's office and mentions that they are not sure or happy about being a boy or girl.

And just that quickly, with those first few confusing steps down the hall, little Bobby who his parents call Robert, has taken the first steps to becoming Roberta, all before the final bell rings. And somewhere in a classroom, a drag queen smiles as another child gets his or her assignments.

But, hell what's the big deal? That's just boys being boys, until they're not.

Counting all the VOTES in my film Class

It's been attributed to Stalin, the importance, not of who is voting but who is counting the votes. *"It's not who votes but who counts the votes"* that really matters.

In my film classes, I was in charge of counting all the votes that should be counted in my class.

In one strange way, with my tongue planted firmly in my cheek, *I was the Stalin of my class*. I counted the votes. I was in charge and always had been in charge of counting the votes and rating the films that we watched together in my film appreciation classes.

The process was old school. Good old-fashioned paper ballots were my mode of voting. Same day voting. With no mail in ballots. Most everyone voted in person on the day of class. The film electorate would handwrite their scores, rating the film 1-100 and anonymously deliver their verdict to me. I would place their votes in one of my popcorn holders. I would then read my review of the movie, complete with my rated score. The following week, I would share their tabulated scores a mean average with the class.

While the chances for mistakes were possible, especially in pre-COVID-19 days, when I taught three classes and had the chance of influencing an outcome, I was pretty confident I got the votes right. It was not rigged. It was not perfect. And it was the way I counted the votes for years at the Longboat Key Education Center. And I can say that the system works, provided one thing is a given. *The people counting the votes are fair and honest.*

In this case – it was me. Naturally, I think I'm a straight shooter who doesn't fudge the results.

As far as how the next presidential election goes? I'm not so sure how it will turn out. And I'm definitely not confident in the vote totals because I don't know any of the people counting the votes. I'm pretty sure they won't let me or people like me count the votes to make sure it's a free and fair election. And, sadly that's something they know they can always count on.

How I See Films & How I teach my students to See and Love Them

I am a film teacher and I like it. And from what I gather, I'm pretty good at it. My classes are usually packed with lifelong learning students, mostly folks who have lived a good life and who are now in retirement, basking in the sunlight of their twilight years, playing golf, tennis, and something called pickleball – while occasionally taking classes at the Long Boat Key Education Center to sharpen their minds.

Over more than a decade of many sold out classes, I can proudly state that I taught hundreds of classes and thousands of students on the art of cinema. In many ways, I taught them how to see and appreciate films, any and all films, but especially great films, classic films, and films that truly have something to say. Worthy pieces of art that defined and fit the description of what writer Arthur Knight, in his book *"The Liveliest Art,"* accurately anoints film "as the greatest art form."

In our classes and through the art of conversation we explored why certain films worked and others did not. We went for the "movie ride" together, a phrase I coined and would use over and over with an array of film enthusiasts, asking them if they went on the ride emotionally? Did they connect with the character? Did they relate to the story? Did they feel something? And I would pronounce, "If the film made you laugh, cry, and think, then it most definitely could qualify as a classic." I would cite my film-reviewing god, Roger Ebert, who would say, *"Film is the empathy machine."* Finally I would lay down my very liberal rules of coming to the class with an open mind and open heart, and warned them to never read reviews before seeing the film assigned. My rationale was simple. I didn't want to know what the paid reviewers from *Rolling Stone* or *The New York Times* thought of said movie, I wanted to know what they thought and, most importantly, what they felt. I didn't want them to be tainted or swayed, but instead, I wanted them to take on the role of the reviewer and tell me what they saw.

In my unscientific but forthright system, at the end of a robust discussion, I would hand out sheets of paper, and they would each assign a number 1-100, rating the film we had just discussed. The value system was wide-ranging for a variety of reasons. It meant that the proper weight and importance could be added to the great films separating them in many delineations and deviations from movies that were merely pablum or, even worse, repulsive.

For reference I would often cite my disdain for sequels and comic book movies, stating as an example, *Dirty Grandpa* with Robert DeNiro as a 1 or *Meet the Fockers* as a 20. Over the years it got many laughs and was part of my movie shtick. On the other side, I would state unequivocally that *Citizen Kane, Godfather I and II, City Lights, and Casablanca, amongst other classics,* deserved a 100 rating. And then I would add —channeling my inner and outer Don Rickles, "If you don't get these films and don't give them a 100 score, then perhaps this class isn't for you and maybe you would be happier taking the Kanasta, or *Mahjong class offered here.*"

It was an offer that they couldn't refuse over the many years that I taught at the school where we connected. The teacher with his students. And the students with their teacher.

We had more laughs. More good times. Shared some tears. And we created many great scenes together as we embarked on making more good experiences. All the while talking about good, bad and ugly films. And by the way, since I mentioned it, that western classic, *The Good, The Bad and The Ugly* by Clint Eastwood deserves an honest and well deserved 94.

After my students had submitted their scores into my popcorn holder, I would read the review that I wrote. As we discussed the film, I would try to hold my movie cards as close as possible and firmly to my chest so that they would not be influenced by my bias – either my love or disdain for a certain film. You know, the kind of practice – straight, down-the-middle reportage that is seen daily on all mainstream news services when discussing their favorite political movie villain of all time– Donald J. Trump. *NOT!*

Through the years I did my journalistic best to stay objective and remain open to other people's opinions regarding film. And I did something that was hard to do – largely for over a decade, I never, ever, ever, ever felt comfortable enough to share my political leanings with my largely left leaning class of accomplished people. Something in my gut told me to shut my mouth and lend thy ear and not the opinion –even as people in the early days trashed Bush, lionized Obama, and eventually - unable to contain themselves, compared Trump to Hitler.

Those ridiculous diatribes were not met with great objection by yours truly.

Like one of my film heroes, Charlie Chaplin, I remained silent. I knew to shut my mouth. Something in my gut told me – "What will you gain by engaging?"

It would be akin to arguing with someone who claimed that *Meet the Fockers* was great and better than masterpieces such as *Some Like it Hot* or *City Lights*.

Ludicrous. So I listened to my gut, shut my mouth and taught my film classes while sharing my wisdom and love of film.

It would be some time later that I would learn first-hand how truly right I was all along about coming out of my independent, conservative and common sense closet, and why I should always listen to my gut when it comes to great films and the body politic.

Loyalty – Means Same Thing to Most People including President Trump

In these crazy *Orwellian* days when words have meanings and definitions that change more abruptly than the weather on a Minnesota or Michigan afternoon, it's interesting to note that President Trump has always put a lot of value in one word -

Loyalty. Loyalty, I had heard that simple seven-letter word meant as much to him as any other in his colorful lexicon when it came time to judge whether someone was worthy of his time, money, or most importantly - his own loyalty.

To Donald J. Trump, when it came to *Loyalty* –the word and what it meant was - **HUGE**. The Cambridge Dictionary describes the quality of being loyal this way. "His loyalty was never in question."

Other definitions state that "LOYALTY implies a faithfulness that is steadfast in the face of any temptation to renounce, desert, or betray." Betray. An interesting word that President Trump has felt the sting of a time or two.

Another example points out that he "valued the *loyalty* of his friends."

Trump for sure values the loyalty of his friends and supporters almost to a fault, as evidenced by the hurt he feels when that bond of loyalty is betrayed by a friend, colleague, or supporter.

Historically speaking, "Medieval knights took an oath of loyalty to their lord." Finally, words that are synonymous with loyalty are FIDELITY, ALLEGIANCE, DEVOTION, PIETY, a faithfulness to something to which one is bound by a pledge or duty.

ALLEGIANCE suggests an adherence like that of citizens to their country. Or in Trump's case- a President's allegiance to the people. And the other way around, the people's allegiance to a President and to, as he would say – a movement. And from both, a natural allegiance or loyalty to the Constitution.

For sure, this definition or implementation of the word loyalty in action applied to President Trump's relationship with a certain successful Governor from Florida. In this case, there are two takes on the word loyalty and what it means to both men. One a rising political star from the Sunshine State, and the other is the biggest political force felt in America and the world for, dare we say - ages, and that's still a long time – no matter whatever definition one uses.

Theirs a story of loyalty, allegiance, betrayal, and finally reconciliation. A tale of mentor and mentee. Of teacher and student. A tale of two power brokers. A yarn about two guys and how they define loyalty. The story of a President and a governor. A powerful leader and a one-time loyal follower. A narrative with many twists and turns. A plot line compelling in its telling. Defining Loyalty and America: The Don and Ron story.

They first met when Ron DeSantis was running to be the Republican nominee for governor for the great state of Florida. At the time, the young congressman was far behind in the polls and Trump famously tells the story something like this. Trump endorsed via his favorite mode at the time, *"Ron is strong on Borders, tough on Crime & big on Cutting Taxes - Loves our Military & our Vets. He will be a Great Governor & has my full Endorsement!"* Trump tweeted.

As they say the rest is history. DeSantis won the race and the President, not shy to take credit for his endorsement, would in the coming days spout things off like, "I gave him my endorsement, and he shot up like a rocket."

Then 2020 happened, and the popular president named Trump lost or had the election stolen from him, depending on your point of view by a mummy named Biden, The crack in the door, and the seemingly tight grip Trump held on the Republican Party and MAGA nation was loosening. DeSantis saw his chance and opportunity especially after his overwhelming reelection as the Florida Governor in 2022. He was the new face and brand of the MAGA movement, the heir apparent to the throne. At least that's what those working for the Governor thought and what Ron believed. Trouble is, no one bothered to tell the King of MAGA nation.

Listening to bad advice from others, falling in love with his press clippings and bathing in the perfume of a big victory, DeSantis abandoned the vow to not run against the man who was largely responsible for him coming out of nowhere and winning in the first place.

Needless to say I was stunned by his bold move and his lack of reading the room and tea leaves, and that comes from someone who admires and respects both President Trump and Governor DeSantis.

I relate to the concept of loyalty with the *shoe on the other foot* scenario that I repeat, is often cited by noted barrister Alan Dershowitz. To me loyalty is a pretty big deal. I've been stung by the blade of disloyal friends or comrades who turned my trust into a weapon and stuck into my back a time or two. I'm also pretty damn sure once I've given my loyalty to someone who deserved it, I never abandoned my pledge of loyalty. In a sentence. I have never been disloyal. Yes I can relate and definitely think that the governor, as much as I admire him, was disloyal to President Trump.

And while I loved Ron DeSantis and the job he did for my adopted state of Florida…I was taken aback by his lack of loyalty. And I felt that in the end, it would lead to his undoing and potentially the end of a skyrocketing career. Call it an inflated sense of self, listening to the wrong advisors, or just not remembering who brought you to the dance – I sensed early on that the Governor would run and based on my own experience. Let me explain.

Having been frustrated with the launch of my book GET Trump, in which I was literally shut out by Facebook to market prior to the 2020 election – I planned on relaunching the book with a foreword by none other than Ron DeSantis. It was a no brainer. Actually a pretty savvy idea. The eventual heir apparent to MAGA nation, the man President Trump helped and whose campaign for governor he helped make great again, spewing the forward for my book – it was a great idea and I had the ear of someone close to DeSantis. While I had friends throughout my life in both low and high places, I never had anyone this close to the man who ran our great sunshine state and the man who, if he played his cards right, could easily be the next president of the United States.

The plan was easy. Get my book, Get Trump to Mr. DeSantis and let him write a new forward to my book. I had placed the book in the hands of a dear friend who supported both President Trump and Governor DeSantis had, in fact, hosted a fundraiser for him in his home, and he assured me he could get it to Ron.

I signed a copy of the book and left a personal note as to how much it would mean to me to have words on our great President as the new Foreword to my book. Well over many patient and frustrated days where many calls and inquiries were made to the parties that could make this happen, the call never came.

And that's when I knew that Ron DeSantis would run for President. Way before many knew in the public, I knew that the writing was on the wall, because the writing of an endorsement for Mr. Trump would not be in my book. I'm not saying that was the sole or main reason, but Ron could not have written a positive forward and then turned around and ran for President.

This tale is a cautionary one. A story about two men who wanted to do great things for America and the state of the country. And sadly, it's a tale of a lost opportunity where ambition was put above loyalty. The lessons are many, but in my heart and mind, I know this to be true.

Where does this story end? Having run a spirited campaign yet one that could not unseat the popular former President, Ron suspended his campaign and eventually did the right thing by endorsing President Trump in his effort to unseat the disaster that is BIDEN. One hopes that the mending of these fences can help catapult Trump to victory in 2024. While it will most assuredly be the last time the man from Queens can run for office, future runs by Ron should not be ruled out of the question.

Like President Trump, who is in the midst of making one of the biggest comebacks in political history, a comeback by DeSantis may be on the horizon. A horizon where this rising son's future may rise once again. At a place and time when he can seize the day and help continue making America greater, just like he did in Florida.

Babylon- Not just a raunchy Film of Yesteryear but The State of Film Industry Today

The great Howard Hawks had a way of measuring what makes a great movie.

The iconic director said, *"Three great scenes and no bad scenes."*

And he should know.

Hawks started out in the silent era and went on to capture the minds and hearts of cinema-attending Americans in a variety of genres and through silence and sound – in both black and white and in color. Hawks classics include *His Girl Friday, To Have and Have Not, Bringing up Baby, Red River, Scarface, The Big Sleep and Rio Bravo,* to name a few.

And aside from all of these works containing three great scenes and no bad ones – all of the aforementioned Hawks films clock in at under three hours, nine minutes – the length of Damien Chazelle's recent film Babylon, which depicts Hollywood's transition from silence to sound.

Why the accomplished Chazelle, he of *Whiplash, La La Land and First Man* fame, would need three hours to tell this version of his Hollywood story is perhaps the greatest mystery posed to all associated with the film *Babylon*. From that greenlighting it's telling to all those working on the film – all collaborating to produce an original and decadent tale, filled with many scenes and way too many obscene scenes, period. A film lacking class. And one that fails, because well you take the pick – good taste or simply the necessary discipline and acumen to cut – as Hawks and other legends would have- the unnecessary and bloated scenes in Babylon- a film about Hollywood's early days that could have been a great film - but is not.

And there are many reasons it falls short.

Unfortunately, while there are probably more than three good scenes in Babylon –there are at the same time not only one- but many bad scenes in the film.

As stated, there are many good scenes. Perhaps Brad Pitt as the fading silent star being informed that it was over by the venomous gossip-spewing columnist –who tells *Jack Conrad* that his time is up—is the best scene in this overwrought epic.

It's my favorite. My favorite character aside from Diego Calva's Manny, is Jovan Adepo, playing Sidney Palmer, who not only blows jazz hot notes but has incredible character in doing so. They are the rare bright spots in this dark tale of Hollywood's early days.

But there is a bigger problem with the film Babylon —that echoes true warnings for today's *Bronze Age of Cinema* and to dwindling numbers of cinema-goers everywhere.

They simply can't help themselves or don't know how to help themselves. Or perhaps they don't care about helping themselves and their cause and calling. That simply stated, is to entertain, if not engage, the public for a couple of hours as a means to escape their humdrum lives. And there is something else they profess in the film as their goal – *"make films for those common folks out there in the dark who don't have a voice while giving them something they can relate to."*

But if this is the best that they could come up with in three plus hours, saddled with a budget of over 80 Million dollars, equipped with a respected director and two big stars —then Hollywood is doomed. And not doomed in a small way – but in a big way, facing a bigger challenge than even those faced in the early days by the pioneers who transitioned from silence to sound. Yet Babylon's problem in the micro and Hollywood's problem in the macro is the same. And it all comes down to taste – as in good taste. In the end it is their charge to produce something that can provoke and evoke – but not turn off the public with these forms of excessive film masturbation —seen in scene after scene of Babylon - pleasuring themselves but not the public – who, after all - do pay for their salaries and buy the popcorn.

For sure, Babylon is full of extremes and guilty of excess. And in the final credits, it is a paradox. As is Hollywood itself. Yet Babylon is well shot. Originally directed. Sublimely edited. Featuring spectacular sets and many wonderful performances. But because – no one would YELL CUT - and that would be the responsibility of the director-it is largely a wasted effort. And because of that, this film, in the end is overdone, over told and just plain over the top in its execution- a trait that is not uncommon in today's Hollywood.

That is not shocking. And that is the problem with this Babylon on the screen and the one that houses the Hollywood sign in the real Babylon, Hollywood, California- a place that once birthed the *Golden Age of Cinema.*

Chazelle's Babylon is meant to shock you. And to one-up itself in scene after scene, aiming the shock gun- that is, the movie camera and projector at the poor – guy or gal, perhaps on an antiquated concept called a date, who have plopped down their hard-earned bucks- to escape to the Cineplex for a night of- wait for it – entertainment.

Harry Cohn- the old studio head of Columbia Pictures who brought Capra classics, *Mr. Smith Goes to Washington, and It Happened One Night, to the silver screen,* had his own rule. It was connected to his backside and represented not only where he stood in the movies- but, most importantly, where he sat.

When Mr. Cohn would squirm in his seat –he knew that it wasn't working on the screen.

While watching Babylon - I squirmed at least 50 times in my seat.

Shocked not so much at what I saw- but in the totality of what I saw. A great scene followed by more debauchery. Question. How many Elephants do you want defecating into the camera? And how many golden showers you want in scene three? And how many midgets you want dancing with a blown up penis in the next scene? The answer to Hollywood and to Chazelle seems to be "HOW MANY YOU GOT?"

As the disjointed storytelling continued to be filled with a roulette wheel of scenes- "Take a spin and see if you get a good one, a great one or a gross one" – it became a personal challenge to me – this recent trip to the theatre to see Babylon. A real challenge. Could I get through it? I played games with myself as I squirmed some more in my seat. Where is this going to end I asked myself. And finally - Will it ever end?

Then the answer came to me. It didn't matter.

This wasn't a film that they made for me anyway–someone who loves and appreciates the craft of storytelling and the rich f not checkered, past of Tinsel Town.

This was for them. The insiders. With their supposed inside jokes meant to titillate and tease not the audience but themselves. You can almost hear them saying – *"Can you believe we got an elephant, a midget, and a mansion full of hedonists in that one shot?"*

How else can you explain that God-awful series of scenes involving a wigged-out Toby Maguire on a day pass to Dante's Inferno? Easy. The former Spiderman actor was a co-producer on the film- and one of the big shots who green-lit this mess and contributed by being a part of one of the worst sequences in recent memory.

But sadly in Babylon – that is not the exception but the rule.

And while it is true that Margo Robbie and the character Nellie LaRoy that she plays in Babylon are both stars – that is not enough to save a film and possibly a place called Hollywood.

Because, in the end they can't help themselves from doing this to themselves.

In the end, Chazelle gives the audience a love letter- maybe it's a Mea Culpa. Anyway he jams in this sequence filled with iconic Hollywood scenes in a magical montage – even shoehorning a moment of sentimentality from the iconic *Singin' In the Rain* – a movie masterpiece viewed by one of the only sympathetic characters in the film – Manny – played beautifully by Diego Calva.

It's an attempt to balance his jaded and grotesque view of Hollywood with a little sugar. But it is too little, too late- to save this movie, and I'm afraid perhaps Hollywood. The box office numbers are in for Babylon – and they are a disaster.

And somewhere in a Hollywood office, in an executive suite with a long table surrounded by many chairs – filled with many empty suits they will point their fingers at the usual suspects as to why Babylon failed.

But they don't want to know the real reason. Not really. Anyway, the story is almost over. And just in time.

Because all the Elephants have escaped. And anyway, there's a shortage of midgets, and it's hard, if not impossible, to find anyone who can fight a snake.

But not to worry - they've probably never heard of Howard Hawks anyway.

DEI – DIDN'T EARN IT

DEI- It's supposed to stand for *diversity, equity and inclusion*. At least, that's how it's packaged to sell as a concept and an idea that we're supposed to like and embrace.

Thumbnail sketch. It's *dumb, engaging, idiots*. Okay that's a bit harsh. But it is a dumb way to get the best people put in the best and most important jobs, essential jobs they called them during COVID-19, but don't get me started.

Do you want to hire someone who knows how to fly a plane or do you want to hire someone who checks the DEI Box of your choice as someone we would look good hiring to fit our quotient of Diversity, Equity, and Inclusivity?

Well, that's an easy one for me. I want the best pilot period. Don't care about his politics. His or her Gender? Their skin pigmentation. Their religion. Hell, even what hockey team they pull for to win the Stanley Cup.

At the risk of offending at least five groups of people, I want the best damn pilot flying the plane for me, regardless of (get ready to be triggered snowflakes) regardless of the fact that they are a *Transgender, Muslim, Democrat, Pittsburgh Penguin hockey fan*. Listen if this guy or gal or whatever is the best pilot and knows better than anyone else how to fly and land a plane- I'll hire them.

I know that's only four groups I offended but let me try one more.

You are having a heart valve replacement surgery and you are worried about the prognosis. Do you trust your surgery with the award-winning Baylor Medical School graduate Patel V. Patel, a native of India, who also studied at Harvard Medical School and did an internship at Johns Hopkins University? Or do you put your heart in the hands of the City College Grad, who did a brief stint at *United Medical Center in Washington, D.C just because they are a gay, Jewish, Socialist, New York Yankees fan from the Bronx?* Now that's checking a lot of boxes- even a Bronx box.

Well any reasonable person would go with the Baylor grad. The only thing that makes sense in this world that often lacks common sense is to go with the ones with credentials - THEY earned it.

They won my respect and the job of flying me home safely. And if needed, and if I can afford the heart surgery, earned my trust to mess with my heart valve procedure.

DEI stands for Didn't Earn It.

It is box-checking on steroids, and you know what happens when you do that? A bunch of innocent people end up in a box dead because you want to be all-inclusive, diverse, and equitable in handing out misery.

That's the thing about this philosophy with roots in socialism. As Churchill once said, *"The inherent vice of capitalism is the unequal sharing of blessings. The inherent virtue of Socialism is the equal sharing of miseries."* And that's all DEI truly is: a repackaging and equal sharing of miseries.

No one earned anything. They were rewarded for looking a certain way, having a certain color skin, and not having a particular skill set, like being able to fly and land a plane or perform open heart surgery.

Diverse, Equitable, and Inclusive at all costs equals an Invitation to a United Disaster

Do you really care if your heart surgeon is from Asia or India? How about the firemen who are called to put out the orange and red flames that engulf your home? Do you care if they are black or white? How about the cops who are called to your home if you are being robbed in the middle of the night?

Finally, the next time you fly the friendly skies - do you care if your pilot is black or white?

There is only one right answer to all those questions. The right moral and logical one is simple to answer - for those who are not woke, don't lack a moral compass, or haven't completely lost their marbles.

You want the best and most qualified person- Period. To cut you open on the operating table, put the flames out as your home burns, arrest a criminal who puts your family in danger, and land the plane you are flying safely.

If we have come to this DEI metric, where skills, talents and attributes are superseded by skin tone, gender diversity, and quotas, then we are all doomed. And nothing dishes out misery in equal shares quite like employing a pilot not because he possesses a competent skill set to fly and land a plane but because they looks a certain way. Nonsensical and ridiculous are not serious enough words to describe this date with destiny that doesn't end well if we continue to go on this DEI trip.

What looms is continued incompetence. An equal sharing of misery. What is lacking is initiative. Hard work. Dedication. The best person for the job gets the job. A meritocracy. *"A government or holding of power selected on the basis of their ability."* What a refreshing idea and way to govern and reward the brightest and the best among us.

In one definition of meritocracy, noted, "Britain is a meritocracy, and every one *with skill and imagination may aspire to reach the highest level.*"

Aspire to the highest level?

Like a pilot who wants to fly planes because he likes their shape and thinks it would be fun. Or some hot shots like Tom Cruise in Top Gun, who have the skills to fly like an eagle.

What will they say about America many years from now if we continue on this flight to absurdity by simply rewarding those who haven't earned it but look the part.

DEI – It stands for Diversity, Exclusivity and Inclusivity. But it's a bad idea and more aptly, should stand for *Didn't Earn It*.

I smiled at an old ad that the great actor John Houseman did for the investment firm Smith Barney. Having come from his work in the theatre and working alongside his colleague and the boy genius Orson Welles on the masterpiece Citizen Kane, Houseman, needless to say, brought a bit of gravitas to the Smith Barney investment ad. The result is an iconic, effective, and memorable commercial.

In it Houseman closes the spot:

"Smith Barney, They make money the old-fashioned way. They earn it."

"They earn it."

A sound principle to trust, whether investing dollars or choosing the best pilots and doctors

Everything Everywhere All at Once (AKA) Nothing, Nowhere All at the same time

When a film wins seven Oscars, including one for BEST Picture, it's supposed to be special and deliver on taking the viewer somewhere special – perhaps even places that they've never imagined or been to before.

On both accounts - ***Everything Everywhere All at Once*** delivers on those demands.

What it doesn't deliver- at least to this reviewer and film enthusiast is a cogent film odyssey worthy of the accolades it's been lauded by seemingly by everyone, everywhere, and all at once during award season.

Everything Everywhere All at Once is touted by some as an absurdist comedy-drama film written and directed by Daniel Kwan and Daniel Scheinert (collectively known as "The Two "Daniels").

In a nutshell – *"the story follows Evelyn Wang, a Chinese-American immigrant who, while being audited by the IRS, must connect with parallel universe versions of herself to prevent a powerful being from destroying the multiverse."*

Now that convenient description-while concise if not compelling - doesn't even begin to hint at what the filmgoer will actually encounter on screen for over 2 hours of 19 minutes of storytelling.

In that time, and over two screenings on the big screen- I watched ***Everything Everywhere All at Once.*** I chose this path and not the easier one at home - as some of my colleagues had done to take in the movie- which allowed them to pause and take in the story in small bites.

For multiple reasons -but largely because of one reason – I chose to take in the movie a second time –largely because of the juxtaposition of comments and everything I heard everywhere all at once about the film. From the negative buzz I had received from a multitude of mature film folks who had over the years valued my opinion- so we'll call them youngsters -who also seemed to value my film acumen.

With that said, I entered the movie theatre for the second time, with some trepidation and, of course, my own bias and opinion after watching it for the first time.

That time the movie- as stated in its own narrative- made me feel like a piece of…. shit.

I felt accosted, jumped was filled at the same time with brilliant and ridiculous images. A storyline that, at best, if not hard to follow, was at least exhausting. Special effects and universe jumping in an attempt to allow an array of characters, but especially the protagonist Evelyn, to self-actualize. All sounding possible on paper perhaps - but all to me, at least, were overdone, over the top, and just too much to process in the film universe where I dwelled.

As I purchased my film ticket for the second time from a young, slightly overweight tattooed ticket taker who had failed make-up 101 – and who slightly resembled a bedazzled Joy from the movie, she volunteered her own review of the movie.

"It was fantastic."

Perhaps it was an age thing, I thought to myself. Some of the younger generations were embracing this movie, as the movie's title suggests, as "having everything."

On that, maybe she was right. The movie did have everything. An everything bagel of solutions and how to live your best life all wrapped up concisely– ok, not so concisely in this slickly shot and edited – gumbo of assembled emotions on film that, at its heart- is a movie about family and the pressures we place on each other to live our best lives. On husbands and wives who fail to see the value in each other, on daughters and mothers, and on daughters and fathers who fail to accept each other and the choices that they made in their lives –that caused the other pain in the life they lived.

Michelle Yeoh stars as Evelyn Quan Yang, with Stephanie Hsu, Ke Huy Quan, Jenny Slate, Harry Shum Jr., James Hong, and Jamie Lee Curtis in supporting roles. All the performances are fine to the degree that they are digestible. I actually felt some empathy toward Evelyn and her wacky, underachieving, and overachieving husband —depending on the universe and place in the story. And even a tinge of empathy for Joy in between all the universe jumping. Still, for the most part, it was a mixed bag of laundry that did not all come out nicely as the movie washed over me.

Still I settled in for the second time, with as open a mind as possible- and I began to take on the story-this time without my Milk Duds and Licorice.

In a theatre filled with few patrons – I heard the occasional laugh and sigh. I watched as the images were shot at me.

As I had experienced the first time- the opening of the film was quite good and had me interested. In the family. Their life at the laundry mat. Their problem with the IRS. Their pulling together. It was tangible. Something and some people I could care about.

Then something happened. The elevator ride. It changed everything, everywhere, all at once for me. When Ke Huy Quan as Waymond Wang, alerts Evelyn of her special powers to universe jump and, in effect, change her circumstances in life – the movie was once again over for me.

With each passing moment and universe change – I became more disinterested in the plight of the characters.

The more they all hit their green buttons —after doing something gross and absurd to grant them this universe-jumping skill- the more I became bored and, in time, insulted and infuriated.

For some- a feast of special effects. For others, a nightmarish ride they were unable to escape that included an overdose of special effects. Highlights or lowlights depending on which universe you related, include Hot Dog Fingers, Phallic symbols used in one of the many Kung Fu Fights, and, of course, Sex Toys that were used to their end and, in fact, in the end -as in rear end -to tell their story. And finally, just because they could - a powerful- all-knowing and encompassing EVERYTHING BAGEL.

Once again, they are right. The film is many things and all at the same time. Intelligent and dumb. Sophisticated and simple. Obnoxious and poignant. Joyous and depressing. Over the top and Subtle- Ok, Not subtle. More a video game than even a movie.

What it is not –is a great film. Not in any way. Not in any place. Not in any universe.

And for the kid who portends to know and love films – especially the classics- in the end, no pun intended - it was too much. So much so that it has accomplished a rare feat- I was once a hot dog and bagel enthusiast- I can't look at those two staples the same way after viewing the movie.

The film claims, and I'm paraphrasing -that "Nothing Matters." That in some way our failures of what we have become – continue to show us all what 'Small pieces of shit we are and have become over millions of years."

And in that way, they are right.

Because in some ways their film is a self-fulfilling prophesy- at least as far as the film industry is concerned. With both feet planted solidly on the ground – like one of those rocks in their cute, deep, and philosophical take on the universe –yet replete with googly eyes – I will leave you this take.

They have managed to create a movie that the Academy Awards rewarded loudly and proudly.

A movie with big images, big sounds, and big messages- yet a movie that I feel is a big piece of ….You fill in the blank.

That it won as many Academy awards *as Lawrence of Arabia, All About Eve and Schindler's List* to name a few - is both a tragedy and injustice in any universe. That the directors named Daniels have exactly one more BEST DIRECTOR Award than Alfred Hitchcock and Orson Welles combined leaves me grasping for my green button- and an escape to another film universe.

One in which – contrary to one of the film's messages - Some things matter.

Especially when making great films- of which Everything, Everywhere All at Once - is not.

In films, great films -these things matter, at least to me and maybe some of us.

A great script. Disciplined Direction. Editing with a purpose. Sublime performances.

Characters we can care about. Give me – "Something, Somewhere and over the course of the two or so hours," that I can relate to. Don't bombard me with images and trite messages.

Now I will "be kind" - one of the messages the film conveys in its telling.

For those who enjoyed the movie. Great. Glad you could make some sense of an effort that was filled with much nonsense and poor execution. I'm happy for you. But sad for the bigger picture to come –and not to a theatre near you, that sadly, I feel in time, will hit the planet that is Hollywood all at once.

With their dependence on a world market that includes a heavy lean and influence from CHINA- it will continue to take them – the power brokers in Tinsel-Town down a path and to a universe that they can't return from and far, far away from their once loyal movie fans.

As I watched the BOLD End Title slide one fan exclaimed, "Thank God."

Was it a cry for help? Or was he just hitting his green button to escape to a universe of better movies and films crafted by the likes of Ford, Wilder, Coppola, Welles, Capra, Kubrick, Spielberg and Hitch? I felt sad for him. Yet I related to this faceless stranger in this disconnected place - an empty movie palace where few patrons now attend. A place that is now nothing, nowhere – all at the same time.

Mock election back when I was a Kid -Now mocking us and our elections

When I voted as a six year old on the playground of my youth, it was not a serious vote. Some may say that it was a fake vote. Actually it was a mock election, and now, many years later, they mock us with their fake elections.

Back then when I didn't know *"shit from Shinola"* regarding politics and everything else because well, I was six, and I hadn't lived yet.

Having lived the last five decades and doing a bit of living and learning, it's safe to say regarding our politics and those who view us from the power centers of government, it's pretty much gone from *"Shinola to shit."*

During those wonder years of my youth and the tumultuous1960's, things were a mess, yet even with the upheaval- the assassinations of King, JFK, RFK, and the horrors of Viet-Nam, our country was in some strange way not as unhinged as we all are today. At least back then, if you told someone that you were voting for the other guy or the other party –both parties weren't so easily insulted. Our skin was thicker back then, even as anti-war and civil rights protests mounted. At least those protesters were sincere in voicing their opinions and even listening to yours, and no one could hide in the cowardice of anonymity on the internet.

Now today they mock you if you wear a *Red MAGA* hat and worse yet will attack you like a mob. That's not the fruit that all those who protested the end of wars and civil rights would have hoped for when they took their movement to the streets.

In 1968, LBJ abandoned his run to become the president because he had lost touch with the office and the American people, and the war that he helped prolong had gotten the best of him while it took the lives of some 55,000 of our best.

It left America at a crossroads and with a choice come election day. With RFK sadly gone, the victim of an assassin's bullet, at the voting booth, America was left with a choice between the Democrat on the ticket, the incumbent VP from Minnesota, Hubert Horatio Humphrey, the Independent on the ticket, a polarizing figure George Wallace from Alabama and the loyal steady-handed VP of Ike's Administration and narrow loser to JFK in 1960, Richard Milhous Nixon.

At the polls, Nixon won in a landslide. And at our mock election on the grounds of my elementary school, Stevens T. Mason, in our mock election, I voted for Humphrey. A vote that I was mocked for back then – just as many of our votes and standing for our liberties and republic are mocked today – because they think we don't know *Shit from Shinola*.

Poor Things: They just can't help themselves & can't help but F-up OSCARS

Poor Things. They can't help themselves.

They have no shame. And that's not new or news.

It's a tired story. One they remake every year. Especially come Oscar time. In the olden and golden days Tinsel Town, it seemed like the entire world watched in awe and reverence as the show beamed around the planet from this place called Hollywood.

But that was then… "Now is Now"…to take a line from Wim Wenders sublime *Perfect Days*.

And right now – Hollywood, like much of the world, is a sad and sick place.

It's no longer the dream factory built on stories of hope and inspiration and has instead turned unashamed and undaunted into their preferred narrative of doom and gloom.

More often than not they churn out and reward stories that …are, quite frankly, my dear, WEIRD FOR THE SAKE OF BEING WEIRD.

Take POOR THINGS for one example. But more on this reworking of FRANKENSTEIN later. Still the facts and plot of their story are always predictable. And on nights like these, their Teleprompters are always loaded with an agenda

They celebrate with glee- BARBIE, a chick flick on steroids as a revelation to the feminism movement, and if there was any doubt before, they lay out their plan to totally emasculate men in bright pink outfits. By the way this is redundant- KEN never did have any balls in the first place. But their goal is to remove them from the rest of us.

At the same time, the vapid and talentless host – some clown named Kimmel attacks a woman who delivered a response to the angry, feeble and demented president who delivered the most divisive State of the Union address in the history of the United States.

But they are good stewards of their agenda and their advocacy.

Their plot foreshadowed at the beginning of the evening to GET TRUMP later, a set up by this joke on a mother and newly elected congresswoman delivering her response to a crazy, corrupt, and angry president and his rant of madness and lies.

They always stick to their script even when they go off script. And in some ways it makes for an interesting, if not entertaining, night. You just never know how low they will go.

As the evening plays on – the story becomes clearer. The messaging no longer hidden. The awards are given out to the crowd. Films and movies are celebrated. Some choices are popular and some not so much.

In delving out the best actress to Emma Stone – for *Poor Things*...the poor things in Hollywood are making a statement. It's not obvious to the untrained eye, but it is - to many of those who have tuned out of watching this annual show that supposedly celebrates the best that motion pictures can offer.

It too, is an offer that those in flyover country have continued to easily refuse by staying away in droves from the films that Hollywood produces. In the case of POOR THINGS - a peculiar interpretation of Frankenstein, the agenda obvious.

Like a mad scientist, with their new toys, both BARBIE and Bella there is a new chance to recreate and breathe new life into all things that they perceive as good and beautiful.

And while doing so – remove all those things that hamper their narrative of transforming America into the kind of place with no memory of what it was, no shame of what is good and acceptable –but a whole new movie moving forward where there is no God, but a multiple of genders and where men, especially white men are evil, replaceable, and if allowed to exist at all –are in dire need of a makeover.

A favorite part of any Oscar show for years has been the clips, as in film clips. Film clips of nominees doing their thing, showing why they deserved to be nominated. How they stacked up against other performances and finally tribute clips, salt, and peppered throughout the evening gave the show gravitas. And no place was there such made-for-Hollywood TV moment as the *Lifetime Oscar Award or the Irving Thalberg Award.* Presented to biggies in the business who is synonymous with the medium in a way- where the star awarded was someone so big – a Charlie Chaplin, Cary Grant, or *Alfred Hitchcock*, it made for something that was akin to watching any scene from *The Godfather* or *Casablanca*. A moment not to be missed. A moment to merely be remembered for all time and from here to eternity.

Another great part of every Oscar show is when Hollywood celebrates the lifework of those in the industry who have contributed significantly to the story of the silver screen but who have sadly passed away in the previous year leading up to the show. A perfect opportunity to remember all those *from set designers to writers, actors and producers, editors and make-up artists, and everyone in between* who had passed but had contributed significantly to the ongoing story that is Hollywood. Done perfectly, one would see a montage of images of artists and stars accompanied with their names and contributions displayed as a tasteful musical piece by someone named Bach, Beethoven, Mozart or the like, and led by a conductor leading an orchestra as the images fade seamlessly from one to another. Done poorly, someone is always left off the list, on the cutting room floor and rightfully those who know the deceased are rightfully outraged for the omission. Done as a disaster, as in the 2024 Oscar show, the producers didn't know what they wanted to accomplish. They cut back and forth, splitting the shots on the screen with live dancers performing Andrea Bocelli singing, and partial shots of the audience viewing the screen inside the auditorium. Total disaster of *Towering Inferno* magnitude. An overproduced nightmare. The audience could not make out the names and images of those who had passed in this final film tribute and fiasco that outraged many. The solution is simple. Simply show a beautiful shot of those who had passed in one continuous montage as the orchestra plays beautiful and timeless music.

But the thing is- Hollywood either doesn't know how to produce or no longer wants to produce moments like these because they no longer care about Hollywood's rich history. In that way, they are tearing down their own statues, much like the zombie-like protesters who tore our history down by removing statues that they didn't like or approve of.

Either way, the lessons, the history, and those special cinematic moments designed to create a memory are either botched or cut from the story. And the result is those moments are gone. There is no time for them on the big show that is the OSCARS. The script has changed. A rewrite done. The Oscars no longer a place to celebrate movies and our love of them but a place to simply deliver a message or further an agenda.

Still, there is good news for those who love and embrace the new Hollywood in dwindling numbers. While there was no time to rightfully honor those gifted artists who made Hollywood a place of magic and where dreams did indeed come true, there was time for the Oscar host, Jimmy Kimmel, to read a lengthy critical tweet at the end of the show by former president Donald J. Trump.

In this movie, there is always time to *get Trump* and all those who follow him. And the sad thing is, as the Trump Movie continues to play in their head and not for nothing…but The Donald should get some kind of award for helping to cut them out of their own narrative while helping to produce his own epic movie about a people, a place, and an American dream called MAKE AMERICA GREAT AGAIN.

VICE- Film and *Proof* Vice President wasn't a straight cat

"Bootsy" was my cat, and I loved him dearly. He was a rescue. All of our cats are rescues. But this one was even a little more special, maybe because of the road or many roads it took for him to land at home with us.

My girlfriend Katherine, a fabulous actress was doing the David Auburn play Proof in West Palm Beach, and that in itself was not strange. She had done the play to rave reviews in St. Petersburg, Florida, at the American Stage twice to rave reviews with a stellar cast. That she decided to do it again was unusual even for her, someone who eats, sleeps, and breathes theatre.

The real reason and proof of why she did it, would be spelled out in the coming days and years.

"Bootsy" came to us, through a circuitous route. During her days of rehearsing *Proof*, along her journey, she'd walk to and from the theater, and she noticed a rather large black and white cat sleeping on the red and blue recycling bins.

Well, that was all she had to see. The cat, she said, had a little "Baby Doll" in him and Katherine had a little Jane Goodall in her, with her love of animals. A love that was only matched by her love of theatre. That this cat had an unusual marking, a large red blot that we would later learn was affiliated with Feline HIV, only intrigued her and attracted her more to his plight.

That he slept on recycling bins would not do with her. She had to act and act like she did, taking the cat off the bin while leaving a note to the owner, saying that she would try to get him some medical attention.

Long story short. *Proof* closed to good reviews, in a production not as moving as the St. Pete productions, *proving* that sometimes you truly can't go home again. That was not true for the cat we would come to name "Bootsy" because of his large feet. After getting some medical attention for him courtesy of a generous donor at the theater and trying as she could for months to find a new loving home for the cat on the East Coast in the West Palm Area, *Bootsy* eventually landed at home with us on the West Coast of Florida. There he flourished with love from a big sister cat, Maisey, who we rescued on the church grounds behind our house, and a little black and white cat named *Buttons* that Katherine rescued while doing a world premiere of *Charm*, a fabulous play at the Orlando Shakespeare Theatre.

Yet still more *proof* of Katherine's love of animals.

Back to *Bootsy*. He would stay with us for years. In many ways was the sweetest cat we ever had. Definitely the best greeter. A great front-of-the-house cat. A *Toots Shor* kind of cat, someone who you placed at the front of your home or establishment because he was good with people.

And naturally, he was good with my mom, herself a real people pleaser. My mom got Bootsy, and Bootsy got my mom. And when my mom visited, she gave him his nickname- *Trump* endeared him even more to me and millions of us in MAGA nation who dig this cat named Trump.

Sadly in time, Bootsy developed a brain tumor. We were devastated. With Katherine out of town doing a show in Tennessee and with a heavy heart and our Bootsy suffering, I made the fateful call late at night. I would take him and say my last goodbye to him. I was a mess. This cat loved me, and I loved him. He loved us, and we loved him. We had a bond that was formed from the first time we met. Now, it would be the last time.

Not myself -crushed and heartbroken – on that same sad day, I had to force myself to see VICE, a film about DICK CHENEY, for my film class which would gather the next day.

Through the prism of a broken heart, I watched what I thought was a largely unfair portrayal of a man who I largely admired for his acumen in all things military. Back then in the Bush era, I was largely supportive of his efforts to *battle terrorists over there, so that we wouldn't have to fight them over here.* Now, in retrospect, I see the folly of my perceptions.

At the time I saw Vice – I still, unwisely, held Dick Cheney in high regard. He had fooled me and all of us with his jive talk of WMDs. This Cheney cat, unlike my *Bootsy* was no straight shooter.

I was fooled by him and the narrative that they wanted to sell us on Iraq and WMDS.

As I watched Vice I thought a lot of my great cat *Bootsy*. He was authentic. An original. A great greeter. A people person of a cat. *Bootsy* was straight, unlike this dick named Cheney, who was never straight with us.

Now, in viewing Vice, I still see it as a bad, uneven movie with a great performance by Christian Bale as Mr. Cheney. But now, strangely, a few short years later, many of those on the left have softened on their opinion of this dick named Cheney and this President named Bush, who they hated back in the day and who both lied us into one of those endless wars America is good at getting into. You know those *Endless Wars* - that guys like the war-mongering Dick Cheney and his inauthentic daughter Liz Cheney salivate over and see as merely real business opportunities.

Now, many years later – I am not sure of many things, but I am sure of these.

There were no WMDs in Iraq. They had no real PROOF. They just lied and told us they were there so that they could make the case for one of those long wars that Trump never got us into.

And for strange reasons, stranger than *"politics make strange bedfellows,"* they are all taking a cat nap together. The *Neo-Cons*. The *Liberal Cons*. And the Con men who will lie us into the *next conflict, police action or good old fashioned war* that is bad for everybody- especially the American people.

With the phoniness of a used car salesman on a lonesome highway, they sleep together, eat at the trough together, and attend the same cocktail parties together while selling out Americans from Motown to my cat, *Bootsy's hometown of West Palm*. Together, like a bunch of wild cats, they attack this man named Trump. While their breeds and breeding are different, *these Re-pub-li-cats, Demo-cats*, and *Independent Alley cats* are allied in their one and only goal: They are engaged in a ferocious and unseemly catfight that has only one goal. *Destroy this powerful and authentic cat named Donald and one movement named MAGA.*

And while he didn't attend any Trump rallies, my cat *Bootsy* was a proud member of the MAGA movement in his own special way.

As I think of these phonies who hate America and Americans but love the industrial military complex who line their pockets, I think of a cool cat I loved named *Bootsy*. My cat *Bootsy* was the real deal and a lot like the man who made America Great once and will do so again, Donald J. Trump.

Want proof? Just ask my mom.

She didn't call *Bootsy* Trump for nothing.

What About-ISMS – and ISMS period?

That's one of the ways how we compare insane claims and counter a point in a particular argument.

"But what about this…But what about what he did… But what about what she said…"

For example, they start with, *"Donald Trump is a liar."* To which the Trump supporter is left with no other choice but to say: "What about Biden?" "What about Obama?" "What about Hillary?" And that's a good example of how the phrase –"What About-isms," is used and used correctly as a comparative analysis.

The other way *Isms* are used is simply to divide a people and a nation. Often, when I seek clarity in making my arguments, I find an ally in an old friend and filmmaker I respect and admire, gaining great wisdom, joy, and bits of treasure in the words and works of legendary filmmaker Frank Capra.

In his 1938 classic, *"You Can't Take It with You,"* Lionel Barrymore as Grandpa Martin Vanderhoff talks about ISMS.

Grandpa Martin Vanderhoff: *"Penny, why don't you write a play about Ism-Mania?"*

Penny Sycamore: *"Ism-Mania?"*

Grandpa Martin Vanderhoff: *"Yeah, sure, you know, Communism, Fascism, Voodooism, everybody's got an -ism these days."*

Penny Sycamore: "Oh"

[laughs]

Penny Sycamore: *"I thought it was an itch or something."*

Grandpa Martin Vanderhoff: *"Well, it's just as catching. When things go a little bad nowadays, you go out, get yourself an -ism and you're in business."*[19]

ISM is, in fact, big business, and Isms affect all our lives.

Isms. Big business. For sure. But even a better way to disarm someone from making their points in a debate on, for example, who should get the job of being the next president of the United States. Sexism and Racism. Two of the biggest ISMs.

If you thought they were vital talking points during the Biden administration, well, you have not seen anything yet. With Kamala Harris as the presumptive Democrat nominee for president, get ready for the onslaught.

Get ready for: *you ain't black if you don't vote for Kamala.*

Get ready for: *you can't call yourself a woman if you don't love you some Kamala.*

And the reason is simple. She has nothing else to run on and only has things like being the border czar that she's running away from. Yet she is willingly running with the narrative of having brown skin and being a woman. On that we could always count on. And with those two talking points not based on policy or accomplishments, she is entitled to hurl in the direction of anyone who brings up her shortcomings or lack of accomplishments- two of those ISMS.

Sexism and Racism.

Not sure which one she will lead with but she will no doubt use them both.

If you can't find your way to voting for her simply because she's a woman –they will accuse you of sexism. They may dress it up and call you a misogynist because they can. And it's all because you don't want to vote for a woman in their eyes. Where before many in her party had a tough time identifying what a woman is – they will now run her in bright lights as the candidate who you are obligated to vote for so that they can break the glass ceiling.

If you can't find your way to voting for her simply because she is a person of color – they will accuse you of being a racist and racism. As I sadly contemplated the coronation of Queen Kamala, I thought of a man named King. *"I have a dream that my four little children will one day live in a nation where they will not be judged by the color of their skin but by the content of their character."*

Content of character. Not judged by the color of your skin or your particular sex but by the ability to get the job done. Wonder what Dr. King would think of the likes of MSNBC's Joy Reid –a noted race hustler. Her answer is as weird as it is expected.

Taking to Tik-Tok Reid posted: "Given just the stratospheric entrance of Vice President Kamala Harris into the presidential campaign, and *she has now secured enough delegates to become the nominee, you're going to look real crazy being on the other side of that line, particularly as a person of color, but really as anyone who claims to have any connection to the culture. You're going to look real weird and real lonely on that side,"* she added. *"You're really going to look crazy being on that side given the cultural phenomenon of Vice President Kamala Devi Harris. She's about to make history. She's about to become the first woman president. The door needs to close behind Amber [Rose], and she looked crazy over there. But shut the door behind her,"* Reid said, reigniting her feud with Rose, whom she criticized after she spoke at the Republican National Convention last week. *She's racially ambiguous. I don't want to say she's black because she has said she's not, so I don't want to say 'this black woman,'"* Reid said following Rose's speech. *"This woman who is of whatever race that she has claimed, she's said she's not black, but [the RNC] brought somebody whose whole career is based in black culture."* Her whole culture came from black culture, even though she said she's not a black person herself, and the fact that she is now the person they're using to try to recruit young people of color and to say that this is the person who is the endorser of Donald Trump who you should trust when she won't even claim the culture that brought her to the table, I'm dubious that this will work," Reid said.

Rose fired back on X, accusing the MSNBC host of "race baiting."

"Hi @JoyAnnReid: *"I've never said I wasn't black. I said I identify as biracial,"* Rose responded in a now-deleted tweet. *"I'm not going to invalid my white father to make you feel more comfortable. Stop being a race baiter your president does enough race baiting for all of us."*[20]

As I digested this disagreement between two people who see Trump and Harris differently, I thought of the words of one of our great leaders, stated by one Kamala Harris as visions of glass ceilings stopped breaking around me.

"I can imagine what can be, unburdened by what has been."

That may or may not be true, but to most serious people it sounds like pure nonsense no matter the race or sex of the person who's saying it. And it points out one Ism that we don't need in the White House – *Idiot-ism.*

Investigating the Investigators

As I mentioned in an earlier chapter, there is a statement attributed to Stalin about voting that is terribly profound. *"It's not who votes that's important. It's who counts the votes."*

So true. And so it follows logically that the importance of any investigation is secondary to who is conducting the investigation. And that brings me to a seminal point, "Who's investigating the investigators?" We have heard about fact-checkers in the shadows checking our every word on social media sites - but who is checking the fact-checkers?

It's a creepy concept and without a doubt, a powerful form of censorship.

Don't like what someone is saying? No problem.

Label it *misinformation or disinformation*. Or better yet call it *HATE Speech*.

As the great communicator, Charlie Brown often said, "Good Grief."

Another great communicator who also like to play with kites like our friend Charlie did, Ben Franklin warned us that we were a *"Republic, if we could keep it,"* and well that's a whole other story.

The intention of our three tiered government with a legislative, executive and judicial branch was in essence built on the concept of checks and balances. The goal was a limited power that prevented the whole thing from going off the rails. The system would prevent or dissuade one branch from putting their thumb on the scales and tipping the direction of the country to far in one or another direction. This thing or idea called America was a big ship and while being nimble enough to avoid many icebergs ahead, should turn slow enough as to not knock any of *We the people* off the side of the ship and from our deck chairs as we lived our lives of liberty while pursuing our individual happiness.

An America should change and progress, but not drastically overnight or within the time frame of one administration, as to render it unrecognizable to its citizenry today or its founding fathers many yesterdays ago.

That is why the making of any laws or the passing of any bills should be an arduous process. Change should come and must come to improve the country as a whole, but it should not come swiftly as to make those riding on America's ship seasick.

Today, many of us are sick to our stomachs and want to vomit at the changing of America seemingly overnight, in the dark of night, as those in power pass bloated, unread bills that are not in the best interest of the American people, but instead are in the best interest of special interest groups who lobby and yield power and influence over them.

The whole point is gridlock.

Gordon Gecko's mantra of - *"Greed is Good,"* about America in the film Wall Street is good and his point of view. But the founders had their own vision about this place and they intended for there to be gridlock. You could see them saying, *"Gridlock for the lack of better word, is good for America,"*

Gridlock for passing bills. Gridlock for impeachment. Gridlock for changing laws. *Gridlock* for changing the face of America. Gridlock for changing America. Sorry, Barack; Hope and Change was a good slogan and bumper sticker. We should always have hope because hope is a good thing, but change, well, that should come slowly, gradually, and deliberately. Change should come only after sober consideration and examination in the light of day by thoughtful representative lawmakers who have in mind what is best for the constitution and their constituents.

Change not initiated in the middle of the night as America sleeps and Illegal immigrants flood over the border.

And finally, that change should be vetted, researched, and *investigated* with one purpose in mind and one question always asked.

Why is this bill here on the hill and who will it help?

In the world we live in today, we have many who want to change America and the foundations that made it great in the first place. There are some who feel the Constitution to be an antiquated document and the principles woven into the sacred blueprint for America are not suited for our time.

They, not the pronoun, but the people behind this movement, want to amend or change core values that most Americans find as vital to us as a nation as the blood that runs through our veins. Casually, they talk of their radical views of eliminating the First Amendment as if they were ordering a latte at Starbucks.

Without thought and lacking critical thinking, these unwise and unprepared citizens can be heard saying things like this.

"We must ban all hate speech." "The First Amendment is overrated and should be abolished."

"The First Amendment is okay as far as it goes. And I'm for it, if I agree with their opinion."

"The First Amendment leads to disinformation and misinformation."

"The First Amendment is dangerous."

This is a composite of what many uniformed citizens, who no doubt either skipped, were not offered, or didn't give a damn about the basic principles they never learned in their civics class. And now, many of these faceless folks anonymously sit in the land of social media, rendering an opinion and verdict like a judge as to what is allowed to be said and what is not. They love information. But distrust and are afraid of misinformation and disinformation.

They are not as afraid of it as they are of climate change, but it is close. Granted, misinformation and disinformation are something that we should be concerned about. All of us. Recently, we lived through a period of rampant Misinformation and Disinformation.

I will simply call them the *Covid-19 Election Years*.

During this time, if one questioned, say, the effectiveness of masks, social distancing, lockdowns, Hydroxychloroquine, Ivermectin, or the pros and cons of the COVID-19 shots, they were shadow-banned, canceled, or tagged with a banner stating that they were a purveyor of misinformation.

Foreshadowing bigger, more devious deeds –to come, like climate change mandates or the next series of vaccine mandates. They are threats to our democracy, our republic, and our pursuit of happiness.

So the next time you get ready to vote or read a headline about a bill being passed or some politician spouting off that you must get the jab, wear the latest and greatest mask or stay locked up at home –first ask yourself some questions.

Who and why are they passing the bills? Who's telling you that masks work? Who's telling you the shots work and instigating a mandate to take them? Who is counting the votes? Who is calling it misinformation and disinformation?

And finally the most important question of them all - who is investigating the investigators?

Conservative Liberal Independent Patriot

I'm conservative, ala Ronnie Reagan. I'm liberal in the classic Kennedy sense. Independent in my Greek heritage and as a journalist. And yes, I consider myself a patriot.

Conservative Liberal Independent Patriot.

For short. A *CLIP*. That's what I am, and that's what I think Donald Trump is too.

In essence –what I call a Patriot. Meaning that regarding many things like our Constitution I'm conservative. First and Second Amendments are there for a reason- many good reasons.

One to respect our free speech. I'm big on that. It's not there for things we say that pretty much everyone can agree with, like: *"You're puppy is cute."* It's there to protect us all whether they say *"Donald Trump is a great and dangerous dictator,"* or *"Hillary Clinton is the most Deplorable candidate to ever run for President."*

Two views and two examples of free speech. The First Amendment is one of the big reasons I'm such a big FILM & MOVIE Guy. I love film, so I would also like to *identify* as a *FILM CLIP. Get it?* I don't play identity politics, but this is my own label and my own Brand.

And well, here are some of my favorite 249 Films, not all American, that I love in no particular order (except for the first 5) to represent every year of this great place called America as it celebrates its 249th birthday in 2025. And while I don't consider myself a film expert- I actually abhor the term- I do know quite a lot about films and what makes a good film. So enjoy my list if you can. And feel free to disagree —even get mad. It's not the gospel on film. Just one of my gospels. In honor of two men I truly respect, Dennis Prager, who did a fine film with Adam Corolla making a film called NO SAFE SPACES that every American who loves liberty should see. And in honor of our 45th and hopefully 47th President of the United States, here is my list; the first 46 or so are in the right order, the rest tie for 47th place. If you don't get the film or get my list – that's okay- both Dennis and I would rather have clarity to agreement. And by the way – President Trump is a big fan of Citizen Kane, but he's also a fan of the Godfather films because he is, after all, a Don.

1 *Citizen Kane*
2 *Godfather I and II*
3 *Casablanca*
4 *It's a Wonderful Life*
5 *City Lights*
6 *Sunset Boulevard*
7 *Shawshank Redemption*
8 *Coming Home (2014) Asian*
9 *Wizard of Oz*
10 *Young Frankenstein*
11 *Singin' in the Rain*
12 *Vertigo*
13 *Mr. Smith Goes to Washington*
14 *The Searchers*
15 *Best in Show*
16 *Dr. Strangelove*
17 *North By Northwest*
18 *One Flew Over The Cuckoo's Nest*
19 *The Graduate*
20 *Zorba the Greek*
21 *Treasure of the Sierra Madre*
22 *Yankee Doodle Dandy*
23 *On the Waterfront*
24 *Grapes Of Wrath*
25 *Double Indemnity*

26 Maltese Falcon
27 An American in Paris
28 Red River
29 Rear Window
30 Psycho
31 Gone With The Wind
32 Lawrence Of Arabia
33 The Hustler
34 Salesman
35 Sideways
36 Locke
37 Lucky
38 Lean on Pete
39 Parasite
40 Shadow of a Doubt
41 The End of the Tour
42 White Heat
43 Goodfellas
44 Saving Private Ryan
45 Field of Dreams
46 12 Angry Men;
47 The Rider; Pale Rider; Mustang; The Last Waltz; Some Like it Hot; Spartacus; To Kill a Mockingbird; Notorious; Network;; The Florida Project; Pride of the Yankees
Arthur; Chinatown; A Place in the Sun; Strangers on a Train; The Little Foxes;; The Gold Rush; The General; Bicycle Thieves; Manhattan; Hannah and Her Sisters, Seven Samurai, Meet Jon Doe; Mr. Deeds Goes To Town; The Conversation; Glengarry Glen Ross; Waiting For Guffman; Touch of Evil; Mildred Pierce; Angels with Dirty Faces; A Bronx Tale; Woman of the Year; Philadelphia Story; Philadelphia; Schindler's List; Capernaum; A Separation; Life is Beautiful; From Here to Eternity; To Have and Have Not; The Natural Streetcar Named Desire; Sullivan's Travels; All About Eve; Being There; Gladiator; Passion for the Christ; The Big Chill; A Bronx Tale; 100 As Good As It Gets; When Harry Met Sally Modern Times; This is Spinal Tap; The Heiress; A Space Odyssey; Roman Holiday; His Girl Friday; Paths of Glory; Crimes and Misdemeanors; Gentleman's Agreement; Rebecca; Roaring Twenties; Showboat; Big Sleep; Moonlight; Moonstruck; West Side Story; Sound of Music; Best Years of Our Life; Lady Eve; The Killers; Out of The Past; Cool

Hand Luke; Sweet Smell of Success; Pulp Fiction; Once upon A time In Hollywood; The Verdict; Dog Day Afternoon; Scent of a Woman; Good Will Hunting; Dead Poet's Society; Lincoln; The Candidate; Manchurian Candidate; Mask; Bonnie & Clyde; The Best Man; Ghost and Mrs. Muir; Humoresque; Devil and Daniel Webster; Mrs. Miniver; Miracle Worker; Trading Places; All the President's Men; The Birds; Night of the Living Dead; Cinema Paradiso; Outlaw Josey Wales; The Good, the Bad and the Ugly; The Sting; Jaws; Rocky; American Beauty; The Ten Commandments; Ben Hur; King of Kings; Shane; McCabe and Mrs. Miller; Fistful of Dollars; Butch Cassidy and the Sundance Kid; 8 1/2 .

High Noon; The Revenant: She Wore a Yellow Ribbon; The Postman Always Rings Twice Way out West; Sons of the Desert; The Circus; Limelight; Amour; 45 Years; Bambi; Toy Story; Snow White and the Seven Dwarfs; The Wrestler; Pope of Greenwich Village; Diner; La La Land; Whiplash; Green Book; In the Heat of the Night; Guess Who's Coming to Dinner?; The Odd Couple; The Apartment; Fargo; Miller's Crossing; Hard Day's Night; Wild Tales; Little Miss Sunshine; Frankenstein; The Past; Shoplifters; Cold War; The Insult; Jo-Jo Rabbit; Roma; Leave No Trace; Free Solo; The Music Box; La Dolce Vita; Sleepless in Seattle; Close Encounters of the Third Kind; ET; Mudbound; Three Billboards Outside of Ebbing Missouri; 1917; Uncut Gems; I, Tonya; Inside Out; The Big Short; American Hustle; About Schmidt; Descendants; Great Expectations; Planes, Trains and Automobiles; Breakfast Club; Trading Places; Ford versus Ferrari; Boyhood; Birdman; Social Network; The Fighter; American Sniper; The Last Flag Flying; Gilda; Manchester by the Sea; No Country for old Men; Cast Away; United 93; Annie Hall; Brave Heart; The Man Who Shot Liberty Valance; Forest Gump; Blues Brothers; Grease; From Here To Eternity; Saturday Night Fever: Laura; Boys Town; The Player; At Eternity's Gate; My Cousin Vinny; Johnny Come Lately; Harvey; Great Dictator; It Happened One Night; You Can't Take It with You; Perfect Days; Zone of Interest; Anatomy of a Fall, Elvis & Godfather III.

My Next Book is a T-Shirt

It was a typical hot summer Florida day in the Sunshine State. But not really. There was never anything typical when the man named Donald Trump came to your town. Yet it was here where he decided to be on this day before the 4th of July 2021. Just months after a day, January 6th, that many on the left will have you believe is the opposite of the 4th of July. They would have you believe that one day *stood for independence* while the other day *stood for insurrection*. What they failed to miss was the point that both days represented important markers in our history, days comprised of concerned disgruntled citizens seeking liberty and exercising their unalienable rights. In the case of January 6th, it was to peacefully and patriotically protest an election. On July 4th it was to declare independence.

Yes, but on this 4th of July weekend, it was just a little bit hotter and steamier as the former President prepared to take the stage before an estimated 45,000 loyal followers. Special too, because it was a day that welcomed back the former President to one of the reddest and hottest regions of the United States. And most importantly it was the first real chance after the election of 2020 and J6 for everyone to show up and show the former president how much they were behind him and the MAGA movement.

The day was filled with extreme heat, intermittent showers, and an emotionally charged appearance by the man who many felt had been wronged by a rigged election. Those there, myself included, were trying to lend support for their president and the movement in oppressive heat.

I, too, was there for another reason: to sell copies of my GET TRUMP book. I had arrived in the early morning hours to scope out the scene. After connecting with one of the vendors who was loaded to the hilt with all things MAGA, I negotiated, leaving my books at her booth. It would give me a great spot and base to pitch my books to many in Trump's base. A comfortable place from where I could pitch my prose in print on a president that I not only supported and respected but also loved.

My pitching area was the small road Ringling Blvd. that was parallel to the entrance of the large outdoor area behind Robarts Arena, where I attended my first Trump rally, oh so many years before.

On that day, the day before the 2016 Election, I stood in line for hours in the very spot where I was now pitching my words and my perspective on the 45th president.

So much time had passed. So much has happened to all of us in these six years. An escalator ride into the race. A stunning upset win on Election Day over a Hall of Shame swamp creature. The trials. The Tribulations. The persecutions. The Impeachments. The Rallies. The Peaceful and Not So Peaceful Protests. The apparent stolen election. January 6th, and now this.

That seemed like a hundred years ago.

A lot of things had changed but there were still things you could count on –the heat in Florida on a July day and the passion of the throngs of MAGA supporters all there to see their hero, no matter what the weather or circumstances.

Through sweltering heat, storms, and even lightning strikes, the show went on. I moved around the big space – finding a choice locale behind the speakers, which ensured great angles of the man and a chance to be seen on TV – but that's not why I was there. I was there to see and support the MAGA man. And as he joked in true Trump-like fashion, telling the women in the audience that they "looked beautiful and were a mess" all in the same sentence. We all knew what he meant and laughed.

Such were the conditions of the day. Heat. Sweltering at times. Rain. Often in buckets. A sauna and a rainstorm. It was like being a kid running through the sprinkler on a hot summer day.

I sat. I watched. I listened. I laughed. I cried. And I became inspired. They might have stolen the election from him, but he was still the happy warrior. The man who did the work while whistling with a smile and not a grimace. And in doing so – those who had gathered – close to 50,000 loyalists (60 or 70 thousand if you're Trump). You see we get and know our man and understand his need to embellish a little. Hell, he's a storyteller. And all storytellers embellish a bit. At least the good ones do. We don't hold it against him. We hold him closer because of this. It endears him to us. And us to him. We love him for confronting the "Fake News Press" and daring them to "turn their cameras" on the HUGE crowd who had gathered to celebrate our independence and see the man who was ensuring that it continued.

Fireworks topped off a day filled with much color, pomp and circumstance with a group of people who now were a movement and always would be. A movement that would continue to try and make America great again on hot days, cold days, rainy days and even days when the storms were brewing.

Before and after the rally, I found myself on that same narrow road named Ringling. I thought of the circus magnate who put Sarasota on the map and how he pitched his circus all over America to become a household name to the masses. Now, with books in hand, I was pitching my book on the man I had come to understand and count on, in his telling of the American story while providing hope for the American dream.

As I sold a few books, for which I was internally grateful to MAGA nation who passed right by me on the way in and out of the event, I heard a voice beckoning from a man down the way who was selling something with a rhythmic cadence that was quite frankly mesmerizing.

Joe and the Ho Got to Go! Joe and the Ho Got to Go! Joe and the Ho Got to Go!

His T-shirt sales were brisk, and his pitch was perfect. Seven words. Sold perfectly

I thought of that the other day when Biden finally dropped out of the 2024 race.

Well - one down and one to go.

On that hot day in July I learned a lot about selling from a couple of masters in selling. One man who knew how to sell his vision for his country created a movement. And the other man who was damn good at selling T-shirts.

And one important lesson learned and why *my next book will be a T-shirt*.

Where are the Jews?

It bothered me when I first heard it. The news from *Hollywood* regarding the opening of the Academy Museum of Motion Pictures. The big take away and this is a spoiler alert –

is that they missed and messed up the story. The folks in charge of unveiling, in essence, "their latest movie" failed to tell the story of how and by whom this place called Hollywood was founded. As hard as it is to believe – THEY LEFT OUT THE JEWS! Surely, that had to be a misprint. But sadly, it was not. It was a story that they rolled out that was not thought through nor executed, and thus, it was not well received. And that, my friends, can be attributed to what dooms most Hollywood films, the failure to have a good foundation and instead produce a film from a bad screenplay chock full of bad writing. And, of course, its own battle with trying to be politically correct and too WOKE.

In writing the story of Hollywood, you simply can't leave out the Jews. Not if you want to maintain credibility. But that's just what they did. The Academy Museum ignored *"Hollywood's Founding Fathers"* in Hollywood. It is a place where the American story was developed, manufactured, and distributed to the American public and the world at large, largely by the Jews. Yet the most recent narrative on its beginnings has received terrible reviews for not getting the story right. Or at least right - right out of the gate.

Bad storytelling is not something new to Hollywood. There are bad scripts and revisionist history in the land of rewrites. But remember one thing – you can't write the story of Hollywood without the JEWS. But somehow, in the W*oke days* that we're living in today's America, as the museum opened, they forgot one thing - that is essential in any accurate and moving telling of how Hollywood's story was formed. In their effort to be inclusive of everyone else to the point of bending themselves backward into a pretzel, they *forgot the Jews!*

Four months after the center's splashy opening big donors and showbiz veterans were still scratching their heads on the omission of Hollywood's "founding fathers." At an opening gala, stars from Lady Gaga to Brad Pitt and other A-list stars mingled maskless inside the 33,000-square-foot space on Wilshire Boulevard. And as they did, many donors and influential Academy members, some who already had received private tours, were outraged. Outraged that this telling of Hollywood's origin story — wherein a group of mostly Jewish émigrés fled persecution in their home countries to create what would become a multibillion-dollar, American-led industry — was conspicuously absent.

Anti-Defamation League CEO Jonathan Greenblatt, who was on hand for the gala, was immediately struck by the lapse. *"I would've hoped that any honest historical assessment of the motion picture industry — its origins, its development, its growth — would include the role that Jews played in building the industry from the ground up,"* he says. *"As I walked through, I literally turned to the person I was there with and said to him, 'Where are the Jews?'* The omission was glaring.... echoing from Hollywood's C-suites to the halls of academia. *"It's sort of like building a museum dedicated to Renaissance painting, and ignoring the Italians,"* says Hollywood historian and Brandeis University professor Thomas Doherty. *"That generation of early moguls — Carl Laemmle, Jack Warner, we know all their names — is a terrific story of upward mobility, living the American dream. It's one of the great contributions of American Jews to American culture."*

Instead of focusing on tributes to those Old Hollywood pioneers, the dozen-plus exhibits that would open to the public five days later included more contemporary-skewing fare, such as *Director's Inspiration: Spike Lee* and *Installation: Pedro Almodóvar*. Behind the scenes, a full revolt was afoot, sources say, with some patrons threatening to pull future support for the institution. Says one prominent Academy member who declined to be named: *"You left the museum with the impression that the film industry was created 10 years ago. They erased the past. And I find it appalling."*[21]

Erasing the history. Tearing down statues. Removing Aunt Jemima from the store shelf. All are part of a society that must *wake up from the WOKE Horror movie playing all across America*. The Academy scrambled to correct their mistake, the way a nervous director re-cuts a film after a bad night in front of a tough preview audience, promising to add "a long-planned exhibit on the so-called founding fathers and the birth of the studio system," which will mark the first and only permanent exhibition in the collection.

A rewrite was in order. Script doctors worked to undo the harm, but some damage had already been done. "By not including the founding fathers out of the gate, they were making a massive statement," says Triller co-founder and Academy member Ryan Kavanaugh. *"As the grandson of Holocaust survivors, it's just shocking that they erased the contributions of a group who faced severe anti-Semitism — they couldn't get bank loans, they couldn't own homes in L.A., and yet they still created this industry that is the bedrock of the L.A. economy and touches people around the world. Instead of, 'Look at what they were able to do,' it's just wiped out. It goes against everything that our industry says they stand for."*

Sadly, it was the beginning of coming attractions worldwide. Anti-Semitism was ready to rear its ugly head yet again, not by omission at a museum opening, but instead by commission as organized Anti-Israel and Pro-Palestine protests were coming soon to a campus near you and on the supposed grounds of higher education, where the brightest and best amongst us should value a real history lesson. Here, with their advanced studies, surely they could get a fair review of the story of a people and place called Israel. But something strange happened along the way. In Academia, like Hollywood, they too *forgot the Jews* in their story. Instead, the narrative shifted and was rewritten, and the story that was GREEN LIGHTED was the other story, which had Palestine and even HAMAS cast as sympathetic figures suffering at the hands of the big bad and evil villain - Israel. In their story, they glossed over October 7th, the massacre of Jews, and the taking of hostages. Their movie *GET ISRAEL* was opening on campuses all across the land as their promotion departments and PR campaigns kicked into full gear. Boldly and loudly, they yelled at the top of their lungs with veins bursting and hate-filled hearts on campuses all over America. Pro-Palestine became the norm, and the film that they were opening that they hoped would do Big Box Office.

What's not normal and should never be accepted is the casual and blatant omission of the facts that our forefathers fought for to create this republic. Whether it's Hollywood, academia or government, when telling the American story – we must never forget the script that was written by great men and acted on by great men to create a great movie and country that is America. And we must remember their ghosts. Sharon

Rosen Leib wrote in *The Forward:* "*At the museum, [Jews] are ghosts. Their presence hangs over the halls — there would literally be no museum, no industry, without them."*

Today there are many ghosts and one Holy Ghost hanging over America, watching over us to see that we do the right things to make it great again. Just as there would be no America without its founding fathers, there would be no Hollywood without the Jews who founded it. The Jews who were the driving forces behind *Paramount, 20th Century Fox, Warner Brothers, Universal, Columbia, and Metro-Goldwyn-Mayer* shared a very 20th-century sense of being Jewish in America. They were assimilationists who considered themselves American above all else and who molded Hollywood to reflect and shape their American ideals.

"Above all things, they wanted to be regarded as Americans, not Jews," Neal Gabler wrote in his definitive 1988 history, "An Empire of Their Own: How the Jews Invented Hollywood." *Louis B. Mayer, a co-founder of MGM, went so far as to claim that his birth papers had been lost during immigration and to declare his birthday henceforth as the Fourth of July.* [22]

MGM's Mayer was born on the fourth of July. A real Yankee Doodle Dandy. A lover of country and flag. A lover of America. A maker of movies. A Jew and an American. One wonders what old Louie would think of today's political climate and make of students yelling anti-Semitic slurs at campuses like Harvard and Columbia. I know what Capra would do. The populist director who worked at Columbia Studios, for you guessed it - a Jew named Harry Cohen, who ran the studio, would make a film. Old Frank would hit the issue head-on. I think Louie B and some of those other Jewish moguls might even join the director. They'd already have a working title. *WHERE ARE THE JEWS?*

It's a story about a *Mr. Smith-like character, starring someone like Jimmy Stewart or Gary Cooper (Good luck trying to cast him today),* who sounds alarm bells on what's going on all over the country. Righting the wrongs of the forgotten men and women, he helps Americans first with their American dreams but doesn't forget friends like Israel as his resolve helps keep the Middle East safe. Still, he's put through the paces by a corrupt deep state that paints him as a bad guy instead of the hero he really is. Through it all, the fake stories, fake impeachment trials, and real assassination attempts, he keeps his faith and fights for the American people.

At the climax of the film, on election night, he looks over the results that at one time held such promise. He lifts his eyes to the TV screen for the results. The contingency plan he supported through thick and then they didn't show up at the polls. As he processes the numbers, he shakes his head and mumbles to himself, "*Where are the Jews?*"

v. Joe Biden – A Presidential Puppet Like No Other

STORYTELLING 101- DESTROYING AMERICA:
The Unbelievable Rise of Joe Biden

Protecting Joe's boy at all cost while failing to provide security for RFK's boy

BIDEN TIME

A GUY NAMED JOE & A case of intentional F-Ups?

LOVE OF ICE CREAM and the real scoop on BIDEN and TRUMP

Storytelling 101- Destroying America: The Unbelievable Rise of Joe Biden

It's a story that even Hollywood would label as being overwritten

The secret of all great stories is the story. It can't be overwritten or underwritten. But it must be written. That is why I've always told my film students that the most important ingredient to creating a great story for the silver screen or streaming is the Screenplay. (Teleplay – if you're talking TV.)

The screenplay is the foundation on which all great films are made. Think Casablanca, Citizen Kane, and The Godfather, all great stories and films – built upon a wonderful structure. And that structure starts with a good or great script.

Sure, the actors matter. Getting a great cinematographer to shoot your film is important. A wise and seasoned editor can help sort out the story. Music and the score can heighten moments and create mood. And finally, it helps to have a guy named Hitch, Capra, or Coppola at the helm to direct your project. But if you don't have the story- a viable and believable story that people can follow- some call it a sound narrative – then you have a shaky foundation.

Speaking of a shaky foundation, that brings me to the Joe Biden Story- or, in this case, *"The Unlikely and Unbelievable Rise of Joe Biden."*

This is not a great script and is a story built upon a shaky foundation and a shaky man named Joe Biden- the protagonist of this story. A story that the writers want you to believe in. A story that they insist you relate to the story even with a most unbelievable hero at its center. In this case, the rise of a man named Joe Biden. *A man who is better at making things up than making things happen.* A man who can't read the teleprompter in front of him. A man who often botches his lines. A man who can barely get the words out of his mouth, and when he does, you need an interpreter to understand him and this language we'll call *BIDEN-ESE* that he struggles to unleash upon anyone within earshot.

Not only is what he's saying unintelligible, but it is often delivered in strange cadences, hues, and various tones ranging from Creepy Whispers to *Cringe-worthy yelling.*

What JFK had in spades, clueless Joe lacks in bushels. He is not only the worst communicator to serve as President, but he may also be the worst communicator ever elected to any office, anywhere. That goes for crooked small-town mayors, inept upstate aldermen, city council folks with ADHD, and Harvard Presidents with PHDs.

Biden makes the struggling Senator from Pennsylvania, John Fetterman, look like a Nobel laureate. That's no small feat and hard to accomplish in any language.

This script handed to the man who, good for him, overcame stuttering but could not overcome his propensity to lie early and often. A man who, in one of his previous runs for President, aborted his quest for the Oval Office due to his ability to plagiarize, once again, early and often. And for those of you who don't have a college degree, plagiarizing is a fancy way of saying he stole someone else's work and words and passed them off as his own. Sound familiar? It's kind of like stealing votes and taking credit for winning an election that you really didn't win. The only difference is back then, Joe knew exactly what he was doing. Today, not so sure. But somebody, actually more likely a group of somebodies, knows exactly what they are doing even if Joe doesn't.

And that's simply this. Their mandate is clear and calculated in its execution, as Biden is fuzzy and foggy in his delivery of the message. One policy is all that matters to all of them pulling the strings and writing Joe's lines. Ironically, they have the right guy in the lead part. A part he was made for and hand-picked to play. *Central casting done by Washington.* Because let's face it, other than this role, what else could this actor named Joe do in his current condition?

Mr. and Mrs. America- a question for you all while watching this play out at home.

In any of your businesses, jobs and occupations, out of all the positions that you are aware of out there in the marketplace- is there one job that you can honestly say you would hire this guy to fill? That's what we thought.

Let's face it. This is the only thing he can do: play a role in this *horror-suspense-adventure disaster film with Armageddon overtones*.

And the plot? The plot is simple. *Destroy America*.

Protecting Joe's boy at all cost while failing to provide security for RFK's boy

The statue of RFK sits ominously in the shadow of a man and a shadow government as the sun streams into the White House. All the while, the frail and failing man who lives there, called the President, tries to string two sentences together.

And when he pulls it off, those within earshot wince and grimace as the words don't flow as much as they ooze from this mentally deficient and decaying old man. Even in bronze, the statue of RFK that adorns his residence, while mute, speaks more clearly and with greater lucidity than sleepy, creepy, and now *crooked Joe*. And everyone knows it. That's one of the good things about a statue - there are no wasted words soaked in lies and hyperbole. Just a statement, some may say, a *profile* in *courage and a bust to look at, take in, evaluate, and value what the man it represented* stood for at another time and place in our history.

In this case, the oddly placed bronze statue seems even stranger because it is often seen in the same room with this man, Joe Biden, the President of the United States. A man who appears more like a resident than a president and someone who so desperately wants to be perceived as presidential in photo ops like these but who, in reality, looks and acts old and out of touch. Kind of *like a lifeless statue or bronze figure —only with less life*.

Yet, all the while, the man with vacant eyes and fading faculties struggles to be relevant and appear presidential. As he makes his failed attempts to fool the few not in on the charade, he glances at it and surely is bothered by the bronze statue that accompanies him in this house. Struggling in his feeble brain – he tries to put two and two together and under his breath, mumbles and asks himself a question: *"Who is this guy? His name is on the tip of my tongue."* And that's not a place where his rarely cogent thoughts go to flourish. That's a place they travel to – to be bumbled, forgotten, or just die a slow death like this man propped up on the fancy couch in a White House. He looks vacantly at the statue of the young lion of liberalism, a man many in a Democrat party of years gone by would have made king had we been a monarchy instead of a republic. Now today, decades after his tragic death, when he was taken by an assassin's bullet as he campaigned to become President, a statue of Bobby Kennedy pays homage to a man and an iconic Democrat who once captured the hearts, minds, and zeitgeist of a younger more hopeful American generation. An America that is fading fast but not as fast as the fading man named Joe, who stares at the bronze statue.

The words of RFK echo in the White House and into the empty head of the statue-like president named Biden. *"Some men see things as they are and say why. I dream things that never were and say why not."*

And some men don't see things at all. Some men can't even ask why things have gotten so bad. And some men, like this empty suit sitting here, are unable to dream of big ideas but instead are installed as part of a national nightmare, sculpted not artistically but tragically, because some in real power, the ones buying the clay, said, *"Why Not?"*

The result? A skeleton of a man who so wants to be believed and trusted as a leader sits within a camera shot of the impressive bronze of Robert Fitzgerald Kennedy, a man who so many wanted so badly to be President. He stares blankly at world leaders, reporters with no intent of asking tough questions and at an old bronze of a man who could have historically changed the course of American history in a positive way- had he lived. But just as the great poets, philosophers, and keepers of history often surmise, sadly, *it was not to be*. Still, in moments like these, when a dignitary or friendly chum in Congress comes knocking, the fast-fading figure, who is anything but the silver knight, the golden boy, or a figure who will ever be remembered justly in bronze, poses on demand. It is the one thing this stiff from Delaware does with ease. Pose. Posing first as a Senator for an unthinkable six terms, then as Vice-President for eight years, and now he poses with the sincerity of a *Used Car salesman* who needs his end-of-the-month sale and is on a test drive with a naïve buyer as his sales manager watches in the wings, to see if he can close the deal.

In this case, *his sales manager* is a man with a funny name who used to live here. He, too, is cleverly hidden away nearby in a back office, perhaps in the shadows of a darkened basement, but yet close enough and with enough light for him to see and pull the puppet strings that are connected to this shell of a man who is trying so hard to act – well like a man who is worthy of the pomp and circumstance, that his Presidential role defines.

In this room, with the sun streaming in, with all the appointments of the proper drape and tightly woven Persian rug setting the scene, designed to make the man who they installed here as President feel as comfortable as possible for his close-up and his photo op. Often on a couch, his legs crossed with the air of someone F. Scott Fitzgerald would have written about, and with an accompanying ethos of aristocracy mixed in with a common man's touch, the mummy-like figure struggles to find the right tone. He has given up on words and merely aims for the right look. He feigns that fake smile that he thinks charmed the masses enough to land him here, allowing him to forge his way into this room, an imposter looking at real portraits of real Presidents named Lincoln, Washington, and Jackson and staring at a real bronze statue of Bobby Kennedy, a man who many think should have been President.

For a moment, distracted, he loses his place, but that upsets exactly no one. And that's hardly news. The rule and not the exception. When you make as many gaffes as he does, that is the norm. The expected f-up from this man who Obama once said, "Don't worry, Joe will F it up."

With a tug from the man in the basement pulling the strings so he won't F-up as much, the puppet struggles to stay focused. But this is no easy task, even for a two-term President to pull off.

Still as the stiff sits and tries to look presidential, he tries not to be distracted by the many cameras or reporters who are usually kept a safe distance away from him. He's used to that, to the handlers and those being handled. His soft focus leads him to glance at the profile and bronze of the man from Massachusetts, this man named Bobby Kennedy.

What's he thinking as he stares at the statue? Is he thinking about inflation?

Or the next flavor of ice cream that he would be tucked into bed with later on this night - if he's a good boy? Or is he thinking about his boy Hunter? Or perhaps, and this is a long shot, is he thinking about the son of the bronze figure who adorns his surroundings at the White House, Bobby Kennedy Jr? Bobby Kennedy Jr?

He's a man that this man named Joe would not dare be seen in the same room with, the son of the bronze figure who still casts a long shadow over him. A man whose daddy and Uncle were both assassinated, one when he was President and one when he was running to become president.

Now, the man who can barely think has done the unthinkable – by denying secret service protection to this man named Kennedy - Robert Kennedy Jr., the son of the man represented in the bronze statue who haunts him and who is running to become President and replace him in this very room and house.

Yes, this empty suit of a man with a broken moral compass who bumbled the Afghanistan evacuation, causing the lives of 13 American heroes and thousands of other Americans to be stranded in a strange land because of his failed plan, sits and stares.

Perhaps he's thinking about that?

Or maybe he's thinking about the consequences of a broken border that allowed millions to literally break into America and bring with them contributions to child trafficking, a pipeline of fentanyl to pour into America and cause an estimated 100,000 loss of lives to a tested drug produced by the Chinese.

Or perhaps he was thinking about the man he was running away from (no, not Donald Trump, he's already given orders to get Trump) but the Democrat with the pedigree - Bobby Kennedy Jr. Maybe he was thinking about two brothers named Jack and Bobby Kennedy? And why he has not provided secret service detail to Bobby's boy - even with all the irony and the possibility of a potential looming tragedy hanging over him, drifting ever so slowly in and out of his head just like a Chinese Spy Balloon once drifted slowly across America.

Still, always still, sits the hollow man, frozen like a statue pondering, a real-life Hamlet figure, only less decisive. Then suddenly, in a moment of clarity, it hits him, as a rare empathy gene connects with a fading synapse. Eureka!

"I would want my boy Hunter to be protected by the Secret Service if he were running for President."

Giving him the benefit of the doubt, perhaps Joe was indeed thinking about that after all. About Jack, Bobby, and maybe even what the bronze figure would think of his mistreatment of his boy?

Maybe that's it. What the man with a vacant look does know - and God knows he doesn't know much, is simply this.

Somewhere deep inside, all those lies concocted in this soulless and talentless entity that make up his mummifying being consist the elements that make up this fake, plastic, and vapid excuse of a man. The clay, if you will. Clay that was molded, shaped, and manipulated – not by a loving and giving God, but instead by a posse of puppeteers - evil puppet masters pulling the strings. No longer content to tell the man with the fading brain how high to jump anymore; or which policies to install and which destructive bills to sign, but merely tugging lightly on the strings in the hope that this broken down puppet merely fades away.

His job almost done now. The destruction almost complete. His usefulness exhausted. The man with the huge ambition and the minuscule intellect sits there almost helpless on the designer couch that was installed and placed here, as was he, to fit into this conjured environment. Yes, the man who could lie on command and did all he was commanded to do has worn out his welcome and his usefulness. Yes, *Sleepy Joe's* job is almost complete. And that job was simply this – destroy and do as much damage to a country that was built by great patriotic men and women who had passion and vision. Two qualities of many virtuous ones that he sorely lacks. Yet, as his empty shark-like eyes peer around the White House, something catches his fading attention. It is a rare voice that sneaks a question past those who guard him, this hapless and feeble figure.

"Mr. President, What is the accomplishment that you are most proud of in your Presidency?"

"Was it Built Back Better?"

Stunned. Shocked. That the question was allowed to be asked in the first place, in this of all places, he smiles, that used car salesman of a smile in the direction of the sycophantic press and puppet masters who fill the room in the White House.

He struggles to get out a reply. But that is not new and instead the new and accepted norm. Still, as the man is escorted out of the scene by his handlers, the man who never should have been president catches a glimpse of the bronze statue – and a likeness of the man who many had hoped would be.

But just as the poets, philosophers, and political historians will write and wax, with both a twinge of sadness and wonder, *"It wasn't meant to be."*

The fading man is fixated on the statue, and strangely, their eyes meet.

The man made of bronze and this stone like leader. They both know the answer to the unanswered question. The man whose presidency was a bust and the bust of a man, *Robert Kennedy, who really could have built back America better.*

BIDEN TIME

America had been bogged down in Afghanistan for a *long time*. It was the result of one of those *endless wars* that America had the propensity to stumble into time after time. Years ago, to another generation, it was *Viet Nam*, then to another *Iraq*, and now finally, it was *Afghanistan*. They were all places where young American servicemen and women went to die needlessly for a variety of reasons, bearing the spoiled fruit of a foreign policy that consisted of one part schizophrenia and another bigger part made up by greedy profiteers who all had a shared interest and stock in the military-industrial complex.

It was something that a man nicknamed Ike warned all of us about in his farewell address before leaving as President after serving two terms and after leading America's fight that defeated real fascists and real Nazis in World War II.

President Dwight D. Eisenhower's exit speech was developed after 21 painstaking drafts because the man who led men into battle wanted to leave behind thoughtful and wise words for future generations of Americans to consider and weigh before plunging into dangerous waters.

It has been noted famously that "everyone liked Ike," but most importantly, one of his greatest contributions to his fellow Americans is perhaps these words he left all Americans with as he exited the political stage for public life in 1961. And they are words that many who comprise the growing military-industrial complex undoubtedly won't like. Yet his words serve as a cautionary tale for sure, given by a man with courage, wisdom, and a love for his country –at a time in our nation's history that was "a solemn moment in a decidedly un-solemn time," warning a nation "giddy with prosperity, infatuated with youth and glamour, and aiming increasingly for the easy life."

Ike's farewell speech is packed with wisdom, critical thinking, and common sense, virtues sadly and dangerously lacking today in many of the men and women who make up the establishment in Washington at this critical time in our history.

Some words from a man named Ike as he exited the political stage right.

"As we peer into society's future, we – you and I, and our government – must avoid the impulse to live only for today, plundering for our own ease and convenience the precious resources of tomorrow. We cannot mortgage the material assets of our grandchildren without risking the loss also of their political and spiritual heritage. We want democracy to survive for all generations to come, not to become the insolvent phantom of tomorrow."

Despite his military background and being the only general to be elected president in the 20th century, he warned the nation with regard to the corrupting influence of what he describes as the *"military-industrial complex."*

"Until the latest of our world conflicts, the United States had no armaments industry. American makers of plowshares could, with time and as required, make swords as well. But we can no longer risk emergency improvisation of national defense. We have been compelled to create a permanent armaments industry of vast proportions. Added to this, three and a half million men and women are directly engaged in the defense establishment. We annually spend on military security alone more than the net income of all United States corporations.

Now this conjunction of an immense military establishment and a large arms industry is new in the American experience. The total influence—economic, political, even spiritual—is felt in every city, every Statehouse, every office of the Federal government. We recognize the imperative need for this development. Yet, we must not fail to comprehend its grave implications. Our toil, resources, and livelihood are all involved. So is the very structure of our society.

In the councils of government, we must guard against the acquisition of unwarranted influence, whether sought or unsought, by the military-industrial complex. The potential for the disastrous rise of misplaced power exists and will persist. We must never let the weight of this combination endanger our liberties or democratic processes. We should take nothing for granted. Only an alert and knowledgeable citizenry can compel the proper meshing of the huge industrial and military machinery of defense with our peaceful methods and goals so that security and liberty may prosper together."

And if that wasn't enough sage advice, he also *expressed his concern for corruption of the scientific process* as part of this centralization of funding in the Federal government, and vice versa:

"Akin to, and largely responsible for the sweeping changes in our industrial-military posture, has been the technological revolution during recent decades.

In this revolution, research has become central; it has also become more formalized, complex, and costly. A steadily increasing share is conducted for, by, or at the direction of the Federal government.

The prospect of domination of the nation's scholars by Federal employment, project allocation, and the power of money is ever present and is gravely to be regarded.

> *Yet in holding scientific discovery in respect, as we should, we must also be alert to the equal and opposite danger that public policy could itself become the captive of a scientific-technological elite."*[23]

Thoughts by wise man with vision given some 60 years ago.

Now, six decades later, at another place and time in our nation's history, those heady thoughts and topics were the furthest thing from the mind of a man named Joe Biden, as he nervously peered down at his watch.

In a strange and criminal gesture, the man, largely responsible for the fate of the 13 corpses of military heroes who were now lying in state in his presence after dying on his watch - was sneaking a peek at the time! The empty suit was peering at his wristwatch.

Looking down at his watch!

All while dead soldiers and patriots whose time had run out because of him and his poor decision-making, lack of leadership, no plan, and bad timing.

Revolting. Disrespectful. Obscene. Grotesque. Deplorable. One wonders if Hillary thinks this is a deplorable action. Anyway, all these words fall short of describing the despicable actions of *this pretend President named Joe.*

Time yourself and think about the action for a minute.

Gazing at his watch? What was he thinking? Hell, was he even capable of thinking?

At this point in time, the questions persisted, *"Could the man in charge be running America – and who was, in fact, the commander in chief in charge of the military and someone who dealt with the growing military-industrial complex on a daily basis –did he even know what day it was and could he even still tell time?"*

These were the thoughts many family, friends, and patriots of the fallen war heroes had as they watched Biden look at his watch.

13 *dead American heroes, and this clown wants to know the right time?*

Well, it was the right time and about time people on both sides of the aisle, those with Rs next to their name and those with Ds, woke up to this one fact.

At no time ever was this guy named Joe Biden ever qualified or cogent enough to lead America through even calm times, let alone times filled with treacherous storms on the horizon.

There is no polite way of saying this, but Joe Biden was always dumb, and now he's just getting dumber. Or more forgetful. Or less energetic. Or simply just overwhelmed by the job and responsibility if you are kind, or *"doing the best he can and a better job than Trump"* if you are dishonest and work as a political hack for MSNBC, CNN, and now even large parts of FOX.

To those in the press covering this guy in BIDEN TIME, just one question, and please answer honestly. Whatever metric you plug in and rate anyone in public service, civil service, or simply a performance report on how the Starbucks manager does his job fetching you your fancy lattes before you go live on your broadcasts: Is this guy running the whole shebang called the United States of America in his right mind? And one follow-up question. Do you trust him with the responsibility of making the decisions that impact the well-being of your children and grandchildren's lives and the future of America?

Take your time, grab a cup of Joe, and think about that for a minute.

So as these 13 American patriots were eulogized, many also pondered what the great timekeepers, the historians, those charged with the responsibility of keeping time, would say about this era of American leadership. Would they reflect on this time fairly? Would they reflect and report accurately as they surely wondered out loud if the feeble man was up to the task at hand as enemies gathered while setting their collective clocks waiting to pounce at the right time - on the man and country whose timing was terribly off?

Only time will tell.

But for right now, at this moment in time, the picture and the scene could not have looked any worse for America and this President, as the plan to leave Afghanistan and one of those endless wars was terribly and tragically botched.

Before looking at how the Biden Administration pulled out of Afghanistan in August 2021, let's first take a look at how we became entangled in this mess in the first place.

- 9/11 Attacks on America September 2001
- Hunt for perpetrators of terrorist attack masterminded by Osama Bin Laden
- Linkage to Iraq Weapons of Mass Destruction
- Entanglement in War with Iraq March 2003
- Actual War with Afghanistan 2001-2014
- Formal War ends with Afghanistan on December 28,2014
- Reduced Forces/approx13,000 troops remain/train Afghan troops until 2020
- Drawdown of troops from 2020 to 2021
- Hasty withdrawal from Afghanistan in August 2021

Those are merely nine bullet points of an endless war, make that endless wars - that we should not and would not have become entangled in, in the first place, had Donald J. Trump been in office. And just think that within those nine bullet points - how many bullets and bombs were fired and detonated during this endless war and how many lives, treasure, and time were lost by yet another bumbled mission.

A timeline was set by President Trump. And while there was no actual date set when America would finally leave the region, a time period when America would finally leave was agreed upon and we were in good faith working toward making that happen. A plan was in place and all things were in order, as much order as can be expected in this part of the world. It was not calm, but it was not a chaotic mess either. That would come later on Biden's watch. America would leave and take with it the footprint of their involvement *in yet another Viet-Nam like Endless war. And then all of a sudden, as if someone was working a stopwatch* – there was apparently a rush to get America and Americans out of Afghanistan.

But why? What was the rush?

God only knows we rushed into this quagmire; what was the rationale of this impotent administration? Should we maintain the symmetry and rush out? Apparently so, according to those who held power and made these types of decisions in the Biden Administration.

The optics. It was and always had to be about the optics to these guys lurking in the shadows- handling the narrative and puppet strings on this President. With an anniversary on the horizon – commemorating September 11th - that was something the Biden regime wanted to take full advantage of for all the world to see. Their goal-seeking headlines would read something like this: *"Old Scranton Joe – a man of the American people finally got us out of Endless War!"* Where all those other presidents failed, from political dynasties like Bush and Clinton and those who attended Ivy League schools and had the gravitas of Obama and the bluster negotiating skills of Trump- it took old Amtrak Joe to live up to his word and get us out of this never-ending nightmare. That would be the spin. Or something close to that. In time, they could surely massage the details of the withdrawal, but the message was clear from those pulling the strings –it was time to go. We had to go. We had to get out. And we had to be out by the 20th anniversary of that fateful date, September 11, 2021. That was non-negotiable. No if, ands, or buts. It had to happen by that deadline. A date that would live in infamy – and ironically, a date where it all started and led to our engagement and entanglement into yet another endless war.

It had been nearly 20 years. And America had remained in the quicksand and quagmire of epic proportions for too long, a war that destroyed the legacy of one president, cast doubt on another, and had fallen deeply out of favor with a country that, while pro-military, was now weary of this failed mission.

Now, after all that time, it was time to leave after all those lives lost on all sides. And all that time lost and treasure squandered.

When Trump took over, he spoke frankly in pure unapologetic Trump tones to the Taliban.

And the leader of the Taliban named ABDUL asked Trump: *"Why are you showing me a picture of my house?"*

When it was decided that we would leave, and for the longest time, some 18 months – while Trump led *"No American*

Soldier was killed in the war or conflict" —that had now lasted nearly 20 years and over four administrations.

Still, in the end, even our patience for endless wars ran out. It was something our enemies could count on time and time again. Our enemies merely waited us out, knowing we would ultimately fail the test. Our will and our dedication to the mission were questioned- and eventually broken –in time, just another endless war we would have to leave.

Surely, to a man named Trump, who watched over many years, came the realization that "While we have watched in America, *they have the TIME."*

Note taken. From Afghanistan and the Taliban and other endless wars.

That is why Trump is so anti-endless wars. Trump knows deep down in his gut that America, led by feckless leaders, doesn't have the stomach and mettle to enter and exit a war the right way- ala FDR and Ike. In other words, WIN THE WAR and WIN THE PEACE. And Trump knew that other thing, that other than being good for those in the *Industrial Military Complex* —endless wars are bad for America and the American people.

Still, as Biden bumbled the exit from the Afghanistan quagmire, turning it into *Dej vu -Vietnam all over again,* he blamed his predecessor.

Biden blames Trump time and time again for all his woes.

BIDEN: "Inherited a Deadline ...Not a plan." "Inherited a Vaccine ...not a plan."

So as Biden looked at his watch, this hapless, helpless, and hopeless excuse for a leader, many Americans thought of a man with high energy from another place and time, when America was great, and the man named Ike led the Allies to a victory and offered advice on his way out the door.

Old Ike knew how to make an exit, and many wondered what he would think of this poorly executed exit strategy in which American lives were lost, other Americans shamelessly stranded, and finally, equipment produced and purchased by American tax dollars from and for the circular Military

Industrial Complex- he warned us about - were simply left behind.

What would Ike think of all those jets, guns, and tanks being left behind for the enemy?

They were questions many would have liked to ask a former four-star general and two-term president named IKE, who warned us about these potential coming attractions and scenes like these a long time ago.

So as one old man, who was the commander in chief, looked at his watch, one had to wonder —what was the rush? Where was he going? And, in fact, where was America headed?

I thought of that man from another time. A man named Ike. What would Ike think?

It's a damn good bet that *Ike wouldn't like* what he saw on that day when America left Afghanistan. What would he think of all those he led into battle – the lineage of the 13 men and women left to die in vain as people glanced at their timepieces?

Surely it would not give him peace of mind. And most assuredly the often brash leader would give them a piece of his mind. He would do so with the wisdom of the past and the warnings of the future. How successful could America be in whatever endeavors, both foreign and domestic that it undertook with this man named Biden in charge?

Where was America going? And would America ever be great again? Only time will tell.

But one thing was sure: it was time for America and American Patriots to step up and answer the alarm because time was running out for *all of us*.

And there was no time left for clock watchers and those who rushed us into endless wars time and time again.

A GUY NAMED JOE & A case of intentional F-Ups?

Name me one thing that this guy named Joe got right?

It was a question I posed to someone who should know better. A smart person. Name one thing his guy named JOE has done that's good for America and has put America first.

No one could fail so miserably —unless it was, of course, intentional and even planned, not by poor average Joe, because at this point, he can't make a plan to exit a 12-foot by 12-foot stage without any drama- the plan comes from those who pull his strings.

It is those in the background who make this mummy of man smirk, even stumble to the stage with a cocktail of medicine to shout then whisper then shout again – delivering at times something that resembles English and other times pig Latin and yet other times even a little bit of baby talk. Delivered by hapless Joe in various cadences and tones – but always with a mad, angry, evil undertone – directed at a good portion of the good folks out there who wear red caps, want to Make America Great Again – and are guilty of the one crime he can't tolerate- they voted for that other guy, and they don't get Joe, but they get all the *Bullshit*.

Words from a man who was supposed to unite us, bring us together, be civil, grandfatherly, old Scranton Joe, a man of the people – standing there propped up by – you fill in the blank...and yelling something incoherent at half – make that more than half of America- that they are bad and evil people. That's what this guy, this shell of a man —who deals in shell companies, sounds like- *a man yelling at much of America to get off his White House Lawn.*

Come to think of it, the guy who yelled at me when I was younger when my baseball came sailing over his fence and into his yard was much nicer. At least much nicer than Joe. But let's face it, that's pretty easy because this guy yelling at many of us in America is not a nice guy. And he's definitely not a good president in the way that all presidents should be judged.

By their accomplishments and how they handled the job of being President.

WHO ARE THE 33% who think BIDEN SLEEPY JOE DID A GOOD JOB LEAVING AFGHANISTAN?

I saw the shortcomings of this career politician many years ago, first as a Senator when he was much younger and cockier. Smirking - while playing his part in the high-tech lynching of Judge Clarence Thomas. Then later as a plagiarist and then a failed Senator spewing division amongst the races with his

"Jungle Fever" comments, and finally as the Vice President of Pandering – the sidekick to the first black President –who himself stated in so many words, that *there wasn't anything that this guy named Joe couldn't F-UP*.

You all remember that, don't you?

As he ran for president in 2020, I scratched my head and wondered. This guy? Really? You've got to be kidding. Then I realized something that surely anyone with a brain, which Joe sadly doesn't have – must be able to see. He's incapable, incompetent, and inept. Always has been. Now, even more so.

But one thing Joe Biden never was – a man with a strong backbone. He was always someone who was easy to manipulate.

Can you imagine Tulsi Gabbard being a puppet and manipulated like that?

No F***ing way. In another time and place, when the Democrats were reasonable and for the people…the American people…Tulsi Gabbard would have been the heir apparent to the Kennedy legacies. Once the rising star of the Democrat party - she was cast aside because she wouldn't let them attach strings to her and treat her like a puppet.

Nor can one imagine the egotist billionaire Michael Bloomberg being strung along.

What about Bernie? Mayor Pete? Pocahontas? Getting warmer. More malleable. Not quite as Gumby-like as Joe - but getting closer. Kamala Harris. Nice Choice. Rumors attribute her ability to bend herself into a pretzel as being the reason she rose to her lofty positions of Senator and VP Harris in the first place.

What about Joe? Scranton and gaffe a minute, Joe?

Puppet extraordinaire. An innate ability to lie on demand. Unlike the wooden puppet Pinocchio, whose nose grew every time he lied – Joe has lied so often that it's been baked into the cake as being "That's Joe being Joe." A liar like no other. He presents himself as a common man, which he is not. He's more sinister and cynical than the common everyday citizen. Yet he is presented as empathetic –which he's not. His great allure is that his combination of unforced errors and lies can easily be brushed away and excused because of his lack of memory, smarts, and the fact that he's a team player and will do whatever takes as long it helps team BIDEN. America and Team America? Not so much.

Joe Biden. The perfect choice. The best puppet, period. And that's why he was the chosen one.

Hence, the golden parachute offer from the Dems as he was bumbling and stumbling his way through yet another campaign. Rescued at the last minute, with a lifeline thrown to him by Jim Clyburn, like a rope offered to someone who's drowning- Biden grabbed the rope and has been attached ever since.

The perfect puppet. The man who could and has f***ed up pretty much everything in America since literally "taking" office. Immigration. Intentional manmade disaster and invasion greenlit by Joe and his puppeteers. Inflation. A result of Joe's impotent policies and business acumen.

A foreign policy that presents America as weak…thus igniting hot wars and chaos worldwide. An energy policy that has most Americans paying twice the amount for a gallon of gas compared to when the orange man was in office.

Rise in Crime with unsafe streets in cities and towns all over America. Death of the American dream as home ownership becomes out of reach for many Americans seeking their first home. Creation of a worried, scared and insecure population who are uneasy about their and America's future.

Once again – answer the question, "Can you name one thing he's got right?" But as you do, remember what Obama said about his one-time VP. "Don't underestimate Joe's ability to F-things up."

Truer words were never spoken. All that remains to be understood and known is this. Are these F-Ups intentional or the result of bad policies, terrible decisions and a poorly executed plan or the result of the puppeteers pulling too strongly on the puppet's strings?

Or maybe –just maybe, all of the above.

LOVE OF ICE CREAM and the real scoop on BIDEN and TRUMP

Even ice cream in Washington, DC, is political.

Biden loves his ice cream. And the press loves to cover old sleepy Joe licking a scoop or two even as he discusses war-torn lands in Ukraine and Gaza. As he takes another lick he feigns answering a question on what he's going to do next regarding these hot beds of chaos. As he gets down to the final bite – a reporter may ask him a really tough one like what his favorite flavor is – and the stunned Joe will concentrate and spit out between licks – *Graeter's Chocolate Chip*.

And there you have it. The real scoop on the Biden presidency. A charade. A presidency built on melting concepts and a frozen man. A time in our history when all of us felt like the man who was supposed to be our fearless leader had suffered some form of brain freeze. Too much ice cream? Or just neurons not firing to capacity. Whatever it was, what it wasn't was comfortable to watch in any way. Sad how so many of his handlers could participate in the charade and the daily dose of elderly abuse…rewarded at the end of the day with two scoops of Joe's favorite ice cream if he was a good boy.

No one, and I mean no one, is guiltier of perpetrating the elderly abuse than Dr. Jill Biden. Joe's supposed better half and the individual most responsible for Joe Biden and America being in our current dangerous and treacherous position. Surely she sees what's happening to her man and our country on his supposed watch. Or maybe she doesn't. Or maybe she has just believed the lie so long or is so drunken with the power –that she can't help herself or the president. Or maybe she is just plain evil. The Real Scoop. It's probably a little bit of all the aforementioned flavors.

On Flag Day 2024, incidentally Donald Trump's 78th Birthday, Joe Biden's campaign put out a snarky ad designed as a birthday wish and shot against the former President.

"Happy 78th birthday, Donald. Take it from one old guy to another: Age is just a number. This election, however, is a choice."

It's an obvious attempt to put Biden in the same league in terms of age as his predecessor.

Dr. Jill continued the attempt in a rant on the campaign trail.

"This isn't just about stopping an extremist, and this election is most certainly not about age," the first lady said at an event in Green Bay, Wisconsin. "Joe and that other guy are essentially the same age. Let's not be fooled. But what this election is about, it's about the character of the person leading our country." "Joe Biden is a healthy, wise 81-year-old ready and willing to work for you every day to make our future better," she added. "Joe isn't one of the most effective presidents of our lives in spite of his age, but because of it."[24]

Hey Jill, here's the news scoop. Not an ice cream scoop. Are you looking at the same picture and the same president? He's practically melting right in front of our eyes. Your assertion that Trump and your husband, Joe, are essentially the same age is preposterous. In terms of their cognitive or physical abilities are miles apart. Age is just a number? True. But comparing Trump and Biden is like comparing a baby and a seasoned businessman and asking one of them to run your country. Needless to say, Biden is the baby in this example and always has been.

Or if that example doesn't work -try this one. Saying these two men are similar in skill sets or the ability to get the job done is ludicrous. It's like comparing *Hagen Dazs* ice cream with that frozen concoction at the bottom of the gas station freezer. Sure, they're both ice creams, but one is top of the line, a brand built on being top quality- and the other is just a frozen mess.

If you have to be told which one is the frozen mess at the bottom of the freezer, then, well, your brain might be frozen, just like Joe's. And you'll have to go to bed without any ice cream.

VI. Out to *Get Trump, America, and You*

Creating an Illusion of Power

Swamp creatures Goals Simplified: Get one of TRUMP's Own *TO GET TRUMP*

Indicting a "Ham sandwich named Trump" at the *Swamp Diner*

As your neighborhood and World Crumbles – They're still out to GET Trump

I'm Cancelled but they Can't Cancel Us All

Creating an Illusion of Power

The *LEFT* creates an illusion of power…blowing up their importance… While brainwashing a good portion, but not a majority of the United States, that they're bigger than they are.

They play big. But they don't think big. And they don't think very *BIGLY* of you and me.

As a matter of fact, they hardly think of us at all.

And when they do, most assuredly, they do so with their label handy and ready to brand us all with their favorite pejorative of the moment – tar and feathering us with one big brush and in more flavors than Baskin Robins. Here's a scoop –that's really no scoop at all. Whether you're the *Deplorable in Ohio*…. The *Irredeemable Flyover in Hick country, or the Super MAGA racist south of the Mason Dixon line –they see us all as one blob or mob, and make no mistake,* they HATE us all equally. In that way they have fulfilled the DEI aspect of their mantra. D for Diverse – They hate us all, no matter who we are or where we come from. E for Equity – meaning they hate each and every one of us with the same passion – but at least they do it equally and in the same proportion. Finally, I – is for Inclusive, and they most assuredly want to include us all in their hate fest of all things Trump and MAGA.

It's the same way the Nazis saw the Jews. Make no mistake about it. That's how they view us. Because we are red-hatted with a slogan that they hate- MAKE AMERICA GREAT AGAIN, we have become the easy target of their hatred.

Helping to shape that monolithic narrative, no one does more damage and is as dumb in doing so than, perhaps Joy Behar, who many on the right have accurately labeled "Joyless Behar."

Joy-less matching *Fading Joe* stride for panful stride in both being mental midgets. Excuse me – intellectually challenged individuals. Joy spreading as much hate as Joe spreads bullshit. Both spreading lies. Both adept at spreading hate and doing so early and often – just how they vote in Chicago- as the old saying goes.

Joy spreads her hate and lies from her morning perch on a feckless TV show -The VIEW…where she shares her nest with fellow hate bomb throwers Whoopi Goldberg, Sonny Holsten, and a crew of other misinformed ladies who have one thing in common. Trump Derangement Syndrome. They all have TDS at various stages as they take their stage. Their combined lack of knowledge about the world combines with their Trump and MAGA hating rhetoric to make for television that is skewed in its view and unwatchable to anyone with any brain cells and sense of fairness. So bad that if given the choice in how if I should ever have to be tortured - I would gladly be water boarded than be forced to watch a full hour of The View.

Recently Bill Maher made an appearance on THE VIEW to plug his latest book. Maher, forever a critic of Donald Trump, offered some insight to Joyless Behar that almost made her head explode calling her out for her unhinged comment that all TRUMP supporters should place a swastika on their cap.

"I'm not going to defend Donald Trump ever, but I would never say that we should put the swastika on the cap because I think you can hate Donald Trump, you can't hate everybody who likes him. It's half the country. I don't want to live in that country, I don't want to live in the country where I hate half the country - and I don't hate half the country."[25]

I remember time when Joy was not so much *"In hate"* with the Donald, even touching and playing with the Donald's infamous hair on one of his many appearances on the View. But that's when the View had a different point of view and when the founder of *The View*, Barbara Walters was still with us and considered a friend of the real estate developer from Queens. Many people were in that camp. Trump fans. Trump friends. They're still there - and there are more of them. They're just not the same people who they once were. Those in camp Trump now are less apt to want to hobnob with the man with the big ego and brand. These folks are more grounded and more concerned with America's future and care less about sharing a ride in a Trump chopper or a photo opportunity at Mar-a-Lago.

Sure, the view on the current version of The View is skewed, slanted, and represents a slice of America, but not the biggest slice of the American pie. The ladies on The View stand out, quite frankly, because they are not outstanding.

They are merely unhinged and have their hatred of all things TRUMP, including those who follow him and will vote for the 45th President of the United States, down to a cult-like ceremony based on ad hominem attacks and stoking fear in the electorate and their viewers.

And it is this fear that drives their narrative and has driven them crazy. And it is because they fear him and his voters that they try to diminish him and the MAGA nation at every turn.

Still, it must be remembered that they are not the majority. They just want you, me, and the rest of us to think they are and to think that most people HATE Trump. In the end, they are a small sample, of a small-minded group of elites controlling a good portion of the narrative.

That's one of the reasons they won't show the size of the Trump crowds. Their rationale – if you don't show the crowds over the airwaves to America – people won't see the movement, and people won't connect with him, and magically, they will disappear as if they weren't there.

But we all know that they are there. Packed into arenas that they won't dare show you. On college campuses where, students with a conservative point of view are not encouraged to speak up. In voting groups in black and Latino neighborhoods who have been conditioned to vote one way – not realizing that they have been voting against their interests and for people who don't give a damn about them.

The Democrat party is worried because they know that their emperor not only doesn't look good in his new clothes but that he's probably soiled them as he tripped up the stairs heading to a speech he can't make.

It's merely an illusion. Their president is not powerful or competent. His supporters are impotent. Their tent is small and getting smaller. And their apathetic support of a pathetic candidate and man whose supporters can fit into a corner of one of Trump's mega MAGA rallies.

No, they don't have the numbers. They just give you the illusion that they do. Kind of like saying old sleepy Joe is the sharpest guy in the room with the most energy. But what room are they talking about?

An empty one. Probably one with no windows. But one equipped with a big TV that's no doubt tuned to The View. Apparently, the president can really relate to Whoopi and gets great joy from watching Joy. As for those Trump rallies on TV, Biden can't bear to watch because of his fear of crowds.

Swamp Creatures Goals Simplified: Get one of TRUMP's Own *TO GET TRUMP*

They couldn't get him. Not really. Not with all their endless, baseless attacks that they hurled in the direction of the *Great Orange One*- could they deliver the knock-out blow.

For years, oh, how they tried.

From those apparently on the outside looking in – a cadre of usual suspects from political swamp creatures – wearing both R's and D's next to their names. From Hollywood. Hell, even from late-night TV. And, of course – from that special breed of swamp creatures –those in the Media Elite- baptized forever as FAKE NEWS propagandists by the man from Mar-a-Lago.

From inside gutless woke corporate American board rooms and in the once hallowed halls of Academia, they went after him- with an all-out assault to take him and his voters out while making, not America Great Again – but by making them, him and his movement irrelevant. *Oh say can you see how hard they tried to get Trump?*

But it was hard to do- if not impossible. Not from where they stood. Because we, the people, didn't trust them. Still, they piled on - bringing *the art of the accusation* to a new low. They did anything they could in an effort to cancel or GET him.

He was labeled a racist. Branded anti-sematic. Construed to be a misogynist. Accused of leading a movement of White supremacists to take over the country. In between called a tax cheat and a traitor who sold out his country to RUSSIA. Those wanting to GET TRUMP would dress up their insults with the usually heated language – calling him a liar, an unhinged egomaniac who was transphobic, xenophobic, and stupid.

They accused him not of making AMERICA Great again – but of making America a hateful, divisive place. When they were measured- they called the outsider who busted through the gates of their club- someone who was simply not PRESIDENTIAL.

And they were right. He was not Presidential in the traditional sense.

What President of any company- or business, and that's what America in the end is- doesn't take a salary. The man was not presidential in the way he negotiated with friend and foe alike, both foreign and domestic.

He simply came to Washington to serve.

The American people. America. Forgotten Americans, for sure. But his hand reached across the land to invite every man, woman, and all Americans into his tent and movement. His offer to serve all Americans was extended to everyone. RACE did not matter. Nor Religion or Sexual Orientation. Hell, he didn't care if you were a Democrat, Republican, Independent, loved the Green Party, and even carried a copy of the Communist Manifesto under your arm.

If you were an AMERICAN, that's all the businessman from Queens cared about.

In his eyes, he came to serve all Americans with two simple mantras

America First. Make America Great Again.

Their hatred of all things Orange and all things Trump – led to two specious, unjust impeachments and a never-ending battle to destroy the man that close to 140 million Americans voted for over two Presidential elections.

And the reason was simple. They feared him. They feared his movement. And they feared the folks who voted for him and stood by him – through thick and thin. That was their dilemma. Appeal to his base without anointing him –who they found to be a base character. Get those who voted for him and got him to abandon him and trade him in.

So they donned their best Donald Trump salesman hat and like the used car dealers that they are tried to move his voters into a new model. The old reliable model- the Donald had too many miles on him. According to them – he would not be able to get them where they all wanted to go in the first place –A better and Greater America. So they made their sales pitches to the voters as they began to *kick the tires* –while considering other candidates (cars).

But they were not a salesman- these folks. A good car salesman –allows you to pick the make, model –hell even the color of the car. They don't tell you that you HAVE TO BUY THIS CAR- because they hate the other car.

They let the buyers make the decision themselves or at least give them the impression that they made up their own minds and are driving away with not only the best car that they could afford – but the one that they truly liked from the car lot that is the upcoming election.

Indicting a "Ham sandwich named Trump" at the *Swamp Diner*

There is an old saying in legal circles that states, *"You can indict a ham sandwich."*

The meaning? You can find a crime or an appearance of a crime if you look hard enough, or you can contort yourself, your case, and your hatred for the defendant into a pretzel and hence bring charges against anyone. The thing is, those string of indictments hurled in Trump's direction as he was running for President were not merely designed to stop Trump; they were meant as a warning and notice to you and me.

Sure, Trump is the main target out front, but make no mistake, they are coming for all of us.

Indictment Trump, Indictment You, Indictment Me!

The Trump series of indictments could have been filed years ago…why now? You know why.

It's because it's Donald Trump. And yes, it's because he's running for president. But the real reason they went after him and contorted into pretzels with charges that would make the best soft pretzel salesman in the Big Apple jealous - was that he was a threat.

He could win and would win if they didn't stop him. Yes, he would surely become the 47th President of the United

States if they didn't stop him- if they didn't get Trump. And they couldn't have that. So they twisted and stretched the four cases into a pretzel that looked like a gun and pointed it in the direction of the former president.

And thus four specious cases were brought up against Trump. One is more ridiculous than the other.

What's next? *There is a rumor, but at this point, only a rumor that a very ambitious young district attorney wannabe in the swing state of North Carolina wants to bring charges against the former President because he didn't return a library book to the Queen's library of his youth. And it's now 60 years late.*

Ima Beach, when questioned about this seemingly petty charge, wasn't smiling when she addressed members of the press. "*I'm going to throw the book at him. No pun intended,*" Beach, who some see as a rising star with a bright political future, then took questions from the media for over an hour on the footsteps of the Library in Charlotte, North Carolina.

When asked - why now?

Laughing at first, she brushed off the question with a *"Why Not." "It's Donald Trump."*

Then the savvy prosecutor paused and looked at the learned press, "To all of you, Lesbians, Gays, Transgender, Queer, Questioning, and Intersex folks out there in the press, did I miss anyone? I just want you to know, as long as Donald Trump walks the earth free with late library books in his possession, I want you to know I won't only get the books back, but I will get Trump."

The alleged three books that Donald Trump took out and hasn't returned are *Atlas Shrugged* and *The Fountainhead*, both by Ayn Rand and George Orwell's *1984*.

Truth is, and it's not coming from the *Ministry of the Truth*, they have indicted four Huge HAM SANDWICHES Named Trump. Yes, the Donald is a Ham sandwich - they can't help but indict.

And if that saying is true, about "being able to indict a ham sandwich," then history will show that during the run-up to the election of 2024, they indicted the biggest, hugest HAM sandwich they could find —merely because who he was and yes because he was running to become the President of the United States.

The biggest ham sandwich ever indicted ...the 45th and hopefully the 47th President of the United States, Donald J. Trump.

In indicting him, they are sending a signal to all of America, in essence, what's next on the menu if they stay in power. They are telling anyone paying the least bit of attention that if they can do this to the big cheese, the HAM Sandwich that is Trump, then they can do it to you, me, and everyone else in America. Simply by using the DOJ as a weapon and being creative like a great sandwich maker in one of the famous *KATZ-like delis – they can and will get all of us on whatever trumped-up* charges that they can come up with in their kitchen at the Swamp DINER. *The Swamp Diner*, where corruption and politicization is served 24 hours a day to anyone who wants to make America Great Again.

On their menu, they have the *J-6er special*, an all-you-can-eat buffet for political prisoners and hostages from that day who can dine on bread, water, and a lack of due process.

They also serve an *outrageous sampler platter imported from the southern border*, a spicy dish of freebies to anyone who is here illegally, complete with an extra serving of a free dessert to any illegal who, just by being here, resulted in a violent crime, such as robbery, rape or murder upon one of those taxpaying American citizens, struggling with inflated monthly bills who can't get a seat at the insider's table.

Sound absurd? No more absurd than the four indictments against the former president.

And no more absurd than *indicting a Ham Sandwich*.

As your neighborhood and World Crumbles – They're still out to GET Trump

As your neighborhood crumbles and the world is pushed to the brink of World War III – one thing is certain in this crazy upside-down world –there is always time to Get Trump. Nothing can deter that. Not the threat of nuclear war, exploding crime numbers, and inflation crushing the poor and middle class...there's always one thing on their agenda, something they have time for and make a priority on their TO DO List. And that is to GET Trump at any cost.

With crime rates rising in New York City, district attorney Alvin Bragg, notorious for reducing sentences on felons to misdemeanors, twisted himself into a pretzel in order to get Trump. He did a trick that would impress David Copperfield –taking a potential misdemeanor in which the statute of limitations had run out to produce 34 felony counts against the former president. It was allegedly and basically a paper filing crime –if you could find a crime at all that could be defined clearly by anyone familiar with the case –including those on the jury.

All the while, as Trump was facing the force of a government throwing the book at him while using taxpayer dollars and precious court time - *many illegal aliens, excuse me, undocumented or better yet, non-citizens,* committed violent crimes on the streets of New York City and cities all across America – as one DA with severe TDS (Trump Derangement Syndrome) failed to prioritize his job to the citizenry.

Protecting the people. Punishing the serious, dangerous, and repeat offenders.

Somehow, in the upside-down state of things in America and the Justice system, a man named Donald Trump, a former President and a man with a rich history in New York, brought many jobs while creating many iconic structures in a city known for its share – jumped to the front of the – *"Most likely to be Prosecuted"* Line.

Ahead of rapists. Ahead of robbers. Ahead of even murderers.

And all for one reason. Make that three reasons.

He was Donald J. Trump. He had decided to run for president. And he was the odds-on favorite to win re-election in 2024. That was all the evidence needed to get Trump. The son of bitch was capable and probably going to win if he ran for president.

And that was always a crime – at least to a DA named Bragg. But make no mistake – this is nothing to brag about.

It's an act that warrants hanging your head in shame. This specious prosecution and conviction will be overturned and seen for the sham that it is. A miscarriage of justice. A waste of time and treasure. And a case of a DA wrongly prosecuting an innocent and good man simply because he was seeking to make America great again.

As May ended with the disgraceful conviction of the 45th President on 34 felony counts, crime from illegal aliens ramped up in June and in broad daylight.

An Ecuadorian migrant held two 13-year-olds, a girl and a boy, at knifepoint in a Queens park as they walked home from school. He was arrested Tuesday for allegedly sexually assaulting the girl and stealing the teens' phones. The Ecuadorian molester, identified as Christian Geovanny Inga-Landi, was nabbed outside a deli on 108th St. when good Samaritans recognized him from sketches circulated by police.

Gruesome crimes are taking place across the nation and have fueled opposition to illegal migration among every voter demographic. Rachel Morin, 37, a mother of five, was raped and bludgeoned to death on a hiking trail in Maryland. The 23-year-old illegal immigrant from El Salvador charged with that crime is believed to have previously murdered a woman in his home country and attacked a 9-year-old girl and her mother in a Los Angeles home invasion.

Sanctuary city laws have been blamed for opening America up to an epidemic of crimes committed by repeat offenders who entered illegally, while New York's over-the-top generosity makes the crime wave even more infuriating. The Ecuadorian mugger captured Tuesday gave a taxpayer-supported shelter as his address, as many arrested migrants do. He was walking around Queens, enjoying the good life on our tab, until he was recognized and captured.[26]

Walking around Queens. The birthplace of one Donald Trump. A New Yorker's New Yorker, if there ever was one. One can picture him, a much younger man, making his bones here, walking around the borough while taking his first steps toward climbing the ladder to a successful business, TV, and political career.

And now, as he sat here in his late seventies, this former and potentially future president was stoic yet frustrated in the fight. That much you could see on his worn face. Knowing that this, as well as the other trials, were built on a political agenda and not on actual crimes, angered him. Yet he did his best to hide it. And the fact that he had been found guilty in this New York courtroom led by a Trump-hating judge and in front of a jury that, according to him, *"Mother Theresa could not get a fair trial in front of,"* surely disappointed him. Maybe even made him a little sad.

But in moments like these, Trump does what all good leaders do. He looks to the future and the road ahead. Not only that, there were rallies to do, a campaign to run, and a country to save. The rallies make no doubt about it, they were the cure to whatever ailed the president. It gave him a chance to get with the people. And it gave him a chance to try out new talking points and new material with his beloved crowd. It was a place, this place and court of public opinion, where the president was not only innocent, but if he was guilty of anything – he was guilty of trying to Make America Great Again.

That was his crime.

At his rallies, he would often laugh at the absurdity of it all, looking toward the heavens and joking that his late parents are "looking down" and seeing their son be indicted "more than" Al Capone. "My mother and father, they're looking down – 'my son got indicted more than Alphonse Capone," he said at Iowa Rally.

At a campaign rally in Reno, Nevada, Trump railed against the indictments — two of which were brought at the federal level and two at the state level — claiming they are "over bullshit" and are politically motivated.

"Did anybody ever hear of the great Alphonse Capone, Al Capone, great, great head of the mafia, right? Mean, Scarface. He had a scar that went from here to here, and he didn't mind at all. But he was a rough guy," Trump said to the crowd of his supporters. *"Now, I heard he was indicted once — a couple of people told me a few times more — but I was indicted four times,"* Trump added.

Trump underscored how dangerous Capone was — seemingly to make the point that his indictments were unjust.

"If he had dinner with you and if he didn't like the way you smiled at him at dinner, he would kill you. You'd be dead. By the time you walked out of the nice restaurant, you would be dead," Trump said of Capone. *"He got indicted once. I got indicted four times."*[27]

"Over bullshit, I got indicted," Trump added.

Pure Trump.

The politician? Sure. The Entertainer? Absolutely. The man who the people entrusted with their mission and movement. He was someone whom they believed in. Someone who could not be booed off the stage or put in a cage. Finally, he was someone who would take a hit for them and get back up no matter how many times they tried to get him.

And even as the world crumbles around you, it's good to know that someone is ready, willing, and able to take the stage and fight no matter what they throw at him.

I'm Cancelled - But they can't Cancel All of Us

It finally happened. As I feared it would. I was canceled by people who I thought liked me, respected me, and got me. I was canceled by a large number of my film students whom I had taught the fine art of cinema to for years. Let me repeat that – for years. I had taught many of these people for over a decade. We would meet at least 15- 30 times a year which equated to 150 to over 300 classes. Obviously, it was not a fly-by-night relationship, but one I felt was built on trust and respect.

Over the years, I'd teach them to view films differently. I challenged them to respect each film. Dive into each scene and see them through both an open heart and with eyes wide open. Largely because of my love of cinema – an extension really of my deep devotion to our First Amendment- I welcomed all films and opinions. Not saying I love all films –nor respect all films- just that I respect everyone's right to put down on film their vision and version of a story that they have a right to tell.

That is why I always encouraged my film students not to read reviews – but to instead go into the film with an open mind and not be flooded by opinions as to whether a film was worthy or not.

Being worthy or not? It was a question I posed about myself as I faced dwindling class sizes due in part to the rebooting of the movie industry after Covid-19, an increase in streaming at home, which was killing the box office of all cinema, and finally, a lack of good movies out there that people wanted to see.

Still, I wondered why the attendance in my classes was down.

Surely it couldn't have all been about Covid-19? I had adjusted by scheduling films that could be streamed on line. I had always dealt with a lack of great products that were being produced in Hollywood, and because of that scoured the film landscape to find, if not great films, then at least interesting films that could arouse an interesting film discussion and something to talk about.

One thing I never talked about in my classes was politics. I had known, deep down all along, that had they known my propensity to lean to the conservative side – that some folks would potentially cancel me.

Sadly it turns out my instincts were right.

After COVID-19, as my classes slowly started to reform, while teaching one of my remaining loyal classes who continued despite the fact that they had learned that I was, in fact, someone who wrote a book about and probably supported the 45th president – I got my review.

In my mind, I had wondered why some of the most verbal voices and personalities I paid the most attention to, like the group of women who I nicknamed the witches because of their ability to kill a movie with their often sharp, tough, and wicked commentary, didn't sign up for my classes. Occasionally, I would call them *murderers row* for the same reason. It was all in fun. And part of my shtick that most people in the class had come to enjoy. Many times, we'd walk out of the class, and many of the students, who were now retired and living in Florida in their golden years, thanked me, often with an enthusiastic smile and sometimes a tear, for creating a memorable experience. I remember Dr. Givant, a great fan of mine, and the class often saying, "*Gussie baby, I don't know how you do it. The film we talked about was not that good, but from it, you pulled out and created a wonderful discussion and experience."*

It was an experience that I would come to reproduce many times over many years. I'd probably taught a total of nearly 1000 classes over the years to many different people from all over the country. It was a gratifying experience.

And then I thought of the faces who were no longer in my classes. Sadly, over the summer between seasons, I would get word that some of my students had passed away. That always saddened me. And I thought back to all the great film discussions we had together. This was different. Apparently, they had passed on me, as in canceled me as their teacher.

I thought that's what might have happened, but I was never really sure. Not until a very nice and loyal couple who had taken my classes each year for 14 years came into an almost empty class one day in 2021 and shared their insight.

Having taught them in a particular class that was packed and often had a waiting list to join, I posed the question. "What happened to the witches? What happened to so and so? What happened to all those folks from my 1 pm class?"

Not wanting to hurt me but still wanting to tell the truth, they gave me their review.

"They're not coming back."

"When they found out you wrote the book on Trump…many of them decided to not come back."

"They couldn't take that fact…that you were a Trump supporter."

And just like that I had been initiated into cancel culture. And I was canceled. I was canceled not because of anything bad that I did. I was not canceled for breaking the law. And I was not canceled because of my sexual orientation, my religion, or even the way that I taught. I was canceled because I wrote a comprehensive book about a man named Trump, whom I would come to know and respect through my research and reportage as both a journalist and an American.

It hurt me. Made me sad. Bothered me. That I meant so little to them, that after all that time I could be eliminated from their lives because of the way I felt about a certain candidate. That I was an independent, a journalist, and an American who sought the truth and tried to remain objective in my pursuit of it - I felt betrayed by the failing score that they had given me.

The teacher whose movie reviews they applauded openly at the end of each class. That I stressed the importance of everyone's voice was my secret to success. I encouraged everyone to speak their mind and tell me what they thought.

Well, now they were telling me what they thought- loud and clear with their silence and by not showing up. Still, I leaned on that old showbiz axiom that the "show must go on." It did. But sadly, without some of them. Not going to tell you that I don't miss some of them because I do.

Yes. I still feel hurt by them, the people who took my film classes whom I loved and who I thought loved me. Their intolerance of my beliefs and right to have them still left me scratching my head.

Ours is a movie without an ending. Open-ended. Where we don't know how it ends. Still, I would like to play one more scene with them and ask them all one question.

I knew pretty much all along how they felt politically, but I never held it against them.

Why did they hold my political beliefs against me?

If you have the answer, I'd like to know. It would make for a great discussion that I'd like to play out in a scene from our unfinished film.

VII. We the People and Our American Dreams

A Tale of two Borders —Mexico, Ukraine and a Forgotten Ohio Town

America is a COWBOY

Can we be Civil?

Love of Patriots on the Radio…and the One who told you the REST OF THE STORY

History is watching and smelling the BS…and so are we Pops

Enough, I'd Had Enough

Big Three Music Icons -Soulful Singers with fans more MAGA than they think

California – State of Mine -Yearning for days when Frank & Jack Played Here

Missing Rush on the Radio

Beef or Crickets? It's what's for Dinner

Transgender- What about Babies- aren't they transitioning in the Womb

If Pop were Alive —He'd be writing MAGA Anthems

A Tale of Two Borders —Mexico, Ukraine and a Forgotten Ohio Town

They will defend their border, but not ours.

One more time. They will send money to defend a foreign border, but they will not send money to defend our own border.

Why? You know why. We all do.

It's part of a plan to destroy and re-shape America in their own image.

There's no other way to explain the millions of *Alien Immigrants (AI)*, the real AI that we should all fear —who are and have been crashing our border during the *unlawful BIDEN regime*.

It should surprise absolutely no one that that was the plan all along devised by Crooked Joe and his puppet masters. They will do anything to gain the office – i.e. stealing an election – and they will do anything to keep that power, concocting new and more sinister ways to destroy the Republic.

No Joke. Come on, man. You know those are the facts, and facts are stubborn things.

Joe told everyone what he intended to do as he ran, make that stumbled for the nomination to be President. During the first Democratic primary debate, Joe Biden said that if he were elected president, migrants should "*immediately surge to the border.*" The migrants took him up on it.

"What I would do as president is several more things," Biden said at the first Democratic primary debate for the 2020 election. "I would, in fact, make sure that there is... We immediately surge to the border, all those people who are seeking asylum." And that's just what he did when he moved into the White House. He made it easier for all illegal aliens to move into America by reversing the immigration policies of former president Donald Trump.

Biden labeled those policies as "cruel" and "inhumane." But what should those policies be called that this President has implemented in his nearly four years in office? Those that have led to an unprecedented border surge and the highest number of border crossings—and roughly 10 to 20 million (you fill in the number) of illegal aliens —the most in U.S. history.

Making matters worse, Biden ended Title 42, a Trump-era rule that expedites illegal immigrant expulsions. In a moment of rare honesty, Biden admitted that the border is "going to be chaotic," while embattled Homeland Security Secretary Alejandro Mayorkas admitted that Title 42's end will "strain our workforce, our communities, and our entire system."[28]

So why do it? Why did they do it? And if they retain power, why will they continue to do it?

Once again, you know the answers.

Their moments of caring or pretending to care what's going on at the border range from the obscene to the absurd. But all of their responses share common attributes. They are insincere, and they are made with an agenda. While downplaying the crisis at the border as migrants flood the border, they use euphemisms like calling the surges "seasonal." At other times, they flat-out lie and say the border is "secure." When the optics get so bad that even those in their own party admit to the damage, they do the one thing that comes naturally: they suddenly remember there are black folks in America at election time that need pandering. They shift the blame to Trump and Republicans, but especially Trump. Eureka! They're finally calling a spiraling situation at the border – what it was as soon as Biden took office – *a crisis*.

But make no mistake - it was a crisis that could not have been prevented with this one guy named Joe in charge. Or the ones pulling his strings and creating these absurd and anti-American policies intended to create chaos and the crisis in the first place.

A crisis and chaos that was intended all along. Even Biden's dim-witted press secretary Karine Jean-Pierre, after delivering falsehoods about illegal immigration being down by "90 percent," acknowledged that *"there are challenges at the border."*

Challenges at the border? That's like being on the Titanic and complaining about the music the band's playing as the ship sinks.

The press secretary, in a moment of hall of fame gaslighting, actually said to a room of so-called journalists that make up the White House Press Corps that immigration is "something that the president has taken seriously from day one." *Something that the president has taken seriously from day one?* Yes, something he's taken seriously to consider and destroyed since day one. All part of a plan. A bigger plan that doesn't concern you and me. A plan designed to help those who are in power stay in power. Secure behind their gates with a border built between them and we, the people. Yet, as one border is ignored, which is the gateway into our country, a border in a foreign land takes precedence. That border is paramount to the larger plan. That border must be addressed. That border and that cause must be a priority for America. Of course, that border, the one *THEY* are concerned with, is the one that adds more blocks between John Q Public and the Washington elites, establishment, and globalists. The Ukrainian border and sovereignty take priority and precedence over our own. The border that borders our southern flank – not so much. Hard to believe? Open your eyes and ears.

It's all there in black and white: our commitment to Ukraine, their border and people, and their rights to their freedoms and liberties. And in one of his most impassioned focused moments – the pretender in chief echoed the quiet part out loud in terms of commitment to a people, not the American people, the Ukrainian people.

Joe Biden delivered a speech on July 12, 2023, that was abundantly clear on where he stood for the Ukrainian people.

"Our commitment to Ukraine will not weaken. We will stand for liberty and freedom today, tomorrow, and for as long as it takes. (Applause.) We all want this war to end on just terms — terms that uphold the basic principles of the United Nations Charter that we all signed up to: sovereignty, territorial integrity." [29]

Territorial Integrity?

We, the people in the United States, wonder what that means to those along our border and throughout our land who have been impacted by this invasion of illegal immigrants into our country because of an impotent and corrupt administration.

Don't have an answer? Don't worry; take your time, as long as it takes, because the disintegrating situation at our border isn't changing anytime soon. And hopefully we can hang on until the changing of the chief border guard takes place in November 2024.

As Long as it takes… What does that phrase even mean?

Well it depends on which parts of the world the leader of the free world is speaking to and about at the time.

In regards to Ukraine and the aid to that region of the world and our involvement in seemingly yet another one of those endless wars, it means we're there until we get the job done. That much is clear in the messaging as he mumbles, stumbles, and blurts out an occasional sound bite that the media can take and understand but, most importantly, sell to the American people, the world, and the forces behind the scenes pulling the strings and benefiting from his effort and our effort *OVER THERE*.

And anything resembling a clear and cohesive message emanating from the loins of this guy named Joe, well that's not an easy thing to get.

"*AS LONG AS IT TAKES.*"

But how about aid to the American people? And a little attention to those other *Palestinians,* the ones in East Palestine, Ohio.

While Biden moves in slow motion most of the time, his response to those in East Palestine, Ohio, which encountered a terrible natural disaster, was hardly attentive. He moved without urgency and at a glacier's pace. He seemed to be saying to these Americans, who were obviously more MAGA and not a part of the electorate that made up his base, "You'll wait to get a visit, and you'll be grateful for waiting."

It took President Biden months to visit the people of East Palestine, Ohio impacted by a real environmental crisis, not one conjured up that may or may not happen thousands of years from now.

Waiting with patience while suffering and for as long as it takes were the people of East Palestine, Ohio. That's what these good, mainly poor American people endured. But here's the question. Should the people, any of the American people, have to wait that long to get relief from their president?

Doesn't seem right. Does it? But that's the reality. Strangers in strange lands move to the front of the line for relief and attention from America and their leader, while Americans have to wait for as long as it takes.

Not sure about this, but it makes you think that those in East Palestine, Ohio, would gladly trade places with the Palestinians in the Middle East, just for the attention, a little help, and to be thought of first.

America is a COWBOY

The Story of the Rugged Individualist…And why they keep trying to Kill John Wayne

The left hates the Duke. John Ford too. Mostly, they hate men. Real men. Those who ride horses and those who don't. In Hollywood, they used to be played by guys like Gary Cooper, Jimmy Stewart, and John Wayne – and then Clint Eastwood.

Today they are all busy trying to kill all the Cowboys and even the Indians, as in *Cleveland Indians and Washington Redskins* in sports. While polls showed that Native Americans overwhelmingly were against changing the nicknames Redskins and Indians to Commanders and Guardians, respectively, The National Football League and Major League Baseball buckled to the pressure of the "woke" mob.

And it was during this time we were all introduced to terms like "Toxic Masculinity."

"Toxic Masculinity" is the stuff that the boys who stormed the beaches on D-day were made of, the stuff that firemen who rush into a burning building to rescue a child are made of, and the stuff that cowboys who tamed the West were made of.

If the great evil or threat to society and the left is *Toxic Masculinity*, then what do we call the hero who definitely won't be allowed and is actually forbidden to arrive on a horse to save the day?

Here are some ideas that may fit their agenda and fit into their *Woke Lexicon Handbook*.

Harmless Femininity…Nontoxic Femininity…Safe Gender Neutrality. To the left, they all work. Some better or sexier… marketing-wise. Wait, I can't say that. Let's just say some get the job done better by confusing the public and playing identity politics. But I must say that *Safe Gender Neutrality* is starting to grow on me. Sounds like a *United Nations term,* so replete with *Utopian drivel* that it almost seems like an actual place.

What's your solution, Madame Secretary or Prime Minister or President?

"Well, we think that once we achieve a state of Safe Gender Neutrality, then everything will fall into place." It's the kind of statement I could see the likes of Kamala Harris turning into one of her patented word salads where she succeeds in dizzying the crowd with the daffiness of her oratorical skills, saying nothing as her lips and tongue work endlessly while her brain is disengaged and parked in neutral.

"I feel that the real danger of Toxic Masculinity has met its match with the safe arrival of Safe Gender Neutrality. Safe Gender Neutrality is not a physical place yet, but it should be. It's a state of mind and a state where everyone can be treated the same regardless of their sex, race, or gender because here, in the state of Safe Gender Neutrality, there are no rules, no genders, no sexism – just a place that's safe and neutral – a place kind of like Switzerland – only with better weather. I can't wait to go there. Everyone is welcome except those who are Toxically Masculine and, of course, **Safe Gender Neutrality Deniers***. We welcome all Safe Gender Neutralists with open hearts and arms."*

And with that potential speech, Kamala Harris could thrust her intellect and gravitas into a cause that she could stand behind or under…you take the pick because from what we've heard from her early days ascending in Oakland politics and literally the body politic, she is as flexible as a Romanian gymnast and can contort her mind, mouth and tongue into many positions.

The whole issue is that men and women are different. Always have been and always will be. And that's the way it will always be unless we continue on the track of social engineering their differences into insignificance and oblivion, creating a lie, blurring the truth that's as devastating and misleading as a mirage in the desert is to some thirsty cowboy.

Speaking of cowboys. I love them. Miss them. And you know what? So does America.

And you know who misses him the most? Women. They miss John Wayne. The Duke. And, of course, they miss the American cowboy. With all his bravery, ruggedness, independence, imperfections, and all that toxic masculinity.

The American cowboy who saved the world on a stormy day in June on a beach so many miles from home. The American cowboy who conquered the West. The American cowboy riding alone on his horse…up at sunrise and riding into the sunset…against the wind…gritting his teeth and always getting the job done.

Yes America is a cowboy. Sadly a cowboy that's been missing from the American landscape for too long. But the good news is the American cowboy is saddling up. And he's getting ready to ride again and fight again for the American people.

Now all we have to do is find some way to bring back John Ford from his heavenly Monument Valley to shoot the picture.

Can we be Civil?

A Man Named Jack, Filled with HATE, gives me the Answer.

It was a question posed to me by a man who walked along the street where I was now working – as I *schlepped* a painting from one gallery to another. He was a man I knew, not well, but our paths had crossed over the years in the media. He hosted a sports radio show with a friend of mine. And I had appeared as a guest and chimed in on my love of sports and as the movie guy.

We never talked politics. Yet here on the street now, almost a year after the 2020 Election – this man who was walking his two dogs did not look happy. It didn't add up. A beautiful day in sunny Sarasota. Walking your dogs on what is always the sunny side of the street.

Yet a scowl from the man who I will call Jack. But why?

Then I realized why. It was me.

My "Hi Jack" greeting was met with a sour face and a single-sentence retort.

"Can we be civil?"

Taken aback by the comment yet seeking understanding, I pressed for an answer.

"What are you talking about, Jack?"

"You know," he said.

"I don't know what you're talking about," I continued.

Then it hit me. "You're talking about Trump," I said.

"Yes," he said.

"Well, as I remember it- Jack, you attacked me on FACEBOOK last year," I countered.

"I Hate Trump," he said, his face unfriendly and in direct contrast to the two beautiful creatures he was walking.

"I know. You attacked me for writing a book on him last year," I shot back.

"I hate Trump. How could you…write…" he countered.

"Did you even read the book Jack?"

"No, I don't need to read it. He's the worst. I hate him."

Taken aback by the outburst – but not shocked by it – I paused and gave his dogs a friendly pet.

"You should save your hate for people who really deserve it. For people like Hitler," I countered.

"He's worse THAN HITLER," he said angrily.

The conversation was, in effect, over.

And the question to his original question, *"Can we be civil?"* was answered.

"Worse than Hitler. Your hatred clouds your judgment. You're unhinged."

"But if you ever want to come on my show or debate this anytime and anyplace –I'd be glad to sit down with you," I retorted.

Not answering - he continued down the street as his original question hung in the air like a dark cloud.

"Can we be civil?"

The answer is, sadly – NO.

If the starting point is *"Trump is worse than Hitler,"* then I'm afraid there is no place that we can meet on either side of the street for a civil discussion.

Forget about meeting in the middle of the road. Those days are gone.

For writing a comprehensive book on Trump and then trying to promote the book I was - in essence canceled by this man named Jack and accused of not being civil.

That was the new normal. He was not interested in my point of view or the fact that I had 452 endnotes in my well-researched and balanced book.

He only saw me as one of those people. One of those people conveniently packaged and labeled into a category. A *Trumpster. A card-carrying member of the MAGA movement. A Hater. A follower of a man that he hated and whom he compared to a mass murderer- named Hitler.*

Stunned and a little shocked, I shook my head and continued with my day

I watched him cross the street with his four-legged friends, and they seemed to be smiling.

Maybe they weren't listening. Or maybe they read my book? Or maybe they were independents? Or maybe, just maybe, they were, God forbid – part of the movement - *MAGA dogs* just out for a walk on the sunny side of the street on a sunny afternoon in the sunshine state.

Love of Patriots on the Radio…and the One who told you the REST OF THE STORY

Growing up in the radio-rich environment of Detroit, Michigan, we often listened to WJR's *"The Great Voice of The Great Lakes."* Radio giants like J.P McCarthy brightened up the mornings, and Ernie Harwell sublimely called Tiger ball games over the rarified air of WJR. And then there was PAUL HARVEY and his "Rest of the Story" reveals something that you thought you knew about —but didn't until you heard the rest of the story from Mr. Harvey.

Because he was both a radio commentator and a columnist, he had his own deep, moral, and fair take on what was going on in this land and place he loved called America.

Paul Harvey penned and read the following essay, **Finding My Way: If I was the Devil** over the Airwaves, "suggesting America's problems in the mid-'60s could be traced back to people not working hard, being dishonest, getting divorced, getting high, getting abortions, and getting out of church."

Harvey's take "the devil must be having a field day in America watching it happen."

Both then and especially now.

With slightly updated, more modern satanic strategies, I came across a man who offered his take 55 years after the original.

"If I was the devil…

I would take down the United States as the beacon of light to a world starving for moral leadership and turn our nation into an angry, tit-for-tat, money-grubbing bully that throws its weight around simply because it can. I would create a Tower of Babel unlike any seen since the 11th chapter of Genesis, wherein our own language is confused to the point that we can no longer agree on what basic words mean—words like honor, fairness, patriot, freedom, compromise, and common sense. I would create an electronic infrastructure that provides fertile ground for those who wish to plant the seeds of secret conspiracies in government, politics, science, history, and art so as to leave a society facing desperately difficult decisions without the ability to even define its problems.

I would take down the middle class, the linchpin that holds a democracy together, and create a nation rapidly dividing into haves and have-nots, each with its own angry mythologies about the other, and both ready to take or defend what they need to sustain life at the point of a gun. And speaking of mythologies, I would spread the lie that those on the bottom rungs of society are there solely because they are inferior in their mental capacity and drive to succeed and, therefore, deserve the kind of poverty and hunger that snuffs out genuine hope of a better future.

I would create programming capable of being watched in secret, where numbing profanity and crude sexual content gradually erode our sense of what normal behavior looks, sounds, and feels like. I would take the idea of a "culture of life" and turn it on its head by inducing a passionate demand for the birth of every fetus, followed by the crass shoulder-shrugging denial of the health and nutritional support needed to help the new life thrive—and then loudly mock anyone who notices the hypocrisy of such a morally bankrupt position.

In the process, I would elevate and enshrine the words of Cain, who asked God with rhetorical anger and sarcasm, "Am I my brother's keeper?" and I would burn those words in the hearts of as many millions as I could convince that the answer is a fist-pounding, thundering no.

I would do everything in my power to destroy the carefully balanced natural world that He created for His children, and I would enjoy discovering that out of everything on my list, this was the easiest to accomplish—since all that's necessary for its success are the twin appeals of corporate profits and today's individual convenience and comfort.

And as my power grew, I would make the utterly ridiculous appear completely reasonable. For example, assigning germs to political parties.

And speaking of germs, if I was the devil, I'd revel in injecting the human race with the one germ against which there will never be herd immunity: fear. And I would laugh as I watched the germ of fear slowly and relentlessly drive us all mad.

And I'd mess with supply chains. Remember toilet paper? I do. Fun times.

So…yeah. That's what I'd do if I was the devil. It probably wouldn't even be that hard. Most of the heavy lifting has already been done."

History is watching and smelling the BS…and so are we Pops

The old man with the penchant for gaffes and low energy made his way to the platform in the August body where all the DC insiders met to discuss the State of the Union and send a message out to WE THE PEOPLE – that the state of the Union is strong- no matter what the true condition of the nation was in at this particular point in time.

And on this particular night, March 7, 2024, as I was driving back from Palm Beach and a trip where I met, albeit briefly, with one of the great political minds of our time, Dick Morris, even while listening on the radio, I could smell all the BULLSHIT beamed out from Washington to the rest of the world.

Thankfully, I was unable to see the old man who played the role of President on the screen...I could only hear him...through my radio feed and the friendly comments of NPR—who, for the most part, see nothing wrong with the delivery, the message, or the policies of this feeble and scrawny man from "Scranton."

Those in the Washington bubble, the elites, media, and others who dwell in his orbit, for the most part, have been in the tank for this guy who has never served the people, and I use that term loosely but has, in fact, served himself to second, third and fourth helpings of insider perks and privilege profiting the Biden family name. Had old Joe been a cow, one of the many I passed as I drove home from the East Coast across the state that claims to have more cattle per capita than any state in the union, he would have been branded as "Corrupt" or "Ours" because he truly was bought and paid for by those who are in power. The very definition of the *Washington Swamp* personified. And he was definitely what the man named Trump from Mar-a-Lago, a place I drove by on my short day trip, was talking about when he entered the Washington scene back in 2016.

Joe Biden is a history lesson, in fact, a microcosm of what is wrong with this place called Washington. A man with low intellect and even less talent. And a man with no moral compass, or any compass at all – as noted recently –this guy could get lost and not find his way out of a 12 x 12 room with one door and one entrance.

As he made his entrance into the politically charged arena for hopefully his last State of the Union, he was surprisingly energized- which for him is headline news. As I heard the description of him coming into the chamber – the NPR clan was describing the scene as if they were watching their grandfather about ready to carve the Thanksgiving Turkey for the last time.

"He's making some faces at some of his friends. Hugging others. And pushing back at the likes of Marjorie Taylor Greene who is wearing a red hat...a red Make America Great Again hat."

For the most part, their description was saccharine and reverent of the man and the office he held.

But it was there underneath, all the BS that they were so adept at delivering to the American people. An all-you-can-eat buffet of Bull Shit – which they hoped the public would take in time and time again as a narrative that *"This President was not only fit for the job, gosh darn it, Old Joe looked pretty good for his age."*

Yes, it was their underneath. Even if it wasn't said out loud or into a plugged-in microphone. Their concern about his faculties, his fragile nature and his ability to stitch together a thought or cohesive sentence without stumbling or mumbling. And it all added up and contributed to their one and ultimate fear. This guy, their aging, decrepit candidate, could not beat Trump in the upcoming general election. They doubted, even the most loyal or delusional of them, who were drinking the KOOL-AID intravenously, that Joe's days were numbered and had to be replaced on the ticket if they were going to be able to GET TRUMP in November 2024.

Oh sure, occasionally, in passing, they'd bring up the fact that many in his party were concerned with his age…but they'd shrug it off and refer to someone saying off the record…"there's nothing we can do about his age."

This was, in essence, an audition or a job interview as much as it was a State of the Union address.

And that there was the crux of their task…how to paint and present this guy as competent…hell was he able to even finish a speech…forget about four more years.

Still, the chants of four more years rang through the chamber.

Or was it four more beers? Because to see this horror show that was the Biden term play out and be replayed over and spun by the media and supporters, who, regardless of whatever misstep, mishap, or plain old catastrophe he was responsible for, shrugged off as "Nothing to see here…The old guy is doing pretty good," - it would help to be drunk.

Hearing them cover for him with *"He's doing a pretty good job"* was hard to take.

Thank God for at least for this leg of the Biden journey. I could not see the picture. Watching the Biden presidency play out was, for most of us, quite sobering indeed.

Perhaps they didn't know or care that some of us had been sobered up with big pots of black coffee and over many years of destructive policies. We could clearly see just what he and his regime had done to our country and to we the people. And we knew or at least hoped that history would report in time the charade of this man, his administration, and all those who went along with the narrative and listened to the spoon-fed lies of a first-class bullshit artist- named Joe Biden.

As I drove and listened to the BS on the radio, I gazed out my windows and caught many glimpses of cows, just being cows, as the magnificent sunshine began to fade and the sun set on them, creating a stunning, authentic slice of the American landscape. Cows merely grazing or resting as the sun sets on them with night falling. The kind of thing old Jack Kerouac wrote about as he watched the road unfold before him. A soothing scene of the land, undaunted and unspoiled by man's fingerprints. Just cows being cows and doing what cows do. Appearing to stare right at me at times as I glanced at them. On occasion, I'd open the window and take in the warm breezeless Florida air, filled with humidity, the fragrance of palms, and, of course, real Bullshit. But to me, it was refreshing in some weird way. Their bullshit. Natural. Honest. And while its pungent smell filled my nostrils, it did not repulse me – for it was real.

Then I closed the window and began to listen to bullshit that was not real. But fake. And the smell was unbearable, served by a master bullshit artist and an old man —who once claimed to be a professor. He was not. BS by a feeble bullshit artist who took bullshitting to another level with his claims over the years. He also was not there marching with Nelson Mandela or at Selma with Martin Luther King Jr.

And by this time – hell, I'm really not sure *Corn Pop* ever existed.

We were all aware by now, that he didn't write the speeches he was found guilty of plagiarizing that forced him to drop out of a presidential race in the past. And while it's certain he didn't write this State of the Union speech that he attempted to deliver as only he could, this was, even for him, fresh bullshit.

Still, it was presented with much of the same Biden style and lack of clarity, even if it was at times more energetic. Disjointed. Delivered with Anger. Filled with many gaffes. Sometimes shouted. Sometimes whispered but filled with many lines of bullshit or tall tales -that some who don't paint in euphemisms – call outright lies.

When it was all said and done, the speech was like many State of the Union addresses. Filled with bullshit. Partisan applause. And one angry man sometimes yelling and sometimes whispering. But through it all, delivering a master class in bullshit.

In the speech, he told the *American people- "that history would be watching."*

On that, he was right. We have been for some time. And so were some of the four-legged creatures in cow pastures that dotted my car ride. As I opened up the window on my ride home, I swear, but as the cows in the yonder, who were listening to the BS emanating from the pulpit to a town full of bull shit artists and the American people who he'd been bullshitting for decades - they turned away. *The cows turned away.* I thought that was telling. Apparently, not only can they smell bullshit from roughly a thousand miles away from a place that thrives on it, Washington DC, but they also know when they have had enough of it.

Even for cows, there is only so much bullshit you can take. On this night, as they chewed their cud and left their deposits -even for them, it was too much. They could tolerate no more because, let's face it, they were used to real pure BS, and they knew where it came from. Not the fake shit, from some bat-shit angry old man spreading it over the airwaves and dished to the American people like it was honey.

Yes, Pops, America, and history would be watching. But sorry, the cows won't be. They'll be too busy dropping their own real BS in a field where it belongs and not on the American people.

Enough, I'd Had Enough

They were two nice people ... two nice Jewish people who appeared to like me very much and who often came into the shop where I worked. Over the years, they never bought anything. That never bothered me. They just liked to come in and browse a bit. We often exchanged pleasantries as they dropped into the shop when they were in town. I suppose they just liked my company and conversation, and I enjoyed theirs as well. Often, the subject of movies came up, and I opined about this film or that film and, of course, proudly shared my movie name, "Gussie Spielberg Mollasis," that my film students had come to know me by. Once in a while, I'd share some of my shtick that I shared with my film classes. "Want to know my two favorite Jews?" I said. They smiled as I delivered my punch line, "*Larry David and Jesus*...The worst and the best...The Alpha and the Omega." They got a kick out of that and laughed. They were not the least bit offended. That was refreshing in a time when *wokeness* has sadly ruled the day when it came to discussing anything controversial and with comedy, suffering greatly because some people were so easily offended by a joke.

Still, as folks would come in and out of the shop, I steered clear of steering right into heavy-laden topics. It was not good for business. That was why I usually stayed clear of discussing politics for all the right reasons with pretty much everybody who entered through our doors.

Late one Saturday night, as I was closing, "the nice Jewish couple" stepped into the shop, and the subject came up. The topic touched on the most recent chapter about a region that could fill books on a place that has always been steeped in chaotic, disruptive, and typical terror-laden happenings. *The Middle East*. A holy place where the three major monotheistic religions of the world, Judaism, Christianity, and Islam, cite as their birthplace. Yet a horrid place where there has been hardly any lasting peace for the people who live there. Discussing the place and taking a side almost as treacherous as living next door to neighbors there who didn't see your point of view. A place built on a combination of philosophies - ranging from a revenge-filled "eye for an eye" mentality to one of forgiveness and "turning the other cheek."

As I was turning off the shop lights we talked of the October 7th attack in Israel.

"Upside down world. Sad. Tragic. Evil," I said while I proceeded to do my nightly tasks closing up the art gallery. They merely shook their heads with sadness.

"*Terrible. Horrible. Barbaric,*" he said as his wife nodded in agreement.

The summation was accurate. It always was in describing this place. And it always had been for thousands of years.

The subject then turned to the topic of leadership. "What do you think of Netanyahu and the job he's doing?" The Jewish man, who I will call Isaac, answered in silence but with an expression of disapproval that told me he was no fan of the man leading Israel through these latest pages of history.

"You don't like him?" I confirmed. He nodded no.

His wife, who I will call Sarah, said nothing, but I could tell she was pretty much on the same page with her husband in regard to the opinion of the Prime Minister of Israel.

Not stunned but informed by their lack of support for him, I blurted out, "The whole world is in a mess. Wars. Hot spots. Conflicts everywhere. What do you expect? Look at the leader we now have in office."

With the words out of my mouth, my whole relationship changed with the nice Jewish couple.

"He wasn't as bad as the last guy," the words shot back, stopping me in my tracks as I hung a final painting. As I gathered the fish food to feed our four fish who swim in a Chinese Bowl nearby, my look must have said it all, my disapproval with the comment.

"*You got to be kidding?*" "*Trump is worse than Biden?*"

In shock, but not really, I repeated the statement. Then we were off to the races, and I knew, as the words poured out of my mouth, that our relationship would never be the same.

I don't know exactly when it happened, the moment when I fell off the pedestal that they placed me on, going from someone they admired to someone they were disappointed in, but it happened that quickly. And the sad thing is – I felt the same way about them as the words emptied out of me.

"*Donald J. Trump. There has been no better friend to Israel in the White House than Trump. Maybe Truman at the beginning,*" I said.

Well this was the beginning of the end of our pleasant relationship.

"He nodded no," as his wife seemed to nod in agreement with me.

"He moved the Capital of Israel to Jerusalem as others promised. He was the only one who delivered."

She nodded and said, "Isaac, he's right about that."

Finally, I added, *"The Abraham Accords. Trump did that. There was peace in the Middle East. Israel had treaties with four neighbors: Bahrain, the United Arab Emirates, Morocco, and Sudan. There wasn't the chaos that there was today in the world."*

Once again, Sarah nodded quietly in agreement. Isaac just turned away and looked down.

"You like Trump?" he said, unable to hide his disappointment in me no longer.

"Yes, I like Trump. But more than that, I trust him more with handling the big problems going on in our country and around the world," I said, *"Don't you?"*

"I can't stand him," he said unapologetically.

"Ok that's your right. But you must admit that the world and America was in better shape on his watch. No Endless wars on his watch. Ukraine would not have happened had he been president. October 7th and the attack on Israel would not have happened either. And he would have never left Afghanistan like Biden did, in a chaotic mess."

"And don't start me about the immigration mess and the invasion to our southern border."

Once again, Isaac looked down, and, as Sarah quietly said, "You have a good point," he disapprovingly shot back.

'He's lacks character."

To which I shot back, *"Lack of character, Biden is a plagiarist, a professional liar, corrupt lifetime politician… and not only that, he's a pedophile-check him out."*

The words rocked my former friend. The cease-fire was over.

Enough, I had enough. Had enough of keeping my mouth shut while being polite and force-fed a smorgasbord of lies. With the flurry of our conversation came a sudden chilling in the air. I could instantly feel the change in their attitude toward me as easily as they saw and felt a change in the weather on a fall Michigan afternoon. The warmth was gone.

Where before they looked me in the eye, they now looked away.

I tried to circle back and summarize.

"What I'm trying to say, is that Donald Trump is a much stronger and better leader for America and the world was much safer and in less distress under his watch. And he's always been a loyal friend and supporter of Israel."

Once again, I seemed to break through a bit with Sarah, not so much with Isaac.

Then, they made some sort of hasty excuse and abruptly made their way toward the door. As they were leaving, Sarah looked sadly at me.

I looked back and countered, *"That's why I went to DC on the 6th of January. I was there to peacefully protest and object to what I felt was a stolen election. I know that my country isn't always right, and it was my right as an American to speak my peace. I live by Reagan's mantra now- trust but verify."*

Isaac was already out the door with a cool goodbye.

Sarah turned back and sadly looked and me and said, "It's been a tough day for Isaac. You're *the second one today* who he's had to deal with on this."

My look must have spoken volumes. Yet, I thought to myself, *"Second one today?" "What the hell does that mean?"*

Sensing that I needed some time of closure, she shared. "You're the second one today. You're the second friend or person Isaac respects who expressed these sentiments about Trump."

"Oh, I see," I said as I turned away and turned off the remaining lights in the shop.

As the nice Jewish couple left, I could see that they were sad and disappointed in me and my beliefs. And while I knew that they could no longer see the sadness reflected in my eyes, I came to realize one other thing. And that other thing that we both knew but never expressed was that we would probably never see each other again. And that was sad, I thought as I headed home. They really could never see and accept me for who I really was in the first place, in this place, a darkened gallery that was closing on a late Saturday night somewhere in America.

Big Three Music Icons -Soulful Singers with fans more MAGA than they think

One of my favorite memories in life is going to a concert. Especially in the good old days when concerts were affordable, and the stars would just play the music for all their fans, and it wasn't so damn political.

Loved to see all the great bands and acts in my hometown of Detroit, Michigan.

Saw the great band from Boston – The *J.Geils* band, 13 times. To them and fellow Detroiters like me and my sister, they were our adopted sons dishing out soulful, lengthy sets led by the incomparable frontman Peter Wolf. My lovely sister was our concert connection and fed us the great tickets that she got from some guy named Tony for a paltry scalper's fee of five bucks over the price of regular priced ticket! We saw the best bands in the best seats, all for around 20 bucks!

My sister loved the band Journey with the same passion and had a super crush on the lead singer, Steve Perry. For us, going to concerts was a *House Party,* and *we couldn't stop believing* that those times would ever end. Sadly, they did. But ah, the beauty of that time. Simpler. A little more innocent. Better because we were younger. But better because it was better. Together, we went on our rock and roll journey, seeing at least 100 or so concerts. Armed usually with my 35mm camera and a heart yearning to see great acts and feel soulful music, we traversed to *Cobo Hall, Joe Louis Arena, The Palace of Auburn Hills, The Silverdome, Pine Knob, Masonic Temple, The Royal Oak Music Theater, The State Fair Grounds and the Fox Theater* -and everywhere else we could jam with our rock and roll heroes. As we got older – and as our musical tastes changed and bands broke up we still went to concerts - but not as often and for a lot more money.

But back then – for the best seats…and when I say best seats – I usually mean inside 20 rows, often inside ten rows. Up close and personal so that we could see and feel the music.

We loved them all. One weekend, when the Pontiac Silverdome hosted the Super Bowl in 1981, I remember going to three eclectic shows that were booked to celebrate Detroit hosting the big game with big-name acts. *Frank Sinatra. Diana Ross and Rod Stewart.* All witnessed up close and personal in the span of four days.

Wow! Seeing Frank sing My Way, listening to Diana sing Baby Love and watching Rod the bod kick a soccer ball into the audience – as he sang to Maggie May- well, it doesn't get much better than that.

Not 100% sure – but I don't remember any of them ever getting political. They knew that their fans represented all stripes and many opinions.

We saw everyone from the *Stones to Elton John, and from Queen to Sir Paul McCartney. Alice Cooper. Foreigner. Aerosmith, AC/DC, Van Halen, Cheap Trick. Ted Nugent. Billy Joel. Prince. David Bowie, The Who and Michael Jackson* - just to mention a few.

Then there were three soulful regional acts that stood out over the years and seemed to sing for we the people with a little more feeling. Putting in that extra effort for the hardworking and hard-rocking people of the motor city and folks like that all over America.

Three real guys. Authentic. Raw. Blue collar. Old school. Forever cool

Tom Petty, Bob Seger, and Bruce Springsteen. Three icons. Three acts from different parts of the country. Tom from Florida, Bob from Michigan, and Bruce from Jersey.

Three rockers who were not ever overtly political.

Tom Petty was one of them, the boy from Gainesville, Florida, who sadly left us too early and whose music I still enjoy immensely on his Sirius station. I only saw Tom once in the early days when he warmed up for Journey. I always knew he was going to make it big because he was extremely talented and real, and through his words and music, he related to his fans.

I felt the same way about the other two rockers in this trinity of hardworking iconic solo acts that were backed by legendary bands.

Bob Seger and the Silver Bullet Band.

Bruce Springsteen and E Street Band.

Tom Petty and the Heartbreakers.

For most of my life, they provided a soundtrack of my life that rocked me, lifted me, and often soothed my broken heart. But most of all, they provided music that I could relate to, and in them found a friend who felt got me because, quite frankly, I got them.

It was a simple bargain. They loved playing their music. I loved listening to their music.

Can't tell you how many times I got lost in the lyrics and rhythms of Seger's *Night Moves* or *Like a Rock*. In many ways, I feel like I'm still the same, but I'm older now but still running against the wind.

Bruce Springsteen and the E-Street Band. Caught his River tour in Detroit in 1980. I was blown away by his three-plus hour act as he seemed to be saying to all of us in the motor city- "I know how hard you work for your money; I'm going to be putting in some overtime for you, *Detroit."*

And that's what he did. That's when I fell in love with Bruce in the same way I loved that band from Boston, The J. Geils band, who would play for over three hours and then come out for three, four, and even five encores after the lights were turned on.

Couldn't get enough of them all, and I loved them all for their music and what they did for all of us. For many of us, a record or song represents a time long ago when everything was possible, when we were in love with that special someone, and when there was more road in front of us than behind us.

Listening to Tom singing *Free Falling*, or Bruce on *Thunder Road*, or Bob on *Mainstreet*, we were transformed and transported magically to those places in our hearts and minds – by guitar-playing troubadours with powerful penned poems put beautifully to music.

Petty's classic *Southern Accent* depicts a boy from the south. And no matter where I am – when I hear that tune, I tune everything else out.

> *There's a southern accent, where I come from*
> *The young 'uns call it country*
> *The Yankees call it dumb*

So authentic in all his work. That's why I continue to listen.

Listening to our own Bob Seger play anything from *Ramblin Man to Beautiful Loser* we felt like he was ours, the star and Michigan Boy we were now sharing with the rest of the planet. We were proud of Bob and his Silver Bullet band as more popular songs like *Old Time Rock and Roll* and *Hollywood Nights* introduced him to the world.

And Springsteen. The Boss. The more I got into Bruce, the more layers I found. Discovering his *Born to Run* album was akin to me stumbling onto Brando's *On the Waterfront*. A revelation. Something I could relate to because the Boss could relate to us. I will never forget playing his THE RISING album hundreds of times as a way of healing in the aftermath of that fateful day, 9/11 when the towers fell. For that album alone, I owe the Boss a ton of gratitude for helping me shed buckets of honest tears as I listened to this soulful, spiritual, and righteous album. Listening to it was like attending my solemn and beautiful Saturday night Greek Orthodox Easter service with my Mom and dad and *little concert-going sister*. It healed me. It encouraged me. Made me think. It gave me hope. And through it – *The Rising* did something magical and mysterious. It offered me a sacrament with one of my rock and roll gods and a communion of sorts that offered me a chance to rise above the chaos that was 9/11 and heal with both the Boss and the Lord's help through those sad, angry, and fearful times.

Petty, the boy from Florida; Seger, the boy from Michigan; and Springsteen, the boy from Jersey.

They spoke to all of us all across America with their music. And because of that we all wanted to listen to and enjoy their music. They were all working-class guys delivering gritty, soulful music that appealed to their regional fans and the masses worldwide – for one important reason: *"They were authentic and empathized with their fans."*

They were not playing down to their fans. They were playing with them and for them.

All of them. For all of us. Music can be so damn uniting.

Then, the tune changed. Don't know when exactly. But the record skipped. And in doing so scratched and bruised a few fans along the way- including me.

The music still might have been great but it was presented with sharp notes against and for certain political candidates. Now, classic ballads were accompanied by diatribes.

Now music, especially 60's and 70's folk and rock music, has always been something that could incorporate strands of rebellion with a goal of changing the world for the greater good. And there is nothing wrong with that – in fact, it's a good reason to produce the poetry in the first place. No better example than Bob Dylan for doing that and doing it well with great intentions in creating a positive change while waking up a sleepy world. Dylan sang about the man. Honestly. Authentically. Writing whatever he wanted from his point of view in an effort to right a world that had gone wrong and had gone off the rails leaving many behind with much blood on the tracks.

So it was natural, when Springsteen grabbed the torch from Dylan as he sang about the faces of the forgotten folks in the crowd. He wrote about the plight of the common man. The forgotten man and woman. The hopeless. The homeless. The Jobless. The people who had been marginalized by big corporations, by big government, and anything that made the common man smaller.

Bruce sang about that and for many of the same types of people who now attend Trump rallies.

Ironically, many of those attending a Trump rally and much of MAGA nation had much in common with those who at one time attended a Boss concert. They were there for many of the same reasons. To listen. But also to be heard. To be encouraged. To be enlightened. To be entertained. To be seen and recognized by a man who saw them and who heard their voices. The voices of the many strangers who were forgotten or abused and misused by *the man.*

Sound familiar. It should.

In his victory speech following the 2016 Election, Donald Trump said his win came courtesy of a *"movement comprised of Americans from all races, religions, backgrounds, and beliefs, who want and expect our government to serve the people and serve the people it will."*

Trump said the *"the forgotten men and women of our country will be forgotten no longer."* He also promised to *"finally take care of our great veterans,"* and said he will *"harness the creative talents of our people and will call upon our best and brightest to leverage their tremendous talent for the benefit of all."* 1

Trump vowed that the U.S. will have *"the strongest economy anywhere in the world."* And the same time, *"we will get along with all other nations willing to get along with us,"* and Trump expects to have *"great, great relationships"* with them."[30]

That chord, the last one, about ending endless wars, while not expressed in his victory speech specifically, is a theme repeated, like an encore, at almost every Trump speech since he first started his "Tour" of America.

The encore ENDING ENDLESS WARS is one that he always plays loud and clear for his supporters, akin to how the Boss plays *Born to Run* for his fans. Standards that both their fans demand with messages that resonate with them.

In a 2020 speech, Trump told the graduating class of West Point that *"the job of the American soldier is not to rebuild foreign nations but "defend, and defend strongly, our nation from foreign enemies."*

"We are ending the era of endless wars," Trump said. *"It is not the job of American forces to solve ancient conflicts in faraway lands that many people have not even heard of."*[31]

The themes of the forgotten men and women and ending endless wars in places where we don't belong, they too are echoed in Springsteen's Anthem *Born in The USA.*

Born down in a dead man's town
The first kick I took was when I hit the ground
End up like a dog that's been beat too much

'Til you spend half your life just coverin' up, now

Born in the U.S.A.
I was born in the U.S.A.
I was born in the U.S.A.
Born in the U.S.A. now

Got in a little hometown jam
So they put a rifle in my hand
Sent me off to a foreign land
To go and kill the yellow man

Born in the U.S.A.
I was born in the U.S.A.
I was born in the U.S.A.
I was born in the U.S.A.

Come back home to the refinery
Hirin' man says, "Son, if it was up to me"
Went down to see my V.A. man
He said, "Son, don't you understand," now[32]

Today, those sons, daughters, mothers and fathers of the American Dream, understand "the VA man" and comprise this mosaic of America's forgotten men, women and a movement sweeping through and touring this great land of ours. And one thing is clear, as they mouth the words of the common song they're all singing with a man named Trump, who while not a singer, is someone who is their rock star – and someone who not only sees them but gets them. All of them. The way the Boss got many of them not so long ago.

Perhaps not so strangely, Comedian Bill Maher, who is a bit of rock star in his own right for providing a platform where those who disagree with each other don't have to hate each other, enlightened a joyless Trump hater on the nuance of public discourse and debate. Maher who is no fan of Trump, summed up the divisive country we live in as he confronted Joy Behar about placing all of Trump's supporters in one convenient *hate* box. During an appearance on *The VIEW* Bill Maher objected to an earlier comment from Behar when she had suggested that Trump supporters "might as well put a swastika" on their MAGA hats. *"I'm not going to defend Donald Trump ever, but I would never say that we should put the swastika on the cap because I think you can hate Donald Trump, you can't hate everybody who likes him. It's half the country. I don't want to live in that country, I don't want to live in the country where I hate half the country - and I don't hate half the country,"* he said. [33]

Roughly half the country who love Trump and half the country who hate Trump and many who still want to hear some good rock and roll music from a man called the Boss. The same forgotten men and women who The Boss wrote and sang about during a time not so long ago when America just wanted to get together and listen to the music.

California – State of Mine - Yearning for days when Frank & Jack Played Here

I loved California. As I child- I thought of it as the promised-land.

Today, sadly, it is largely a disaster. And that's a shame.

Still, there are many who want to use it as a model of what America should strive to be.

And if they had echoed this statement about a California that used to exist- then they would be right. But sadly, the LEFT and their left-leaning policies have destroyed the land of milk, honey, and dreams that was California for many.

To many, it represented a place that was magical, and nowhere was there more magic than in a town called Hollywood. But sadly that Hollywood is gone. And gone with them and the wind are all the legends. When I was a kid, and I saw that old Hollywood sign, it meant something different. It was magical. Almost mystical – this place called California.

Visited it many times –especially in the 1980's and 1990's. Met the great actor Jimmy Stewart in front of his home in Beverly Hills. Shot marketing videos in Palm Springs in the 1990s. Traveled up and down its beautiful coast from San Diego to San Francisco a number of times. Highway One along the coastline in California runs south to north through Big Sur and misty fog and the brilliance of Carmel and

Monterey- God's country. Spectacular, some say, the greatest confluence of land and sea on the planet. Who knows? I just knew it was a sight to take in. Can't think of Pebble Beach without thinking about my Uncle Pierre, who loved golf and California as much as anybody. Caught ball games in LA, Anaheim, and Oakland. California was always special to me. Loved it from La Jolla to Santa Barbara, some of my favorite places on earth. Haven't been there for years. And I don't know if I ever will get back there. But there was a time when the mere mention of the word California would send a thrill up my spine.

Had a history with some of my family there. My Uncle Pete, a very sharp man, was a hotelier and did quite well in California in his heyday, owning a number of hotels and motels when California was California. My Uncle Pierre made his way to Palm Springs and ended up managing the Eldorado Country Club – the home to the Bob Hope Desert Open for years. Legend has it -my uncle Pierre, while playing a round of golf with Jack Lemmon, Gerald Ford, and Bob Hope – to namedrop a few names, actually told Bob Hope after watching the great comedian swing, "There's no hope for that swing."

Sadly, I'm afraid there isn't much hope for making California great again. Not unless, of course, they can remove Governor Newsom – NEW–SCUM in Donald Trump's book of nicknames and one of my favorites- and sadly, Newsom, one of the favorites of the DEMS to take the baton from sleepy Joe if not this year, then in the future.

But really, do you want America to look like California? I want California to look like California when it was California of old. When Sinatra played in Palm Springs his pal Jack Kennedy was supposed to come and stay at his Palm Springs property- but ended up breaking Frank's heart by staying with the Republican crooner- Bing Crosby – because of political pressures.

Wow – how things have changed in California and the body politic. Back then, Francis Albert was a true blue Democrat who threw his support behind JFK and worked his ass off campaigning for him. In time, as the chairman grew older, he once again threw his support behind another politician and one time Democrat, this time working his tail off to help his friend and fellow Republican Ronnie Reagan get elected President.

The former governor loved California, as did Frank. Who didn't love that California?

Sadly, that California is gone. Gone too, are the days that I would have loved to frolic here under the palms with the summer wind blowing in and the Jack Daniels flowing, when men were men and women were glad they were.

California represents a certain light and energy. Now only a dream to many of us.

I get sad when I see pictures of San Francisco. How dirty it had become. Shameful.

I remember my Uncle Pierre telling me many times, "My boy, there is no place like California; you can go from Palms to Pines on the same day. It's got everything. It's paradise."

Now my uncle Pierre is gone. So is my Uncle Pete. Still, when I think of California, I can't help but think of these two men, and one night, I shared a wonderful memory with them - that can only happen in America and in California

The scene - a darkened restaurant after the sun went down in the desert town of Palm Springs.

I had told both by uncles that I wanted to go to a very special restaurant that was located on Frank Sinatra Drive. The place was *Chaplin*'s, and it was owned by the son of the iconic movie legend Charlie Chaplin, Sydney Chaplin.

Once inside my two uncles who were both restaurant men, having worked at some of the best restaurants around the USA – started talking about the business. The "*Do you remember this place and that place*" turned into a diatribe on joints that didn't make it because *the "owner didn't know and watch his business."* They always talked about guys who didn't know their business. And for the most part, I was amused, even though I didn't know the business, and quite frankly, it was none of my business. And that's when I saw him sitting near the bar. Sydney Chaplin. The son of the great silent movie comedian. I recognized him a little bit from his role in *Limelight*, which he played in with his dad, and silent movie great Buster Keaton.

At first, as I approached him- I was a little speechless and silent like his legendary father. Then, I got my nerve up to introduce myself. I looked over at my two uncles who were going down memory lane, talking shop, and remember my Uncle Pierre being a little shocked – "Pete, I didn't know you worked at *"Chasens."*

Well, that was all very interesting, but I'd had a lifetime of talking about the restaurant business. What I wanted to do was talk a little bit about something I really loved *–show business*. And who better to talk with about that than the son of a man who created it and who'd been there and seen it all?

As I looked around the dark and simple restaurant with a nice, prominent, masculine square bar – I noticed that there were no pictures of the man who shared the name of the joint in the desert.

"No pictures of Charlie Chaplin in Chaplin's," I thought silently to myself.

Then, as if to break my thought, I heard his voice introduce himself to me.

"I'm Sydney Chaplin, welcome to Chaplin's."

Well, we started talking in that dark Palm Springs restaurant and bar about show business and, of course, about his father. And I must say I was in heaven. My Uncle Pierre was right. California was paradise.

"My father hated Christmas because when he was young, he was always so poor and remembered Christmas as being lean, sharing oranges with his brother," he said to me as I took a drink and told a tale about his famous father.

I looked over at my Uncles, still talking about restaurants, and then back at Sydney.

"It's ironic that he died on Christmas day."

He spoke of his father as "someone being hard to get to know" but he also spoke with reverence of his talent. *"He was a perfectionist and a genius. No one could do what he did, before or since."*

As our conversation came to a gradual end, a gracious handshake was offered, and I thanked him for his hospitality and for sharing a little bit of his father with me.

"No problem, I'm glad you enjoyed the stories," he said as he made his way to another customer at the other end of the bar. *"Enjoy your time in the springs."* There was a spring in my step as I made my way back to my uncles, who were still talking about the restaurant business.

My Uncle Pete was smiling as the ash from his cigarette fell to the ground, missing the ashtray on the bar, when he asked me, *"What did you guys talk about?"*

I smiled back, *"What else - The Movies"*

"Charlie Chaplin," I mouthed softly. *"His father was Charlie Chaplin. There is no Hollywood without the Little Tramp."*

He smiled back, *"I got to know Paulette Goddard pretty well when I worked at the Beverly Hills Hotel,"* he said.

I smiled back, as a soft piano played a tune and us out into the still warm Palm Springs night.

A memory of California from days gone by. About some men I loved and miss and a place called California that I still dream about.

Missing Rush on the Radio

His voice was always the right voice. A voice that surely was the voice of the political right. And his voice is the one sorely missing from the airwaves, and the voice many of us in America and MAGA-land miss the most today during these depressing times that all of us who love America are living through.

The voice of Rush Limbaugh – a voice of wisdom and political acumen that, in Rush's words, could *"read the stitches on a fastball thrown 95 miles per hour."*

Rush was that good, that sharp and that accurate in his assessments of all things regarding the body politic – but most assuredly a voice and man who knew the political left as well as anyone.

Wonder what Rush would be thinking today of the crazy political landscape?

How would he read the current Biden drama?

What would be the next act in this Shakespearean play?

Who were the traitors? When would the heroes appear to save the republic?

Would justice be served? Would we, the people, triumph?

Would we continue to be, as Franklin said...a Republic if we could keep it?

Rush would have the right answers and the right take on every question.

El Rushbo would know what the next moves would be from the dysfunctional left and the smart moves that the right would need to make to defeat them. Rush was always playing the long game. Playing political grandmaster chess while his competition was playing checkers, sometimes Chinese checkers.

Rush was always there with an insight that would calm you. As soon as I heard his bumper theme music, the iconic song Chrissie Hynde and *The Pretenders*, called *My City Was Gone*, I was psyched and ready for my political therapy session with the maestro.

The funny thing is that theme music forever associated with the show was almost silenced. Even though Rush used the song with the permission of one of the most legendary female performers, her publishing company actually tried to take it away.

"The publishing firm tried to take it away, and she interceded and told them, effectively, to pound sand; that, if I wanted to continue to use it, I would have her permission to use it," said Rush.

It wasn't the only time "The Pretenders' Chrissie Hynde went to bat for Rush and his pal Donald Trump, as she praised Trump for Honoring Rush Limbaugh at the State of the Union address— Despite Being a LIBERAL Herself — Because Her Dad Loved the Pundit and She Believes in the 'Right to Disagree.'" Hynde says that her late father, Melville, "would have loved Trump's presidency, would have absolutely adored Trump, and would have just been excited as he could be when Trump presented to me the Medal of Freedom at the State of the Union."

Their union wasn't always as harmonious as one of her anthems, and admitted that she 'didn't always see eye-to-eye' with her father and that they 'argued a lot.' Hynde would say, "But isn't that the American way? The right to disagree without having your head chopped off?" [34]

That line stuck in my throat like her bumper music stuck in my heart.

"The right to disagree without having your head chopped off."

It played over and over in my mind as I remembered Rush over a recent lost weekend in America, when one of his Palm Beach neighbors, a man the rock star's dad Melville admired so much, Donald Trump, almost lost his life at a rally.

As this particular Monday approached in July of 2024, following the chaos and violence, while Rush had been gone for years, it was still his voice that I longed to hear- to greet me and help me make sense of it all.

I'm damn sure I'm not the only one. The right side of the nation longs to hear his common sense and brilliant take on the crazy, evil, and dangerous times we are living in. And I know that President Trump would tune in – hell, he would call in.

With Rush, the result was predictable even if the analysis was not. All of a sudden, you'd feel a little better, smarter, and wiser for having tuned in. And so it went on for years until his great voice was silenced by a killer named Cancer. And we are all poorer for it – those who agreed with him and those who did not. A man who earned his Congressional Medal of Honor for his insight and *talent on loan from God*. This was no DEI token accommodation – a piece of metal slung in his direction to meet a quota- he got the award because he consistently was brilliant in discussing what it was to be a conservative and have conservative common sense values. And even if you didn't like or agree with him- you knew it was his right and your right to disagree - without having your head chopped off.

Had Rush been on the radio this upcoming week, oh, I do wish he was, he would have been steady and still able to read the stitches on the 95 mph fastball that was a bullet hurled in the direction of his friend Donald J. Trump's head, on a Saturday afternoon in Pennsylvania.

Rush, for sure, would have been shaken, but like the president who got up and yelled *Fight, Fight, Fight* - after being shot, Rush would have eased up to the EIB microphone and done his duty because he had a job to do and that was to be there for all his loyal listeners who needed him and trusted only him to help make sense out of a senseless day.

One thing would be certain: he would give it his best shot to help us all figure it out. And he was the right man for the job, especially when it came to supporting and understanding a man named Trump. A man he got and a man he admired greatly. Rush got Trump, and Trump got Rush. They got each other in a special way, like few did. Rush was adept at reading people, and he was especially adroit at reading his fellow Palm Beach neighbor better than most. Understanding what made him tick ticked him off, but especially understanding the bond that Trump had formed with his fellow supporters.

If Rush said it once, he said it a thousand times, almost like his iconic Chrissie Hydne music being looped for his show. It was something you came to expect, Rush saying, *"The only one that can separate Donald Trump from his supporters is Donald Trump. The media didn't make him. He built the bond with them, and he's the only one that can break it."*

The bond he built with them was something Rush knew a little bit about and something he had built with his radio listeners for more than three decades.

One day, toward the end, when Rush was sick and getting sicker, I tuned into the show.

I remember saying, *"Let me check and see how our boy is doing."*

On came the iconic bumper music, and then I heard his wife Katherine's voice. She was there with the bad news. It wasn't on the doorstep but instead delivered over the airwaves to the people who got him the most, his loyal listeners who loved, trusted, and listened to him.

As I took in the sad and bad news...the melody from Bye, Bye *Miss American Pie*...entered into my brain. Rush, who loved to spin rock records in his early days as a DJ, would appreciate that.

Sadly, the music that he made over the air stopped. The day had come. His voice was silenced. I cried at the void and the silence. And I have been ever since. Oh, how I miss his voice, the right voice, our choice, and the only voice on the radio that could get it all just right - especially on weekends like these with Monday on the horizon, and a country in chaos and him not there to help us make sense of it all.

Beef or Crickets? It's what's for Dinner

It's no secret that I was raised on meat and potatoes. I am, after all, a *Meat Man's son*. So a good steak – a *New York, Ribeye, or Porterhouse* is the way to get to me.

And hey, I get it. If you don't love or even like to eat meat.

If you're a vegetarian or vegan. I respect your decision to go that way; in fact, I admire your discipline. Me, I can't do it.

I love the scene in *"My Big Fat Greek Wedding"* when Aunt Voula is confronted with a stranger in the strange land of Greeks who doesn't share a taste for meat.

Aunt Voula: *"What do you mean he don't eat no meat?"*
Aunt Voula*: "Oh, okay. Make lamb."*

Well, I also love lamb. My mom's Easter Leg of Lamb is my favorite all-time dinner. If I was ever sentenced to the e*lectric chair* for perhaps voicing my First Amendment rights, for my last supper –lamb would be my choice.

The reason I bring this up, recently, while bringing in some donuts to work for the crew, I was encountered by an interesting situation. Yes, I know that donuts are bad for you, but adhere to the saying – everything in moderation. And anyway, everyone loves donuts.

One day, one of the young ladies who enjoyed the donuts met me at my car as I came into the office and asked me to open my hand. I obliged the strange request. When I opened my hand – it revealed a cricket. Chocolate covered. Whatever. Needless to say, I was grossed out, and I didn't hold back telling her so.

"I bring you Dunkin Donuts and you hand me crickets. Are you out of your mind?"

Her response with a smile, *"They're good for you. And they taste pretty good."*

I looked at her and read her the riot act.

"Listen, you can eat crickets, grasshoppers and cockroaches if you like. But one thing, and let me make this perfectly clear. I will never ever eat a cricket. That's their next move, they want you all to eat crickets while they chomp on cheeseburgers."

She didn't know what I was talking about. But I did.

And so did a guy named Bill Gates.

Cicadas, tarantulas, crickets, and mealworms are just some of the critters that have been reimagined in recipes aimed at curbing the global population's consumption of meats such as beef, production of which has been cited as a major contributor to worldwide pollution.

Microsoft co-founder and billionaire Bill Gates has also weighed in on the issue, encouraging others to eat crickets, not for the sustainability of the planet but because of their supposed health benefits. Health benefits? While the claim can't be verified in 2021, the foundation provided more than **$2.2 million to Insecti Pro Limited "to establish a commercially viable** business for sustainable insect production for food and feed products in East and Central Africa." In 2012 it also granted $100,000 to All Things Bugs, LLC to "develop a method for the efficient production of nutritionally dense food using insect species."

Gates is a big supporter of plant-based meats, investing millions in Impossible Foods, as reported by *Newsweek*. In any case, while Gates' charitable foundation has invested in technologies in insect foods, and has invested heavily in plant-based meat, he doesn't appear to have been directly quoted saying people should eat crickets to stay healthy. [35]

Staying healthy is one thing, but there is no way I'm going to trade in my beef for crickets.

I thought of my dad, the meat man, and what he would think of the crazy times we were living through. A smile crossed my face as I thought of the old ad *Beef it's what's for dinner*. And as far as tomorrow's breakfast, I think I'll stop and get some donuts on the way to work.

Transgender- What about Babies- aren't they transitioning in the Womb

Isn't the baby in the womb…transitioning?

No really. I think it's a good question. And the question for all those who claim to be concerned about the health and well-being of children regarding gender dysphoria and so-called *Gender Affirming Care*.

This question involves the most basic human needs in terms of survival and sustainability.

And while this aspect of transitioning is focused not on gender –but species.

We'll call it *"Species Assigned Valued Evolution" or SAVE*.

Because if you truly are the party or movement that embraces science and uses buzzwords like sustainability – don't you think you should start by defining when a baby is a baby? Use whatever definition you like, but at least define it. And finally, how many genders are there? Is it limitless – like space?

Regarding babies and their transitioning nature, perhaps we can get them a letter, it can be lower case, in what David Chappelle calls the *ALPHABET people's* mantra.

Let's see. Where does it stand now? That famed acronym that defines sexual inclusivity along the fluid, ever-changing, and evolving stages of life?

LGBTQIA.

It pertains collectively to people who identify as lesbian, gay, bisexual, transgender, queer (or questioning their gender), intersex, or asexual (or their allies).

Wow! That's a mouthful. And there must be room for babies to tag on.

There seems to be clarity pertaining to the L, G, B, and T letters.

The L defines lesbians as ranging from, I presume, lipstick lesbians to large Marge and in-charge types. Hope that doesn't get me cancelled.

The G stands for gay. Gay is someone who is attracted sexually to that same sex. From closeted Gays – famous ones like Rock Hudson to the flamboyant types who are great at designing your living room and the conservative types who get married and may even attend a MAGA rally. Sorry if that triggers you- The MAGA stuff not the designer stuff.

The B stands for Bi-Sexual. Those who want more options for dating on Saturday night. Male or female. They dine from both sides of the menu.

The T stands for transgender, and here's where it gets a little tricky, as in T. According to the American Psychological Association, *"Transgender is an umbrella term for persons whose gender identity, gender expression or behavior does not conform to that typically associated with the sex to which they were assigned at birth."* [36]

Got that? Good. Now, the fun part.

Q is for Queer. And also for those questioning their gender. Not sure if a queer who was suspected of a hate crime can be questioned by the police if they're questioning their gender. Well I know for sure that will get me cancelled. Anyway, the Q stands for Queer. ***Queer*** is an umbrella term for people who are not heterosexual or are not cisgender. Originally meaning 'strange' or 'peculiar,' *queer* came to be used pejoratively against LGBT people in the late 19th century. From the late 1980s, queer activists began to reclaim the word as a neutral or positive self-description. [37]

According to Planned Parenthood, I stands for Intersex, an umbrella term that describes bodies that fall outside the strict male/female binary. There are lots of ways someone can be intersex. The general term is used for a variety of situations in which a person is born with reproductive or sexual anatomy that doesn't fit the boxes of "female" or "male." Sometimes doctors do surgeries on Intersex babies and children to make their bodies fit binary ideas of "male" or "female." [38]

Now we're getting somewhere. Still, I noticed a lot of umbrellas in the definitions and wondered if those who fall under the LBGTQIA nomenclature are big fans of Singin' in the Rain.

Anyway, if I hadn't been canceled – that might have done it. But at least they mentioned the possibility of a baby. And what sounds like a baby who is transitioning.

The A part here stands for Asexual or their allies. **Asexuality.** Some parents may be concerned because their teenager appears to have no interest in sexual matters at all. There are various possible causes, among them asexuality, which characterizes about 1% of the population. [39]

Regarding being an ally to someone asexual, here is a primer. According to Stonewall.org, A grey-asexual (grey ace/grey-a) person may experience sexual attraction very rarely or only under specific circumstances. Demi-sexual people only experience sexual attraction after developing a strong emotional bond with someone. Similarly, somebody who is aromantic does not experience romantic attraction, and a grey-romantic person only does very rarely. Demiromantic people are only romantically attracted to those they've emotionally bonded with first. [40]

The IA part of the LBGTQIA is not to be confused with AI –Artificial Intelligence. The danger and benefits of that AI- Artificial Intelligence is being weighed right now with the biggest and brightest minds, and they're all doing tests and studies to see if AI is more a danger and road to doom for humanity or more, dare I say a godsend that will make our world better.

Regarding LBGTQIA, If this all sounds, well, pretty confusing, it is, according to me. But what do I know? I'm a cisgender male who doesn't really know what my pronoun is but has a few questions to ask the alphabet people.

All these terms and definitions for those who are born and fall into these categories. But what about all those LBGTQIA folks who were aborted and didn't get a chance to transition, be fluid, and find and define themselves under one big Umbrella?

I bet you all could find some room in your alphabet for a little baby. Just think of it: LBGTQIAb or LBGTQIA baby! Not bad.

Hell, I bet you a lot of those babies, had they been born and not aborted, could have joined and become a proud letter fitting under your umbrella and bringing new life to your alphabet, and I'm sure a lot of them would have just loved – *Singin' in the Rain.*

If Pop were Alive –He'd be writing MAGA Anthems

My dad has been gone now for almost 25 years. And there isn't a single day I don't miss or think about him. Sometimes, a passing thought triggers the memory. A Sinatra song. A sports clip from an old ballgame. When I'm praying in church and anytime I talk with my mom. And a lot of times when I see Trump, with his endless energy, battling on his American journey, I think of my dad. I wonder what he would have thought taking this all in. I think my dad would have related a lot to Trump for he never quit, always get up and fight type of attitude. My dad was a lot like that. Like Trump, he was an early riser. Hard worker. A businessman. Brash. Bold. Good hearted. Mischievous. Armed with a great sense of humor. Smart. Often misunderstood. A patriot who loved America. A man with a sense of purpose. A doer and a dreamer. Yes, my pop would have gotten the former Queens businessman.

And I'm pretty sure had he lived, my dad, who was a hardworking meat man from Motown who dabbled in writing great songs, more than likely would have written a tune or two for the former and potential future president.

He wasn't an overly political guy. He loved Kennedy and was lukewarm about Nixon. He liked Ronnie and was amused by the Clinton show. In the 2000 election, in which he would not live to vote, he wasn't crazy about Bush or Gore. Now, in retrospect, I feel kind of the same way.

Still – had he lived, he would have thrived during these times. He would have watched the rallies. Been aggravated with many of the issues plaguing America. He would have connected with the man in the red MAGA hat named Trump.

And he would probably written a song or two and tried to get them to his campaign.

He would have been upset when he saw Trump shot at the rally. I'm sure that would have triggered something in him, a flashback to the time when a young man named Jack Kennedy was taken from us with an assassin's bullet. That would have bothered the hell out of him. But it would have gotten him to write something when he saw Donald Trump get up and pump his fists –while mouthing…fight…fight…fight!

That very gesture reminded me a lot of my dad. Fists pumping like that, I saw him do it many times. Imploring me to keep fighting. A gesture to all of us to keep going after our dreams. It was a gesture that would have moved my dad to write something great again to celebrate America and our president.

But it was not meant to be as my pop watched the scene play out from his roost in heaven, probably shaking his head all the time at what's happened to our America – all the while imploring us in Trump-like fashion to fight…fight…fight.

In some way, I hope and pray that those words would and could come to me as they did to him so often in song. I will pray on it and hope to see if my dad sends me the right words worthy of sharing with President Trump, great words and music to help Make America Great Again.

I'll keep you posted.

My dad serving during the Korean War. Stationed in Panama, here he is with movie star Debbie Reynolds representing a time when Hollywood was truly magical.

A shot of me – early MAGA. Way before the rallies, I was wearing the right color and ready to make America fun again.

A shot of three different elections. The numbers just don't add up.

My friend Marcia and me on Election Night 2020 before the pause in vote counting.

Me standing near The Washington Monument listening to the President's speech on January 6th 2021, asking to "peacefully and patriotically protest."

I'm making my way toward the Capitol on January 6th 2021. Things still pretty normal, but that's "weird" I can't find any bathrooms.

The revelry and right of patriots having their voices heard at the Capitol on January 6, 2021.

Meeting a patriot I came to know as General George Washington on January 6, 2021.

My friend Mike a Marine and a Flag maker with the beautiful wood flag he made for President Trump who he shares a birthday with on June 14th which naturally is Flag Day.

The hand written letter with the hand crafted Flag he made and sent to President Trump which expressed "how proud he was to support him."

VIII. Time for a Rewrite and New Leading Man or Woman?

The Real Manchurian Candidate in the Basement

No Debate Here- Trump won, Biden Done, Dr. Jill to Blame for Elderly Abuse

Time for a New Script – A New Actor, Candidate and Head Dummy?

Not Being There

The Real Manchurian Candidate in the Basement

He said it smugly, off the cuff, in a rare moment of transparency without the help of the teleprompter prompting him. That's when the man named Barack was most authentic and most dangerous to his cause – destroying America or, in his words- *fundamentally transforming America*.

With his two terms behind him – and living in the time of Trump, the man with the made-for-Hollywood smile mused as he was asked by a reporter if he could, and the Constitution permitted it, look forward to a third term.

"I've said this before, people would ask me, 'Knowing what you know now, do you wish you had a third term?' And I used to say, 'You know what, if I could make an arrangement where I had a stand-in, a front-man or a front-woman and they had an earpiece in and I was just in my basement with my sweats looking through the stuff and I could sort of deliver the lines, but somebody else was doing all the talking and ceremony, I would be fine with that.' Because I found the work fascinating. I mean, I write about the — even on my worst days, I found puzzling out, you know, these big, complicated, difficult issues, especially if you were working with some great people, to be professionally really satisfying. But I do not miss having to wear a tie every day."[41]

No – he didn't have to wear a tie while he was helping pull the strings on his puppet-in-chief named Joe during his day-to-day operations. And he didn't have to go to all those events and press conferences. He would have more time to fill out March Madness Basketball brackets and, just for fun and getting no credit, continue to fundamentally transform America from the shadows and not in the bright light. One thing he would have to do, however, was wearing one of those suits or tuxedos with a bow tie at the Hollywood fundraiser that he hosted with George Clooney and Julia Roberts. There, he would be joined by two big headliners and A-listers both coming to the rescue; they hoped for the man with nothing in his head who was always a B-picture player at best.

At these events, he would be guaranteed one other thing. Top billing. He was and would always be the biggest star in the room, any room, even a room filled with Hollywood's top leading men and women. And he knew it. He couldn't help it, and they couldn't help falling back in love with the man with the strange name when he flashed his Hollywood smile.

A smile that was always camera-ready and the stuff leading actors could bank on. And if Barack Obama was anything, he was a major player in this story and narrative and not just a lowly supporting character player.

That was Joe Biden.

He was and always would be an inept character actor who always lacked character. Now, he was forgetting lines at warp speed. And while many of these actors were doing their best to act like nothing was wrong with Joe – while trying to tell those all across America "that it was their eyes or to "please adjust their TV sets or smartphone screens." They kept telling you Joe was fine until you saw him in public at a meeting with able-bodied world leaders, or at a press conference with a friendly press spoon-feeding him softball questions – or more shockingly, here at a fundraiser with A-listers where you really noticed the fade, right before your eyes of the non-candidate and non-person named Joe.

Here on this "Hollywood set," with all the Hollywood pretty people led by the Pretty Woman herself, Georgie Boy, and even an appearance by Jack Black, donning something resembling an American flag overall ensemble that wasn't going to win him any best-dressed award, Biden looked even more pathetic and feeble than usual.

While they were all there to raise funds for his disastrous run for president, what must have crossed some of the minds of some of these *Hollywood Types*, was that they could now relate to the folklore horror stories of Hollywood investors being convinced to pony up dollars for cinematic turds like *Heaven's Gate* which lost 144 Million and *John Carter* which lost 255 Million!

While the fading and feeble man on the stage was not named John Carter but Joe Biden, there is no doubt this old man was waiting near Heaven's Gate or some other gate to make an exit. Make no mistake, it was still a shit show, and the elevator pitch was for the turd on the stage, which ironically looked like he was soiling himself, as the original Manchurian Candidate entered stage left to the rescue just in time like

SUPERMAN - to help his former and current underlying off the stage.

It was not the money shot that they all came to see. It was pathetically orchestrated, and as *Clueless Joe* was led off, actually pushed off the stage by his former and current boss, it was, I must say, a little sad. Yet it was not sad in the way good Hollywood movies make you feel. And in was not fulfilling in the way great Hollywood films like *Shawshank Redemption* give us hope. Nor was it overly thrilling, and it certainly wasn't a good old-fashioned western, or a good buddy road picture or suspenseful in a Hitchcock kind of way,

What this was, in fact, was an enlightening look at Hollywood, the elites, and an indictment on our whole political system that was infiltrated with *not only one Manchurian Candidate* but a whole country filled with many Manchurian candidates.

What was most frightening in this political thriller was not that many had gone undercover to grab and maintain their power, ala Sinatra's original Manchurian Candidate; perhaps even more frightful were that these actors, i.e., politicians who were reading their lines out loud with the spotlight on them, in a film called *America -A Crumbling Republic.*

They were putting on their show, hiding in plain sight for all to see and document if they dared lift their heads out of their smartphones to pay the least bit of attention. In this documentary, one film I wish the *Maysles Brothers* could have covered to lend their brilliance to in terms of direction and restraint – but especially their pursuit of the unvarnished raw truth.

Still, I wonder where and how the movie ends, not only for Joe but for all of us.

As we watch some of the final scenes portraying the useful idiot, foreshadowing produced by all those behind the scenes, Joe is being shown the door as he shuffles, stumbles, or is pushed off the stage and into the sunset by a Manchurian Candidate who has always had Joe's ear.

No Debate Here- Trump won, Biden Done, Dr. Jill to Blame for Elderly Abuse

Don't act shocked ...because if you are...you have either not been paying attention...or you're delusional...or worse yet, you've believed their narrative all along, the one by the mainstream media fed to you courtesy of the most incompetent, dishonest and manipulative administration ever as they've been pulling the strings of a puppet, not a man, poorly playing the role of a president. Let's face it: the man named Joe Biden is gone and has been fading into oblivion for a long time. They just didn't want you to know about it. But that all changed on a debate stage on a June night in 2024 in Georgia, when a narrative of lies hiding in plain sight crashed head-on with the ugly, unvarnished truth. *Joe Biden is no more capable of being the president of the United States, than is your toddler or first grader.*

On this night, the biggest lie that they had ever been told to an American electorate came tumbling down and was exposed for all to see. Joe Biden was sick, weak, demented, and incapable of stringing together two coherent sentences without stumbling, freezing, or losing his train of thought.

The thing, *you know the thing*, is that many of us, the honest and fair ones, those paying even a little bit of attention, had already known this to be true. We didn't need fact-checkers to validate what we have seen with our own eyes for years. It was the media, apparently wrapped in their insulated *Trump derangement syndrome* bubble, complete with a layer of agenda, propaganda, and one thick layer of dishonesty, who suddenly discovered on this night that Joe Biden was old, impossible at times to understand, and finally not qualified to be a greeter at WalMart, much less the leader of the free world.

Like *Louie in Casablanca*, who was shocked to find that gambling took place at *Rick's Café Americain*, the establishment and elites of Washington and the media were "shocked, shocked" to see this version of Joe. But were they really? The signs had been there for years. The stumbles. The falls. His uneven nature. His stares into nowhere as he was unable to take the stairs up Air Force One.

Still, those around the president, his advisors, confidants, aides, and friends are the ones most responsible for perpetrating this dangerous charade, one in which the nuclear codes were assigned to this man, who could barely manage a TV remote. But make no mistake - there is one person who stands out, herself not an outstanding person, who is most responsible for this shameless, evil, and unconscionable power grab – "*Dr. Jill Biden.*"

She is at fault for allowing this to happen. She is the guiltiest one of all for allowing this elder abuse to go on daily for years – and all on her watch. And finally, Dr. Jill Biden is guilty of lying to all of us and playing Russian roulette with the well-being, security, and future of Americans in red states and blue states -everywhere from Peoria to Philadelphia. *Hey man, you do know that Jill is a Philly Girl?*

Still, Dr. Jill is not completely at fault for creating this myth of a man built on a foundation of lies. Joe Biden is responsible for the phony, incredibly dishonest, corrupt, and vacant leader that Joe Biden has become. He accomplished much of that by being the inauthentic and shallow human being that he has always been, which has allowed him to thrive in the Washington swamp for 50 years - by being a guy who could take advantage of any good opportunity as long as it was good for Joe.

For years, the plan was clear and simple. *All the President's Men – pardon me, the puppet's men and women, would surround him and protect him from seeing the American people, but most importantly, from being seen by the American people.* Those closest to him continued to pull his strings as a means of protecting him but as part of a bigger master plan and master manipulation.

They had only one purpose now - taking advantage of Joe. Were they slowly walking him out onto a stage in an effort to fool the audience one more time to use him? Or were they finally exposing him on purpose to the public for what he always was all along- an empty Washington suit, now sadly with an empty brain to match? As he shuffled onto the debate stage, faintly ever so faintly, one could hear TAPS being played in the background. And as his strings were pulled harder, and they found it more difficult to move the puppet; still in frustration, they continued to try the levers. After all, this was Showtime, and the show had to go on. The debate, after all, was a go —even if Joe wasn't. And they had already spent a good amount of time prepping their man for this night.

In the lead-up to the debate, Joe's gang leaked how Joe was not only working hard for the American people, but hell, he was working hard to get ready for the debate. The puppet's chief supporter and propagandist – his own wife, Dr. Jill told everyone in America who could stomach sitting through the talk show THE VIEW her views on her man Joey and predicted how things would go on debate night.

"This election is not about age because like -- I mean Donald Trump's going to be, what, 78. And Joe is 81. They're basically the same age,' the first lady said.

'This election is about character. So, you have two choices. You have my husband, Joe, who you all know who has integrity, he's strong, he's steady, he's a leader. He's smart. He's energetic or you have chaos. 'They will turn off the mics so somebody can't ramble or scream at somebody, you know, not that my husband would be the one doing that and so that's already been negotiated.'

'I think the American people deserve a debate because you need to see your choices. You need to see Trump and you need to see the president and you need to see the differences, and my husband -- and you're going to see how smart he is and the experience he has and then you'll see somebody who, like you're saying... can't put a sentence together.' [42]

Dr. Jill's prediction didn't age well. And sadly, neither has Joe.

But you know whose assessment of Biden has aged like a fine wine? Special Counsel Hur's take on President Biden serves as a bell ringing clearly in a wilderness of lies and liars - even if the actual audio recordings of his meeting with the frail Commander in Chief have been hidden from the public.

The special counsel raised Biden's age and memory in explaining why he didn't bring charges.

"We have also considered that, at trial, Mr. Biden would likely present himself to a jury, as he did during our interview of him, as a sympathetic, well-meaning, elderly man with a poor memory," Hur

wrote. *"Mr. Biden's memory also appeared to have significant limitations," Hur wrote in another passage, adding that his conversations with his ghost writer "from 2017 are often painfully slow, with Mr. Biden struggling to remember events and straining at times to read and relay his own notebook entries."*[43]

Still, they prepared. They had no choice. Everything seemed ready, even if their candidate was not, for the earliest-ever presidential debate at the end of June, strangely before either man had even claimed their nomination. The procedures and protocols were in place. A cocktail of medicine was prepared for the man from Delaware. Tons of rest on the schedule so Joe could be on his toes to battle the bully from Queens. It did not matter that the world kept spinning out of control with hot wars, illegal immigrants crashing a border, and inflation continuing to threaten the middle class; there was a debate scheduled, and Joe needed to be ready for it. The world, America and Americans and their problems could wait. The top priority was the debate now. And Joe was going to do it and he needed lots of debate prep. They all knew that while Joe was used to studying, he wasn't always the best student. To counter that, he would have recited answers to questions at his ready. Questions his friends in the press do doubt had already probably provided the fading president. His cause was their cause now, and even if he was a lost cause, pre-debate, they were all in on their guy named Joe –for the one reason that mattered most. He was not TRUMP! And this was all their one and final hope, that the puppet could help them - pull it off for one more night - and for four more years.

Yet deep down, the puppet masters knew what many of us knew for years – and that was that the puppet was old, broken down, and tired. They knew deep down it was over, even if the puppet did not. Yet they put him out there anyway to perform. And that is probably the sickest indictment on a long list of evil actions dictated to the puppet by the puppet masters. They kept putting him out there. Kept abusing him and all of us. And when all of us looked on in horror and at the spectacle. They acted shocked, playing us all for puppets.

Anyone viewing the event will never forget the sad, macabre, and evil scene. And in saying that, while my humanity and faith allow me to feel a little bit sorry for the man named Biden, what emotion I most feel today in America for all Americans is anger.

Anger that they tried it. Anger that they thought they could get away with it – like forever. *And anger at what lengths they would go to stay in power, as they continued to try and get Trump, get Joe and get all of us.*

But make no mistake, as many watched the train wreck that was Joe Biden crash into their living rooms in big towns and small towns all over America, some were seeing the puppet abuse for the first time, while for many others, the scene was a rerun of an old tired show.

And the show was over for Joe Biden and *his chief puppet master, Dr. Jill Biden*, whether they knew it or not.

To say that it was just a bad debate night is to say the Captain of The Titanic veered off track a little bit. Still, some in the complicit media shamelessly continued spinning, trying to make the night about Trump "stretching the truth and telling lies" as a way to cover up for Biden's disastrous night.

As if to show that Biden could not be more off his game, Joe kept pushing a number of times the old "good people on both sides" argument that the elderly Biden used as a motivation to run in the first place. When Joe heard that, he had to run. The fact is, that's not what was heard or said at all. What has come to be known as the *"Charlottesville Lie"* had been debunked by a Trump-hating media that included debate host CNN and noted fact checker – SNOPES. Still, Old Joe pressed on retelling it, even on this night, saying that the reason he ran for president was because of *Charlottesville*. In essence, Joe got into the race based on a lie. Only time would tell if he would leave the race because a bigger one told about him and the American people for years.

And that lie was that Joe Biden was competent, in charge, could be trusted, and possessed the mental faculties to handle the toughest job in the world. Even after the debate, some of his handlers were still spinning in his universe, saying Joe was *"effective from the hours of 10 am to 4pm."*

After that with Joe it is pretty much a crap shoot. Kind of like his performance on debate night. And the trouble with "Joe's part-time competence" is that the bad actors, terrorists, world leaders, and deep state players who want America's harm don't time their mischief on banker's hours when Joe is supposedly at the top of his game.

Make no mistake- that's what this has been all along – a game. A game of lies where they have played on all of us - *We the people*.

And if they want to make it about lies, the biggest one told is the one they tried to pull off by putting *Sleepy, Creepy, Corrupt or Scranton Joe* out there in the first place. This group of puppeteers had been covering up for the failing Adult Living Facility (ALF) bound Biden for years. His whole candidacy and in essence his whole presidency- was built on this giant lie. According to them- *Joe Biden was healthy, competent, energetic, and had no cognitive difficulties.* To use a Biden maxim – That's MALARKEY.

Lies. Lies. And more lies. Sold, packaged, and served to us in the form of a puppet named Joe.

On this night, one other thing became crystal clear and an obvious truth to anyone watching.

There was a clear winner. One man was more capable. One man is not at all capable. One man is a leader. And one man who had to be led off the stage at the end of the night. One man could be president for four more years. And one man who would have trouble staying awake for four more hours.

One man who failed to build America back better. One man with a vision and plan to make America great again. There is no debate as to what we all saw on the debate stage on this night in America.

Two men. One a president. One a puppet.

One unscientific flash poll conducted right after the debate asked people who won the debate. The results were a convincing 67% to 33%, with Trump winning the debate.

That's not shocking. But what is still shocking to many are the 33% who THINK BIDEN WON! Really? The obvious question is, "Who are these people?"

What person in their right mind (right mind being the key phrase), after watching this debate debacle take place in real-time with their own eyes, while witnessing that Biden was not in his right mind —say that he WON?

Who are these people? The 33% or whatever real number this represents – do they still feel this man is capable of holding down the office of the presidency for four plus more years? While we don't know all their names, I know one, an important one, who supposedly has Joe's best interests at heart, even if she doesn't have America's – and that's Dr. Jill Biden.

She should have known better and, in fact, did know better. *Shame on her.*

She must have seen the decline behind the scenes, where the American public was not granted access, this obvious and troubling decline of her man Joe. She is, after all, a doctor. But unlike a great woman who stands behind her man or by his side, she threw him aside for reasons she can only answer in her heart and conscience. She continued to chime the BIG LIES over days, weeks, months, and years - that her guy was fine and that he was "virile, energetic, the smartest one in the room" and able to handle the biggest job in the world, even as he struggled to form coherent sentences. Dr. Jill echoed the talking points of the Biden administration and all those on the payroll paid to protect their investment and job security that was in the hands and faculties of this frail lifetime politician and fading president.

In a moment that will live in infamy, after the debate and at a small public post-debate "rally" and before possibly some of those 33% that feel that Joe Biden did a good job and won the debate, Dr. Jill Biden brought out her show pony and *her favorite ignored and abused patient*, and like the great grade school teacher that she is, showed her Joey off to the rest of the class.

And with no class - she screeched in a way that reminded many Americans of a Clinton named Hillary, and that's hardly ever a good thing. *"Didn't the president do a great job? Yes!"* said Jill Biden to supporters who gathered at the hotel after Joe stepped on stage. After a brief pause, the crowd started chanting, *"Four more years!"* before Jill joined in on the chant.

"Joe you did such a great job," she went on. *"You answered every question, you knew all the facts."* Then she turned to the crowd to ask, *"And what did Trump do?"*

"Lie!" they all shouted in unison.[44]

While how many falsehoods or lies Donald J. Trump or Joe Biden told on the debate stage that night is up for debate, one truth is self-evident.

What is not a lie and just the unvarnished truth is simply this. Much of the *Democrat party, the Biden Administration, Vice-President Kamala Harris, some of our agencies and departments in our own government, judges, big segments of the main street media, much of Academia and Hollywood, some members of the clergy, some of his supposed closest friends and advisors and most atrociously and unforgivably the First Lady Dr. Jill Biden, have been part of the COVER UP and THE BIG LIE, by covering for this man and lying to the American public for years about his abilities to serve the American people.*

And that is an unforgivable act and not one that's up for debate.

Time for a New Script – A New Actor, Candidate and Head Dummy?

They'd written themselves into a corner. Not only could their leading man not lead…but he could not memorize his lines…hell he couldn't even read his lines.

And just as a producer would want to replace an actor who couldn't remember his lines or bring their studio a big box office return …the writing was on the wall, and they, too, would have to reject and replace him before their big movie opened on Election Day all over America.

The early debate? Was it a chance for their leading man to clear one last hurdle and get them over their finish line, or was it an audition for higher-ups to see if their leading man had enough energy and was capable of handling the very important lead role they had handed him?

Their strategy was foolproof, they thought, except for the fact that those financing the big picture- got greedy. They thought they could drag Joe out and have him star in the sequel to *Get Trump*.

Their marketing strategy was to put Joe out there and have him *pull off maybe two acceptable debates*, then hide him as much as possible from the public until *their ELECTION MOVIE* opened. The producers would do a minimum of press to create a mystique about their candidate. And if things didn't go well, they would lie and cheat about the box office numbers (votes) when *Joe Biden II* opened to the public.

But like all sequels except Godfather II, this sequel was destined to fail.

Like a fading silent movie star in the old movie days before talkies, whose careers crashed because their *high pitched or heavily accented voice* didn't quite match up with the persona that they had been presenting to public, anytime this leading man named Joe Biden opened his mouth, those in back offices who controlled the show worried, never knowing what would come out of his mouth. More often than not it was the disjointed voice of a weak old man, who at best mumbled and garbled in some sort of language- often called *Bidenese* to the point of incomprehension to those out there in the dark listening. At worst, a non-sequitur in the league of *"We finally beat Medicare"* or a statement so ripe and ridiculous that you almost felt sorry for the doddering, evil, and corrupt old man who was at least the figurehead in destroying America.

In July of 2024, after the debate... President Biden described himself as the *"first black woman to serve with a black president"* once again twisting his words, his latest gaffe as he scrambled to reassure voters he was still fit to lead. [45]

Still fit to lead or time to get a new lead to finish the movie?

But the sad and the really sick thing about all this post-debate posturing is simply this.

The only reason they wanted to replace Biden is because they know now more than ever - that he can't defeat Donald Trump. No way, no how.

They could care less if all of America is in danger and has been in danger ever since this fading man took the oath years ago, a zombie-like figure who could barely walk and talk yet an individual who was put in charge of our foreign and domestic policies. Any reasonable person, fair person, or simply any person who loved America and his fellow human being – should have been able to see and figure out this picture easily. The movie that they have produced and presented to America has been wrong, evil, and dangerous to everyone, and there is much blame to go around. True, there is much blood, not only on Joe Biden's hands and blood money to divvy up to those who've been pulling the strings on their puppet candidate.

Blood money earned and much blood on their hands for this demonic dereliction of duty.

As the failing man couldn't put two sentences together, thirteen of our finest soldiers died on his watch. Still, this *commander in thief* at the disastrous debate claimed that no soldiers died while he was in charge. Biden in charge? That's a joke. Biden needs a charge. Like a depleted EV Vehicle just trying to make it to the next charging station, the man they were trying to drag across the finish line – was now a reluctant puppet who not only ran out of steam on a hot Georgia debate stage but now he's steamed that his own puppet masters, who gave him the role in the first place, want to cut the strings and replace him with shinier, younger and more saleable puppet.

On this there is no room for debate. The man named Biden is replaceable and always has been. He just never knew it or wanted to acknowledge that in his fleeing moments of cogency.

And now the producers of this movie, knowing that their test previews are revealing a disaster come election and box office day – want to change the lead. *The left now have an urgent wake-up call to change their head dummy before it is too late and for all the wrong reasons.*

Not one of them wanted to replace him as inflation climbed.

Not one of them wanted to replace him as our borders became infested and invaded by illegal aliens who robbed, raped, and killed innocent Americans.

Not one of them wanted to replace him after the disastrous and shameful Afghanistan evacuation that brought back memories of Viet Nam, as 13 of America's finest died and others were shamelessly left behind along with billions of dollars of military equipment for the Taliban.

No one wanted to replace him as the world broke into wars, as bad actors were encouraged to act in various regions, while the commander-in-chief showed weakness by sleeping at the wheel.

None of those were good enough reasons for his supporters, fundraisers, aides, or simply those pulling the strings to pull Joe off the political stage and cease his power. The sick, sinister, and sleazy reason they wanted to rescue power from him now is because - THEY THINK TRUMP WILL WIN IN A LANDSLIDE COME NOVEMBER!

And one of the reasons why they know and believe this is that deep down, they know that Trump, sans the cheating and rigging, already won a landslide victory in 2020 over *Basement Boy Joe*.

Now, all of sudden - they want to replace sleepy, creepy, corrupt, incapable and cognitively challenged Joe. Why now? Why the urgency now?

Well, they need to get the new leading man or woman cast in the role of President to see if they can pull out a big box office vote on ELECTION DAY.

That much is obvious. You don't have to be a Washington or Hollywood insider to figure out that plot point. But who tells him? Who nudges the lead actor, paints the picture, and tells sleepy Joe, "Listen, kid," contrary to Bob Evans of Paramount, "Kid, you're not staying in the picture.

Who? Who gets that job? Well as President Trump would say, it better be someone from central casting. So that's just what they did – they got together in smoke-filled rooms where insiders from both Washington and Hollywood swapped swamp stories. And between cigars and whatever else you could imagine – the decision was made and central casting called.

"Let's get George to do it." "Everyone likes George." "Let George tell Joe."

And just like that, George Clooney was cast in his latest role to tell old Joe that it was over.

It's rich and ironic that one of the great leading men of our time, George Clooney, the Hollywood elite personified, himself a big Biden fundraiser, was the one to come out in big Hollywood headlines and tell Joe that he had lost his part and that the studio that was the swamp was looking for a new leading actor – a new kid and star that could put fannies not in the seats of a movie house but draw them in droves to the voting booths on election day.

"I'm a lifelong Democrat; I make no apologies for that. I'm proud of what my party represents and what it stands for. As part of my participation in the democratic process and in support of my chosen candidate, I have led some of the biggest fund-raisers in my party's history. Barack Obama in 2012. Hillary Clinton in 2016. Joe Biden in 2020. Last month I co-hosted the single largest fund-raiser supporting any Democratic candidate ever, for President Biden's re-election. I say all of this only to express how much I believe in this process and how profound I think this moment is.

I love Joe Biden. As a senator. As a vice president and as president. I consider him a friend, and I believe in him. Believe in his character. Believe in his morals. In the last four years, he's won many of the battles he's faced.

But the one battle he cannot win is the fight against time. None of us can. It's devastating to say it, but the Joe Biden I was with three weeks ago at the fund-raiser was not the Joe "big F-ing deal" Biden of 2010. He wasn't even the Joe Biden of 2020. He was the same man we all witnessed at the debate.

Was he tired? Yes. A cold? Maybe. But our party leaders need to stop telling us that 51 million people didn't see what we just saw. We're all so terrified by the prospect of a second Trump term that we've opted to ignore every warning sign. The George Stephanopoulos interview only reinforced what we saw the week before. As Democrats, we collectively hold our breath or turn down the volume whenever we see the president, whom we respect, walk off Air Force One or walk back to a mic to answer an unscripted question.

Is it fair to point these things out? It has to be. This is about age. Nothing more. But also nothing that can be reversed. We are not going to win in November with this president. On top of that, we won't win the

House, and we're going to lose the Senate. This isn't only my opinion; this is the opinion of every senator and Congress member and governor who I've spoken with in private. Every single one, irrespective of what he or she is saying publicly.

We love to talk about how the Republican Party has ceded all power, and all of the traits that made it so formidable with Ronald Reagan and George H. W. Bush, to a single person who seeks to hold on to the presidency, and yet most of our members of Congress are opting to wait and see if the dam breaks. But the dam has broken. We can put our heads in the sand and pray for a miracle in November, or we can speak the truth."[46]

Well by George, those were some of the sentiments that someone wrote, no doubt for George to act out for the public. That it was just a few weeks before that they had gathered to give Joe all that money to star as president for the sequel – and that they had to help him off the stage is a nice touch of foreshadowing.

But one thing that can never be foreshadowed is the truth. The truth that *"not so old and still handsome George"* talks about. The truth has a way of rearing its ugly, unvarnished head for all to see at the strangest times. In Hollywood, they're called *Happy Accidents*. Happy Accidents, those little unscripted moments that are not in the script that an actor accidentally stumbles upon that often times are better than the words in original screenplay or script. A good director will mine that moment and leave it in the final draft as a moment of authenticity that connects with the audience.

And that happy accident has been revealed now that the script has been changed. The story had a re-write. The old washed-up lifetime politician was given a not-so-subtle hint that his services were no longer needed.

But here is the plot twist and the catch – *Joe don't want to leave*. And *goshdarnit* he's going to do anything he can to hold onto his power. Rumor has it he loves all the ice cream that they serve at the White House 24/7.

Echoing his inner Leonardo DiCaprio, who in Wall Street said *he wasn't leaving*- the former Delaware Senator mumbled something to the effect of – HE'S NOT LEAVING.

Whether Joe stays or goes is yet to be determined. And who they would replace him with is mere conjecture.

There is, however, a couple of truths that can be learned from *Joe Biden II*.

Both Hollywood and Washington don't care about the truth. Nor do they care about you - the people out there in the movie seats struggling to pay your bills and hang on to your pursuit of happiness all across America. They don't care about the movies, either. They care only about two things- both the studio heads and the heads of government.

Money and Power. And whoever gets them the most of it gets the part. Keep that in mind the next time they cast their next political thriller and put out a big cattle call audition for the leading role –that of a head dummy.

Not Being There

Peter Sellers was brilliant playing Chauncey Gardiner in the iconic and brilliant 1979 Hal Ashby film *Being There*.

His interpretation of the hapless and wise gardener who rises to power by offering sound and simple advice to those in power. He is taken into their confidence by spewing metaphoric gems like these. President "Bobby": Mr. Gardner, do you agree with Ben, or do you think that we can stimulate growth through temporary incentives?

[Long pause]

Chance the Gardener: As long as the roots are not severed, all is well. And all will be well in the garden.

President "Bobby": In the garden.

Chance the Gardener: Yes. In the garden, growth has it seasons. First comes spring and summer, but then we have fall and winter. And then we get spring and summer again.

President "Bobby": Spring and summer.

Chance the Gardener: Yes.

President "Bobby": Then fall and winter.

Chance the Gardener: Yes.

Benjamin Rand: I think what our insightful young friend is saying is that we welcome the inevitable seasons of nature, but we're upset by the seasons of our economy.

Chance the Gardener: Yes! There will be growth in the spring!

Benjamin Rand: Hmm!

Chance the Gardener: Hmm!

President "Bobby": Hm. Well, Mr. Gardner, I must admit that is one of the most refreshing and optimistic statements I've heard in a very, very long time.

[Benjamin Rand applauds]

President "Bobby": I admire your good, solid sense. That's precisely what we lack on Capitol Hill.[47]

Good, solid sense. That's exactly what we lack on Capitol Hill and by the man who occupies the White House. But that was a movie and because this isn't a movie and the guy who is playing the resident in the *White House* it's enough to scare the hell out of many us.

Even when he finally decides to get out or someone decides he should get out of the 2024 race, he wants to hang around like some zombie while hanging a "*sword* of *Damocles*" around all our necks. With this Damocles sword, "you live your life under a constant threat which you know about, but can't avoid."

The truth could no longer be avoided. This cat was out of the basement. And he didn't look good. But he hadn't looked good for a long time. Still, now, no one could avoid the fact that the man who was occupying the office was really not there.

There was nothing funny about this film. Nothing poetic. Nothing hopeful in how the story ends. This was no Hollywood classic starring the iconic Peter Sellers. This was the reality at 1600 Pennsylvania Avenue. You didn't have to be there inside the White House or in closed-door meetings to see this man cognitively decaying in front of us.

One thing is certain – this story – The Joe Biden story would not end well. Everyone knew that. But it will most certainly end. And the funny thing is, really more the ironic thing is that when it actually ends – he will not be there at all and hasn't been there for a long time.

IX. Usual Suspects Act Out Their Narrative

Joe Changes his Fading Mind, Not for Hope and Change, but for more Change

What did you know about Joe and When Did You Know it?

Who is the Real Threat to Democracy?

Joe Changes his Fading Mind, Not for Hope and Change, but for more Change

The more they told him that he had to go, the more the career politician named Joe dug in his heels and said NO. And for him, that's quite a feat for a man who can barely stay on his feet. Through a debate debacle, failed relaunches with friendly media personalities who had been looking the other way for years...a stab in the back from his former boss, a Hollywood leading man who demanded they get a new leading man for the party and rats from his Democratic party jumping ship quicker than a hustler jumps an unknowing tourist in the French Quarter - the old man struggling with cognitive difficulties had had enough and decided to call it quits.

Or that's what they wanted you to believe.

But how he did it was a bit peculiar –even for Joe and this highly dysfunctional administration.

In a tweet? Excuse me on X. That didn't sound like Joe. Hell, you could understand Trump teasing his exit –if that man even quit, which is a possibility. You could see Donald teasing in all CAPS. HUGE NEWS FROM THE GREATEST PRESIDENT IN HISTORY!

But Joe? To quit on the social media site. It doesn't jive.

And to do it on National Ice Cream Day? That wasn't the kind of scoop most people saw coming on Joe's favorite holiday and a sleepy Sunday afternoon, as the aging and ailing president was holed up in his home state with yet another bout with COVID-19. Even with all the booster shots he got- Joe was still getting Covid-19. There were two truths and staples you could count on – make that three as long as Joe was "in charge."

1. *He was going to get his ice cream.*
2. *He was going to get Covid-19 again and again.*
3. *He was going to get himself in trouble anytime he tried to put two sentences together.*

If you add the fourth GET—getting Trump- he would probably have to settle for getting Trump out of office with his miraculous campaign strategy that led to gathering all those 81 million votes with the basement strategy.

Now, presumably – the man from Scranton was back in the basement –but this time with a pen in one hand and maybe an ice cream cone in the other, offering this note;

"My Fellow Americans,

Over the past three and a half years, we have made great progress as a Nation.

Today, America has the strongest economy in the world. We've made historic investments in rebuilding our Nation, in lowering prescription drug costs for seniors, and in expanding affordable health care to a record number of Americans. We've provided critically needed care to a million veterans exposed to toxic substances. Passed the first gun safety law in 30 years. Appointed the first African American woman to the Supreme Court. And passed the most significant climate legislation in the history of the world. America has never been better positioned to lead than we are today. I know none of this could have been done without you, the American people. Together, we overcame a once in a century pandemic and the worst economic crisis since the Great Depression. We've protected and preserved our Democracy. And we've revitalized and strengthened our alliances around the world.

It has been the greatest honor of my life to serve as your President. And while it has been my intention to seek reelection, I believe it is in the best interest of my party and the country for me to stand down and to focus solely on fulfilling my duties as President for the remainder of my term.

I will speak to the Nation later this week in more detail about my decision.

For now, let me express my deepest gratitude to all those who have worked so hard to see me reelected. I want to thank Vice President Kamala Harris for being an extraordinary partner in all this work. And let me express my heartfelt appreciation to the American people for the faith and trust you have placed in me.

I believe today what I always have: that there is nothing America can't do — when we do it together. We just have to remember we are the United States of America."

– Joe Biden[48]

The note. Full of boasting from the supposed humble servant, hyperbole, lies, the usual assortment of Biden claims that don't wash, and one final line that was as ironic as it was absurd.

"*...There is nothing America can't do — when we do it together. We just have to remember we are the United States of America.*"

One of the most divisive, incompetent men ever to sit in the Oval Office was reminding us of who we were as Americans. But it is Joe in his feeble, fading, and evil mind that perhaps wrote the note for himself —especially the last line, "*We just have to remember we are the United States of America.*"

For a man who had trouble remembering anything, was he really reminding us of who we were?

Because who we were was not who they said we were, as he shouted, whispered, and signed into policy, actions throughout his tenure that vilified the forgotten men and women in America.

Joe Biden – the career politician, was stepping away from it all now. Not with the gallop of a hero who had done his job well and for the will of the people, but a man limping home unseen as he dips into the ice cream in the basement of his mind.

But why the note now? It caught some of his aides off guard. Was he delivered a Sicilian message of sorts from *one the Capos* in DC- who made him an offer he couldn't refuse? "Joe, either what's left of your brain or your signature will be on this note."

According to some reports old Joe was visited by the head of the Pelosi crime family, none other than *"The Godmother,"* Nancy Pelosi. Allegedly, she ended up all but threatening to rake Biden over the coals if he didn't drop his campaign, the source said.

"Nancy made clear that they could do this the easy way or the hard way," a source told Politico. "It was about to be the hard way." [49]

The hard way. Not only for Joe – but for all of us in the country who have had to suffer through this presidency and watching this man fade away before our eyes all the while the media and those actually running things – have told us how great a shape Joe was in.

Some have said that his resignation signature doesn't match other Biden signatures. But does it really matter? Does anyone think that this guy, who probably doesn't know his name most of the time, is the one signing all those bills and executive orders? Sure, he probably scratched his signature down – as an aide in the shadow pushed it across his desk. But did he really know what he was signing or saying?

But still to sign off here and now in the middle of the afternoon, on a sleepy Sunday, just one week after his presumptive opponent in the upcoming election came within an inch of losing his life to an assassin's bullets. The timing. Not Joe's. Theirs. The handlers. They had to change the narrative.

All that coverage of the man who, after being shot at by an assassin's bullets, raised his hands in defiance. Quite frankly, it was driving them all nuts. They had to kill that Trump story and heroic narrative, but how would they do it with their weak puppet?

There was no defiant gene left in their candidate and the man in the basement. That, too, had been vanquished – the stubborn, power-hungry Biden was softened up and defiant no more – perhaps by an extra scoop of soft serve ice cream with sprinkles. Or perhaps someone brought him the headlines of the day, not a fish wrapped in a newspaper – but the latest polls telling him that there was no path for him to get to the White House. Those stubborn polls –was that the final argument that made Joe write the note?

What had made the stubborn donkey of a man change his failing and stubborn mind? Was it perhaps *His voice* that he finally heard, that of the almighty who convinced Joe to get out of office and abandon the 14.5 million voters who voted for him? Or was it something else? There is an old adage that applies to all matters where corruption runs rampant. And it is this. "Follow the Money." Joe was always good at that.

Experts say that Joe is out now because the donor class in the *vape-filled rooms has* cut off the money. But I beg to differ. True, it is about the money. It always has been about the money for those in power and especially for good old Scranton Joe. The love of money. The Bible warns us. In an often misquoted passage, "Money is not the root of all evil," "It's the Love of Money that's the root of all evil."

And all these *Greedy Government Grifters* love their money. None more than the man from Scranton. Yes, the donor money may have stopped flowing to his campaign, but it will continue to flow to the man named Joe holed up in his basement in Delaware in the form of some golden parachute that probably includes the promise of a bigger Presidential Library and other perks

That's why he signed the note. Because there's time left on the clock, and Joe still needs the money to buy more ice cream he has yet to enjoy.

What did you know about Joe and When Did You Know it?

This is for all of you in the power centers of Washington, and the media centers all over the country. This is for all his handlers who mishandled him for years. This is for all those who worked with, for, and in the service of a man named Joe Biden, the 46th president of the United States.

But mostly, this is for the two main ladies in Joe's life. His wife, Dr. Jill Biden, and Kamala Harris, his work wife and Vice President.

Just one question.

"*What did you know about Joe and When Did You Know it?*"

Today that question is paramount in getting to the truth in what many consider the greatest political cover-up since, well, the mother of all cover-ups – *Watergate*.

Back then, as the whole "Watergate thing" was coming into focus as a presidency was unraveling, they investigated Richard Milhous Nixon, a man that the left was salivating about getting for years. Yet it was someone from Nixon's own party, a loyal and respected Republican, Howard Baker, who uttered his immortal line about Watergate:

"*What did the president know, and when did he know it?*"

A line that would capture the zeitgeist of the time. And a line that still plays today.

It was late June 1973. Senator Baker was the ranking Republican on the special Senate committee convened to investigate the 1972 break-in at the Democratic National Committee headquarters at the Watergate office building.

What Baker sought was an eventual answer to the question we all know to be true now - that President Richard Nixon had conspired to cover up White House involvement in that infamous break-in early after its discovery. But the country did not know that at the time. And Baker didn't either.

And that is where we stand today, sans the formal hearing.

We have all seen the evidence of the decaying man in the White House – fading and falling right in front of our eyes, yet accompanied by a strange and inaccurate voiceover from those who wanted the charade to play on.

"There's nothing wrong with Joe."

"He's fit as a fiddle."

Most of the voices sang from one chorus and one song sheet. Evidence of *Operation Mockingbird*, if there ever was one.

And while many were involved in this particular cover-up, *the lie that Joe Biden was okay*, ironically, it was us, the extremists who made up MAGA who questioned him, who were considered too unhinged and delusional.

There were, however, two lead advocates, advisors, and confidants – who stood out and sang the praises a little louder, stronger, and always out of tune to accompany and counteract the picture we all saw of Joe Biden's condition – as being not only good enough to serve as president, but that he was in fact, some sort of "Superman" behind the scenes.

Joe's First Lady and his VEEP Kamala Harris.

While many were complicit, these two were even more complicit in the cover-up that involved lying to Americans.

Both had ringside seats in the making of policy and history. And both had a responsibility to be straight with the man in the White House and with the American people.

But only one of them was voted into office by the voters and carried the duty of doing what was truly in the best interest of the American people. Sure, there is shame and blame that falls on the slinking shoulders of Dr. Jill for failing to do what was in the best interest of her man —but it is Kamala Harris who was bound by the Constitution not to stick by her man, but by her country.

That is precisely what the 25th Amendment is designed to do: be a tool and remedy to help the country remove a sick president who is not only a harm to himself but, most importantly, a danger to his country.

Yet she not only stood mute when she should have spoken up- she actually lied and was complicit in covering up his shortcomings and cognitive decline.

"I'll tell you, the reality of it is, and I've spent a lot of time with Biden, be it in the Oval Office, in the Situation Room and other places — he is extraordinarily smart. He has the ability to see around the corner in terms of what might be the challenges we face as a nation or globally," Harris told a reporter.[50]

When special counsel Hur chose not to bring criminal charges following a 15-month investigation into Biden's handling of classified documents because the president cooperated. Hur said Biden would be difficult to convict and described him as a *"well-meaning, elderly man with a poor memory"* who was not able to recall to investigators when his son, Beau Biden, died.

Harris rushed to Biden's defense stating, *"The way that the president's demeanor in that report was characterized could not be more wrong on the facts and (is) clearly politically motivated,"* she said. [51]

Politically motivated? That sounds like a good description of Kamala Harris and her aspirations.

Questions to Harris over Biden's mental competency were raised frequently beginning in the fall of 2023 and she often deflected any concerns over his fitness ahead of the election year. *"Let's not get distracted. Let's look at whether we have a president that's actually produced, and followed through on his commitments and especially on long-standing issues that needed to be addressed,"* Harris said. *"Joe Biden has done that. That's the measure of the man. Not what's on his birth certificate in terms of his age." "So this whole issue that they are raising about his age is, again, because they've got nothing to run on,"* Harris said during a one-on-one with Katie Couric during her podcast, *Next Question with Katie Couric*. "*And I just think that we've got to get beyond this, because I think ultimately, what the American people deserve is that their leaders perform by way of solutions and uplifting the condition of their lives.*"

Even after *Biden's Debate Disaster* where the world had not had "*The Emperor has no new clothes*' moment, but instead had a "*The president has a cognitive problem*" for all to see awakening, Harris made excuses attributing his shocking performance to "slow start."

"*Last night, President Joe Biden and Donald Trump had their first debate, and earlier today the president said himself it was not his best performance,*" Harris told voters in Las Vegas after the debate. "*This race will not be decided by one night in June.*" [52]

But this was not about one night in June. An off night. She was right about that. His competency to do the job should not be based on one night in June, but instead on many nights and days in June, and many days over past three plus years in which the president appeared to not be quite up to snuff and able to perform sharply at the most demanding job on the planet. And that's being kind.

A cross-section of the American people had already appeared to make up their minds on the state of the mind and ability of President Biden to run the country.

More than 6 in 10 Americans say President Biden does not have the mental sharpness or physical health to serve effectively, according to a Washington Post-ABC News poll. About a third of Americans (32 percent) say Biden has the mental sharpness to be effective in the White House, while 54 percent say the same of Trump. And one-third (33 percent) say Biden is in good enough physical health for the job; while 64 percent say that about Trump, the leading Republican candidate. About 7 in 10 independents say Biden lacks the mental sharpness and physical health to serve effectively, and about 1 in 5 Democrats say the same. The vast majority of Republicans (94 percent) say Biden lacks the mental sharpness to be president. [53]

Mental sharpness to be President?

That statement, in regards to that being posed in the same sentence with Joe Biden is absurd.

To me, Joe Biden never had the mental sharpness to be president. Not in the 1980s when he ran. Not when he was Obama's VP and then when he was passed over in 2016 by his boss. And certainly not when he ran last time from the basement during the 2020 Election. Why no early debate that year? We all know the answers and we know what we see and have seen under this regime.

And there is only one truth about this lying administration, and the man propped up to lead it. Joe Biden was and always has been a political creature and candidate who lacked the essential mental sharpness to run this country. Now, sadly, it's only worsened by some major cognitive decline, and that's something that most everyone can plainly see and something most everyone can say and admit to out loud. The charade can stop. The alarm bells have been rung. Not because we should *ALL* be questioning his fitness to work for us and fulfill his duties as President, but because he can't in no way beat Donald Trump in an election taking place in the fall of 2024.

What did I know about Joe and when did I know it?

My answer. Simple. Easy. Like most honest Americans who've had their eyes open. Mine were opened long ago by a man named Joe Biden. What I know now, I knew way back then before he ran last time. This Joe was not up to the job. No way. No how. Not ever. How do I know for sure? I ran into a guy named Corn Pop, and he told me all about Joe.

"No joke man, you know…the thing…those things that prove to be self-evident…"

Who is the Real Threat to Democracy?

They shout it so often now and put it in a variety of fonts on all their publications and at the top of headlines on their news shows. Gone to the B-block were the headlines that Trump was worse than Hitler, Putin's pal, a racist, misogynist, and a white supremacist. Hell, even the *fake felon branding* could be abandoned to the silver medal position of the left's hyperbole to Get Trump. They had something juicer. More inflammatory. Something that could be crystalized in one succinct hateful and dangerous talking point, or one bullet point in a politician's speech or news anchor's story – and hell, even be packed into a few actual real bullets that were shot in the direction of the former president on a warm July afternoon at a Trump rally.

"Trump is a threat to Democracy."

He was dangerous. And had to be stopped at all costs because he was a danger to us all.

And on one Saturday afternoon, at least one loner and delusional young man took it upon himself to counter this *real threat to Democracy* that everyone in the press was raging about by shooting eight rounds into the threat's direction and at the head of one Donald J. Trump.

That the political heat had been turned up for so long, as before Trump ran for the first time in 2016, and had never been toned down was troubling. But it did not bother those on the left who made a mountain out of a molehill of every mean Trump tweet. That was never their issue with him. They hated him because they feared him not for what he would do not to our democracy, correctly stated, our Constitutional Republic; they feared, hated, and had to get him for what he had threatened to do to their hold on power.

That's why they always concocted the conspiracy theories and pushed the impeachments and indictments, none of which would have been brought up had he decided not to run. About Trump, they knew this deep in their deep-state hearts if they still had hearts. Trump was not a threat to democracy; he was a threat to them, and they were the actual embodiment of the only real threat to democracy.

The projectionists. They were good at it – spinning this narrative of *Trump being a Threat to Democracy*. And from their projectionist booth, they projected all the dangers of Trump – living and breathing in the body – the actions that they had acted on over the last nine years.

From fake Russian dossiers to get Trump to rigging the primary election in 2016 to Get Bernie and install Hillary as the candidate. Rinse and repeat. They installed a mummified man named Biden as a moderate for the primary of 2020, once again *Getting Bernie* because he was too much a socialist, and America was not yet ready for a full-fledged socialist who presented so. Before the presidential election of 2020, they killed the Hunter Biden Laptop story in the press, providing the kind of election interference that was powerful and cheating done in such a way that even as you were cheating, you could feel good about it because you were doing something noble to combat the threat that Donald Trump was – this Orange threat to our Red, White, and Blue Democracy.

As the presidential election season rolled on, a plan was already in place to deal with their Joe problem. An early debate with Joe and Donald in June 2024 would allow a lot of America to get the picture that many of us were sure we had seen of this man who could barely manage the task of getting off a simple stage.

This was bigger than all that. It was about Joe getting off the political stage. It had to be done, not because it was dangerous that he had ruined the American economy, or that millions of illegal aliens were invading our border, or that he misled a disastrous evacuation from Afghanistan where 13 of our finest soldiers were slaughtered on his watch; or finally, because Joe who could barely tell you what a football was, yet he was now in this state and mind and still handling the nuclear football. It wasn't because of all those dangers to our democracy that Joe had to go – it was because of something handsome leading man named George from Hollywood, a crafty politician named Barack, and an evil witch named Nancy had known all along about this rotting man. There was an expiration date on this melon of a man, and it was already well beyond the expiration date for Joe to be in power.

And that other thing – those who so cared for democracy and for *keeping the Republic* as Franklin had warned, were now focused on the real threat to democracy in the person of Donald Trump-and could barely see themselves in the mirrorless vape-filled rooms as they busily averted and sidestepped the people who had voted for him. In their effort to save democracy, they had become the thing they feared or at least said they feared. They had become a threat to Democracy.

That they never allowed anyone to run in the primary and gave people a choice; they shrugged their shoulders and said what they always said about we the people, regardless of party affiliation. *"We know better than the people."* And some of them would think it, if not say it off the record and in quiet corners of the swamp. *"The people are the real threat to Democracy."*

And in keeping with their earlier narrative chock full of rigged primaries and hand-selecting puppets to serve who served them and not the people, the order was made.

Joe had to go. It could be done the easy way or the hard way – but in some way, he had to step aside.

That over 14 million voted for Joe Biden in the primary was a non-factor. Some claimed that these folks were disenfranchised voters who meant little to those who were concerned with protecting the republic and the real threat to democracy. And not only that, Trump's nearly 75 million voters got over it the last time. Get over it. They seemed to be saying. We have a country to save. But from who and whom?

As they were getting ready to undemocratically replace their guy because he *couldn't beat the guy who was a threat to democracy*, the irony was lost on them. Yet their story was not lost on those paying attention as the script flipped in the last scene, and they became that thing they warned us about, a real threat to democracy.

X. Orwellian Ministry of Lies

Deep Fakes or Cheap Fakes? Made up Names on How They want us to see Biden

FOX now a different Animal - Used to get Trump Now it wants to *GET TRUMP*

Elite Three Stooges Gather for Their Close-Up as America Crumbles in the Big Picture

Many Years from Now, Many Climate Fear Mongers Still Living Past Their Bleak Predictions

A Place and Time Stranger than fiction Destined to Doom US All

Seeking the TRUTH- Not a Ministry of Truth

Deep Fakes or Cheap Fakes? Made up Names on How They want us to see Biden

The press secretary, with a propensity for leading confusing, confrontational, and content-lacking press conferences, smugly released her new phrases as if she had just discovered gold and an answer as to what was ailing her boss's campaign.

"Deep fakes." "Cheap fakes."

That was the rationale and cause behind all those gaffe-laden, stumbling, bumbling, and incoherent moments that we thought we had all witnessed with our own eyes, of President Biden. Those moments flashed on the screen of well, Joe just being Joe.

We were now being told that the images being beamed to us on our TVs and Smart phones were being manipulated. That the man, who looked shaky at best, was actually a steady hand with a quick, gifted wit and the agility and energy of an Olympic athlete. And that the pictures that we were seeing- well, we really hadn't seen them after all. They were all made up by forces who were designed to *get Biden.*

The three time fall up the stair on the way up to Air Force One. That's hard to do.

The fall off the leisurely bike ride on one of his what seems like 100 vacations.

The fall on the stage at the Air Force commencement in Colorado. [54]

The Mangling of the English language as to not be able to get two sentences together without a gaffe or uncomfortable long pause.

Creating his own words, in perhaps his own tongue that we can call "BIDENESE" because no one knows what the hell he's saying on a great number of occasions.

His inability to exit a stage without causing a scene or giving the impression he needs directions.

General look of confusion and blank expression that he wears constantly on his face.

Wavering, weak and wobbly walks to and from any event that he attends with constant need of handlers who must see to it that JOE doesn't get lost.

Fragile, uneven, unclear and with a lack of focus. An old man fading away before our eyes and a man who does not build any sincere confidence in any person, organization, people, military or country that he is supposed to be leading.

We have all seen this version of Joe Biden. Actually, it's a version that's been around for a while.

But the press secretary, herself a recipient of the DEI movement, is someone who has no business being in charge of guiding a press conference. With that, she shares common ground with her boss, Joe, who also has no business being put in the position of dealing with America and America's business.

But that's not what Press Secretary Karine Jean-Pierre thinks or at least wants us to believe.

Pay no attention to your lying eyes. These images of her boss are *made up, contrived, and the creation of right-leaning opposition research types who not only want to make the President look bad*, they want him to look hapless and helpless.

When asked about a recent series of videos, which stemmed from Biden's trip to France, his visit to Italy last week, and his stop at a fundraiser, that purportedly show Biden being guided off stage or standing motionless, Jean-Pierre pushed back and said they were being spread in "bad faith" as she referenced a *Washington Post* article that called the footage "cheap fake" videos.

"Ironically several cheap fakes actually attack the president for thanking troops - that is what they are attacking the president for. Both in Normandy this happened and again in Italy. I think it tells you everything that we need to know about how desperate Republicans are here. And instead of talking about the president's performance in office, and what I mean by that is his legislative wins, what he's been able to do for the American people across the country, we're seeing these deep fakes, these manipulated videos. And it is, again, done in bad faith," Jean-Pierre said.

Charlie Kirk, founder and president of conservative organization Turning Point USA, slammed the remarks as he wrote on X, *"Unbelievable!! Karine Jean-Pierre is blaming DEEP FAKES for all of the videos going around exposing how old, feeble, and senile Joe Biden looks anytime he steps out into public. This sums up the White House comms strategy in one video: Don't believe your lying eyes!"*

X user and Republican Brittany (@bccover) wrote, *"Definition of a cheap fake: is an AV manipulation created with cheaper, more accessible software (or, none at all). Cheap fakes can be rendered through Photoshop, lookalikes, re-contextualizing footage, speeding, or slowing....So far, the WH comms team has gotten away with writing off these videos that make Biden's decline very obvious as "cheap fakes". The question is, will they get away with using that excuse for another 4.5 months?"*

MAGA-based talk show *The Nunn Report* wrote on X, "WTF is a 'cheap fake'? Misinformation Disinformation- The lying has not yet begun." In an emailed statement to *Newsweek*, Jean-Pierre said, *"They are fakes—cheap fakes. That is the point."* [55]

And the point is clear. They want to blur the line between truth and lies and have those of us who have watched this career politician bumble his way into the top job and head puppet in chief precisely because of his propensity to commit to gaffes early and often. And for years they wrote it off as Joe being Joe. But Obama knows just how badly Joe can F up something even with him pulling the strings. So the new strategy is to cast doubt upon all those incidents starring Joe in a series of bloopers. The thing is – they forget that we have been privy to this guy's antics, missteps, and plain lies for many years. We've seen it and him fail and fall for years.

And it's not a case of age or years, yet that's another line they want to blur as they try to portray these two men as equals cognitively. They are not. Not even close. Can you ever imagine Biden doing one rally a week, let alone two or three in a day? In regards to press conferences – Joe simply doesn't give them. And when he does, they are filled with softball questions from a friendly pro-Biden press who have his back. Hell, some believe, more often than not, that the questions are rehearsed and who Biden will call on is predetermined and assigned. With Trump, who gives and gives many interviews to a press hostile to him, think little Georgie Stephanopoulos, who practically sat on Trump's lap over a thirty-hour access period, the questions are free to fly in the spirit of The First

Amendment. Can you imagine Biden sitting there day after day after day with a hostile press and Dr. Fauci disputing the effectiveness of drugs that could have helped save countless lives? Can you imagine that? Hell no, Joe. Because it's impossible to compare the two men.

Their mere four years of age difference is not the story, not even a small part of the story. Regarding mental fitness and the ability to handle the job and put in the time that it requires- be honest and look at the two men.

Comb through all the videos you want. All the deep fakes and cheap fakes and all those MAGA Rallies filled with what the press will tell you are white supremacists and racists. Watch the plethora of gaffes, missteps, and preponderance of falls and fails by sleepy Joe. Then watch the Donald catch a few of his mistakes and even outright embellishments of crowd size or two or three. And as you watch him ask yourself a couple questions.

Which of these two men is capable of handling the pressure of this job for four more years?

Who do you want to handle the economy?

Who do you trust to straighten out the immigration disaster that sits at our southern border?

Who will make you feel safer as you walk down any street of America?

Who can handle the world stage and conflicts erupting globally with China, Russia, Iran, North Korea and the Middles East to mention a few - and who has trouble finding their way off a small stage?

Those are real questions that need real consideration and real answers.

There is nothing that's a *cheap fake* or *deep fake* about them.

And no video is necessary to understand what's going on and how chaotic the world is today.

You get the picture. We all do. But sadly, one candidate doesn't even know that the camera has been focused on him all along, and we've seen everything that he's failed to do.

FOX now a different Animal - Used to get Trump Now it wants to *GET TRUMP*

Rush Limbaugh used to say *"that the only one that could separate Donald Trump from his supporters was, in fact, Donald Trump."* The legendary radio talk show's rationale was simple regarding the media's power to accomplish that deed, stating, *"The media can't take down Donald Trump because the media didn't make Donald Trump."* Sure, Trump, forever the master of everything media, used the media to take full advantage of getting "free" coverage of his rallies and stump speeches. But make no mistake – Trump made Trump. From the ground up and from a ground swell of support from all across America. The media were merely a tool he used to sell his ideas and policies while marketing himself to the public. They did not make him. In fact, the truth is more likely – He made them all bigger, more popular, and at times more powerful. And that goes for all or most of the media- including Fox News.

Back then, Fox News did, in fact, GET TRUMP in the way that his supporters got him. They understood his mission and were part of the movement to transform America and try to make it great again. Somewhere along Trump's political odyssey, Fox News shifted their narrative in the coverage of the man who helped them climb to the mountaintop of conservative media in America. The change happened gradually but obviously, and in time, Fox had become *just another media outlet that wanted to Get Trump*. Really no different from CNN or MSNBC.

And as the suits at Fox flipped their script, some of these geniuses actually were surprised that the folks in the heartland –who constituted the majority of the Trump movement were noticing this shift and that they were now inclined to flip the channels.

At first, it started in whispers near the grill at backyard barbecues, from red ball cap-wearing guys with beer bellies asking their Bud-Light drinking buddies if they wanted their burgers medium rare, and then in not-so-hushed tones, *"What the heck is up with Fox?"*

Then it spread to hockey moms who were picking up their kids at an early practice, who asked fellow moms in hushed tones: *"Something's going on with Fox. It's changing."*

When did Fox News change?

Many will say it started on Election Night 2020, with the premature calling of Arizona from the decision desk, when with less than 1% of the vote, the decision team was confident enough to call the consistently Red state of Arizona Blue and for Biden in prime time, while not calling the key battleground and rich electoral prize of Florida for Trump —even though he held insurmountable leads throughout the night.

Then it hit me and many of us who got Trump and who once got Fox. It was part of the plan. Part of their storytelling, talking points, and foreshadowing are set up by a shift starting at the head of their media empire.

Fox News had changed. It's a different animal now.

It started when O'Reilly left, then Megan Kelly, but it really changed for the worse when Tucker Carlson left the network or was forced to leave.

When Tucker left Fox News, it was a shot that they have yet to recover from and possibly never will. Oh sure, there are still good people there. You know who they are. And they're all doing their best as soldiers to balance the news in a mainstream media that overwhelmingly favors the left. Some soldiers for the conservative or common sense agenda that so many in America yearn to return to save the country and our collective sanity are there, like Hannity, a cheerleader for all things Trump. And there is still the scholarly Mark Levine. The loyal Jesse. And Gutfeld. Laura too. The Judge. Still many, too many have shaded their support and played against type and into the hands of the Dems by abandoning and even getting or going after Trump, sometimes more times than not. And we know where that comes from, the boardroom where the power players have shifted to a newer, younger and more progressive version of itself, and where Paul Ryan sits on the board.

And that's why – the real big reason why the purity of the conservative Fox has been deluded with another animal, a

RINO named Paul Ryan. It is bad breeding that has led to less robust ratings while contributing to the ascension of other more conservative Trump-backing networks like NEWSMAX, who get Trump and don't want to get Trump.

Elite Three Stooges Gather for Their Close-Up as America Crumbles in the Big Picture

They sit there so smugly. Two ex-presidents and hopefully soon another ex-president posing and puffing up their plumes as elite donors take portraits and selfies so self-absorbed with themselves that they fail to see the real picture in America, that they are largely responsible for setting up.

Migrants crash over borders, and the lawless kill innocents on our streets in towns and cities all over America. *"Just one more. Get in closer. Smile. Cheese."*

The photographer barking instructions appealing to the vanity of those in this exclusive picture.

But fret not; this is a picture for the few, the very proud, no, not the Marines, but the obscene.

All you need to take a picture with former Presidents Clinton, Obama, and the current President Biden is the ability to fork over $500,000 at this Democrat fundraiser.

Yes, to get a shot with "Joe, Berry, and Billy," you just need a lot of green. Not sure this is the green new deal that Bernie and AOC have been obsessing over, but that's a lot of bread any way you slice it.

Me, I'd rather have a shot with the original *Three Stooges, Moe, Larry and Curly*.

The $500,000 fee is something that the former president could still afford even with all the unjust indictments and appeals draining the Donald's wallet. But that is a picture that the President named Trump would never pose for and one that deep in his soul must make him and anyone with any decency sick to their stomach.

On the same day that Joe, Berry and Billy posed, a man named Trump visited a funeral for a fallen cop in New York, the city that he loves. He didn't pose. He just showed up to offer his support and sympathies while displaying some of that empathy that Joe Biden was supposed to have in spades.

Once again, this wonderful tale of two citizens and Presidents displays the difference between the Washington insider and lifetime politician and the populist outsider businessman turned public servant. The one named Joe Biden went to Washington as a relatively poor man and, after a lifetime in politics, made himself a millionaire, no matter when he left the nation's capital. The other man named Donald J. Trump, went to Washington as a billionaire and left after one term much less wealthy.

As the fiery former president Harry Truman, known for speaking his mind once said, "Show me a man that gets rich by being a politician, and I'll show you a crook." [56]

Yes, the man from Independence, Missouri, who was his own firebrand in the way that Trump is today, had a way with words and a way of cutting through the clutter in Washington. There's no doubt that his cutting words would elicit some pushback from today's press, and one can only wonder what the heck they would say if Donald Trump made that same statement today.

They'd probably sue him and give Harry some hell.

Or at least try to get him indicted for attacking the credibility of all those poor Washington insiders who always have their hands out looking for some funds.

Many Years from Now, Many Climate Fear Mongers Still Living Past Their Bleak Predictions

Those on the left *love the word existential*. It's a fancy word. When I googled it this is what I got. *"Grounded in existence or the experience of existence; empirical."* On the same search, it is referred to as an adjective in the following example: relating to existence – *"the climate crisis is an existential threat to the world."*

And there you have it. The existential threat of a hyperbolic definition creates fear in the masses when used in the hands of those with their own agenda. Many politicians have used it as a rallying cry to scare the population and initiate radical green policies. And of course they use it to divide a nation on yet another topic. When color of skin, class status, religious beliefs or ethnicity won't work at dividing us further into the divided states of America –those in power tweak their *Green New Deal* to benefit themselves while hurting their neighbors around the planet.

No one was better at profiting from such nonsensical rhetoric than Al Gore. Al Gore in producing his film ***An Inconvenient Truth in 2006,*** won an Oscar for best documentary film while being credited for educating people about global warming, reenergizing the environmental movement while grossing nearly 50 million dollars. [57]

But that was only the tip of the iceberg- pun intended. For Al Gore, warning the world that it is on the brink of disaster has been lucrative for him. How lucrative? A lot of greenbacks for Al Gore, backing all things green and anything to do with the Green New Deal. It is believed that Al Gore has made $330m with climate alarmism. After losing to George W. Bush in 2000 he set up a green investment firm now worth $36BN that pays him $2 million m a month... as he warns about 'rain bombs' and 'boiling oceans. Gore has made hundreds of millions through his climate awareness.

Yes, indeed, warning the world that it is on the brink of disaster has been lucrative for Al Gore. He proudly said of his role as a figurehead at the fund when it launched, 'I'm not a stock picker.' Yet it is obvious he has a large stake in all those green profits.

The firm owns millions of shares in companies such as Amazon, Microsoft, Google's parent Alphabet, finance giant Charles Schwab and tractor king John Deere.

While his generated controversy over the years, with outrage that it was shown to school students in the US and UK and Gore's Democratic Party ties were also criticized for politicizing climate issues, the bottom line for Gore has been fat, black, and green with dollars rolling in no matter what the weather. For Al Gore, the climate has always been good for making money by lecturing the world on how humanity was losing the war against climate change.

An alarmist extraordinaire, Gore told the World Economic Forum in 2020: *"This is Thermopylae. This is Agincourt. This is Dunkirk. This is the Battle of the Bulge. This is 9/11. We have to rise to the occasion."* Rising to the occasion for Gore usually means upping his speaking fees to offset his multiple residences, properties, and lifestyle that accompany his green lifestyle.

It did not stop him from being bold as predictions go. Back in 2006, when he was promoting his Oscar-winning documentary, *An Inconvenient Truth* — Gore declared that unless we took "drastic measures" to reduce greenhouse gasses, the world would reach a "point of no return" in a mere ten years. Back then, he called it a "true planetary emergency." Well, ten years passed now it's been 18 years. We're still here, and the climate activists have postponed the apocalypse. Again."

One activist who apparently got the memo is a congresswoman and former bartender AOC, who still parrots the same existential fury that Al Gore does but hasn't yet figured out how to cash in with a big tip for pushing the Green narrative.

Still she tries to create a sense of urgency and fear as to – you guessed it, how much time we all have left if we ignore the greatest existential threat of our lifetime?

"Millennials and people, you know, Gen Z and all these folks that will come after us are looking up, and we're like: 'The world is gonna end in 12 years if we don't address climate change, and your biggest issue is how are we gonna pay for it?'" Ocasio-Cortez asked Coates.

For the young congresswoman from New York, her words in 2019 leave her until around 2031 to figure everything out so she'll be able to deal with the existential threat of Climate Change.

But we shouldn't worry about it too much. It's been reported that should the waters start to rise, the Obamas have extended an open invitation to AOC to vacation at their Martha's Vineyard beachfront home if things get really bad.

But worry not, that day will never come. And one can easily imagine AOC not as a young congresswoman but as an older seasoned political creature still thriving and, on a sunny day into the future, possibly in her 50th year in Congress, warning anyone who will still listen to her about the dangers of climate change to a whole new generation of Americans.

That's the one inconvenient truth. These people who are in charge and are warning us and profiting from trying to scare the shit out of all us have got to go.

It's time for term limits, audits, and investigations into these fear-mongers who represent, to most Americans, the greatest existential threat to us all.

A Place and Time Stranger than fiction Destined to Doom US All

We have come to the end or are nearing the end of a place that once stood for *life, liberty and the pursuit of happiness* in this idea and experiment called America.

When leaders are more concerned with what they call those who enter the land illegally than the murderous act that they commit once they crash our borders-less boundaries, then we are all doomed. And sadly that's exactly where we are in America today.

Standing on a precipice, and two sides of an issue, a metaphor for a place and people representing a lack of vision and policy that threatens to topple us all.

Whatever you think about walls really doesn't really matter.

We are beyond that now.

Where at one time, almost everybody in the Washington body politic thought the same way about those who entered this country illegally. It didn't matter if you were the bluest Democrat Senator –someone like New York's Schumer or the Turtle from the red state of Kentucky – you felt pretty much the same way about those who entered our country illegally. It was wrong and there was a right way to step foot on the land of the free and the home of the brave.

Feeling similar were all the recent presidents *Clinton, Bush, Obama and Trump* –who all saw the issue of border security and immigration pretty much the same way.

In 2022, Bill Clinton echoed sentiments he made while he served as a two term president, telling CNN's Fareed Zakaria, *"... there is a limit to how many migrants any society can take without severe disruption and assistance and our system is based much more on an assumption that things would be more normal."* [58]

And surely judging by his state of the union address in 1995, regarding illegal aliens entering our country, Clinton could not have been clearer on what the costs were to America, saying, *"All Americans ... are rightly disturbed by the large numbers of illegal aliens entering our country. The jobs they hold might otherwise be held by citizens or legal immigrants. The public service they use impose burdens on our taxpayers."* [59]

In an Address to the Nation on Immigration Reform, on May 15, 2006, George W. Bush said, *"We're a nation of laws, and we must enforce our laws. We're also a nation of immigrants, and we must uphold that tradition, which has strengthened our country in so many ways. These are not contradictory goals. America can be a lawful society and a welcoming society at the same time. We will fix the problems created by illegal immigration, and we will deliver a system that is secure, orderly, and fair. So I support comprehensive immigration reform that will accomplish five clear objectives.*[60]

Sadly, while ambitious and well thought out, those five objectives were never executed fully with the result being the immigration issue was kicked further down the road and onto another administration's to do or not to do list. Perhaps the list was too big or got lost in all that had to be done, but Obama's eight years in office, left behind a mixed legacy on immigration tainted political impasse and half-fulfilled promises. Congress did not pass comprehensive immigration during Obama's administration; a bipartisan Senate plan stalled in the House. But Obama broke new ground in creating DACA, which gave more than 800,000 young undocumented immigrants known as DREAMERS a lifeline, with temporary work permits and protection from deportation. At the same time, more immigrants were forcibly removed from the United States under Obama than any other president. More than 2.8 million undocumented immigrants have been deported over the last eight years. [61]

During his administration Trump fulfilled much of his promise to build hundreds of miles of the wall at the southern border, while implementing the *"Remain in Mexico"* program that curbed illegal immigration into the United States.

In campaigning for re-election in 2024, Donald Trump will terminate Biden/ Harris open border policies on his first day back in office, restoring the full set of his first term's strong border policies including ending "catch and release."

Between the beginning of the Biden presidency in January 2021 and the end of September 2023, the Border Patrol released around 3.3 million illegal border crossers into the country. And that number would have been much larger if millions of illegal crossers had not been expelled pursuant to the Title 42 pandemic order.[62]

One can only guess at the number of Illegal aliens given red carpet treatment over the Biden/Harris years who cruised into America and over its invisible border. Is it 10 Million? 15 Million? 20 Million?

And at this point does it really matter? What does matter is recognizing the motivation, make that the motive or plan of an administration and a policy that obviously was designed and built to do one thing. Create chaos by ALLOWING Illegal Aliens to INVADE America – as if they owned the place. And in many ways they already do. These illegal aliens are welcomed with open arms, debit cards, plush hotels and a ticket into the American dream, all for jumping the line. And as they enter in America by breaking the law as their first act on the road to being an American citizen, they succeed at accomplishing something that the DEMS shout Donald Trump can never be - and that's *above the law*.

As these true outlaws and illegal aliens make their way into America, *unleashing a planned chaos*, one look no further than the 46th President of the United States named Biden and the forces behind him that have forced this horrid and dangerous policy on all of us.

When Joe Biden ran for President, he said that if he were elected president, migrants should *"immediately surge to the border."* The migrants took him up on it. *"What I would do as president is several more things,"* Biden said at the first Democratic primary debate for the 2020 election. "*I would in fact make sure that there is… We immediately surge to the border, all those people who are seeking asylum.*"63

With the invite, came the surge and a planned catastrophe that could have been predicted. But this irresponsible and tragic outcome, that is the invasion of millions of illegals at our southern border is not by accident or because someone left fireworks and matches with unattended children. This is intentional.

A formal invitation from the bumbler in office inviting all those to America as if it were a party. The thing, you know the thing, it was not a birthday party but a recruiting tool and welcome to the neighborhood party courtesy of the Democrat Party – Kind of Party.

And this party and those attending are for the most part not young children. Many of those, sadly disappear into the darkness of child trafficking. Those breaking into America for the most part are men, younger men from all over the world – from China to Iraq and from Mexico to South America. All recruited to be in time, good democrats and loyal Democrat voters. But first as soldiers of this regime – their first job is creating chaos at the border and eventually in their new homeland.

Many of these "asylum seekers" have records, are dangerous criminals, and are the dregs of society in the countries that they are fleeing. And for some, their second act of breaking the law on American soil is committing a violent crime like robbery, rape, or murder.

The family and friends of Laken Riley got an up close and personal look at the results of Joe Biden's immigration policy. Riley, a 22-year-old nursing student, was killed by Jose Ibarra while she was out for a jog on Feb. 22, 2024. Jose Ibarra, a man who never should have been allowed into the United States in the first place and most likely would have never made it into America to take this innocent life had President Trump's immigration policies not been overturned by Joe Biden. The tragic and preventable slaying is a direct result of a chaotic and feckless Biden-Harris border policy.

In March 2024, former President Donald Trump met with the family of Laken Riley backstage before speaking at a rally in Georgia on Saturday. *"I met her beautiful mother and family backstage,"* Trump told the crowd in Rome. "*They said she was like the best. She was always the best to us. They admit that she was the best, and she was the first in her class. She was going to be the best nurse. She was the best nursing student. She was always the best. She was the brightest light in every room, they told me."* He added, *"She was the whole world to her parents and to her sister and just to the whole family."*[64]

A whole world turned upside down. The tragic loss of one special life and a bright light in our world. All at the hands of an evil act an evil actor and an evil policy that made this tragedy possible.

And the thing, *you know the thing*, that Joe Biden was most concerned with as he made his hopefully last state of the union address in 2024, while butchering the name of the Laken Riley with blood on his hands. He was concerned about all the pushback that he got for calling the person who murdered Laken Riley, *an illegal alien*.

Not so concerned with the crime. Or the death of an innocent young American woman and future great nurse. Old Joe got all concerned when the press questioned him on calling this monster who killed the best and brightest amongst us – an ILLEGAL ALIEN.

President Biden expressed regret for using the word "illegal" to describe an undocumented immigrant who has been charged in the killing of a 22-year-old nursing student in Georgia, agreeing with his progressive critics that it was an inappropriate term.

Mr. Biden used the word during an unscripted colloquy with Republicans during his State of the Union address… and then came under fire from immigration supporters who consider the term dehumanizing. *"I shouldn't have used 'illegal,' it's 'undocumented,'"* Mr. Biden said on Saturday interview with Jonathan Capehart from MSNBC. "*And look, when I spoke about the difference between Trump and me, one of the things I talked about in the border was his, the way he talks about 'vermin,' the way he talks about these people 'polluting the blood,' "* he said, adding, *"I talked about what I'm not going to do. What I won't do. I'm not going to treat any, any, any of these people with disrespect."*[65]

Respect. And Disrespect. When the resident who occupies the White House is more concerned with what he calls the murderer than the act of murder, then we are all in a heap of trouble. The word police have entered Joe's brain, what's left of it anyway, and the narrative that lives there continues to confirm the greatness of George Orwell's writing, further validating him as a hauntingly great predictor of things to come in the future, showing just how far the authoritarian state will go to mind control you and rewrite history.

Trump, as he usually does had his own clear and concise take on the whole matter.

"Joe Biden went on television and apologized for calling Laken's murderer an illegal," he said to loud jeers and boos. *"Biden should be apologizing for apologizing to this killer."*[66]

Still, with apologies to radio legend Paul Harvey, this is not the end of the story, or the rest of the story, only a part of the story that qualifies as being so sick, unjust, evil, and demented that it is hard to believe it is true.

But true it is.

As it turns out Homeland Security had released the illegal immigrant accused of killing Laken Riley into the U.S. *because it lacked the detention space*, according to his confidential immigration file. Sen. Josh Hawley, Missouri Republican, read key parts of the file into the record at a Senate hearing. The accused murderer and illegal alien was released under Homeland *Security Secretary Alejandro Mayorkas 'power of parole*, which is supposed to be used in limited cases and only when there is an *urgent humanitarian need or a significant benefit to the public*.

Benefit to the public? It's hard to comprehend how any of this can be portrayed to be a benefit to the American public and American people. But in Biden's America, the profane and unthinkable is not only possible but probable.

In the department of *truth is not only stranger than fiction but definitely sicker* than fiction, the smoking gun of how we got here to this upside down place and time at the border to view the immigration mess, must be traced to the language used and the tone set by those in power,

A time when the Biden administration ordered U.S. immigration enforcement agencies to stop using terms such as *"alien," "illegal alien"* and *"assimilation"* when referring to immigrants in the United States, a rebuke of terms widely used under the Trump administration.

Changes detailed in *1984ish memos* sent to department heads at Immigration and Customs Enforcement and Customs and Border Protection, the nation's chief enforcers of federal immigration laws, part of an ongoing effort to reverse President Donald Trump's hardline policies and advance President Biden's efforts to build a more "humane" immigration system.

Among the changes: "Alien" will become "noncitizen or migrant," "illegal" will become "undocumented," and "assimilation" will change to "integration."

The memos sent a clear signal to a pair of law enforcement agencies — and their associated labor unions, which endorsed Trump's presidential candidacy — that under the Biden administration, their approach must change. *"As the nation's premier law enforcement agency, we set a tone and example for our country and partners across the world,"* Troy Miller, CBP's top official, said in his memo. *"We enforce our nation's laws while also maintaining the dignity of every individual with whom we interact. The words we use matter and will serve to further confer that dignity to those in our custody."*

House Minority Leader at the time, Kevin McCarthy (R-Calif.), tweeted: *"President Biden is more concerned about Border Patrol's vocabulary than he is about solving the border crisis. These backwards priorities are only making the situation worse."* Democrats and advocates for immigrants praised the new policy. *"Words matter,"* tweeted Rep. Jesús "Chuy" García (D-Ill.), calling the new terms *"a small but important step."* [67]

Dignity for those in custody? Yes, for those who invaded the border, but not those who entered our capitol on January 6th. *Words matter?* To this crew, they certainly do, evidently a lot more than action. And *finally new terms - a small important step?* A step leading us further into chaos, down a rabbit hole, and into an upside-down world where words and laws lose their meaning and effectiveness and to a *place and time in our history so evil that it is destined to doom us all.*

And somewhere in this picture, I see a vision of George Orwell, but I can't tell if he is laughing or crying or if he's just mouthing the words, *"I told you so."*

But worry not, it's all left to your interpretation and your own definitions of the truth and how you see the story taking place. And the scary part is that it's not a work of fiction called *1984*, but a reality we all live in a place called America in *2024*.

Seeking the TRUTH- Not a Ministry of Truth

"The Party told you to reject the Evidence of your eyes and ears. It was their final and most essential command" - George Orwell 1984

Somewhere, George Orwell must be smiling and or grinding his teeth.

THE TRUTH. It was something the great writer was fascinated with, especially in his iconic novel *1984*. Truth. What is it? Where can we find it? And how do we know when someone is telling the truth? To some, there is one truth. To others, they have their own truth with different definitions depending on their personal narrative and circumstances. The Truth –it is something that many seekers have sought over the ages.

And for sure, depending on the times, it's been defined differently by those various seekers.

The Truth as portrayed in the religious films celebrating The Lord, like *Jesus of Nazareth …The Passion of the Christ…and King of Kings* is pretty consistent.

If God is your pilot- then it's evident and clear what is the Truth.

Regarding Pontius Pilate's take – "What is Truth?" "Pilate apparently went along with the idea **that truth is relative**. For him, it was "truth" that Jesus was innocent, but for the Jews, it was "truth" that Jesus was guilty."So Pilate, in all "fairness," washed his hands and let the Jews follow their truth. [68]

In Orwell's iconic masterpiece, 1984…he sees the manipulation of the truth and language as a powerful way to mind control the masses. His use of the bastardization of definitions is eye-opening and eerie in that he could have been talking about the times we are living in today. His indictment of totalitarian regimes and authoritarian figures and governments controlling the people is dark, demonic, and a stern wake-up call to a WOKE generation, who are eager to please their new masters by punishing those who disagree with them.

And they will leave no stone or tweet or Facebook message unturned in pursuit of setting the record straight. If you made a gay joke at a family barbecue –they're coming for you, you homophobe. If you called some female beautiful, or honey, or darling, you may be hung as a sexist. And if you dared to disagree with the current regime in power and you happen to be wearing a red MAGA hat, *you're probably headed to room 101*. You get the point. In today's upside world, where statues are torn down to erase history and definitions of words change like the weather in Chicago, and the truth is transactional, a look back at the words of Orwell's 1984 is as haunting as they are accurate. But the truth is they are chilling. See how many you think apply to today's America.

"Who controls the past controls the future. Who controls the present controls the past."

"War is peace. Freedom is slavery. Ignorance is strength."

"The best books… are those that tell you what you know already."

"If you want to keep a secret, you must also hide it from yourself."

"But if thought corrupts language, language can also corrupt thought."

"If you want a picture of the future, imagine a boot stamping on a human face—forever."

"Doublethink means the power of holding two contradictory beliefs in one's mind simultaneously, and accepting both of them."

"It was a bright cold day in April, and the clocks were striking thirteen."[69]

The clocks are striking 13. Melting like some *Dali painting*. Ringing haphazardly like you were in some kind of nut house or listening to *Pink Floyd*. A nightmare. Constant. And one that never ends. Not the truth. Most definitely not that. Quite the opposite. A lie is portrayed as the truth. And told over and over and over until it is woven into the landscape.

A place where no one knows or cares to remember what the truth is. A land where the truth has come to die, buried in a sea of lies in a place called America, post Obama, post Biden, and post-Harris. A land that once sought it and fought for it and now a place that doesn't know what the word means at all —not after 1984, but in 2024.

XI. Only One Man Can Save The Republic

A President like No Other

What Would You Do (WWYD) ---If The Presidential Election was stolen from you?

"If Trump watched his mouth…Then What?" Then they'd Still Hate Him

Shots Fired, Shots Missed, Shots Deflected and One more shot to get things right

Trump Hears You Loud and Clear

There is lot of Hate Out There… But there's also a lot of Love

A President like No Other

I often wondered how he does it. How does this man named Donald J. Trump keep going? How does he keep fighting all those who have declared war on him and everything, MAGA?

Well, the answer is both simple and complex. The easy answer is – *He has done it. Or he has been chosen to do it.* That somehow, he has been equipped with armor and the intestinal fortitude that allows him to do it. But that doesn't explain why he does it. That answer is actually easier.

He does it because he loves America and truly wants to make America great again.

For some, that may seem far-fetched, even delusional, but that is the answer. And that is why he fights for this America, his America, for all the Americans out there who love America and get America, and against those who HATE America and want to GET America. He is the worst enemy of the globalists. The elites, too – regardless of party.

A billionaire –who at times is the bull in the China shop and a bull period to CHINA- because he has to be, and at other times just a man bullish on America and grateful for all America has done for him and his family.

To others, merely a bullshit artist. And at times, that description is true. Sure, he'll inflate the size of his crowds at one of his rallies. He'll claim that any one of his buildings that are branded Trump is the greatest building of all time, right up there with the Parthenon, The Pyramids, *and The Taj Mahal*. Hell, Trump liked the iconic building in India so much that he usurped its name and created the *Trump Taj Mahal* in Atlantic City.

But how many real estate agents or developers do you know who don't talk about their properties or listings a bit? Trump got in trouble for just that, in one of his sham indictments where the ultra-bias judge, obviously with a lack of sense or real estate acumen, valued Mar-a-Lago at just 18 million dollars! Hell, the gold toilet seats there are worth at least that. While the actual value is open for debate, similar properties have sold for many times what the judge put his lowball evaluation. And while Trump's evaluation of over a billion dollars may be high – it is closer to being right than the Trump hating judge.

It's just one more example of an injustice that Trump has had to endure in his journey from private life, where he soared to the top of the mountain of success, to public life, where he served the people by draining the swamp. From Mar-a-Lago to the White House to Trump, it's all part of his narrative and one of the great American stories.

But it's a great American story – both his and ours. And above everything else Trump is a storyteller. And his and our story is incomplete. Where does it end? No one knows for sure. His enemies have their desired ending – and have prematurely written it many times. His followers and supporters have their endings, too. Needless to say, their desired outcomes are as different as they could possibly be. And in them, their endings represent how they see America, how they want America to be seen and how and if America will be seen at all in the same light in the future.

Donald J. Trump's vision and ending of the story are optimistic in every sense. He sees America returning to greatness. Not for those who are connected but for the people. He sees America building things better than ever before. He sees more people of all creeds, colors, and backgrounds buying into it, believing in it, and achieving the American dream.

But to him, it's not a greeting card or sentiment expressed tightly on a bumper sticker. He has seen too much and achieved too much. And he has been through too much. Even his rose-colored glasses have become tainted. His eyes have been opened to the way of another world – in a place called Washington and other power centers around the world that really run things. And how he, the outsider, and the outsiders he represented, were never invited on the inside to discuss their pursuit of happiness and live the American dream.

He watched, at first naively, as he was attacked for merely winning an election he wasn't supposed to win- not because he wasn't the better candidate, because he was easily that in both 2016 and 2020, but because he wasn't one of THEM.

That's why they hate him. He's not one of them. And neither are any of us in MAGA nation.

And decades from now —when those concerned with weaving or painting the narrative that was America in the late 20th Century and the first third of the 21st Century – his name will be dominant and uttered on page after page for what his vision of America was – and what he wanted it to be again. And that is great. The kid from Queens merely wanted America to be great again.

Whether we get back there or not – well we shall have to wait and see. Only time will tell.

And hopefully, in the telling of the American story and the shaping of our history many years from now, in classrooms where they still revere men named Lincoln and Washington- students will read about how America rose to greatness again because of a movement called MAGA and man named Trump - a President like no other.

What Would You Do (WWYD) ---If The Presidential Election was stolen from you?

What would you do if you were Donald J. Trump and you felt and knew in your heart that the election was stolen?

What if you won the Masters and someone tried to steal your Green jacket? What if you won the Stanley Cup, and the other team hijacked it as it was being handed to you? What if they stole your Oscar or your Grammy...or Emmy or your Tony as you broke into your acceptance speech? What if you won the Nobel Peace Prize, and they tried to take it away from you? Pretty sure a fight would break out, and you might even punch the guy in the nose who tried to steal your Nobel Peace Prize.

What if you got nearly 75 million votes, almost 12 million more than the first time you won, and they stole the Presidency from you?

What would you do? Good question, right?

I know that many of us would like to think that we would be able to rise above it and shake hands with the victor and say, "That's okay. We'll get you next time."

But this is no Stanley Cup playoff. Yet, in the pursuit of Lord Stanley's Cup, we see the best example of sportsmanship and being a good sport on full display. Two opponents, after beating each other up literally and figuratively, sometimes for seven games, develop a pure hatred for each other in pursuit of capturing the sports world's most revered and cherished trophy. Then, after one of them wins the Cup and their opponent is left bleeding, nursing a multitude of undisclosed wounds at the hands of their opponents, they line up at center ice and shake hands.

Incredible. Good sportsmanship. Being both good winners and good losers.

And do you know why they are able to just do it, suck up that pain, and say those guys played a hell of a series? They're able to look each other square in the eye and say CONGRATULATIONS – often holding back tears because the one team won the contest fairly and squarely. And while they may have just been in a war fighting to the end, both teams, through ceremony and tradition, line up to shake hands. It's the greatest lesson of how we should all act when we win and when we lose.

But what if one of the teams cheated? Used some trick, some illegal means that allowed them, that guaranteed them the Stanley Cup, no matter how hard the other team dug in the corner for the puck, no matter how many incredible plays their best players made and how many great saves their legendary goalie made.

What then? What would they do? I'm pretty sure all hell would break loose.

Inquiries would be made, and many hockey players would be yelling at the tops of their lungs:

"WHAT THE PUCK?" Well that's exactly the situation Donald Trump was put in.

He worked his ass not only as President for four years and with no salary to boot but on most metrics, he made America Great Again – until the Pandemic, make that *plandemic* reared its ugly head. And all things considered, when the true history comes out, Trump handled that pretty damn well.

He campaigned like he was playing in overtime of a game seven Stanley Cup game for the Cup. All the while, his opponent was sleeping on the bench or hiding in the locker room, giving no effort and attracting no crowds while the Donald played to full houses. Then, on election night – the equivalent of a game seven playoff, the game – i.e., the vote counting was suddenly paused, and bam – over the next few days – Biden was handed enough votes to win the Stanley Cup, make that the Presidency.

How would you feel?

And considering everything- he's made the Stanley Cup handshakes a distant second in terms of sportsmanship. In many ways, Trump has been magnanimous.

The election was stolen. He knows it. They know it. Everyone with half a brain knows it. And that's why they fear running against him again and why they are hell-bent on trying anything to prevent him from gaining office again.

So the next time you think about Trump and how he's making such a big deal about the 2020 election, ask yourself that question. What if the election and the presidency of the United States were stolen from you? What would you do?

Well I think I know how I'd act. And it wouldn't be pretty.

Come to think of it, I know quite a few hockey teams over the years, like all of them, and many of the greatest hockey players ever who would have turned into madmen had someone tried stealing their Stanley Cup.

Can't imagine Bobby Clarke or Bobby Orr just smiling and saying that's okay. I'm afraid to think of what Rocket Richard would have done. I knew Gordie Howe, Mr. Hockey, who, off the ice, was one of the finest gents ever - on the ice, not so much. I shudder to think what old number 9 would have done had someone tried to cheat him out of his Stanley Cup. There would have been no handshakes and no peaceful transfer of power. This is the Stanley Cup, after all. And this is the Presidency, after all.

Stolen. Rigged. Taken. All things considered – while there have been no handshakes at center ice when you really come to think of how Donald J. Trump has acted, considering he thinks the election was stolen from him. When you consider that, he has acted saintly. Quite saintly indeed and like a real good sport, and no one can blame him for not shaking hands with Joe Biden.

"If Trump watched his mouth…Then What?" They'd Still Hate Him

Then what? Then, he would be more presidential.

So what. If you're still worried about the way Donald J. Trump talks and tweets, you miss the entire point completely. And you don't get what's really happening and how there are real enemies out there planning and plotting to do damage first with their words but most importantly and dangerously with their evil deeds.

Their goal? *GET TRUMP, GET AMERICA, GET YOU & GET ME & GET WE THE PEOPLE*

If Trump has said it once, he has said it a thousand times. This time from back on October 11, 2023, at a speech in Palm Beach, the 45th President of the United States said:

"They want to take away my freedom because I will never let them take away your freedom. It's very simple. I'm not going to let it happen. They want to silence me because I will never let them silence you. And in the end, they're not after me. They're after you, and I happen to be standing in the way. It's my honor to do so.[70]

And why do you think they are all in on getting Trump? Mean tweets? Please.

It's because he's a danger to exposing and dismantling a whole system that is designed to enrich them and not we the people.

The differences between Trump and Biden are startling when you compare their policies, personalities, performance on the job, and finally, how they fill out the role of being president.

The fact that Trump can speak coherently and with lucidity distinguishes him from the dolt and dummy mummy in the White House, who, let's face it, on a good day for Joe, can barely string two cogent sentences together.

I've tried to reason with those who are so filled with TDS-*Trump Derangement Syndrome* –but after a couple of illogical or incoherent sentences of never-ending blind support for Biden– I give up. And they call MAGA folks the cultists. But what are they, a group that includes "TV media personalities" like Joy Reid, who said she would *"vote for" President Biden even if he was "in a coma."*[71] Joining Reid in her blind support was Whoopi Goldberg who shared how far up Joe's backside she was as she shared her scatological view of the choice come election time. "*I don't care if he's pooped his pants. I don't care if he can't put a sentence together. Show me he can't do the job, and then I'll say, okay, maybe it's time to go,"* Goldberg said.[72]

Still, I would fall into a hopeless argument from time to time, trying to talk common sense to the senseless. But lately, I've gotten smarter. Not swinging at those diatribes who say *"TRUMP is worse than Hitler"* and that *"TRUMP is the most dangerous threat to Democracy."*

I know better, most of us do, having lived through the four Trump years and nearly four Biden years. Any reasonable person – someone not unhinged and not filled with TDS when looking at the mere metrics can easily come to the same conclusion. A good friend of mine, a very successful businessman and savvy restaurant guy, shared his way of dealing with folks who have severe cases of TDS.

He merely looks at them as they make their point. After they have stated their hate-filled rant about Trump, he offers a slam dunk argument on something that's not arguable - *"Under Trump, our Southern Border" was in better shape"* or *"Under Trump – Inflation was lower and the cost of living was better for most Americans."*

When they shake their heads in disagreement and say they're voting for Biden anyway, my friend looks at them, then dismisses them with a *"You're not a serious person,"* then exits the scene.

It's a great lesson. They are not serious people. To them, Trump is a serious threat. And while they are not serious people, what they are saying should be taken seriously. One wishes they could get help. Therapy. Attend a Trump rally. Hang out with some MAGA people. Catch the RNC convention and the diverse and powerful speeches of …Rubio, Sanders, Vivak, and Ben Carson. Go to a ballgame or church together with someone you disagree with, and maybe you will see the humanity in your neighbor instead of painting him with a skewed brush.

I know because I don't cancel people – I don't agree with politically. For the most part, I shut my mouth, not because I want to, but because I know that THEY can't take it- an honest conversation about a good man trying to make America great and all the people who make up what he calls a movement.

And it is indeed a movement, moving in the right direction in more ways than one, representing a party that is comprised of authentic, real people. Real working people and real Americans who really love this country and this man named Donald Trump. Still, some want to paint Trump as a dangerous threat to Democracy.

Trump – A danger to Democracy?

He is, if it means he focused the light on the forgotten men and women who have been taken for granted and advantage of by the coastal elites, media elites, elites from academia, and the government elites who thrive in Washington's swamp – then surely Trump is dangerous. Dangerous to them and wrestling their power away.

I regards to who is more dangerous to America, Robert F Kennedy Jr. said, *"Biden is far more dangerous to our Republic than Trump."*

A contrarian opinion was offered by deep-state warmongers like Dick Cheney and Liz Cheney.

Dick Cheney gets the award for exaggeration, and just plain bullshit that makes Trump's tall tales seem like kid's play. *"In our nation's 246-year history, there has never been an individual who has been a greater threat to our republic than Donald J. Trump."* In an ad endorsing his deranged daughter's failed run for Congress, Dick Cheney, The Darth Vader of the Deep State and the man most responsible for an endless war called Iraq is calling Trump the most dangerous man in our history.

That's rich. And so is he. But how did he get that way?

We know how the Donald got rich. By building things – Hotels, luxury residences, golf courses, resorts, a TV legacy, and finally, most importantly – a family.

Dick, well, dick got rich – another old-fashioned way – through his ties with the deep state profiting off endless wars and the military-industrial complex.

The next time you say, "If only he wouldn't tweet this and that…" please stop and think a minute. *They're not after him because of his mean tweets, they're after him because he won't retreat.* Like the iconic Tom Petty song, *HE WON'T BACK DOWN*, not from a fight and not from fighting for the American people.

Yes, Dick Cheney is right on one thing, Donald Trump is the most dangerous man to the deep state. To the American people, he's a champion fighting for all of them, whether they like him or not and no matter if they voted for him or not.

"If Trump would only watch his mouth…Then What?" Then, they would still hate him and his supporters. That may not be presidential to say, but those are the facts –tweeted or not.

Shots Fired, Shots Missed, Shots Deflected and One more shot to get things right

It was inevitable. Can't say I was surprised when I first heard that shots were fired at the 45th President of the United States. They had been shooting at him in one way or another ever since he came down that golden escalator almost a decade ago when he first threw his red MAGA hat into the ring to become president of the United States.

His enemies had been aiming at him for years and, in every possible way, took their shots in a variety of ways. From the Washington power centers in government, from the media elites in their ivory watch towers to the pillars of those who profess to teach *"Knowledge and Wisdom"* in the supposed higher learning places in academia, to those in Hollywood and the music industry stars prancing around on stage as they spewed their hatred for this man and movement and an intolerance for a varying point of view and vision for America.

Shots fired from former presidents, senators, members of Congress, mayors and members of the local school board, Oscar-winning actors, and aging rock stars, all throwing rocks and worse in the direction of man who sacrificed his rich and accomplished lifestyle -to come to Washington- for one simple reason - he wanted to *Make America Great Again.*

And for that —they pumped up anti-Trump rhetoric 24/7 and fired it out to the masses that he was an: *anti- Semite, a xenophobe, a racist, a Nazi, a Fascist, a Russian spy, a traitor, a rapist, a con man and crook, a white supremacist, a dictator and finally an existential threat to our democracy.* A threat to our republic and man worthy of whatever bad thoughts or actions you wanted to fire in his direction. In other words, it was all justified.

The hatred turned into two specious impeachments and four indictments by a weaponized justice system out to get Trump. Still, he stood tall and fought for America and the American people.

Famous actors waxed philosophically that *"it might be a good time for another assassination of a president," a*s a crazed, unfunny comedian held up a model of a severed and bloodied Trump head for all to see and rally behind.

And all in all, their shots were continuously and endlessly fired and deflected away by a warrior of man who would not quit and would not fail. They attempted to reduce the man and his movement into a symbol to be hated.

Then, on a Saturday in July, in a small Pennsylvania town, one of the crazed haters with extreme Trump Derangement Syndrome (TDS) took it into his own hands and used the weapon of his choice as *shots were fired* at the 45th President at a Trump rally.

Sadly, one Trump supporter was tragically killed, and another two were seriously injured at the event. A former Pennsylvania volunteer fire chief, Corey Comperatore, 50, who served as the fire chief for Buffalo Township, was shot and killed by Thomas Matthew Crooks, 20, at the rally while trying to protect his daughters when gunfire rang out during Trump's speech.

"The hatred for one man took the life of the one man we loved the most. He was a hero that shielded his daughters," she wrote on Facebook. *"He truly loved us enough to take a real bullet for us,"* Allyson wrote on Facebook. Comperatore's wife, Helen, echoed her daughter's description of the former fire chief as a "real-life superhero" who protected them.

"Yesterday, what [was meant to] be such an exciting day for my husband, especially, turned into a nightmare for our family," Helen wrote on Facebook. *"What my precious girls had to witness is unforgivable,"* she added. *"He died the hero he always was."*[73]

Former First Lady Melania Trump expressed her sadness and condolences in the aftermath of the tragic event.

To the families of the innocent victims who are now suffering from this heinous act, I humbly offer my sincerest sympathy. Your need to summon your inner strength for such a terrible reason saddens me.

A monster who recognized my husband as an inhuman political machine attempted to ring out Donald's passion – his laughter, ingenuity, love of music, and inspiration. The core facets of my husband's life – his human side – were buried below the political machine. Donald, the generous and caring man who I have been with through the best of times and the worst of times.

Let us not forget that differing opinions, policy, and political games are inferior to love. Our personal, structural, and life commitment – until death – is at serious risk. Political concepts are simple when compared to us, human beings. We are all humans, and fundamentally, instinctively, we want to help one another. American politics are only one vehicle that can uplift our communities. Love, compassion, kindness and empathy are necessities.

And let us remember that when the time comes to look beyond the left and the right, beyond the red and the blue, we all come from families with the passion to fight for a better life together while we are here in this earthly realm.

Dawn is here again. Let us reunite. Now.

This morning, ascend above the hate, the vitriol, and the simple-minded ideas that ignite violence. We all want a world where respect is paramount, family is first, and love transcends. We can realize this world again. Each of us must demand to get it back. We must insist that respect fills the cornerstone of our relationships again.

I am thinking of you, my fellow Americans.

The winds of change have arrived. For those of you who cry in support, I thank you. I commend those of you who have reached out beyond the political divide – thank you for remembering that every single politician is a man or a woman with a loving family."[74]

Miraculously, President Trump was spared as a bullet came within centimeters of taking his life.

A man who has taken many bullets over the years for his movement to make America a better place. As that news came into focus ...much of the proper responses were heard from former presidents and political leaders...many of whom had contributed to painting Trump and his followers as *deplorable human beings and extremists.*

One former Trump ally and the former Attorney General William Barr told Fox News that "*the Democrats have to stop their grossly irresponsible talk about Trump being an existential threat to democracy. He is not."* The statement came just hours after a would-be assassin shot at former President Trump at a campaign rally in Butler, Pennsylvania.[75]

Yet, on the same day, shots were fired, and an innocent man was killed; the hateful rhetoric was alive and not well on social media sites. In one of my feeds on Facebook, someone commented, *"Too bad he missed and missed his chance to make America Great Again."*

Naturally shaken by the remark, I responded, *"You're sick and demented."*

To which she replied, *"Watch your mouth, you don't know me."*

I did not respond back. After all I did know her and what she was all about.

In a word - *Hatred.*

And I knew one other thing: I knew what Donald Trump was all about. He loves this country and he's a fighter who will keep fighting for the American people. Even take a bullet for them and the movement. Defiantly and thankfully, Donald Trump dodged a bullet.

And in the sometimes sad, sick, and evil world we live in, I encountered a restless night as I thought of the day's events that filled me with tears and many moments of reflection.

I knew what I knew. Many people in America love Donald Trump. Many in America hate Donald Trump. That's fine. Actually, it's not, but my point is simply this. Don't hate the man. Argue the policies. I don't hate Joe Biden. I despise and disagree with his policies.

Want to make America Great Again? Let's talk and listen to each other again.

Let's have a debate and a conversation in America.

Be like Bill Maher, who told a hate-filled Joy Behar on The View, who said the "Nazi sign should be affixed to all Trump MAGA hats," "*I think you can hate Donald Trump. You can't hate everybody who likes him- that's half the country. I don't want to live in that country. I want to live in that country where I hate half the country.*"

Shots fired. Shots deflected.

Before I went to bed, I caught Bobby Kennedy Jr eloquently and poignantly discussing the day's events. I was moved by the hopeful and wise words of a man who knows all too well what heightened hatred looks like up close – losing both his father, RFK, a man who was running to become president, and his uncle Jack, JFK, a man who was president – to assassin's bullets.

I don't agree with many of Bobby Kennedy Jr's policies. Some I do. But one thing is for sure - I respect his right to say them, and in many ways, I love and admire his courage to say them.

As I woke up Sunday morning in America, mourning the loss of a true American hero who gave up his life for his family, I went to the only place that I could to help me seek answers- my church.

As I prayed for our country and for a former firefighter and former president, I spoke with my friend George, a bartender, who echoed his thoughts about divine intervention as we looked at a painting of Jesus.

"The Lord is big. And He was watching out for our president."

As the service ended – I spoke with another friend, George, at the altar; he himself is a Biden guy. He grabbed my arm, wished me the best, and emotionally pulled me aside, "*You* know what really scares me? Lots of the sick things many of friends are posting on Facebook —like, that it's too bad he missed."

"*Pray for them,*" I said, borrowing words of The Lord that I learned from many good people I have been blessed to know that have shaped both my American and Greek Orthodox life.

As I was leaving, I crossed myself and tapped on an icon depicting St. George's slaying of the tyrannical Dragon, and I noticed yet another friend named George in the church. One thing is certain: any time you enter any Greek Orthodox Church, you'll find many Georges.

This George, I'll call retired George, was pumping his fist like President Trump did after he was shot. Me and my friend George, the bartender, were moved even from many pews away, inspired by his defiant gesture.

Message sent. Shots fired. Shots missed. Shots deflected all with the help of God's hand.

With his hand, as the man many love and many love to hate pumped his fist in a courageous sign that will live forever as an image of bravery and resolve- I thought of yet another George - George Washington crossing the Delaware. This was Donald J. Trump's moment – his crossing of the Delaware, as he continued on his mission and movement to travel across America with the words and message ingrained in his heart. He nor his movement were not meant to die on this day at the hands of a hate-filled and delusional man firing evil shots.

Resilient with fists pumping – and yelling fight, fight, fight!... the man who many believe was put on earth divinely for this mission... is not a perfect man.... but a man perfect for his times.

Donald J. Trump is a man –who they hate for many reasons, mostly because he is the head of a movement where he and his followers are reduced to not being worthy of life, liberty, and their pursuit of happiness.

One man, a true American hero, came here to this Trump rally like all his supporters do, not with hate in their heart – but with love in their heart for their family, country, and their president.

Sadly, one real American hero did not make it home alive. A day of joy turned to unthinkable pain –in an instant, a dream turned into a nightmare. All within seconds. A trigger was pulled, ignited by the ammo of hate. And now, sadly, this patriot and hero, who represents the best of us, will not be there to share in his little girls' lives. A tragedy of epic proportions. Not only for one American family but for the entire American family. Yet a tragedy and a chance for this trajectory of hate to stop now before it's too late for all of us.

Please pause, ponder, or pray if you do that sort of thing…but definitely think about that the next time you mindlessly shoot your mouth offloaded with pure hate.

Because the lessons are there, while presumably one monster is responsible for the evil deed committed on this day —we all have a hand and must do our part in turning down the temperature and lowering the hate all across this great land.

Because we can't go as if nothing happened- because it will happen again.

What do you think happens when you reduce people to calling them a mindless cult or white- supremacists or worse than Hitler?

You know the routine …you know the drill…you know the drum beat.

So let's take a shot, not with a gun and with bullets, but a shot at being civil.

Because there are many more Saturday afternoons in the years to come in this land all across America and many opportunities for all of us to either return the fire or deflect the hate away from a president, a movement, a country, and from you and me.

Because we are all in the sights, these are merely the latest shots…. and, sadly, not the last. When will we learn? And what will we learn? Will we learn to love thy neighbor? Can we agree to disagree? Will we admit that Trump is NOT a threat to Democracy?

Will we state that Trump is not a fascist or Nazi? And will we agree to disagree - that Donald J. Trump is merely a man and head of a movement of people, running for President who according to his vision, is trying to make America Great again?

Shots fired, shots missed, shots deflected - all on a beautiful day in middle-America.

And yet one more shot- to turn the other cheek, love thy neighbor and remove the bullets of hatred from the chamber in our hearts that we are all capable of firing.

Trump Hears You Loud and Clear

Even with an injured ear – suffered from an assassin's bullet …Trump can hear the American people better than those connected to the *Swamp Network* that infiltrates much of America. Yes contrary to some media narratives, the former president has always been a good listener. And he was still listening to something in his heart, his instinct perhaps to let his fellow Americans know that he was alright, and that the country would be alright – as he yelled *Fight, Fight, Fight* for all of the world to see and hear. The shot seen and heard around the world.

Yet, as an assassin tried to end his life and his movement, while leaving him with an ear injury, resembling a bad impression of the great impressionist painter named Vincent – one thing was clear as the days played out in the summer of 2024- Donald Trump was still listening to the American people. And he always would.

As the debacle of an early debate orchestrated by the Democrats, continued to play out over and over for all of America to see and hear and at the same time the tape of the failed attempt on Trump's life continued to be played and was seen and heard by much of America – one thing remained crystal clear. To anyone who was watching and listening – the sound of truth, like a church bell ringing on a Sunday morning – or Ella Fitzgerald singing anything, could be heard echoing throughout the land.

The lessons were clear. Donald Trump was who he was and who he told you who he was right from the beginning. The other guy? Well, let's say, they hid him and have been hiding who he is and who he has always been, for a long time.

Donald Trump entered the race because he heard the voice of the forgotten men and women in fly over America and all over the nation, whose voices were not heard in Washington.

Donald Trump would be the eyes and ears of all those who were not connected, did not own lobbyists, were true outsiders who wanted, if not a seat at the table, then at least an invite into the process as they pursued their American dream. An American dream that for many had fallen on deaf ears.

The man named Trump put them and America first. First, he fired a symbolic shot across the bow, involving changed policies that would help the forgotten men and women all across America and for everyone to hear if they cared to listen.

The shot was loud enough to be heard in government buildings where Washington insiders made their deals. Places where they brain washed America's children - at our lower and higher learning institutions. And finally the cultural influencers shaping the narrative of hatred for the other. In places like Hollywood where they created slick and sick Hollywood movies where the guy or gal with the Red Hat is the bad guy. It was a tune that was getting old and much of America was tuning out —even before the shots were fired at President Trump in a Pennsylvania field.

A good part or portion of America had hit the mute button. They no longer cared what they were telling and selling them.

They, the hillbillies and hayseeds, the people who took a shower after they got home from work had been watching the movie play out all across America – involving a man they knew, loved and who was their hero- in their American movie. And not only had they stopped believing anything they – the left, the elites, the deep state, the smart people with the double starched shirts said about him or them – they finally stopped listening period.

They only heard his voice. The voice of a leader who not only always saw them- but perhaps most importantly had listened to them.

That point could not have been clearer than the third day of the RNC convention when the families of the 13 murdered American heroes and patriots spoke on the stage to not a dry eye in the house. And one after another —they spoke about how this man named Trump came to lend support, offer sympathies- but most importantly listen to them.

Because just as the picture, even with the sound off, of President Trump's heroic response to the assassination attempt is carved in our memory forever- so too is the Democrat party and their response and remedy for Joe's condition.

They cared not about Joe Biden the man, obviously a fading and feeble figure, they only expressed concern for their guy when they saw and heard his latest trip ups in July of 2024- and realized that there was no way that they could win with this guy and no way in hell they were ever going to beat and Get Trump on election day.

And he dropped out of the race, as he inevitably always would, they, the same cadre of Washington insiders and traitors who inserted the knife in Joe's back, started with their tributes about the man.

In tweets, finely crafted letters and soundbites they all offered a few words on Joe.

They thanked him for healing the nation… which he did not do.

They thanked him for fixing the economy …which he did not do.

They thanked him for bringing decency back to the White House –which he did not do.

Finally they thanked him for all his service on behalf of the American people- which he did if you're name was Biden. All their empty words had come full circle.

NO ONE was listening to them anymore.

But many people in America were listening to a man named Donald Trump.

Many people who would not have given him the time of day – now pledged their vote as they dissected the narrative with their heart. And they saw and could hear everything playing out in perfect time all across America. The man, who the media tried to make into a monster, they found was no monster at all.

In fact, it was they who were the monsters.

The man who was indicted and convicted for fake crimes – was no criminal at all. In fact, it was they who were the criminals.

The man who they impeached and said was a threat to democracy, they came to see that he was not impeachable and no threat to democracy. In fact, it was they who were the real threats to democracy.

The man who they called a villain, they came to joyously see was no villain at all, but in fact was their hero. In fact, it was they who were the real villains all along.

And this all crystalized, appropriately, at a Trump rally, where the man that they had come to see and listen to often did his thing that they all came to see, hear, and love. Here on this Saturday afternoon in Pennsylvania field, he told some of the same jokes, repeated many of the same jabs at the elites, and recited many of the same talking points that many in the crowd could recite themselves.

It did not matter. They believed in him, and they were listening to him.

And they always would. Because, after all - he believed in them.

And he was listening to them all across this great land called America.

And as the assassin's bullet clipped his ear and blood gushed from the patriot's head, even if the sound was turned down on your picture, you could hear Trump's defiant words echoing the fighting spirit of Patrick Henry, *"Fight. Fight, Fight."*

On this day, when his great story and a great movement was almost killed by a man who was not great – but only filled with hate, the legacy of a hero named Trump was recorded for posterity.

Someday, many decades from now, hopefully in an American History classroom, children will be taught the story of a man who was always listening to the American people, first. A man who was always listening to the forgotten men and women in America who thought that no one was listening to them.

And if you listen closely - you'll still be able to hear the sound of that bullet miraculously, whizzing by the ear of a man who sacrificed everything for his country.

Once heard – an unmistakable sound. Sounding a lot like providence and liberty.

But there is one catch – to hear it you have to be listening to the people.

There is lot of Hate Out There… But there's also a lot of Love

The fact that someone took a shot and nearly killed our 45th president and potentially 47th president should sicken every American. It should also make them a bit sad and angry. That's the way I feel. And a bit fearful of the folks who live in our country – no not the MAGA wearing red hatters…but those who simply hate the MAGA red hatters because they support a man named Trump. I dare them to go to a Trump rally – really go to a Trump rally and take an informal poll in your heart and head on one issue and vote on what you see. I think you'll find what I found and what most who attend a Trump rally find – LOVE.

Love of God. Love of country. Love of community. Love of the Flag.

Love of the law. Love of Freedom. Love of a Liberty. Love of Happiness.

Love of a movement. Love of a neighbor. Love of a president.

One person who tested this theory – a died in the wool leftist, former Trump hater and someone who is the last person you'd expect to see and enjoy a Trump rally is a woman named Sasha Stone.

Stone made her "bones" in Hollywood. She knows and loves films and on that I can relate, because I know and love films and the magic that the movies can bring. Sasha Stone, a California girl who studied film at NYU and Columbia University, eventually graduating from UCLA – which is like an "EGOT for Academia film studies." The talented Stone won a Samuel Goldwyn Award writing award at UCLA and was on her way to making living covering Tinsel Town, while scribing for various entertainment industry magazines, including *Variety*, *The Hollywood Reporter*, and *The Wrap*. As a film critic, her big claim to fame was founding a website that covered the Academy Awards called *Oscar watch* –later renamed *Awards Daily* after being sued by the Academy of Motion Picture Arts and Sciences. But hell- if you haven't been sued in Hollywood you can't call yourself a real insider. As part of her leftist street cred she would appear on NPR's Weekend Edition.

The last place that you would expect to find Sasha Stone was at a Trump rally. But in plot twist to her narrative – that no one saw coming- especially her, that's exactly where she found herself.

Six years ago, I stood a few feet away from Joe Biden at a fundraiser and was certain he was the only person who could save this country from Donald Trump in 2020. However, by the end of the election, I would leave the Democratic Party for good. I saw them as corrupt, too powerful, and dangerous to the very democracy they now claim they want to protect. Now, I wake up every morning in a panic that our last best hope of ending the monopoly of power on the Left rests on the imperfect shoulders of Donald Trump. So I guess that finally makes me a Trump supporter.

It was a long, slow slide that started with simply humanizing Trump and the MAGA movement and believe me, just that alone upset my friends and family. They're evil, they believe, because that's what the media tells them every second of every day. I spent a lot of time saying, "I'm not a Trump supporter, but..." I said it so much I began to feel like a coward for saying it. Trump is no better or worse than any politician in America. But we've never lived through an entire oligopoly scaring people against a former and half the country. Because it was never just about Trump, it was always about the people who voted for Trump and chose him to represent them in government. Didn't they matter at all? No, because they were demonized as racists and thrown away like human garbage.

So now I will stand in full support of Trump because I know that this is not a time to hedge or back down. It is a time to stand up to people who have assumed power that does not belong to them. Their election meddling has become the real threat to our democracy. From the raid on Mar-a-Lago to the indictments and now to the show trials, they've left me with no other option than to stand behind the one guy they haven't been able to destroy. [76]

No they haven't been able to destroy him, but boy how have they tried. Stone's podcast – is something I've come to count on – in the way a lost ship at sea counts on a lighthouse during a treacherous storm.

Sure it was her wisdom, poetry, prose and course her love of movies that she brilliantly had woven into her podcasts – that have deeply touched and moved me. But why I connected with her and her show was really simple. She was authentic. She was real. She had heart. And finally she had a change of heart. When she saw that the story that the left had been feeding her all along, had been bullshit, she did the courageous thing and jumped ship. Bravely, adorned with the armor of a fighter, fighting for what is right and true, she took her talented and pure voice to the airwaves in an effort to humanize those people and a president who were demonized by those people she used to hang out with on the coasts.

And that's when I found her on a podcast: Sasha Stone: *Free Thinking through the Fourth Turning.* To say that I'm a fan is not the right word. It's more than that. She was filling a void for me left by the departure of the great Rush Limbaugh who I listened to make sense out of the political landscape. I listen to Dennis Prager and he is my rabbi and moral compass on the radio. When I wanted to rev up – a dose of Michael Savage gets me going. But with Stone it was different. She had come from way over on the other side – from left leaning Hollywood and the land of the media elites where if you wanted to get along or get promoted you shut your mouth and expressed your hatred for the *great Orange Man.*

I too, had my dealings with the left. As a PBS Producer, filmmaker and teacher I had dealt with my frustration and fear of trying to shield my body and soul –from politics –so that I would not be canceled. But eventually it happened anyway. When students whom I had taught film classes to for years, who I presumed loved me, canceled me because of my support of Trump. I like, David O. Selznick, got the memo. While devastated – I was grateful. Awake now. Able to see the whole picture now. I had room to hear and connect with other voices who I get and love, and who get and love me. Stone ends her broadcasts with a phrase from Shakespeare's Hamlet, **"To thine own self be true.**" When I hear it at the end of long day, it is like my light on a stormy night.

Kind of like the man himself. Donald J. Trump. A lighthouse standing taller and through all the storms sending light into a dark world, trying not to save merely a lost ship or panicked sailor but instead sending a signal out trying to save an entire nation. That's what the fist pump and the words *fight, fight, fight came to symbolize*. A defiant gesture. Lifted high in the air for all to see. Those lost. Those suffering. Those Forgotten. They all saw the raised fists from their fighter and their champion. Sure he was knocked down. But he got up.

And he always would get up for the American people.

A man who was knocked down and knocked off the airwaves at Fox, the popular journalist Tucker Carlson, shared a personal story, at the RNC convention of a man who the journalist had come to know and dare I say loved.

"The day after the midterm elections in 2018, Anti-fa came to my house, the Democratic Party's militia, okay? I was at work, it was obvious when I was at work, because it was public. My wife was home alone. They tried to come in through the front door. They terrorized her. She hid in our pantry. It was on television. It was horrible, actually. I'm not whining about it. Wasn't getting shot in the face, but it wrecked our day. And the next morning we're lying in bed, and the phone rings for my wife. And it's Donald Trump. Who's not like a regular text buddy of Donald Trump's? She picks it up. "Hello?"

"Susie, it's Donald Trump." And it's coming through, I could hear it. I'm lying in bed. Whoa. And the first thing he says is, "I'm going to stand guard outside your house." And she goes, "Oh, that's so nice." And he says, I'll never forget this, as long as I live. He says, "There's a lot of hate out there." And she said, "There is, Mr. President." And then he says, "But there's a lot of love." There's a lot of love. And we are seeing that love. I don't think it's human love. And I'll just stop with this. I'm not always convinced that I'm on the right side. I've been on the wrong side many times. You'll never hear me say I'm on God's side or God's with me, or even I'm with God. I want to be; not sure I am. But I will say this, unequivocally

and conclusively, God is among us right now. And I think that's enough. God bless you."[77]

We are all blessed to live in this great country. And we are blessed to have such a great man standing up for all of us to see from sea to shining sea. Yes there is a lot of hate out there. But there is also a lot of love. And no matter how bad the storms get, to find the love, just look for the lighthouse that will guide you to all those red hats at a rally packed full of good people and love.

XII. America – A Republic Rises and Is Made Great Again

Only one question remains unanswered regarding Whoopi's Gas

No Joy in Saying this from the Boy on Joy Road

You do know you're not voting for a woman...a black woman...or... an Indian woman don't you?

Fight, Fight, Fight...For what is Right...Right...Right

As the Movie Plays out – I think of a man named Capra

Only one question remains unanswered regarding Whoopi's Gas

Whoopi Goldberg couldn't help herself – allegedly, she can't when it comes to controlling the gaseous and stinking odor emanating from her being. In Hollywood, she is considered the queen of flatulence. That's, in fact, how the often talented actor got her name. Her propensity to excuse the term – *FART*…and let it rip at any time is something that has made her a household name and fixture while sitting on her "Whoopi cushion" as a co-host for years of the long-running TV show The View.

In recent days, her hatred of a certain man who she not only once tolerated but genuinely gave the impression that she liked has gotten the best of her…perhaps given her indigestion and upset her stomach and other parts of her body. Trouble is – when it comes to Whoopi lately, it's not hard to identify the stink in the room –what's most difficult is identifying which end it's coming out of.

Her mouth or her backside.

While there are endless examples of Whoppi's ability to go low on the show, her lowest point may have occurred on a recent show after the Republic National Convention and just days after an assassin tried to take the life of the former President and former frequent guest of The View Donald J. Trump. Sadly, on that day, a real-life American hero, former Fire Chief Cory Comperatore, lost his life shielding his family from the assassin's bullets.

Sacrifice and Family. They are two words that describe the fallen hero who was a *Mega MAGA* supporter who loved his faith, family and country and a man who also loved President Trump.

Dare I say that Cory was already in heaven as he sat there in the stands surrounded by the love of family and friends in a rural community setting, as the man whom he respected was about to share his love of country with the folks in Butler who had gathered to see him. And that pretty much sums up every one of these MAGA folks who the media like to paint as a cultist mob. The fact of the matter is that those who attend know what these MAGA rallies are all about.

In a word, it is love. Love of country. Love of community. Love of family and love of neighbor. That's what a MAGA rally is about. But they dare not tell you that because it will not only humanize all these faceless MAGA supporters who make up the movement. And it will do something else - it will humanize him, Donald J. Trump, the name, face, and brand of movement that they love to hate.

And because of that, the view of Cory the hero —is one that the mainstream media doesn't want you to see. A very noble and brave man sacrificing for his love of family, community and country. That's also a view that many on the left don't want you to see —of this man named Donald Trump, who sacrificed much to serve his country.

And it's certainly a view that Whoopi Goldberg not only doesn't want you to see, it's one that she demands that you not believe.

On this particular day, Whoopi lived up to the gaseous attributes of her name, spewing hate and bile so repugnant that had someone in the audience called for a doctor, they would hardly have been blamed.

What got under Whoopi's thin skin on this day?

A family moment fit for the family hour and not fitting for the morning hours that The View spews their often hateful and denigrating points of view. What caused Whoopi to practically spontaneously combust on the show was a sweet moment shared by Donald Trump's oldest granddaughter Kai Trump. Here in prime time at the RNC, the eldest daughter of the president's oldest son, Don Jr., spoke from the heart about her grandfather, arguably the most famous man in the world and potentially the next president of the United States.

"To me, he's just a normal grandpa," the 17-year-old daughter of Donald Trump, Jr. said, smiling during her political debut on stage in Milwaukee, Wisconsin. *"He gives us candy and soda when our parents aren't looking. He always wants to know how we're doing in school."*

Kai, an avid golfer with a significant social media following, recently emerged victorious in the ladies' club championship at Trump's golf course in Palm Beach and bonds with her famous grandfather over a mutual love for golf.

"He calls me during the middle of the school day to ask how my golf game is going and tells me all about his," said the 17-year-old. *"But then I have to remind him that I'm in school, and I'll have to call him back later."*

"When we play golf together, if I'm not on his team, he'll try to get inside of my head, and he's always surprised I don't let him get to me," Kai said about her grandfather. *"But I have to remind him, I'm a Trump, too."*[78]

Not exactly sure what words got to Whoopi, but apparently, they seemed to give her gas or worse, the words spoken during the RNC by Trump's eldest grandchild, Kai Trump.

Urging Americans to not fall for the banana in the tailpipe, *"I know his grandchild was up on the thing and they're trying to humanize him and change your idea about who this guy is. Don't fall for that,"* Goldberg said the July 18th episode of "The View."

In Kai's memorable speech, she insisted the media was demonizing Trump, saying her grandfather has been put "through hell" -a repeated talking point within the MAGA campaign *"through hell,"* saying, *"the media makes my grandpa seem like a different person, but I know him for who he is. He's very caring and loving, he truly wants the best for this country."*[79]

Goldberg would have none of it and continued her diatribe that Trump is bad news for the country and has repeated her own talking points to her audience that we're "all in danger" if Trump wins.

But her argument is anything but a winning one. Upset for humanizing a man who only days before took a bullet for liberty only to get up and yell, fight, fight, fight for your country?

It is Whoopi who has come to embody the bile that eats up our country and divides us and is about as appropriate as… a fart in church.

It reminded me of another guest, Tulsi Gabbard, who entered into the den of inequity that is The View. She fought for our country and switched from the Democrat Party because they had changed. Tulsi battled their small and closed-minded arguments with dignity. She pointed to meeting with the newly elected president at Trump Tower to discuss foreign policy with the curious and hard-working Trump. For that, she received a series of tweets and pushback from those on the other side of the aisle – *for daring to humanize Trump*.

What a pathetic view.

At this point, with Whoopi Goldberg and the like, it is difficult to tell where the pungent aroma is emanating from – the mouth or the backside. Certainly, it doesn't come from a loving heart. As we move on together as a country, one hopes that there is still room to disagree on policy and principle and that it doesn't become a crime to try and humanize someone. Because if that's the case, then there is no hope and we are not only sick in our stomachs but in our souls.

Still, when I looked at these two women, Kai and Tulsi, who could have been mother and daughter, one a granddaughter of a former president, the other a war veteran and former Democratic congresswoman, I had hope as I thought about an American hero named Corey. A man who humbles and humanizes us all with his courage. A man who makes us all stand a little stronger and taller. A great man who shielded his family from danger, committing a selfless, brave act, giving us a heroic and heavenly act and the right view in our collective and ongoing fight between good and evil.

No Joy in Saying this from the Boy on Joy Road

I grew up on a street called Joy Road in a place called Redford Township, Michigan. And I must say it was a joyous time. It was largely filled with joy because of the woman who lived there and ruled the roost with a big, kind, giving heart- my beautiful mother Freda.

Her only agenda in life was doing for others. Her family. Her friends. Her church. Her community. Her country. Her world. She invited everyone in no matter what. To her all lives mattered.

That is why it's so hard to hear the name *Joy* used in such a joyless fashion by those in the media and on social media. Three Joys in particular, and I have no joy in saying this, not only give me no joy, but they put no Joy into the world.

Joy Behar – on The View, often called *Joyless Behar*. That this woman is on TV is bad enough, that she continues to constantly spread her joyless gospel to the masses and is sad, sick and a waste of precious time.

Joy Behar sparked furious backlash questioning Trump's Christian faith in wake of the assassination attempt on his life for describing Donald Trump as *'very narcissistic'* after he claimed he survived his assassination attempt because God was 'on his side.'

Trump spoke to the RNC and talked about the fact he shouldn't be here and that G-d intervened. Still Joy would have no part of it symbolically clinging to her rosary as she criticized Trump who only days before had dodged a bullet to save his life. "'What I want to point out, one thing. I'm speaking to fellow Christians, I was raised Catholic. I'm a Christian girl. 'When something like this happens to you like this assassination attempt and you say something like "God was watching me," that is a very unchristian thing to say because it's very narcissistic.'"

Narcissistic or not, *Joyless Behar, is* a nickname given to her by some who can handle watching her and even some of them chimed in on her self-righteous tone. *"If there ever was an example of someone NOT a Christian it would be Joy Behar so she should stop claiming she is... She should be fired. A hateful human being,"* wrote one viewer. [80]

Not to be outmatched in the joyless category is Joy Reid, who sits and spits hatred on MSNBC like a dragon unleashes fire on daily basis. MSNBC host Joy Reid questioned the nature of former President Trump's injuries on Wednesday after he narrowly survived an assassination attempt. *"I have many questions! Like where are the medical reports? What caused Trump's injury and what was the injury? Shrapnel? Glass? A bullet? Where were the three attendees who were shot seated or standing relative to Trump? Why was Trump allowed to stand and pose for photos, fist pumping for nearly ten seconds while asking about his shoe when there could easily have been additional shooters?"* Reid responding to a post wondering why journalists weren't demanding medical information from Trump in the aftermath of the Pennsylvania shooting, as they are from President Biden.[81]

That's pretty low. As joyless as you can get. Man escapes death, leaps to his feet and raises his fist in defiance, yet her hatred prevents her from sharing what should be a universal moment that celebrates the human spirit. But Joy Reid and her fellow joyless TV personality Joy Behar lack spirit, fairness and of course they lack joy. But they are after all famous and seeking controversy.

In the days that followed the Trump Assassination attempt, the Coup to remove Biden and the crowning of Kamala, I laid low on social media not because I was defeated or discouraged but because I was exhausted. As I listened to the chatter, often gritting my teeth at the hatred and stupidity that was proudly posted –when I came across an acquaintance named Joy. I checked in to see if she could inject some "joy" into one of my favorite words with the spirit it so justly deserved. Even with all her Zen-like training, steeped in philosophical metaphysical rants of s guru seemingly in control of her emotions, she too had gone to the dark side ranting from behind her keyboard into the universe how a rapist and felon could not become our next president- excuse me dictator.

I have no joy in saying this, but the boy who grew up on Joy road was just about to give up on the word, when I got a call from mother, in the aftermath of the assassination attempt.

In beautiful Greek, my mother stated her take saying simply, *"O Theos Eivai Megalos"* – which means that G-D is big. And then she added, *The Lord was watching out for him on this day. It wasn't his time. We should all be grateful."*

And just like that I moved from one of my favorite words to another – from *joy* to *gratitude*. All courtesy of my mother, a wise and good woman who sees the world from her beautiful and loving point of view.

You do know you're not voting for a woman...a black woman...or... an Indian woman don't you?

You do know you're not voting for a woman...a black woman...or an Indian woman...you're just voting for another fake human, make that two fake humans who in all actuality are just puppets. And voting for another puppet or two doesn't break any glass ceilings.

Merely changing the puppet at the end of the puppet strings and leaving the same puppet master in charge will provide the same miserable results for America and Americans.

So who's in charge? One thing is certain that Donald J. Trump is in charge of his own thoughts and policies. There are no strings attached to him. You might not like him, you may love him, but one thing we can all agree on is he is his own man. He's no puppet. The farthest thing from it.

Kamala on the other hand follows in the footsteps of the previous puppet in chief named Joe.

And not only is she a puppet just like Joe, but she has copied one of his signature traits- stealing other people's ideas. For Biden plagiarism was his Achilles heel, for "Kamala Cat," she's lifted Trump's "NO TAX ON TIPS" idea, a bold policy idea designed to give those working in the service industry a break. Kamala's real passion all along has been passing legislation that put an extra 88,000 IRS agents on the streets, many of whom would crack down on collecting tips from bartenders, waitresses, waiters and caddies.

Phoniness and an inept business sense are two of the strings attached to this inauthentic puppet.

Her notorious word salads are probably the most real and revealing thing about Harris. In dissecting them, one realizes there is no there, there. Kamala like the true puppet that she is in over her head and has nothing in her head, but dust.

Want a tip? Promise it won't be too taxing. Take a look at her record before you vote. It is filled with enough flip flops to dizzy even the most loyal supporters

Trump says...a politician will usual tell you who they are in the beginning. She is on the record for being an extreme, far left radical. Her policies fitting of a hard core Marxist at the worst and a socialist on steroids at its best. That's why first impressions matter.

It will be the tip of the iceberg of what you get. *Because what you don't see is what you will get.* And what every American voter will get if she becomes president is a road to serfdom.

Eventually, she will be found out, and the strings attached to her will surely be seen by the American people. The puppet can't keep the strings moving forever. Eventually, the mask will be lifted, and the imposter will be found out; one hopes it is just not too late.

Fight, Fight, Fight…For what is Right…Right…Right

They had all been taking shots at him for years. But this was the first time that they used real bullets. For those who know and support, even love Donald J. Trump, you know the level of hate being shot in this man's direction ever since he came down that golden escalator.

Had they known he was going to be this much of a thorn in their sides, they surely would have tried harder to kill him way back before he and the movement took hold.

Still, as the bullet miraculously passed by the former president's head, it would be fascinating to see and hear what they were all saying, those truly responsible for this evil and heinous attack on a man named Trump.

I'm not speaking about the patsy named *Thomas Mathew Crooks*. I'm talking about all the *thieves, traitors, and crooks* who are really behind this attack. They'll want you to believe that this 20-year-old loaner from middle-America with acne and mental problems acted alone as he outfoxed all the alphabet agencies paid to protect the president, a young man whom they brains-washed as a Manchurian Candidate to kill their political enemy and the MAGA movement.

They have all had Trump in their sights for many years. They were there front and center, trying to destroy him, his name, his legacy, his movement, his family, and his country.

They first shot at him with Russian collusion nonsense funded by Hillary. It continued 24/7 in a frenzied manner, an assault on him and his vision of America in a machine gun-like fashion, spraying accusations, shooting in any and all directions, hoping to hit something and get him- Get Trump. After a grotesque Mueller report failed, two specious impeachments and four indictments failed to deter the Donald, they in the deep state and on the left had only one choice left – real bullets.

Real bullets shot at their only real threat to them in their continued remaking and resetting of America. It was not rhetoric now or some conspiracy found at the end of some fringe follower's tweet or post. They knew what they wanted to do, and they knew how they wanted to do it. There was only one man who stood in their way, and on July 13th, 2024, he was standing on a stage in a rural Pennsylvania town named Butler.

It was approximately 6:11 pm when President Trump uncharacteristically pointed to a projection of a chart that showed a spike in illegal border crossings under the man he's running against, President Joe Biden.

"That chart's a couple of months old," Trump told the crowd. *"And if you want to see something really sad —"*

That's when the shots rang out, at least five. Trump clutched his ear as dark-suited Secret Service agents dashed toward him. He dropped to the ground as the agents yelled, *"Get down!"* The thousands of rally-goers packed into the field in front of him moved as one, dropping down as silence spread across the grass, punctuated only by an occasional scream.[82]

Shots fired. Chaos. Shock. An occasional scream. People scurried in many directions. Yet the crowd of red-hatted Americans remained remarkably calm. Perhaps because of the shock of the scene and what they had just seen. The shock of seeing the man, their man named Trump, no longer on the stage with just his name TRUMP resting on a sign and a shaky podium. They were shots seen and heard around the world. And once seen they were ingrained in our memory. The shots that were fired were designed to drastically change our history.

The shot of our president on the ground was apparently hit and bleeding. Shocking. Traumatic. Too much to process. Then, the sudden move. The only one he could make. That only he would make. The move for the movement. Trump rose to his feet as those around him in black suits struggled to keep him down and covered.

The thrust in the air of the fists, from a man who has been shot at for years. This time with real bullets. Bloodied but not beaten. Not ever ready to give up on his fight for America, he triumphantly pumped his fists in the air as he yelled... *Fight, Fight, Fight!*

It is a shot. A photograph. An image of a man who, in his own words, has said, "I'm not supposed to be here," realizing the providence of the moment. It is a shot that will live on in American history. And it is a shot that will be viewed from either a point of view of inspiration, pride, and patriotism or, sadly, one of hate and disdain.

It is a shot of a man and president raising his hands and proclaiming his intention to all those out there in America – that he isn't going anywhere, and neither are the people who attended the rally and have attended rallies like it for years all across this great land.

It is a shot of a missed shot by a delusional young man and the people behind him who hate America and the man on the stage so much that they try to kill him and his movement that he leads with the same bullet. The magic bullet, they thought.

Thankfully, they missed their shot. But the president didn't miss his.

Raising his hands as if to say, "Hey, I'm okay."

And you know what? So is the movement. The one he and the people who attended this rally and rallies like it are fighting and standing up for and that they will never give up on. No matter how many bullets are fired in their direction. And a movement that... *We, the people,* will always stand up and fight, fight, fight for... because it is right, right, right!

As the Movie Plays out – I think of a man named Capra

Often I sit there wondering if this movie will ever end and how it will end. I want to look away because it is too painful to watch. It raises my blood pressure and infuriates me at what's happening to the picture that I have always had of America.

Were we ever perfect? Hell no. But at least we were fair. Or at least I thought we were fair. And we had people in positions in the media who would check on those in power to make sure that *we, the American people,* were getting a fair shake. Never thought I could watch elected officials play favorites with those who didn't belong here in the first place. Illegal immigrants - whose *first acting job* was breaking the law while entering America, as if it was some movie set that they were entitled to visit while starring in a movie that they were never cast in, by those of us doing the financing for this movie called America.

Still, they came in waves – like they were in one of those *Cecil B DeMille* movies – crossing the border and the river in Texas as if they were Jews being led to the Promised Land by Moses. At least Moses parted a sea for the migrants to land in the promised land – and yes, they were truly asylum-seeking refugees.

But these folks don't belong here. Nope. They don't. And they never will. It's funny and ironic that one of the lines in their script that almost everyone in the legacy media, elites, and those swamp monsters in DC often cite as their mantra – "that no one is above the law." Yet when it comes to addressing these actors who came onto the set known as America, with literally their first act breaking the law, to the left, they and their actions are obviously above the law.

Frank Capra, the wonderful three-time Oscar-winning director, himself an Italian immigrant, masterfully told the story of the forgotten and common men and women in his films about America. His stories featured the George and Mary Baileys, John Does, Mr. Deeds, and The Mr. Smiths out there who believed in and achieved the American dream and, even with all the struggles, painted America as a place to certainly pursue life, liberty, and happiness.

And for that, his films, while lauded by many, are dismissed by some as being Capricorn- a pejorative attached to the legendary filmmaker's canon of work. But that's not how many Americans – you know the types – those that don't frequent the movies as much as they once did, the MAGA-wearing forgotten men and women who relate to Stewart's and Capra's Mr. Smith and George Bailey and Cooper's and Capra's John Doe and Mr. Deeds characters. To them, they are alive, if not always well on the screen, these men and women representing an America whose goodness still beats in many of our hearts and whose memory is tucked away for safekeeping.

In his autobiography, *"The Name Above the Title,"* Frank Capra speaks with gratitude and with a debt owed to his brother Ben, who first came to this country and paved the way for his younger brother to come later to the land of milk and honey. And while Capra himself did not find the roads paved in gold, he found true opportunities for his voice to be heard and his stories to be told.

It's a journey that we, as Americans, are grateful the Capra family made. Their trip to America tipped their heart and hopes to a statue in the harbor as they came to our land the right way.

As I think of Capra, I cannot help but think of my grandfather, bringing his five children, including my beautiful mother, to this land of milk and honey. I think of him, brokenhearted and just plain broken after World War II had torn his world apart, coming to America and looking at the Statue of Liberty with no guarantees but with much gratitude.

Then I think of another elderly man who occupies the office of presidency and a look I will never forget when he was asked a question about his potential opponent in the 2024 presidential election. When he was asked a rare pointed question by the press, "If Trump got a fair trial," the evil grimace of a man named BIDEN smirking like the Devil at the question while not ever answering it will be a scene this forgotten man shall never forget.

Mr. Potter has nothing on Joe Biden when it comes to accurately portraying a greedy, powerful, and empty soul – drunk on power. Many of the elites and establishment Potter and Mr. Paine types call his films *Capri-Corn,* while others view them as jewels of inspiration providing hope for the masses.

Capra often explained his films simply, saying, "Not the way life is, but the way life ought to be."

The way life ought to be. Indeed.

How do I want this movie to end? Like a Capra film, of course.

The hero comes to the rescue of we the people, and we, the people, toast him with gratitude in the scene while thanking him for all his efforts. Pure Capra. With the bad guys getting their just deserts and justice and the common men and women getting their fair shot at living and chasing their American dream. A film where *John and Jane Doe* characters everywhere star in their own film where joy, hope —and the pursuit of happiness are alive and well. A movie version and vision of America once seen by grateful immigrants taking in the Statue of Liberty as they looked on with hope in the money shot as the end credits roll.

Capri-corn?

No, just the way it ought to be and the way I hope this movie finishes.

XIII. Good vs Evil & the Only Vote That Counts

Child Trafficking Film, That Sick left leaves Behind like Children at the Border

J-6 Perspective- Sick Sad Feeling of Inevitable Storms, Diminishing Blue Skies and Fog

Twist Plot Twist in Abortion Story - A Sudden thirst for Killing Babies

13 Dead Soldiers, Patriots & Names Forgotten, Honored and Remembered

CAGED BIRDS- Plight of my fellow patriots, brothers, and sisters (The J-6 Hostages)

Ultimate Vote in the End/Choosing between two forces -One Good & One Evil

A True Dream – Attending the Truth Awards

Holy Spirit delivers me the Number: John 316, No- Don 316

The Legacy and Face of MAGA – A tribute to Corey

Out to Get JD Just like Trump by not getting his Hillbilly Elegy

You can't be Serious…or a serious person if you vote for these two clowns

The Distance from JFK to DJT not as far as you think

I was born in Dearborn Michigan

Project Much? Who are the real weirdos?

Does Anyone Remember a Patriot Named Ashli Babbitt?

It's a Conspiracy World After All (Sung to it's a small world) X

MAGA Man A Once Banned Twitter Refuge Becomes X Factor Breaking Internet

The Emperor's New Pant Suit

JFK, RFK & JFK Jr smiling down from above in MAGA Hats

Going Back to Butler…because that's what Leaders do

Get Trump…Get America… Get You…Get Me…

Child Trafficking Film, That Sick left leaves Behind like Children at the Border

A slam dunk. A No-brainer. A place of agreement. A meeting of minds, not in the middle –but in a holy place, where good overcomes evil and common sense should rule the day. A place where good liberals, staunch conservatives, and independent-thinking libertarians can all agree.

"God's children are not for sale." Or at least they should not be for sale.

Hell, even devout atheists –me thinks can agree with that.

But no- in a world so lost in terms of a moral compass, this is not an obvious place of agreement.

That's what I've found out as I viewed the heartbreaking and powerful *"Sound of Freedom,"* and the reaction to the film from an eclectic group of reviewers, Hollywood insiders, and a strange amalgamation of talking and writing heads who've appeared to have come out of their dark closets with one goal in mind: *Crucify this film and deem it fake, exaggerated, and even a lie- or just simply ignore it.*

Well, that's come to be expected in some perverse way in mainstream media. After all, the man portraying the Homeland Security agent and patriot Tim Ballard in the film is Jim Caviezel. And he did, after all, portray Jesus in the most painful and convincing way – in Mel Gibson's "Passion of the Christ," a film ridiculed and, yes, even *crucified* by the world press and Hollywood alike.

Well, like the *Godhead* and man Jesus Christ, whom Jim Caviezel played in *The Passion*, a resurrection was on the horizon, as *The Passion* played much to the dismay of Hollywood to packed houses of the faithful, film lovers, and mere seekers.

Now, fast forward to the times we are living in today. Not the end times hopefully, but who really knows for sure? But unique times never experienced before reflecting perspectives hardly ever seen in our country. A time impacting how the latest chapters, and perhaps last chapters told in our American story and rich history of storytelling in America. Emanating from a place called Hollywood, once ruled by showmen who told and sold tales direct from tinsel town factories that smacked of value and entertainment- and dare I say goodness. A place where projects were green-lit by a studio system – headed by studio moguls - who, yes, wanted to make a buck, but who were also individuals who also wanted to make a difference and even make something good for the common good.

I can't imagine Jack Warner or Irving Thalberg not getting behind and supporting the making and distribution of *Sound of Freedom*.

Actually – I can't understand why anyone would not rally behind this film.

But to paraphrase a line from the iconic *Casablanca:*
"I'm shocked, shocked, that child trafficking is going on here."
"Sir, your profits from your part in our child trafficking enterprise."

The issue is the safety and well-being of children and preventing harm to the most innocent among us. The issue is ugly and obvious and one that is not discussed in polite company –but one that should be talked about in loud voices by *everyone, everywhere and all at once*. No, there can't be two sides to this argument. There are not two sides –when children are being sold into slavery as sex slaves to be used and abused by monsters and have their innocence stolen.

Children. Those with the smallest voice, no choice and without an inability to fight back. Those with the least representation –unless, of course, you count those in the womb. But I won't go there in this argument or review of what I see not only at the movies but all over America.

It concerns the varying values of children. A sliding scale, if you will. The value of our children changes depending on the issue and upon who you are. And please don't use the argument –that *"You don't have kids-therefore you have no right to an opinion."*

That's precisely why I'm going to shout my opinion, blanketed in my film review of SOUND of FREEDOM, at the top of my lungs so that those seeking freedom can see and hear where I stand on this issue at this moment in time, not only in America but all over the world.

Still, you'd think that this was the one place that everyone could agree. Protecting children. This is about preventing children from being abused, raped, and even murdered. This is about stopping them from being worked like slaves at the behest of adults. A no-brainer. A case of good vs. evil – right? But that's not the case. Shockingly, I learned the hard, cold truth that is this. If everyone in the land can't agree 100% to support wholeheartedly the message and the efforts of the filmmakers to expose the evil portrayed in this terrible story – then *there is no hope in America of ever coming together as a nation*. Regarding this issue, there should only be one acceptable outcome pertaining to child trafficking. *Good winning over evil*. Freedom gained over slavery. And children- all children should be valued and protected at any cost- period. And those who do children harm must be punished harshly and severely to the highest extent of the law.

In seeing the film *Sound Of Freedom*, not once but twice – I shook my head at some of the recent reviews I had encountered in the media. I was not shocked at the negative reviews. One is always entitled to their opinion on the value of a particular piece of art – there's that word again- VALUE. With great films as with all art, their value is measured over time. Time will tell if a painting becomes a masterpiece, a building becomes iconic, a piece of music a standard, a sculpture timeless, or a film a classic. Children are God's greatest creation. Our greatest art form. Timeless. Classic - and not for sale.

Back to the film – *Sound of Freedom*. Over the years, surely I have encountered differing opinions from film critics, friends and my film students on particular films –even classics. My years as a film enthusiast, TV host, reviewer, film teacher, and filmmaker have allowed me to wear many hats in the theatre and witness films – (to me, the greatest of all art forms) with varying degrees of passion, disdain, enjoyment, and finally respect.

I take film seriously. I'm blown away by the masters of the medium, from Chaplin to Ford, Francis Ford to Hitch, Wilder to Welles, and from Capra to Spielberg. To those and so many others not mentioned – I always feel I owe you a little bit of my heart and, yes, my childhood for making your tremendous movies and films to engage and inspire me. The movies – is where I got lost and where I found my place to dream. It's where I've had my heart broken, and it's also where I found hope. And throughout the years, the movies were always a place where I could go to dream and a destination where I could find heroes.

There's a word we don't hear often today. *Heroes.* Yet, it's a word that is sadly and sorely lacking today. Gone with the wind are the days, both in America and at the movies, when we were full of them.

And not just in the *John Wayne Cowboy hero kind of way* - although I love the Duke in *Red River* and *The Searchers* and so many others. Nor is this an ode to George Bailey, the heroic everyman played magically by my all-time favorite actor, Jimmy Stewart, in - *It's A Wonderful Life*. And this is not even a tip of the cap to Bogie's Rick Blaine, who sacrifices and sees the love of his life, Ilsa, off at the airport for the greater good in *Casablanca*.

Heroes all. And all worthy of being looked up to and admired. But this isn't about famous heroes portrayed on the silver screen; this is about common heroes. Unsung heroes. Heroes that surprise us. Heroes, as Emerson would say, were heroes "because they were brave five minutes longer." Heroes, yes who we used to read about and see all the time on the big screen. Heroes who once united us all. Heroes who encouraged us to strive to do the common good. A heroic tale. One where we related to the heroes on the screen. Thankful for them just being there —and hopeful that things could be better in an often dark world with the light of the movies casting and producing a flicker of hope in all of us. Hope. A big word in films and movies. Hope – a word we all relate to and one that's hard to live without.

Hope and Heroes.

It's what many of my favorite films and movies were made of.

And that's what the film, *Sound of Freedom* is all about.

Hope and heroes.

So, as I sat there watching Sound of Freedom for the second time with a friend steeped in a similar Cinema upbringing of Capra and classic Hollywood, I asked a simple question as the credits rolled and with tears still rolling down my cheek.

"How could anyone be against this film?"

My thoughtful friend paused and then uttered this: "If you're against this film, *you must be on the other side that's responsible for bringing this evil into the world."*

You're either with me or against me - is a phrase echoed sometimes by those trying to set the argument in absolutes and thus shape and win their argument by positioning themselves on the right side of a "Good versus Evil" construct.

Well, with this film and in this case —it's true. You're either for the film and the children and against the demonic forces who bring on this evil, or you are part of the *Infamnia*. The sides couldn't be more easily drawn or clear. Incidentally, *Infamnia*, if you don't remember, is a phrase echoed in *The Godfather* by Don Corleone referring to drug dealing and pedophilia. Two things are forbidden in The Don's business plan. The Don knew all too well the meaning of *Infamnia*, and he knew that while the world profited on the souls of the addicted and the innocents – on these two subjects —especially pedophilia – the Don would have no part of this blood money in his business plan because to him it was personal and all about the kids.

Another man named Donald Trump knows that the scourge called *Child Trafficking* is infecting the planet and that it must be fought and eliminated. Yet some in the media – Hollywood, and the public square choose to look the other way as an epidemic far more dangerous than a Chinese flu threatens the world's children. When they aren't ignoring this issue all together- they are hurling insults at the producers of the film and those who support it by buying tickets.

One need look no further than an array of commentaries and reviews by many in the Main Street press casting aspersions on a film that was largely conceived and created to shine light on the human trafficking problem and help children.

A film and an issue about - *Good vs. Evil*.

I tried to find the good in the following mostly evil reviews of the film.

"As for the losers, start with everyone who gave their money and two hours and 15 minutes of their life to a story that is at best embellished and, whether intentionally or by coincidence, profiting off conspiracy-fueled mass hysteria." Melanie McFarland, Salon.com

"A blandly competent thriller that finds an easy way into your feelings since it deals with child trafficking (a grave subject matter that has been tragically co-opted as a rallying cry for xenophobic, pro-Trump types." Radheyan Simonpillai, CBC Radio

"The narrative diffuses into an improbable "Heart of Darkness" style river journey. Only kind of dull." Glenn Kenny, New York Times

"To know thousands of adults will absorb Sound of Freedom, this vigilante fever dream, and come away thinking themselves better informed on a hidden civilizational crisis… well, it's profoundly depressing. Worse still, they'll want to spread the word." Miles Klee, Rolling Stone

"A solemn, drawn-out bore." Nick Allen RogerEbert.com

It is at times like these that I especially miss my film guru and review hero, Roger Ebert. I just know in my heart that Roger would have been able to articulate all sides of this film.

While these were negative, if not evil, reviews – still some in the media found the value of the message of the film.

"You won't come away BLOWN AWAY by the film itself, but your jaw will drop, and I feel many people will walk away emotional from that. There's a lot of heartbreaking stuff you learn. It is a solid watch." Zach Pope, Zach Pope Reviews

"But even as the film's pacing starts to thud… its work has been done competently, if not altogether artfully. Sometimes, obvious works just fine." Adam Graham Detroit News

"Sound of Freedom tells us about a reality we cannot ignore: trafficking in minors and child pornography exists worldwide. This feature film deserves all the attention just for daring to talk about such a critical issue." Luis Bond Diario las Américas

"Controversy and filmmaking flaws aside, Sound Of Freedom touches on an important subject that neither side should be politicizing." Rosa Parra" The Daily Chela[83]

The numbers at Rotten Tomatoes, the film review website that compiles an aggregate of film reviews from both critics and consumers alike as of July 27, 2023, lists 70% of the critics giving the film a positive or *Roger Ebert and Gene Siskel- Thumbs Up* to the film; while the audience gave it a rating of 99. This simply means that out of 100 people who saw the film as consumers, -99 gave it a positive review. It also means that out of 100 critics, 70 gave it a positive review, and 30 gave it a negative review. *(Update: As of October 2024, critics lowered their Rotten Tomatoes score to 57 while the audience still gave it a rating of 99.)*

Before I share some more savaging words from the Rolling Stones reviewer, who I find to be a damaged and dim-witted reviewer –let me throw some questions at you.

Should sex with children be allowed?
When is a good time to abuse a puppy or a kitten?
How often should you beat up old people?
The answer to all questions is obviously - NEVER.
Simple if you know the difference between right and wrong.
And the difference between - Good vs Evil.

While Rolling Stones reviewer Klee is probably unable to easily answer questions like these, he is without question an individual who displays an obvious animus toward not only the message and execution of *Sound of Freedom* but also a disdain toward those who supported the film by buying tickets in bushels.

Rolling Stone – Review by Miles Klee

Tim Ballard, Caviezel, and others of their ilk had primed the public to accept Sound of Freedom as a documentary rather than delusion by fomenting moral panic for years over this grossly exaggerated 'epidemic' of child sex trafficking, much of it funneling people into conspiracist rabbit holes and QAnon communities. In short, I was at the movies with people who were there to see their worst fears confirmed."

"It's a stomach-turning experience, fetishizing the torture of its child victims and lingering over lush preludes to their sexual abuse. At times I had the uncomfortable sense that I might be arrested myself just for sitting through it. Nonetheless, the mostly white-haired audience around me could be relied on to gasp, moan in pity, mutter condemnations,

applaud, and bellow 'Amen!' at moments of righteous fury, as when Ballard declares that 'God's children are not for sale.'

"Based On a True Story," I heard from somewhere across the theater.

"The familiar words had appeared on screen, and an elderly man had taken it upon himself to read them aloud to the rest of a sizable audience seated for a matinee showing of the anti-child trafficking thriller Sound of Freedom starring Jim Caviezel. For the seasoned moviegoer, this phrase is a joke — we know that cinema will stretch almost any "truth" to the breaking point — and the rank insincerity of such a pronouncement is the foundation of the prankish opening titles of Fargo. But this crowd, I could tell, would view the events depicted over the next two-plus hours as entirely literal."

"Caviezel, best known for being tortured to death in Mel Gibson's The Passion of the Christ, has become a prominent figure on the conspiracist right, giving speeches and interviews in which he hints at an underground holy war between patriots and a sinister legion of evildoers who are harvesting the blood of children. It's straight-up Q Anon stuff, right down to his use of catchphrases like "The storm is upon us." Here, he gets to act out some of that drama by playing a fictionalized version of Tim Ballard, head of the anti-sex trafficking nonprofit Operation Underground Railroad (O.U.R.), in a feature film that casts the operator as a Batman-style savior for kids sold into the sex trade."

"Ballard himself has dabbled in Q-adjacent conspiracy theories, such as the Wayfair trafficking hoax, while his organization has far-right affinities and a long record of distorting its botched "raids," which rely on bizarre tactics like asking psychics where to find victims for rescue."

"It matters, too, that Sound of Freedom almost never saw the light of day. Completed in 2018, no studio would take it for fear of losing money, according to producer Eduardo Verastegui— with Netflix and Amazon among those who passed. It finally found distribution thanks to Angel Studios, a Utah-based media company that crowdfunds original films and TV series that "amplify light." (Although founded by

Mormon brothers who originally created a content- filtering service to prevent children from seeing violence, nudity and profanity, it claims no formal church affiliation."

"Therefore, to its boosters, the movie checks many satisfying boxes at once. Caviezel, a devout Catholic allegedly blacklisted by the entertainment industry, back for a mythology-burnishing biopic of Ballard, a call to action in an imagined global war against sexual predators; a blow struck at the heart of "woke" Hollywood, the den of iniquity that snubbed it and (lest we forget) is thought to produce the wealthy deviants who serve as villains in this story."

"Meaning it will surely do no good to point out Sound of Freedom's hackneyed white savior narrative. Or its wildly immature assumption that abused and traumatized children go right back to normal once the bad guys are in handcuffs. Or that it enforces stereotypes about trafficking that Angel Studios itself says are less than accurate. To the film's intended viewers, these cannot be flaws — they're the whole appeal."

"There is visible suffering all around us in America. There are poor and unhoused, and people brutalized or killed by police. There are mass shootings, lack of healthcare, climate disasters. And yet, over and over, the far right turns to these sordid fantasies about godless monsters hurting children. Now, as in the 1980s satanic panic, they won't even face the fact that most kids who suffer sexual abuse are harmed not by a shadowy cabal of strangers, but at the hands of a family member. To know thousands of adults will absorb Sound of Freedom, this vigilante fever dream, and come away thinking themselves better informed on a hidden civilizational crisis... well, it's profoundly depressing. Worse still, they'll want to spread the word.'[84]

Not a review as much as a crucifixion of those who are on the right and on the right side of history in the fight between good vs. evil on the movie screens and in the world in general. Mr. Miles Klee is a hapless and hopeless film reviewer. A lost soul from Rolling Stone Magazine. He proves once and for all that while a rolling stone gathers no moss, his reviews you can toss because they have no value and are merely laced with his bias, hatred, and lack of a moral compass that leaves him lost in the wilderness, *with no direction home,* M*iles* away from getting the picture.

Another Hollywood picture depicting the dark side of the atrocities of man is 1961's Judgement at Nuremberg, with Spencer Tracy as Judge Dan Haywood delivering a verdict on the value of human lives in the battle of good vs. evil.

Judge Dan Haywood: *Janning, to be sure, is a tragic figure. We believe he loathed the evil he did. But compassion for the present torture of his soul must not beget forgetfulness of the torture and death of millions by the government of which he was a part. Janning's record and his fate illuminate the most shattering truth that has emerged from this trial. If he and the other defendants were all depraved perverts - if the leaders of the Third Reich were sadistic monsters and maniacs - these events would have no more moral significance than an earthquake or other natural catastrophes. But this trial has shown that under the stress of a national crisis, men - even able and extraordinary men - can delude themselves into the commission of crimes and atrocities so vast and heinous as to stagger the imagination. No one who has sat through this trial can ever forget. The sterilization of men because of their political beliefs... The murder of children... How easily that can happen! There are those in our country today, too, who speak of the "protection" of the country. Of "survival". The answer to that is: survival as what? A country isn't a rock. And it isn't an extension of one's self. It's what it stands for, when standing for something is the most difficult! Before the people of the world - let it now be noted in our decision here that this is what we stand for: justice, truth... and the value of a single human being!"*[85]

One single human being. And one single child. One child abducted, tortured, and held in slavery is one too many and cannot be tolerated.

Critics, like Klee, who point to an *exaggeration* in the number of children being trafficked as being a flaw in the film, have already lost the meaning and point of telling the story in the first place.

They mock the "What if it were your child?" line from the film but fail to really answer the question.

"What if it were your child?"

Another question for those with the broken moral compasses.

What is the number of child trafficking cases that you feel comfortable with?

One? 100? 1000? 10,000? 100,000? 1,000,000?

As with the film *Judgement at Nuremberg* – the weight of the guilty verdict rests with committing a crime so heinous and evil that it impacts *even one life* and not in the fact that during the Holocaust masterminded by the evil Nazi regime in 1930's Germany, where over six million Jews were exterminated. For this inconceivable evil, the judge – so that we could understand – stated that the guilt of the crime rests - *in what we do to one fellow human being.*

The same is true today in regard to worldwide child trafficking. We should all be outraged and called to action. For one life. And for one child's well-being. Obviously the guilt lies with those who mastermind and conduct the evil. But it also rests with *those who know that evil exists and do nothing to stop it*. For those who sit silent today, rationalizing and diminishing evil deeds taking place around them- they must remember only this from the Judgment at Nuremberg.

Do you sit silent for one life or for millions of lives impacted?

What is the magic number that will *trigger* you into action?

And finally, did you crucify the film *The Sound of Freedom* because you thought the numbers of children impacted by human trafficking were exaggerated and part of some right-wing conspiracy?

There was one brave woman, Tara Lee Rodas who could not stay silent any longer. Working in the Biden Administration for Health and Human Services, she came forward to tell the horror stories of child trafficking and what she saw take place at our southern border. Speaking with conviction and clarity as a whistleblower, a congressional hearing, "*The Biden Border Crisis: Exploitation of Unaccompanied Alien Children,*" *examined the unprecedented surge of unaccompanied alien children at the southwest border and how open-border policies enable the exploitation of those children."*

What follows is a transcript of her entire testimony before Congress on April 26, 2023, when she blew the whistle on the evil deeds and doers thriving amongst us – for the only reason you need, not its impact on millions of lives but on one single life – the life of one child.

"It's an honor to be here. I thank you for the invitation to share my testimony. My goal is to inspire action to safeguard the **lives of migrant children, including the staggering 85,000 that are missing**. Today, children will work overnight shifts at slaughterhouses, factories, restaurants to pay their debts to smugglers and traffickers. Today, children will be sold for sex. Today, children will call a hotline to report that they are being abused, neglected, and trafficked. For nearly a decade, unaccompanied children have been suffering in the shadows. I must confess; I knew nothing about their suffering until 2021 when I volunteered to help the Biden Administration on with the crisis at the Southern Border. As part of Operation Artemis, I was deployed to the Pomona Fairplex Emergency Intake Site in California to help the HHS Office of Refugee Resettlement reunite children with sponsors in the US. I thought I was going to help place children in loving homes. Instead, I discovered that children are being trafficked through a sophisticated network that begins with being recruited in home country, smuggled to the US border, and ends when ORR delivers a child to a Sponsors – some sponsors are criminals and traffickers and members of Transnational Criminal Organizations. Some sponsors view children as commodities and assets to be used for earning income - this is why we are witnessing an explosion of labor trafficking. Whether intentional or not, it can be argued that the US Government has become the middleman in a large scale, multi-billion-dollar, child trafficking operation run by bad actors seeking to profit off the lives of children. As for me, my interest is in the safety of the children. I don't view this as a political issue. I view this as a humanitarian issue. My motives are the highest and best. I want to see the children protected, so I want to tell you some what I witnessed at the Pomona Fairplex:

• I saw vulnerable Indigenous children from Guatemala who speak Mayan dialects and can't speak Spanish. That means they can't ask for help in English and they can't ask for help in Spanish. These children become captives to their Sponsors.

• I've sat with Case Managers as they cried, retelling horrific things that were done to children on the journey.

• I saw apartment buildings where 20, 30 & 40 unaccompanied children have been released.

- *I saw sponsors trying to simultaneously sponsor children from multiple ORR sites.*
- *I saw sponsors using multiple addresses to obtain sponsorships of children.*
- *I saw numerous cases of children in debt bondage, and the child knew they had to stay with the sponsor until the debt was paid. Realizing that we were not offering children the American dream but instead putting them into modern-day slavery with wicked overlords was a terrible revelation. These children are a captive victim population with no access to law enforcement or knowledge of their rights. They are extorted, exploited, abused, neglected, and trafficked. This is why I blew the whistle. I've witnessed firsthand the horrors of child trafficking and exploitation. My life will never be the same. But I have hope. I'm counting on you. It's my hope you'll take action to end this crisis and safeguard the lives of these vulnerable children."* People have asked me, *"What would you do to turn the ship around?"* I usually say some of the following:
- *Commit to oversight, transparency, and accountability. #1 Priority for HHS is Oversight. Data from the UC program needs to be examined by expert data analysts. This can quickly be done by experts in the IG Community at the Pandemic Analytics Center of Excellence (PACE). Children could be rescued, and criminals could be prosecuted if the PACE had access to the data in the UC portal.*
- *Stop retaliating against whistleblowers. Stop retaliating against the truth-tellers who are trying to help. As it is written, "A wise man listens to advice, while a fool continues in his folly." HHS needs to be wise.*
- *Change HHS' culture of speed over safety. Speed is the wrong performance measure.*
- *Revamp the vetting process of Sponsors and have Case Managers who are investigators, data analysts, certified fraud examiners, etc.*
- *Reimagine a system where the Sponsor is the accountable party. Sponsors should be required to report to ORR.*

Again, I have hope. I'm counting on you. It's my hope you'll take action to end this crisis and safeguard the lives of these vulnerable children. Thank you for your time and attention to this urgent matter. I'd be happy to answer any questions from the committee. [86]

Brave testimony from a whistleblower. Impassioned. Compassionate. Hopeful. An apolitical call to action. A voice speaking for the voiceless in the fight of good versus evil. It's really that clear and simple to understand.

Good versus Evil.

Currently, whether wittingly or not, the United States government acted as a middleman in this evil deedor using Hollywood terms acted as a Co-Producer or distributor. And while many in Hollywood, the media, academia, and government stand as silent as Charlie Chaplin once did so brilliantly in his films, these evil pictures and stories are being produced all around us and by producers, directors, and actors amongst us in the shadows.

Still, the script can and must change. But it must rest with all of us in the rewrite. We must be more concerned for the well-being of children than breaking a picket line for fellow union SAG and AFTRA members. Where are the many voices —who have platforms to denounce these evils, yelling *ACTION on the set*? Instead, they yell, "Quiet on the set."

Nothing to see here.

And where are the critics who fawn over a *Barbie* movie while at the same time shun and crucify a film made about child trafficking - an unspeakable evil done to children? Little children, many hundreds of thousands, perhaps millions of little girls and little boys, who right now, as you dress in pink and glitter for your Barbie movie night, are having their innocence and lives stolen from them by monsters, not in darkened theatres on the screen– but by real monsters who abuse them in the dark underworld that is child trafficking – a business thriving and doing bigger box office numbers than even Barbie or Oppenheimer combined.

Save the cute phrase *Barbenheimer* branding for your marketing meetings, as kids around the world are branded as commodities to be abused for profit by monsters and big business.

Today, child trafficking is part of a human trafficking business that accounts for an estimated $150 billion industry. An industry that takes advantage of the least protected amongst us- our children. Children who are enslaved and forced to work in deplorable conditions and perform sexual acts with monsters, fighting to survive and leaving them no time to be children and play with actual *Barbies and GI Joes*.

The attack on this movie has been relentless, reminding many of the constant and ferocious persecution of Donald J. Trump that took place ever since he rode down that escalator. To many, that persecution rivaled and reminded many Christians of the persecution their Lord faced when he came to fulfill his promise to save the souls of all the world's sinners in His fight between good and evil.

Now today, Jim Caviezel, the man who portrayed *Jesus* in Mel Gibson's runaway box office smash *Passion of the Christ*, is being targeted viciously for his portrayal of Tim Ballard, a rogue Homeland Security agent battling to fight the evil of child trafficking while saving God's children.

In the film, Caviezel, as Ballard states, *"God's Children are not for sale."*

Well, at least they should not be.

Still, the numbers regarding *human trafficking, forced labor, forced commercial sexual exploitation, and modern slavery are staggering, according to statistics on the United States Department* of State website. Under the section, *International Labor Organization*, a report was released regarding Global Estimates of Modern Slavery in September of *2022.*

This report estimates that, at any given time in 2021, approximately 27.6 million people were in forced labor. Of these, "17.3 million are exploited in the private sector, **6.3 million in forced commercial sexual exploitation**, *and 3.9 million in forced labor imposed by state." The definition of forced labor used in this report is based on ILO Forced Labor Convention, 1930 (No. 29), which states in Article 2.1 that forced labor is "all work or service which is exacted from any person under the menace of any penalty and for which the said person has not offered himself voluntarily. This report also estimates that 49.6 million people were in "modern slavery" at any given time in 2021, but this figure includes both the estimate for forced labor and an estimate for forced marriage. Consistent with current implementation of U.S. law, it is recommended to use only the 27.6 million estimate when referring to human trafficking. While some instances of forced marriage may meet the international or U.S. legal definition of human trafficking, not all cases* do. Note further that the term "modern slavery" is not defined in international or U.S. law.[87]

Whether the numbers are 49.6 million people in Modern Slavery, 27.6 million people in forced labor, 17.3 million exploited in the private sector, or 6.3 million in forced commercial sexual exploitation, the actual numbers should not matter as much as this number - ONE.

Remembering the wisdom of a wise judge at Nuremberg, *"Before the people of the world - let it now be noted in our decision here that this is what we stand for: justice, truth... and the value of a single human being!"* While its value rests in impacting even one life, that trafficking potentially affects millions of children is a shameful, sinful and to quote Don Corleone, an infamnia.

Watching *Sound of Freedom*, impacted by its power, moved to sadness and angered by those savaging the film, I came to the only conclusion that any normal human can reach. You are either on the side of good or evil and either for the film or against it. And if you are muffling out the *Sound of Freedom* – you're complicit in protecting the monsters, aiding the abusers, purveying evil to the masses, and *you are the problem*.

But you are not alone – because no man is an island.

From author John Donne's *No Man is an Island," "any man's death diminishes me because I am involved in Mankind; and therefore never send to know for whom the bell tolls; It tolls for thee."* Hauntingly, metaphorically, part of the narrative in *Sound of Freedom* takes place on an island reminiscent of Epstein Island, where much evil and abuse to children took place.

Yet strangely, at a time when everything is news, 24-7, and everything is a potential Trump indictment, the media are not the least bit curious in pursuing the flight log rich with celebrity names who frequented Epstein's evil island.

And you know why not? It's just a theory, but they're not interested because one man's name is not on that flight log. Donald J. Trump. He never visited Epstein Island. But you know who allegedly did? Bill Clinton. At least 25 times. Hillary too. Bill Gates. Oprah. And many other celebrities and famous, well-to-do people who were probably up to no good.

But you know who is up to doing some good? Jim Caviezel, the man who once played Jesus in a film and who now beats the drum to wake up people in time to fight for the children in *The Sound of Freedom*.

Speaking with Brian Kilmeade on Fox and Friends, he spoke of the child trafficking issue: "We have to do a lot more. And we got to start with Donald Trump...he's got to be in there because he's going to go after the traffickers."

"This is the new Moses," Caviezel said. "I mean, I'm still Jesus, but he's the new Moses. Pharaoh, let my children go free."[88] If you thought they hated Caviezel and Trump before, well, you haven't seen anything yet.

And sadly, to some, it's not *The Sound of Freedom* that they hear but the sound of hatred. But make no mistake. This issue and movie are bigger and more important than any box office number by Marvel or a toy made by Mattel. This is about liberty. Freedom. But most of all it's about the children, all children and in the end one child….and the value of one human being.

Because if you don't know or agree that *"God's children are not for sale,"* then get ready, because soon you will hear a louder sound that at first you won't be able to identify. But then you will. Softly at first, then building like a freight train. The sound of loud drums banging and patriots marching, charging, and gathering to come after all those complicit in this *infamnia*.

J-6 Perspective- Sick Sad Feeling of Inevitable Storms, Diminishing Blue Skies and Fog

It was January 6, 2021. I remember talking to the black woman from Georgia as the scene played out on the Capitol steps. I had seen smoke, a light fog that permeated the DC air and impaired my vision from a distance. There were rumblings from afar – but as I got closer, the scene became not more clear in my mind - but increasingly cloudy.

Some call it the "Fog of War" or, in this case, the "Fog of Protest" or the "Fog of Insurrection" or the "Fog of you fill in the blank."

I'm not going to tell you that I clearly remember everything in a crystal clear fashion.

My head was foggy. But one thing was crystal clear on this sad and sick day in DC – there were many people who saw the day differently…uniquely and from their own perspective skewed by where they sat, who they voted for, what they saw or think they saw, what they didn't see - and finally and perhaps most importantly what the republic and the Constitution meant to them as they watched, the riot, protest or insurrection play out.

That's when I saw her. A black woman was looking down at her phone, preoccupied with something that was blurting across her feed.

I caught her attention, yet she hardly looked up at me as she started to blurt out a headline.

"The Vice-President has just double-crossed the President."

The words, for a moment – hung in the increasingly cloudy DC air.

That's when she looked me straight in the eye and sent a chill down my spine.

"Pence just double-crossed President Trump."

"He's a traitor."

She was, of course, speaking about the actions or inaction that Vice-President Pence held in his hand regarding what could or couldn't be done regarding certifying the election. And while I only saw her briefly I will never forget this black lady who I encountered on the steps of the capitol and at the edge of liberty. She spoke so softly and with great sadness in her voice about a man she loved named Donald Trump and a man named Pence who had done him wrong on a cold day in the nation's capital.

Plot Twist in Abortion Story - A Sudden thirst for Killing Babies

Oh my, how the Abortion story has evolved. -

Evolved, an interesting choice of words when one considers that a baby is evolving when it is in essence growing inside the mother. An evolving narrative to those that at one time claimed that *"Abortion should be safe, legal and rare,"* have changed their view on *how they don't see the baby inside the body* of the *person* carrying the baby.

"Safe, Legal and Rare."

Those were sentiments once coined by none other than *Bill Clinton*. Leave it to *Slick Willie* to come up with a phrase that would save his ass politically - even as it failed to save babies' lives. *Safe, Legal, and Rare was the nuanced mantra that the man from Hope, Arkansas,* was famous for and one that at least provided a *little hope* to some babies.

Nuanced phrases – he perfected them. Who can forget his, *"It depends on what your definition of is, is."* A twist on Bill Clinton's words hauntingly applies today as well. As far as "Safe, Legal and Rare" goes, that was so 1990's.

Still, *how many see the Baby* depends on what their definition of *"What a baby is."* Some see it as a group of congealed flesh. Merely cells attached to their body. But to them – those who are pro-choice it really is nobody and a *no body* that is contained in their body. It's all about the body. And as the old Virginia Slims cigarette advertisement from bygone days proves - we haven't come a long way baby.

And there lies the rub. *They* will not and cannot call it a baby. That is in their talking point. *It's a fetus. It's a well-organized flesh.* God forbid they ever acknowledge that the creature that lives, grows, and evolves within them is a living being. There are many problems with their arguments- aside from the obvious moral one. But if supposedly this is all about the *"right of the mother"* to hold domain over her body- what does one say about the rights of the baby inside the woman?

That is where they need to redefine *what life is and isn't* and *what a baby is or isn't*.

Regarding the left or those who are supposedly pro-choice being the science party –their argument runs into problems when you start calling the creature inside the woman a baby.

When is it *not a clump of flesh, and when is it a baby*? One week? One month? Two months? Three months? Four months? Five months? Six months? Seven months? Eight months? Or Nine months?

What does the ultrasound say? What does the science say? What does God say? What do all those *Passionate Baby Killers* say? No, that's not a punk band. *Poor Lost Souls.* Nor is that a Rock band. But they both work to describe the current extreme left and their thirst for killing babies. *Passionate Baby Killers & Poor Lost Souls.* On this set – I'm not sure who opens. But it doesn't really matter. They're delivering the same somber death-march music that represents a shift in the once moderate democrat party.

What do the latest polls reveal about how Americans feel about abortion?

According to the Gallup Poll conducted from May 1-24, Respondents answered the following question: "Do you think abortions should be legal under any circumstances, legal only under certain circumstances, or illegal in all circumstances?" *50% of the respondents said that abortion should be legal under any circumstances; 35% of the respondents said that abortion should be legal only under certain circumstances; and 12% responded that they should be illegal in all circumstances.* [89]

When asked, with respect to the abortion issue, would you consider yourself to be pro-choice or pro-life? *54% of the respondents considered themselves to be pro-choice, while 41% considered themselves to be pro-life.* The trend for the nation has been in the direction of being more pro-choice. In May of 2021, the gap was 49% pro-choice to 47% pro-life, and in 2018, the question was answered with 48% pro-choice and 48% pro-life. One need go back to 2012 to find the last time the country, at least in a polled survey, was more pro-life, with 50% of the respondents saying they were pro-life and 41% pro-choice.

Whether pro-choice or pro-life, it is a complex question that has divided the country for a number of reasons.

One wonders how many of the respondents who answered pro-choice, based on the fact "that it was their body while claiming bodily autonomy, granted those some slack, who *chose* not to get jabbed with the experimental COVID-19 vaccine. Because if they allowed their neighbors and fellow Americans to choose not to get the shot, then I'm okay with their right to do what they want with the choice of aborting the baby or taking it to full term.

Further, just as President Trump, I make exceptions in that I am pro-life and make exceptions in the case that the mother's life is in danger and if the pregnancy was a result of rape or incest.

I beg to differ with those who say I have no voice, Pro-Choice or Pro-Life, simply because I am a man. David Chappelle, a brilliant comedian who makes light and some points about what's fair in the abortion argument.

If you have a d***, you need to shut the f*** up on this one. Seriously! This is theirs; the right to choose is their unequivocal right. Not only do I believe they have the right to choose, I believe that they shouldn't have to consult anybody, except for a physician, about how they exercise that right.

Gentlemen, that is fair. And ladies, to be fair to us, I also believe that if you decide to have the baby, a man should not have to pay. That's fair. If you can kill this motherf***er, I can at least abandon him. It's my money, my choice. And if I'm wrong, then perhaps we're wrong. So figure that sh-t out for yourselves.[90]

Figure that stuff out for yourselves.

Well, my reasoning is different. I am and always will be taking the side of the baby, female or male, who has no voice – either pro-life or pro-choice in the matter. So, my voice is a choice for the least amongst us.

And finally, I must admit that even as a man, I can relate to being one of those "cat ladies" that J.D. Vance spoke about many years ago when he was running for the senate, stating that the US was being run by Democrats, corporate oligarchs and *"a bunch of childless cat ladies who are miserable at their own lives and the choices that they've made, and so they want to make the rest of the country miserable, too."*

"It's just a basic fact — you look at Kamala Harris, Pete Buttigieg, AOC — the entire future of the Democrats is controlled by people without children," Vance continued. *"And how does it make any sense that we've turned our country over to people who don't really have a direct stake in it?"*[91]

Vance has been raked over the coals for his comments. Yet, there is a lot of truth in what he was implying. His belief that having and creating strong families is a staple of any successful society. The American society is no exception. If the family unit is not valued and having children is not respected –then people make other choices, sometimes choices that they regret. I can relate. It wasn't in the cards for me – my timing was off. I met great people, but it didn't work out, and it wasn't meant to be for me to have kids. It's a great regret of my life. I have cats. And I love them and my country. But I would have liked to have a bigger stake in contributing to the mosaic of the American family. So lay off Mr. Vance; he makes a lot of sense, at least to this cat lady, who is, in fact, a cool male cat from Motown.

What doesn't make sense is this sudden insatiable appetite for abortions.

That you have the right to an abortion is one thing, but to literally foam at the mouth and become unhinged because this is your number one concern and a right you care about. The right to kill a baby. Granted. Go do it. Congratulations. Yes, your baby in your body. *But a baby, nevertheless, that you are killing, you shouldn't be so fucking happy about it.*

The pro-choice side cannot afford to acknowledge the legitimacy of the pro-life argument — that what's being aborted is an innocent human person. If they did, they'd lose the moral high ground. Bill Maher recently illustrated this on his show.

"I don't understand the 15-week thing, or Trump's plan 'let's leave it to the states.' You mean, so killing babies is ok in some states? I can respect the absolutist position. I really can. I scold the Left when they say, 'Oh, you know what? They just hate women. People who aren't pro-choice.' They don't hate women.

[The Left] just made that up. [Pro-life absolutists] think it's murder. And it kind of is. I'm just okay with that. I am. I mean there's 8 billion people in the world. I'm sorry, we won't miss you. That's my position on it."[92]

Sometimes Maher can be so damn refreshingly honest.

So let's call it what it is - MURDER.

Yes, done in the safety and privacy of your own body and in your particular state –but murder, nevertheless. Where before, the goal of abortion was to be *safe, legal, and rare-* today, *it is commonplace, normal,* and a nonchalant practice. Today, abortions are executed akin to someone ordering their Starbucks coffee.

Like many of the limousine and latte liberals who must have their coffees and abortions, the issue of abortion is one the left will never give up because they use it to rile up and rally their base to turn out on Election Day. Or G-d forbid, take a chance at losing your right to kill a baby.

And if killing babies is the goal –it's one that's been highly successful.

More than 63 million abortions are estimated to have taken place in the U.S. since the Supreme Court's 1973 Roe v. Wade ruling that granted federal protections to women seeking to terminate their pregnancies.[93]

Dis-proportionally, the leading consumer of the abortionists' services is the African-American female. According to the 2011 Abortion Surveillance Report issued by the Center for Disease Control, black women make up 14 percent of the childbearing population yet obtain 36.2 percent of reported abortions. Black women have the highest abortion ratio in the country, with 474 abortions per 1,000 live births. Percentages at these levels illustrate that more than 19 million black babies have been aborted since 1973.[94]

19 Million Black babies. Abortion is the biggest cause of black deaths in the history of the United States. Had abortion been done by a white person instead of an unholy act – it would be considered racist and guilty of committing one of the greatest mass murders and hate crimes in history.

So, who are the real radicals? The ones who want to have an abortion on demand in any month right up to birth and even after the baby is born? On that, Trump is right. It is a decision that each of us must make with our own hearts.

My answer has been one guided by the same moral compass as my dear mother. She is pro-life and pro-baby. And we are both guided by the ultimate pro-lifer – Jesus.

Jesus may hate the sin, but he doesn't hate the sinner. And one thing is for sure – The Lord loves all those babies.

13 Dead Soldiers...Patriots and Names to be remembered

They died for nothing. Actually, they died for something a lot greater than most people will ever know or understand about this special breed of human being – *the American Soldier.*

And while their final fate has already been forgotten by many in the mainstream media and by others who never respected or revered their lives in the first place, Americans should never ever forget the names of the 13 American Soldiers who died as a result of a bad war, a botched plan and gross dereliction of duty that is unforgivable.

For their valor and bravery, they should be honored because they not only represented America but the best of us. Their names should be unforgettable and committed to memory in American history classes for generations and throughout this land and country that they died defending.

Marine Corps Staff Sgt. Darin T. Hoover, 31, of Salt Lake City, Utah

Marine Corps Sgt. Johanny Rosariopichardo, 25, of Lawrence, Massachusetts

Marine Corps Sgt. Nicole L. Gee, 23, of Sacramento, California

Marine Corps Cpl. Hunter Lopez, 22, of Indio, California

Marine Corps Cpl. Daegan W. Page, 23, of Omaha, Nebraska

Marine Corps Cpl. Humberto A. Sanchez, 22, of Logansport, Indiana

Marine Corps Lance Cpl. David L. Espinoza, 20, of Rio Bravo, Texas

Marine Corps Lance Cpl. Jared M. Schmitz, 20, of St. Charles, Missouri

Marine Corps Lance Cpl. Rylee J. McCollum, 20, of Jackson, Wyoming

Marine Corps Lance Cpl. Dylan R. Merola, 20, of Rancho Cucamonga, California

Marine Corps Lance Cpl. Kareem M. Nikoui, 20, of Norco, California

Navy Hospitalman Maxton W. Soviak, 22, of Berlin Heights, Ohio

Army Staff Sgt. Ryan C. Knauss, 23, of Corryton, Tennessee.

They died on the last day of the endless Afghanistan war. A war that was finally coming to an end, in a hastily planned and ill-conceived manner, with a predictably disastrous result. As planes rushed out of chaotic scene reminiscent of Saigon and another Endless war called Viet Nam, in which 58,220 American soldiers died.

As this endless war ended with people who were jumping horrendously from aircraft while others struggled to hang on, it was a scene that was too horrible to forget unless you were most of the American press and the Democrat party.

Hanging on. To a narrative and a mission we had no business executing. Hanging on for years to keep the meter running. It's frightening to think just how right the Five Star General named Ike was about all those things he warned us about. This war, the Afghanistan War brought to you by the *MILITARY INDUSTRIAL COMPLEX*. Sadly, the sponsor of many of these unnecessary and endless wars, the kind that a man named Trump always saw as wasteful. Wasteful of time, money, treasure, but mainly of lives. This man named Trump, a sensible alternative and threat to the likes of the Washington establishment who bumbled us in and out of wars time and time again over decades. Trump had a plan in place, but it would not be a rush job. It wouldn't put our soldiers in harm's way. We would leave. But we would leave with dignity and not in a rush. Under Trump, you would not have seen the chaotic scene that happened in August of 2021.

And those 13 patriots would more than likely be alive today.

They say that there is a "Fog of War" in which the details of either a failed or successful mission become lost in translation.

But many say the most important part of any conflict or war to remember is the "Face of War." What is the cost of your actions or inactions? For every face lost, there is a face and story that accompanies an American flag-draped casket to the families of the departed American heroes.

That's something that the man from Queens got before he was president. The cost of war. And that's why he always remembers the names of those who gave their lives for their country. That sounds like that should come naturally to every American president, but sadly, that's not the case.

President Biden with whatever remaining brain cells he had firing, made one bad decision after another, leading to a chaotic exit plan to vacate that went terribly wrong. After nearly 20 years —now they were in a hurry to get out fast. But why? Ah, they had to get out in time for the photo opportunity that represented America getting out by the 20th anniversary of September 11th.

As ludicrous as that sounded - it was the truth.

All the while, a man named Trump watched the catastrophe play out almost in slow motion, and then he picked up a phone. One call he made was to Darin Hoover, the father of a 31-year-old Marine who was killed in Afghanistan, who was not expecting a call from Mr. Trump while Mr. Hoover had declined to meet Mr. Biden.

"It was just very cordial, very understanding [Mr. Trump's call]. He was awesome. He was just talking about the finest of the finest," Mr. Hoover was quoted as saying. *"He said he heard and saw everything that we had said, and he offered his condolences several times, and how sorry he was,"* he added.[95]

Just days after Trump was nearly assassinated, in an emotional moment at the Republican National Convention, Gold Star families of U.S. service members who were killed in an August 2021 terrorist attack at Afghanistan's Kabul airport accused President Joe Biden of "never once" saying their names.

Herman Lopez, the father of U.S. Marine Corps Cpl. Hunter Lopez said each name aloud as the audience stood, repeating the names back:

Marine Corps Lance Cpl. David L. Espinoza. Sgt. Nicole Gee. Staff Sgt. Darin T. Hoover. Staff Sgt. Ryan C. Knauss. Lance Cpl. Rylee J. McCollum. Lance Cpl. Dylan R. Merola. Lance Cpl. Kareem M. Nikoui. Cpl. Daegan W. Page. Sgt. Johanny Rosario Pichardo. Cpl. Humberto A. Sanchez. Lance Cpl. Jared M. Schmitz. Navy Hospitalman Maxton W. Soviak. Cpl. Hunter Lopez. Eleven Marines. One soldier. One sailor.

The call-and-response followed a prerecorded video that featured the families criticizing Biden and Vice President Kamala Harris for the chaotic withdrawal and for how they say the administration treated them afterward.

"*To this day, Joe Biden and Kamala Harris have never mentioned these fallen soldiers' names,*" the RNC narrator said after the video ended.

"*While Joe Biden has refused to recognize their sacrifice, Donald Trump spent six hours in Bedminster (New Jersey) with us,*" Christy Shamblin, the mother of Sgt. Nicole Gee told the crowd.

"*Donald Trump knew all of our children's names. He knew all of their stories.*"

He knew all their stories, and he knew all their names. And so should we.

They are a sad, tragic, important, and proud part of our history. Representing the best part of us and the best in us on a day when we were all represented by the worst of us. Yet with your revered memories, you will continue to serve us while helping us make sense out of this senseless and endless war.

And for that, we shall never forget your names or your stories. An American story with *13 American names* that we will always proudly remember.

And now, as if they had not committed enough shameful and damaging acts to the lives and memories of these American heroes and their families, they lowered the bar. Those on the sick left, made up of the legacy media and a bad part of the Democrat party, actually criticized President Trump for visiting the graves and paying tribute to the fallen patriots at Arlington National Cemetery on the third anniversary of the heinous and shameful withdrawal from

Afghanistan in August 2024. Those who hate the President so much coined it a photo op that disrespected the solemn ground of Arlington, as Trump came and spent time, lots of time, with those mourning their loved ones. That Trump took pictures laying a reef, hugging family members, posing for pictures, and giving a thumbs up, not out of disrespect but out of respect for their service, got under their sick, twisted skin.

More so than even the sick withdrawal executed by leaders named Biden and Harris, who were not leaders at all. Harris, standing on her claim that she wanted to be the last one in the room when big decisions were made, claims proudly that she stands by that botched abortion of a withdrawal.

And here is where Kamala stands on Trump visiting Arlington, labeling it a political photo stunt that disrespected the solemn ground and the soldiers. Meanwhile, she was not there, nor was Biden, who was too busy sunning himself on a Delaware beach. Both are nowhere near the graves of the soldiers and their families as a man and leader who was invited to the event to console them with that thing- you know the thing- empathy that they claim he lacks.

But in the end, it is character that they lack. And thankfully, that's something that many more Americans are waking up to and seeing, just like the families of 13 Patriots who saw that firsthand by the graves of their loved ones.

They saw a president who showed up to honor and commemorate the third anniversary of the attack at Abbey Gate in Afghanistan. What they witnessed was a man who genuinely cared about them and the memory of their lost heroes. They saw a president who knew all their names and always would. And finally, they saw a president, who had he been in office on that fateful day, would have prevented this tragic story from happening in the first place. And that is a picture that everyone now can clearly see coming into focus.

CAGED BIRDS- Plight of my fellow patriots, brothers, sisters (The J-6 Hostages)

Some birds are not meant to be caged, that's all. Their feathers are too bright, their songs too sweet and wild. So you let them go, or when you open the cage to feed them they somehow fly out past you." Stephen King

I don't know how many of my fellow brothers, sisters, and patriots were caged as a result of the happenings at the Capitol on January 6, 2021. It's a number that's impossible to know for sure. And with the sad and evil state of our government today, a government that lies to its people on a regular basis, regarding just about everything, one can never truly believe the numbers with complete confidence.

One thing for certain - the number is too high, even if it's one fellow American and patriot.

At the same time that hardened criminals are having their sentences reduced and illegal Aliens run free across the USA, many committing heinous crimes, patriots are jailed shamefully in a DC prison. Fellow Americans still being held in unconscionable and inhumane conditions now over three years later is unforgivable, unjust, and, to those who are faith-based - a sin. Their Crimes? Many for mainly trespassing onto and into the Capitol; some minor and misdemeanor offenses, and some, a very few charged with violent crimes. Yet, they are bunched and bundled into one convenient *anti –Trump* or *anti- MAGA, or anti-American* narrative that makes these men and women *the usual suspects* and criminals like the dregs of society - making them out to be the worst criminals this side of a Nazi at Nuremberg or a Terrorist at Guantanamo Bay. All painted with the i*nsurrectionist brush* for taking part in what some call an attempt to overthrow the government or overturn an election, while others call it a protest gone wrong, perhaps even orchestrated to go terribly wrong on purpose by some in our very own government.

Whatever you call it – what happened on that day made a mark on America that will be left for interpretation for many years to come by scholars, the body politic, and patriots seeking meaning through debate, and of what truly happened on January 6, 2021?

The long and short of it is this. There are a select few who did something so wrong that warranted the extremely tough sentences handed out like candy by judges and a justice system with an agenda for the alleged acts committed on that day. Many, dare I say most of these caged birds and patriots, linger in godforsaken conditions, unfit for what we do to the worst amongst us. Caged birds held with no trial dates and no hope of justice. Caged birds held under deplorable conditions. *Caged birds imparted with cruel and unusual punishment.* Caged birds receiving "punishment that does not fit the crime." Punishment, shameful to take place at all - in what some still call the greatest country to ever exist and under a justice system supposed to be the gold standard.

Crime and Punishment. Not just something Kafka was fascinated with, but something many of us who live in this country count on as a given, and sadly, many of us take for granted. Throw out the labels. This is not a liberal or conservative question or issue – this is a human being concern and one that should be based on common sense and doing the common good for we the people.

It should be steeped in fairness and with the wisdom of one of our founding fathers, Ben Franklin, *"It is better 100 guilty Persons should escape than that one innocent person should suffer."*[96]

Better the guilty go free than one innocent man suffer?

Heady stuff and a concept filled with *Solomon* like judgment.

But what would you expect from a great man and mind like Franklin?

Is it too much to expect those governing us today to be equipped with the same wisdom and sense of fairness? Unfortunately, I'm afraid so. And sadly, because of that, some of the people who attended that J-6 rally to dispute the results of an election, most assuredly, amongst them are many faceless innocent men and women who suffer.

Most of those protesting patriots who trucked to Washington on the 6th of January 2021 to have their voices heard have largely been silenced and their voices muzzled in one way or another by forces in our government, media, and members of the deep state, who want their narrative to be written that sheds light on one word - insurrection.

But those who are the least bit fair and who have even a cursory working knowledge of a dictionary know that what happened on that day was not an insurrection,

The words "insurrection" and "insurrectionists" have been widely used by news outlets and others to define the storming of the Capitol building and the rioters involved. According to Merriam-Webster, "insurrection" is the "act of revolting against civil authority or an established government." Other definitions, like that of the Cambridge Dictionary, specify the act is usually a violent one. Synonyms include "revolt" or "uprising," according to Merriam-Webster.[97]

What I witnessed on that day was a lot of things, but one thing it was not was an insurrection.

As evidenced by the fact that no one was charged with insurrection.

More than 1,230 people have been charged with federal crimes in the riot, ranging from misdemeanor offenses like trespassing to felonies like assaulting police officers and seditious conspiracy. Roughly 730 people have pleaded guilty to charges, while another roughly 170 have been convicted of at least one charge at a trial decided by a judge or a jury, according to an Associated Press database. Only two defendants have been acquitted of all charges, and those were trials decided by a judge rather than a jury. About 750 people have been sentenced, with almost two-thirds receiving some time behind bars. Prison sentences have ranged from a few days of intermittent confinement to 22 years in prison. The longest sentence was handed down to Enrique Tarrio, the former Proud Boys national chairman who was convicted of seditious conspiracy for what prosecutors described as a plot to stop the transfer of power from Trump, a Republican, to Joe Biden, a Democrat. Many rioters are already out of prison after completing their sentences, including some defendants who engaged in violence. Scott Fairlamb — a New Jersey man who punched a police officer during the riot and was the first Jan. 6 defendant to be sentenced for assaulting law enforcement — was released from Bureau of Prisons' custody in June.[98]

Yet there are also those individuals who, after being taken into custody and while facing a justice system that was hell-bent on lumping them all in together as the worst of worst, were unable to take the injustice and punishment that did not fit the crime.

After all that time, some of these *caged birds* were unable to take the conditions and hang on any longer. And sadly, some of these caged birds took their own lives.

One of these caged birds was named Mathew Perna. And he is one of the many stories of caged birds that they dare not tell. For in the telling of these stories, you might grasp them as individuals…and see them as *Eagles, Cardinals and Doves*. Or as just good Americans and good patriots who flew to Washington to spread their wings and exert their First Amendment rights, refusing to be bunched into convenient categories and labeled by bureaucrats as birds of a feather who flocked together to do harm to a country they all professed to love.

Mathew Perna, a Pennsylvania man, was accused of disorderly conduct at the U.S. Capitol on Jan. 6, 2021, and died from "a broken heart," according to his obituary. His loving Aunt Geri hopes that we will all remember all the caged birds being held by our government. As of this writing, five J-6s have taken their lives. In that time, as America sleeps, many face endless detentions and delayed trials and are held in deplorable conditions, while illegal aliens are caught, captured, and released to the streets to commit violent crimes. They are the truly forgotten men and women who sit and suffer in shameful conditions. They sit in jail cells in the Nation's capital, forgotten men and women waiting for trials and justice that never comes. Some, like Mathew Perna, reached a breaking point and could not hang on any longer, tragically taking their own life.

"His community, which he loved, his country, and the justice system killed his spirit and his zest for life," his family wrote in his obituary. Perna told police that when he reached the top of the steps on the building's west side, he was surprised to find the door open. He claimed he was pushed into the building by a crowd that gathered behind him.

Still, images of video from inside the building showed Perna wearing a red hoodie emblazoned with the phrase "Make America Great Again." He was in the building for 20 minutes and was seen recording the riot on his phone chanting "USA! USA!" with the crowd, the statement of offense said. The same day, he posted a video on Facebook with two others in a hotel room. He claimed that people with Anti-fa were "chiefly" responsible for breaking the doors and the windows at the Capitol, according to court documents. Referring to then-Vice President Mike Pence, Perna then said, according to the documents: "It's not over, trust me. The purpose of today was to expose Pence as a traitor."

Perna was one of the people whose photographs the FBI shared, asking for the public's help to identify them. A person familiar with Perna recognized him and flagged him to the police, saying Perna's Facebook account had posts indicating his support for Trump and QAnon. Perna was a Penn State University graduate who loved to travel and previously lived in Thailand and South Korea, the obituary said.

"Matt did not have a hateful bone in his body. He embraced people of all races, income brackets, and beliefs, never once berating anyone for having a different view," the obituary said. Perna's family supported him as he faced the charges. "His actions last year are not looked down upon, instead his family is grateful and humbled by his courage," the obituary said.[99]

An obituary. Part of the story, and certainly no way for any American eagle to die. And that's just who Mathew Perna was - an American eagle!

As I watched his aunt Geri Perna testify before members of Congress, I felt her pain as she spoke about her nephew and, in essence, Mathew's suicide note:

"On the 25th of February 2022, my nephew Mathew Lawrence Perna went into his garage, placed a rope around his neck, and hanged himself. He was 37 years old, broken, and close to unrecognizable. Matt had stopped going out, stopped sleeping, stopped eating, and was vomiting blood. We are a remarkably close family and we did everything we could but it wasn't enough. I will let Matt tell you why in his own words from a note he wrote on the worst day of his life."

"I sacrificed my freedom when I entered into the Capitol building on January 6th and in despair took my own life the night that I wrote this."

Signed Mathew Perna

"My nephew was extraordinary. He was honest and strong and defined by his love of all people. He should never have been pushed to the point of despair. He had no intention of going into the Capitol when he traveled to DC. In his mind, he was standing up for all of us. Matt believed we are still entitled to free speech in the United States of America and did not think that expressing it would cost him his life."[100]

For entering into the Capitol on January 6th, 2021 Matt was assigned a parole officer that he was required to report to, and the first of many hearings was scheduled. On February 25, 2021, the Grand Jury indicted Matt on four counts:

1. *Obstruction of an Official Proceeding and Aiding and Abetting*

2. *Entering and Remaining in a Restricted Building or Grounds*

3. *Disorderly and Disruptive Conduct in a Restricted Building or Grounds*

4. *Disorderly Conduct in a Capitol Building*

In December 2021, at the behest of his defense attorney, Perna agreed to plead guilty to all four counts. With no criminal record and no violent conduct on January 6, Perna and his family expected a prison sentence of less than a year; Perna's sentencing hearing was scheduled for March 3, the seven-year anniversary of his mother's death.

But Matthew Graves, the U.S. Attorney for the District of Columbia handling every January 6 prosecution, intervened and asked the court to delay Perna's sentencing so his office could make sure Capitol defendants are punished equally. "While every case and every defendant are different, the Government is attempting to ensure that similarly situated January 6 defendants are treated in the same manner," Graves wrote in a motion on February 11. "The Government is attempting to do that in this case, and that requires additional time for the Government's internal review process to be completed."

Very bad news for Perna as Graves' office has sought lengthy prison terms for defendants who plead guilty to the obstruction felony. In the case of Jacob Chansley, who, like Perna, committed no violent act on January 6 and was allowed into the building by police, Biden's Justice Department sought 51 months in jail and three years of probation.

In sentencing recommendations on obstruction pleas, prosecutors have compared defendants to domestic terrorists and asked judges to act accordingly. *"The need to deter others is especially strong in cases involving domestic terrorism, which the breach of the Capitol certainly was,"* one of Graves' prosecutors wrote in Chansley's sentencing memo. *"The sentence of this Court must drive home this fact for this defendant, and any others who may wish to emulate him: crimes committed against this country and democracy will be prosecuted and punished in accordance with the law."* That appears to be what Graves would have demanded in Perna's case as well.

When Perna learned his sentencing hearing was again delayed, he called his aunt. *"'I am guilty, I am guilty!'"* he told her. *"He said that he deserved whatever punishment they were going to give him. That was the last straw. The constant harassment was too much."*

But that sort of isolation clearly isn't enough to satisfy Biden's Justice Department as it continues to seek revenge against Americans who protested Joe Biden's election on January 6, 2021. Federal prosecutors want jail time even for those charged with low-level misdemeanors such as "parading" at the Capitol. (Perna's original indictment still includes the lie that Kamala Harris was in the building during the protest that day, the basis for thousands of criminal charges. It is unclear whether his lawyer notified the court about the falsehood before accepting the plea offer.)

Matthew Perna was failed by the country he loved, demonized by the news media, tormented by the world's most powerful law enforcement, ignored by political leaders of both parties, and betrayed by a federal judge sworn to defend justice does not appease the whims of a vengeful regime.

"They broke him, they mentally broke him," Geri said through racking sobs as she explained why her loved one ended his life. "He had run out of hope. I know he couldn't take it anymore."[101]

Those are the sad words of an aunt speaking on behalf of her nephew, a fine young boy who didn't have to die the way he did. An eagle relegated to a cage without hope. A bird whose freedom was taken away because he expressed his First Amendment rights. An American who died, not in vain, because his story and many others like it will be told and retold about a time in America when the American justice system became the American Injustice System. Those who wore certain red caps expressed their love and support of a certain political candidate and genuinely were exercising their constitutional right to peacefully protest were treated harshly with cruel and unusual punishment, especially when compared to the criminals who burnt down American cities during the "peaceful protests" in the summer of 2020.

Two tiers of justice? Hardly one for a man named Mathew Perna. A nightmarish system that was an accomplice in the taking of his life. Painted with a crude brush as a terrorist by a system that was out to get him, get you, get me, and get everyone in America who dared support Donald J. Trump.

Draconian. Shameful. Barbaric. Evil. Their actions are shameful and have **no bounds**

An *Injustice System* that rushes to judgement – but slow walks sentencing.

An *Injustice System* that is as lenient to illegal aliens as it is harsh to J-6'rs.

An *Injustice System* that locked up many Americans unjustly just because they were *MAGA*.

An *Injustice System* that cages up our free birds who seek liberty.

An *Injustice System* that thankfully can no longer hurt a man named Mathew Perna.

His cage is finally open, and this American eagle can finally soar high and fly free.

Ultimate Vote in the End/Choosing between two forces -One Good & One Evil

My mother – a very wise woman, has often said to me, *"Once your eyes have been opened, they cannot merely be closed."*

In other words, it's hard to un-see what you have seen- with your own eyes. And what we have all seen over the last few years is beyond tragic and belief. Try to not see what you have seen. Many will tell you not to believe *your own lying eyes*.

Yet you have seen them, Mr. And Mrs. America, because your eyes are open. And you have not only seen them, these tragedies, miscarriages of justice, and lies, but you have also felt them in your heart and mind. And there is no doubt it has sickened most of you. But there is good news. With open eyes, there is always good news on the way.

"My eyes have seen the glory of the coming of the Lord."

In summary, what have you seen in today's America and throughout the entire world? Two forces, really you have seen only two forces at work. No, silly, it's not Democrats and Republicans. It's bigger than that. And those are just labels, anyway. These same two forces have battled for control of the planet called Earth since it was formed, and most importantly, these two factions are fighting to see *where you cast your ultimate vote*.

A vote to determine where your soul is going when it's all over for you, me, and everyone else. The final vote. Good vs. Evil. The one that's always on the ballot. Everywhere. So, which one are you voting for? The Good One or the Evil One.

And, in essence, who will you be casting your vote for or against in November of 2024? So, what are you voting for? Mask and vaccine mandates. Lockdowns and social distancing. Abortion on demand. Fascism in the streets. Censorship of airwaves. Open borders and endless chaos.

Legal immigration or illegal aliens crashing our gates. Law and order or crime-laden cities. Better schools or failing students. American families or corporate fat cats.

Outsiders or Insiders. Bound by chains or freedom. Liberty or lockdowns. War or Peace. Good or Evil. Two candidates, two parties, and two forces.

All on the ballot. The choice and vote is up to all of us this fall.

On whether we rise or fall.

A True Dream – Attending the Truth Awards

The writer wrote. Because that's what writers do, it was both his obligation and his passion. Yet it often pained him to do so. But the rewards were worth it. Those times when he tapped into joy and discovered a true thing buried in a mountain of lies. That's why he wrote. And at this time the only truth he knew about his life - aside from his undying faith in the man from Nazareth - was that this writing was his only therapy.

Not even attempting to get a good night's sleep in today's America, he struggled to grab a few moments of shut-eye while avoiding any and many nightmares. The nightmares always came in a rainbow of colors – some staying with him into the next day. But on the good days – and they were few and far between, he slept, and he dreamt good dreams about life, about liberty, and about the pursuit of happiness. And on very special nights, he dreamt of things near and dear to his heart. Movies and politics often combine the residue of the day into wild dreams. Sometimes, as he tossed and turned, he was shocked at his own dreams.

Not too long ago, he had a dream of *Zombie* children killed by Dr. Fauci coming back and roaming the earth until they forced a deadly shot on the good doctor. He liked that one. Then, there was that dream he had where Donald Trump with a powdered white wig replacing his signature head of hair, fighting alongside *the Founding Fathers* while trying to take back America. He liked that one because he woke up laughing as The Donald removed his white wig in the dream while joking and laughing with Thomas Jefferson and John Adams. "I don't know how you guys wear these things. Sometimes, you just have to accept the hair God has given you."

And on those special nights, he dreamt of a place where he found the truth. The one that really got to him was the one where *Donald is being chosen to fight for the Truth by Moses and Jesus.*

This was such a night. A big and great dream came to him in bright and bold colors.

The scene of the Dream was a huge and important stage somewhere in the United States. A place where palm trees swayed beautifully in the gentle breeze and were lighted up by magnificent sunsets. In the dream, there was a well-built modern building that incorporated all the elements of design and function. A great structure that would make the builders of the *Parthenon, Howard Roark and Frank Lloyd Wright,* smile in agreement that this was one hell of an architectural marvel.

And it had to be. This work of art was hosting the First Annual TRUTH AWARDS, where the best of the best from many fields of Art, Business, Sports, Government, Journalism, Academia, Science, Hollywood, and the Music Industry gathered to receive their Awards for well, being talented of course, but most importantly for that other T- telling the TRUTH to the American people. *Not the whole truth and nothing but the truth.* Hell, no one does that anymore, and the last guy who did that, they put on the cross. In fact, come to think of it, the award looked something like a lower case t.

All these folks who gathered here at the Truth Awards in my dream were here for one purpose, and that was to receive their just deserts. They had each risen to the highest level in their field and, for the most part, and in their hearts, felt like they were telling the truth, or they were so darn good at lying that well, they believed that they were telling the truth.

What's an award show without a great award? And while this was no Oscar, this award, a simple lowercase t with a crown on its top to symbolize the ultimate truth teller from Nazareth. While some were not believers in that truth, they could not avoid this honor they had to attend – because the one truth in their world was this. They were addicted to being recognized, immortalized, slapped on the back with a "that a boy" or a "you're the best." Fame was their drug. And if they were here on this night in this warm and beautiful Florida resort that was a paradise on earth, well, they were somebody. Anybody not here did not really matter.

The proceedings would be broadcast via satellite around the world eclipsing even Elvis Presley's famous Hawaii concert that was beamed to over 1.5 billion people around the world.

Those who attended were not going to miss their chance to pick up their award and the swag bag that accompanied it, and they would not miss out on their chance to be seen around the globe by as many as five billion people.

Truth is, that was a number that their egos could not resist.

That's why they gathered here on this night. Five thousand of the most important and truthful human beings in the United States.

From the Business world, *Bill Gates* and *Mark Zuckerberg* were there.

From the field of Science and Medicine – The esteemed *Dr. Anthony Fauci* was there to receive a lifetime achievement award for his work battling the Covid-19 pandemic.

Also, there was Dr. Rochelle Walensky, the former head of the CDC.

The honorable Joe Biden was there even though he probably didn't know he was there, accompanied by his wife, Dr. Jill Biden.

Also there, yet sitting on the other side of the stage, were former President Barack Obama and his wife Michelle, as well as Bill and Hillary Clinton, George W. Bush, and Dick Cheney, who was there with his daughter Liz Cheney.

From Congress, a literal who's who in truth-tellers. Headed by AOC and her squad, Rashida Tlaib, Ilhan Omar, and others who were there collecting the award for most influential group with the best nickname that had done the most to impact America's trajectory in the shortest amount of time.

The major "truth tellers" with big names and egos to match, named Schumer and Pelosi, were taking their seats, ready to enjoy the praise from their colleagues that was almost as rewarding as being elected to their august bodies in the first place.

The little leaguers –the California contingency who had not only run America into the ground with their atrocious voting record, but their big truth was what they had done with a face-lift on the once great state of California - making it not great again but instead unrecognizable. This group, led by Adam Schiff, Eric Swalwell, and Maxine Waters, sat adjacent to the box that housed Governor of California Gavin Newsom, freshly scrubbed, almost gleaming in his Armani suit with not a hair out of place – ready to accept his BIG T-Award for all the good he had done to his state - once coined the land of milk and honey and the envy of all the rest of the states in the union. He was visited briefly by Kamala Harris, who was now running for president but had her heels dug so deeply in the soil that was California, leaving her impact on the once great state and especially the city of San Francisco. She was overheard saying, "*Hey, I'm sitting near you all. After all, I had a lot to do with what California looks like today. You're not getting all the credit,*" she said before going in a laughing jag.

There were plenty of smiles to go around, backs to be slapped, and fists to be pumped by all those who were there, who knew why they were there.

They were there because they were all great.

In the section set aside for Governors sat former Governor Andrew Cuomo kibitzing with Governor Gretchen Whitmer from Michigan, both there, of course, to receive their TRUTH award for how well they handled the COVID-19 pandemic. Whitmer sat mouth open in respect and a little jealous as Minnesota Governor Tim Walz told her about the *Tampons in Boys Bathrooms Policy*. Yeah, she nodded under her breath, *"We can do that."*

The Media not be to be ignored; their presence was omnipotent at the award show. Phony waves and fake gestures of "I'll call you" were flung in the direction of fellow newsreaders, propaganda makers, and TV personalities. Joy Reid hugged Rachel Maddow, and both sauntered up to *The Morning Joe* table to give hellos and hugs to that crew of early risers – led by Mica and Joe.

From there, you could get a view of THE VIEW table – The TV show which had been on the air since 1997, hosted by a changing troupe of female personalities who told their version of the truth and shared their views in such a manner that one felt either soiled or enlightened by the encounter depending on your particular political stripe and what you perceived the truth to be. Most of the long list of co-hosts gathered. A woman named Elizabeth was not invited, but Rosie showed up and was holding court with the current roster of The View, trading forced smiles between grimaces with her fellow ladies as they tried to get in a word edge-wise – a feat that they all knew was impossible.

Leaders of academia, presidents of famed universities - the Ivy League schools of course, they were all there on this special night of arts and letters. A special award was going to be handed out to Harvard University to honor being chosen as the school that most represented THE TRUTH in academia. Harvard University founded in 1636 as Harvard College and named for its first benefactor, Puritan clergyman John Harvard, it is the oldest institution of higher learning in the United States with its influence, wealth, and rankings have made it one of the most prestigious universities in the world.

(101a)

That everyone knew. Anyone who was someone. And those in the know also knew something else. The very motto for the elite university that thrived in the Commonwealth of Massachusetts and its small charming enclave of Cambridge - stood for truth.

Harvard's motto, in fact, in Latin, is Veritas, which translated to English is *TRUTH*.

What better higher learning institution to honor on this night than HARVARD?

That both Palestinians and Jews alike were protesting the award show outside was a non-issue to those who gathered here on this night that would surely and appropriately be documented in a Maysles Brothers-like documentary.

Fashion icons and publishers of the couture rags like Vogue and such were all there dressed to the nines, as *Truth was on display and what everyone seemed to be wearing on this night and on this runway.*

The Hollywood A-listers and high-end producers could greenlight anything, even today in Hollywood, when few, if any, projects were being made. Robert DeNiro was there getting a Lifetime Achievement Award for Speaking Truth to Power. A montage, not of his great roles in cinema encompassing his journey from the *Mean Streets to Raging Bull or Taxi Driver to Goodfellas*, but instead a brilliantly edited montage of his rants, raves, and monologues aimed at a man named Trump. A man who DeNiro truly hated with all his heart and a man this legendary thespian always told the truth about.

Finally, the big Award of the night was THE MINISTRY OF TRUTH award, given not to one individual but to the collective. To all those who attended, not only would they get a special T-award machete –but all would rise to their feet and salute with a special salute the *giant T* that would be backlit and on stage, infused with all the proper pomp and circumstance of special effects used in any big box office film that Hollywood now specialized in. It would create a moment, dare it be said aloud, to rival Jesus returning high in the clouds. And here and only here, on this stage and in this magnificent arena and in this state of palm trees and euphoria –where these folks assembled, not because they only dealt in truth, but more importantly, they dealt in their truth. A truth that was fed to them – yes, by some higher power. The only truth that mattered – truth created, edited, trusted, and distributed by the Ministry of Truth.

In the dream, the lights dimmed as the opening to the show and credits to the TRUTH awards were brought to a worldwide audience as the sponsors for the show were flashed on the screen. Over the top of the graphics you could hear an announcer's voice, no doubt an AI version of the most trusted voice of the last 100 years – Morgan Freeman.

"The Truth Awards." "Proudly brought to you by *Pfizer.*"

"The World Economic Forum." "The CDC- Center for Disease Control."

"ECN - Electronic Cars Now." "Johnson and Johnson."

"The World Bank." "END FLICKS – The latest and last word in ENTERTAINMENT."

And finally – "*Crickets…it's what for Dinner.*"

With that, the host, also probably an AI amalgamation of beauty, prose, and spirit, a created concoction of pronouns and a blender of genders, an attractive being – being one part George Clooney and one part Pretty Woman Julia Roberts, took the stage in an outfit that was neither a formal tux nor an evening gown but was off-putting just the same as it began to speak.

"We would like to welcome you to the First Annual TRUTH awards, built upon the foundation presented to us first by the Ministry of Truth –from Orwell's masterful and fictitious telling of a Dystopian society. Well, we have got some news for you. That stuff was all true. And tonight – the awards presented to all you truth-tellers gathered here tonight will have a special inscription and truth inscribed by our founding father."

"War is Peace," "Freedom is Slavery," and "Ignorance is Strength."

The entire arena rose to their feet en masse and would not stop cheering. And they might never have stopped had it not been for the convincing and authoritarian voice of *AI Morgan Freeman*, who filled the arena with his voice of power as he told them charmingly:

"Folks, you can get busy sitting, or you can get busy standing. Please have a seat."

THE TRUTH AWARDS were off to a rousing start.

As the evening unfolded, all those in attendance had received their just deserts and slice of the truth after a record seven-hour live show, in which 638 or so dignitaries and the *truthiest* people on the planet were honored on stage, getting their Truth award, the closing music swelled and once again that AI creation of a host appeared to sign off.

On behalf of all those who contributed to bringing you the Truth, not only tonight but always and for all time, thank you for coming, and until we see you next year, remember these three important things from our charter.

"War is Peace," "Freedom is Slavery," "Ignorance is Strength."

And then he added an ad-lib- even the AI version couldn't help himself.

"Trump is Hitler."

"Goodnight!"

As it signed off, a loud rumble sounded almost like an explosion – but only with more natural and gradual building sounds filling the arena.

The rumble continued, and the earth shook.

Screams from the auditorium drowned out the sound of the band as it attempted to play on -Titanic wise, as the event unfolded.

Still, a louder rumble continued, matched only by the movement of the earth, which was moving under the feet of all those who had gathered in this place. Reminiscent of one of those scenes in an old time epic from Hollywood's golden age, something out of *The Ten Commandments* or *Samson and Delilah*, a big finish was coming.

Then in a series of moans emanating from below the earth's surface – the structure, the stage, and all those who had been invited here seeking their truth award were sucked up and swallowed into the earth. A horrific sight. The screams faded underground as the structure and award winners were swallowed up by the hole below them.

Eventually, after a few minutes, there was nothing left but smoke simmering and the last sounds of the earth settling and covering up the hole that had opened and closed all over them.

Then, after a few moments, one started to hear a song, something familiar and patriotic being played in the background as a platform from below the earth started to rise. In the silhouette, a familiar figure framed by beams of red, white, and blue lights flashing accompanied his entrance.

His unmistakable voice accompanied his now recognizable image.

"One thing I always said, you have to build your structure on a good foundation." "And always check for sink holes. Truth is…Everybody knows that."

As the man named Trump spoke to the cameras that were still carrying the event to a worldwide audience, Trump went into a story.

"One of my biggest supporters, who gets me, a Greek kid, I always told him, Do what the Greeks did and make sure you build on rock and not sand. That's why I love the Parthenon and The Lincoln Memorial.

Both built on a hill and on solid ground. Something to look up to far from the Swamp."

Just then, the writer's alarm went off. Awakened from the bazaar dream, he scratched his head, made some coffee, and turned on the TV. Somehow, his station was tuned to MSNBC and *Morning Joe*. Before reflexively changing the channel, he paused. On the screen was the always sanctimonious Scarborough commenting on all things Joe Biden. On this Wednesday after Super Tuesday of the 2024 primary season, a day when Niki Haley was allegedly dropping out of the race and giving up her bid to be president, as she faced the truth that she could not beat Trump, a man from TV named Joe waxed on about a lifetime politician named Joe Biden.

"There's such a, there's such a challenge for the Biden team. Because, as I've said here on the show over the past couple -- I've spent a good bit of time with Joe Biden. I've spent a couple of hours with Joe Biden, sitting, talking, going around the world as far as talking issues, talking the economy, talking inflation, talking."

"And I must say, when I was talking to him, my thought wasn't, oh, poor guy. My thought was, oh, my God, I wish Dr. Brzezinski were on the other side of the table right now, cause these two guys -- I mean, 50 years of experience, and Joe Biden hasn't forgotten it. He may get pissed off at a press conference, and he may be thinking about the Mexican border deal and say Mexico instead of Egypt. He knows what he's talking about; he circles back around and gets to Egypt. He might misplace a word here or there."

"But you talk to him for hours at a time. Is he slower? Does he move slower? Yeah, he moves slower. Is he stiffer? Yeah, he moves stiffer. Does he have trouble walking sometimes? Yeah, so did FDR. We get out of the Depression, we won a G.D. war against, against Nazism and, and, and against the Japanese."

"But comparing that guy's mental state -- I've said it for years now: he's cogent. But I undersold him when I said he was cogent. He's far beyond cogent. In fact, I think he's better than he's ever been intellectually and analytically. Because he's been around for 50 years and, you know, I don't know if people know this or not, Biden used to be a hot head. Sometimes, that Irishman would get in front of the reasoning. Sometimes, he would say things he didn't want to say. This is -- and, and, I don't -- you know what? I don't really care."

"Start your tape right now because I'm about to tell you the truth. And f-you if you can't handle the truth. This version of Biden, intellectually and analytically, is the best Biden ever. Not a close second. And I've known him for years. The Brzezinskis have known him for 50 years. If it weren't the truth, I wouldn't say it." [102]

Holy Spirit delivers me the Number: John 316, No- Don 316

The vision came to me at night, around a week before the 2020 Election

Donald J. Trump would win the 2020 Election- and do so convincingly.

The man that the media was so sure was too divisive to be reelected would win a decisive victory.

The number that was burned into my brain – was 316.

It referred to a similar electoral number the President gathered in 2016. The President would add ten extra electoral votes from Minnesota to his total of 306 from his victorious Presidential bid.

It was also not lost on me that the number that appeared to me in a dream and vision –was spiritual in nature. It seemed to be coming from the Holy Spirit- and the Lord himself.

This was not John 316 – but, in fact, Don 316.

As it turned out, that number did not come to fruition for a lot of reasons that I won't go into here. Donald Trump finished with 232 electoral votes and lost to Joe Biden, who shockingly accumulated 320 electoral votes.

As the vote counting was paused on election night, I got a sick feeling, the opposite feeling that came over me when I saw the number 316. Something had gone wrong. Something was not right. Something along the opposite lines of the Holy Spirit intervening on that election night. And much of America and the world has suffered because of it.

The opposite of good being evil, I still feel that much evil was done on that night and in the many preceding days that headed into that election night. While the Holy Spirit was trying to deliver a message to me on election night, even the Holy Spirit could not compete with the shenanigans of election interference and the opportunity for cheating to occur that excess mail-in balloting delivered.

As we go into this election one hopes that the good and honest forces win out over the evil ones and that a fair and uncompromised election will be delivered to the people of America come this November 2024. It is something that I will be praying for and looking to the Father, The Son, and the Holy Spirit to watch over during this most important presidential election.

The Legacy and Face of MAGA – A tribute to Corey

It was supposed to be a happy day. Most Trump rallies are just that. Days filled with anticipation, enthusiasm, and a joyous celebration for the man named Trump who would be coming to town.

Trump calls it a *"Love Fest."* And that's what they usually are.

On this day, July 13, 2024, it started off that way. Sadly, it would not end that way. Instead, it turned into a tragic day that would forever be marked as an afternoon in American history when America lost a patriot and almost lost a president.

The man lost to us all that day was an American hero named Corey Comperatore and he represented the best of us. A faithful family man. A firefighter. A man who loved his Lord, his family, and his country in that order. There was no other place in the world that he would have rather been on that fateful summer afternoon in America than at a Trump family with his family and his president.

A day like many others for Corey and many other Trump supporters. A chance to see their guy up close and personal as he connected with fellow patriots. A love fest. A joyous day turned tragic in the blink of an eye, the turn of a head, and with bullets reigning down on a happy crowd. On this day, as the bullet flew toward the stage where his president was speaking, Corey threw his family down and covered them heroically with his body, saving their lives while losing his own beautiful life.

That's the kind of man he was, a personification and symbol of a group of good people who are often maligned for their support of a man named Trump and a movement named MAGA. Called a cult by some, in the same way that Christianity is called a monolithic cult by others. Corey, true to the way he lived his life and true to the WORD that he believed in, in his final moments on earth, did something the Lord, his Lord, preached.

"For whoever desires to save his life will lose it, but whoever loses his life for My sake will find it."

In finding it, he defined not only what a hero is but what it means to be a good God-fearing man. He gave his life for his family in the service of the Lord.

And the world noticed the heroic actions taken by him shielding his daughter from the gunfire when he was fatally shot just minutes into former president Trump's speech. A bullet pierced part of Trump's ear as a gunman opened fire at his rally in Butler, Pennsylvania.

Pennsylvania Gov. Josh Shapiro, a Democrat, in a press conference...said that the father of two "*died a hero*" after diving on top of his family. "*He dove protecting his family. Took a bullet for them.*"

"*We lost a fellow Pennsylvanian last night ... I just spoke to Corey's wife and his two daughters. Corey was a girl-dad. Corey was a firefighter. Corey went to church every Sunday. Corey loved his community. Corey loved his family. He was an avid supporter of the former president and so excited to be there last night with him in the community,*" Shapiro told the outlet.

"*Corey's wife asked to share with all of you that Corey died a hero. Corey dove on his family to protect him last night at this rally. Corey was the best of us... May his memory be a blessing,*" Shapiro said.

Randy Reamer, president of Buffalo Township Volunteer Fire Company, where Comperatore served as chief, spoke to *Newsweek*...saying: "*Corey was a great guy, great to work with, fearless. He was a dedicated family man. He loved his family, talked about them often, loved his girls, wife, and his dogs, loved fishing,* Reamer said in a phone interview. "*He was a lifetime member and joined in 1994. He was a great mentor. He had so much knowledge of the fire service it* was mind-boggling. He probably forgot more than most people know. It was great working with him."

Allyson Comperatore, paid tribute to her father, calling him "a real-life superhero." "*He was the best dad a girl could ever ask for. My sister and I never needed for anything ... He could talk and make friends with anyone.* "He loved his family. He truly loved us enough to take a real bullet for us", she wrote, noting that her family has lost "a selfless, loving, husband, father, brother, uncle, son, and friend."

"And I will never stop thinking about him and mourning over him until the day that I die too. July 13th will forever be a day that changed my life. I will never be the same person I was less than 24 hours ago," she wrote. "Dad I love you so much there aren't enough words to express how deep that love goes."

Comperatore's sister said, "*He was a hero that shielded his daughters,*" adding, "*My baby brother just turned 50 and had so much life left to experience...Pray for my sister-in-law, nieces, my mother, sister, me, and his nieces and nephews, as this feels like a terrible nightmare, but we know it is our painful reality.*" [103]

Speaking at the RNC convention just days after the tragic shooting, Senator Marco Rubio, R-Fla., emphasized that politics may matter, but they are not what *"truly matters in our lives and our country."*

"It is our people who must always matter most," he said, making the case that Trump had given voice to everyday Americans, transformed the Republican Party and inspired a movement *"of the people who grow our food and drive our trucks, the people who make our cars and build our homes, the people whose taxes fund our government and whose children fight our wars."*

"Americans like Corey Comperatore... a "loving husband ... described as the best dad a girl could ever ask for ... a man who loved Jesus fiercely and looked after members of his church."

"Corey was one of the millions of everyday Americans who make our country great," Mr. Rubio said. *"He wasn't rich. He wasn't famous. And the only reason why we know his name and story now is because last Saturday he shielded his wife and daughter from an assassin's bullet, and lost his life the way he lived it — a hero."*[104]

A true hero. At the same convention, a solemn President Trump honored the slain retired firefighter by bringing his helmet and jacket onstage for his RNC 2024 speech. Trump then, in a heartfelt moment, poignantly embraced his jacket and kissed the helmet of Comperatore.

"He lost his life selflessly acting as a human shield to protect them from flying bullets," Trump said. *"What a fine man he was."* The former president, growing emotional at points as he recounted the shooting, asked the convention hall to recognize "a moment of silence in honor of our friend, Corey." Trump mentioned that at a fundraising drive had raised $6.3 million for the families of Comperatore and two wounded rally-goers — and brandished a $1 million check he said that a friend had given him for the cause.

"There is no greater love than to lay down one's life for others," he said. *"This is the spirit that forged America in her darkest hours. This is the love that will lead America back to the summit of human achievement and greatness."*[105]

All the tributes paint a picture of a man who will be missed. A portrait of a man who always put his family first. A vignette of a man who believed in the MAGA movement that put America first. He is the face of this MAGA movement that many have come to ridicule as a mob and part of a mindless cult. But Corey Comperatore did not belong to a cult or a mob.

He was a loving family man. A person of deep faith who attended church every Sunday. A good friend. A great American. Proud. Courageous. Selfless. A man to be remembered who lived a life to be emulated. A man to be respected. A real-life hero. The type of man that we all wish we could be. An American soul who we lost on a tragic Saturday afternoon in America while he was doing what came naturally. Celebrating joyfully with his family his love of faith and country. A man who, in his final selfless act, was doing what he always did –putting his family first.

Out to Get JD Just like Trump by not getting his Hillbilly Elegy

If he had come out as a Democrat candidate for President or Vice-President, the left and liberal America would have embraced him enthusiastically. Just as Hollywood and the mainstream media had loved JD and his story before he ran and was elected the Republican Senator of Ohio. And way before Donald J. Trump chose him to be his running mate in the 2024 presidential election.

Sound familiar? We've seen this movie before. Many times, in fact. They all loved Donald J. Trump before he ran for president. New Yorkers. The Hollywood set. TV land. The Publishing World. Both sides of the political aisle - locally and in Washington. Blacks. Whites. Browns. Chinese. Latinos. Gays. Straights. Jews. Christians. People of faith. And non-believers. They all liked, admired, and respected Donald until he wanted to become President.

Same path for J.D. Vance. Before he ran, everyone loved his best-selling book, *Hillbilly Elegy*. It was a real and raw book about a man who pulled himself up from the bottom of poverty in Appalachia and a troubled childhood fraught with a drug-using mother and an abusive upbringing that was far from nurturing. Still, the young man got enough love and watering to grow into a fine young man who served his country as a marine in the Iraq War, graduated from Ohio State University, and eventually got his law degree from Yale University. Not bad for a poor kid whose grandmother, affectionately referred to as Mamaw, had to beg for extra food from social services so the kid could eat. Along the way, he fell in love with a smart and beautiful Indian woman whom he married and is raising a lovely, stable family of his own. Something he longed for so desperately in his youth. Sounds like a storybook ending and one Hollywood loves. Or used to love and make. And that's why they made it into a film with the touted Ronnie Howard, who knows a thing or two about creating that wonderful Hollywood narrative and whose own childhood is embedded in his iconic portrayal of Opie in the classic series The Andy Griffith Show, in a place called Mayberry. A place, by the way, that is central casting for what the folks in the MAGA movement are searching for in our jaded and upside world.

There is a lot of Opie and Andy in what people call making America great again. And tell me, JD Vance isn't a grown-up Opie of sorts and someone Andy would be proud of? Maybe that's why Ron Howard took the movie and placed such great

A-listers – Amy Adams as his drug-using mother and Glen Close as his tough but loving grandmother. How can you hate this story?

I'll tell you how. Let Donald J. Trump pick "Opie" JD Vance as his running mate, and suddenly, the film, the story, and even the best-selling book are open for scrutiny.

Just as they all loved Donald J. Trump, from guys named Al Sharpton, Joe Scarborough, and all those old hens and young chicks on The View once did, now they have no choice but to flip the script.

Can you imagine if this had been Kamala Harris's story? Her actual story. Not the one that stars Willie Brown. But a real inspirational tale of a woman who rose up based on merit. A soulful narrative with roots firmly planted with seeds of hope.

It would be streaming 24 hours a day and be considered the greatest Horatio Alger story ever.

Instead, now they pick at the kid from Appalachia because of a cat lady comment in which he imparts how important the family unit is to him, someone who longed for a normal family life and in essence how important the family unit is in shaping the greater American family – a large country of little towns like Mayberry - if you will.

And stop right there. I don't mean to say that all the towns are populated with white folks like in Mayberry. That was then. And that was TV. I mean that all the towns and cities all across America are filled with people from all backgrounds living in towns that are safe, loving, kind, and neighborly –just like Mayberry.

Regarding the cat lady comment- see if you can figure out what JD means by that. Watch the movie or read the book if you need help. Here's a hint. It's all about creating a stable and loving family that he could be proud of while giving them all a shot at their American dream without having to worry if your mother was going to overdose or if you were going to eat today.

Family it's essential to J.D. Vance just as it is to Donald J. Trump.

And the American family whether a poor white one from Appalachia or a poor black one on Chicago's south side – they are essential and matter to the kid from Queens and the kid from the hills of Kentucky. Some have said that the only ones who can save this country are *the felon and the hillbilly*. *The Felon & the Hillbilly*. That actually sounds like a pretty good TV Series. The first two letters of their names, Trump and Vance, after all, are T and V –together, that is, TV. Coincidence? Well, Donald is a showman, and he does know quite a bit about that medium.

As far as *Hillbilly Elegy* goes. Can't wait to read the book. Thought the film was very good. Knew and expected the critics to savage it just like they did *The Sound of Freedom*. Still, it's a hit once again on Netflix, and the audience on Rotten Tomatoes has given it a very good score of 88.

But this isn't about scores or settling scores.

JD's story works in print and on the screen because it appeals to all of us out there who have wanted to give up but didn't. It appeals to the forgotten men and women in places like the hills where he came from or the streets of Motown, where I came from, who want to be inspired again and grab their part of the American dream. A man named Frank Capra would have loved JD's story, and he would have loved JD and Donald Trump for just those reasons.

He would have loved them for going into all those unsavory and dirty places far from the glitter, digging out a diamond that was rich in character. A story of a young poor kid who fought for his country and against his own doubts on his way to a Big Ten school, Ivy League law school, election to the United States Senate, and quite possibly the next Vice President of the United States.

The J.D. Vance story. It's one hell of an inspirational tale. One that will give you hope. The kind of story Hollywood used to make and when a lot of America was more like a place called Mayberry and hopefully can be once again.

You can't be Serious…or a serious person if you vote for these two clowns

You can't be serious if you are considering voting for Kamala Harris and the newly minted *"White Normie Good Old Boy from Minnesota."* The Dems and mainstream media would have you believe that this Tim Walz character is a straight-down-the-middle mid-westerner. A guy who hunts, fishes, and hangs out at the hardware on Saturday morning. They want you to believe that he's a *"football coach and teacher."* The truth is - he's more of a cuddly Communist who relates more with Tiananmen Square than he is a Midwestern boy from Main Street, USA.

The man who got married on the anniversary of the Tiananmen Square uprising, where death estimates ranged from several hundred to several thousand, so he would always remember the date.

This is the middle-of-the-road guy who watched as his city burned during the peaceful protests of 2020 while he insisted that tampons be supplied in boy's bathrooms and demanded that Illegal aliens be given driver's licenses.

This guy, who calls Trump and Vance weird. He's the one that they want you to believe is the normal guy. You can't be serious if you think he or his running mate is the answer for America. But one thing is certain regarding these two weird presidential candidates named *Harris and Walz,* They are seriously dangerous if they get anywhere near the White House.

And you can't be serious…or a serious person if your main reason for voting for a candidate is because they are a certain gender or have a certain skin pigmentation. Because the pain that is, has been and will be inflicted on the American people, knows no bounds or boundaries when it comes to the amount of potential damage that this dynamic duo can do to this country while making it anything but great.

Regarding the border, the two are tied almost poetically to their borderless views of America. She, the *Border Czar,* who never visited the border. In a contentious interview with NBC's Lester Holt in 2021, the media called her out on her border or lack of border policy.

Harris was in the country to meet with Guatemalan President Alejandro Giammattei and to talk about the root causes of migration to the United States, but has faced criticism—largely from Republicans—for not making a trip to the U.S.-Mexico border.

"The question that has come up and you heard it here and you'll hear it again I'm sure, is, 'why not visit the border? Why not see what Americans are seeing in this crisis,'" Holt asked the Vice President. Harris responded, "We have to deal with what's happening at the border; there's *no question about that. That's not a debatable point. But we have to understand that there's a reason people are arriving at our border and ask what is that reason and then identify the problem so we can fix it."*

Pressing the topic, Holt asked if Harris had any plans to visit the border, and she said, *"At some point, you know, we are going to the border. We've been to the border. So this whole thing about the border, we've been to the border. We've been to the border."* "You haven't been to the border," Holt said. *"And I haven't been to Europe,* Harris said. *"And I mean, I don't understand the point that you're making. I'm not discounting the importance of the border."* [106]

No, she's not discounting the importance of the border; she is merely ignoring it and has ignored it in the greatest and most impeachable dereliction of duty ever by a Vice-President or president for that matter.

What was the *border Czar* doing for the border? It was her one big job. And she blew it. And now, with Orwellian overtones of rewriting history, those who want her elected are trying to ignore the issue by saying she was not the BORDER CZAR in the first place.

Her running mate, a man named Tim Walz, seems to be a perfect match for the less-than-curious Kamala. Where she ignored the border as the Border Czar, her running mate, welcomed those jumping the border illegally and greeted them with open arms of citizenship and even driver's licenses. Hell, he even famously said he would give them a hand and help them get their foot in the door to the country. Minnesota Governor Tim Walz once bashed former President Donald Trump's US-Mexico border policy, telling CNN's Anderson Cooper, *"[Trump] talks about this wall. I always say, 'Let me know how high it is. If it's 25 feet, then I'll invest in the 30-foot-ladder factory.'"*[107]

Harris has infamously been very clear about providing benefits to those who get over the border with or without the help of a ladder provided by Walz to get over the wall. Harris took several progressive stances on immigration when she sought the Democratic presidential nomination in 2020. She wanted immigrants who were in the country illegally to be eligible for government healthcare, and she wanted to decriminalize border crossings. [108]

Their solutions for many of the problems that plague our country are not serious.

They are two peas in a pod. And share the same radical agenda and state of mind. In fact, the states where they were best known, Harris's California and Walz's Minnesota, are similar. Lands blessed with many beautiful natural resources and just plain beautiful places that both Harris and Walz had a great influence in wrecking. Harris contributed to the demise of California, especially San Francisco, with her soft-on-crime stance, while her newly anointed running mate merely "stood down off his ladder" and watched as his twin cities of Minneapolis and St. Paul burned during the summer of 2020.

The results are seriously depressing for both Minnesota and California –as more people are fleeing those states that are making it their new home.

While the people in Minnesota…may be Minnesota nice …they can't be serious people if they voted for a man named Walz who doesn't believe in walls at our southern border. His policies are reckless and left of Kamala and Bernie Sanders. Yet he masquerades as a moderate from Main Street USA with Tiananmen Square sympathies.

They are both dangerous. And like Gavin Newsom in California …true disciples …and believers in their far-left philosophies and policies. And because of that, they are ominous and sobering, and the threat that they pose to America and making it great again – should be taken seriously.

The choice is clear. It's never been clearer. If you want….lower inflation, safer neighborhoods, a secure border, and a more stable world not filled with endless wars, then there is only one serious choice that you can make and one ticket that you can vote for on Election Day.

But if you want America to turn into Minnesota and California, then vote for the laughing candidate and the communist sycophant because you can't be serious.

The Distance from JFK to DJT not as far as you think

The day was November 22, 1963. A day that would forever change America.

It was on this day that a man named Abraham Zapruder stood on a concrete pedestal along Elm Street in Dealey Plaza holding a Model 414 PD Bell & Howell Zoomatic Director Series Camera and waited for John Fitzgerald Kennedy, the 35th President of the United States, to come into view.

What he would shoot on this day would become known as the *Zapruder film*, a footnote on one of the darkest days in our nation's history. As the images of the young, handsome, and smiling president along with his regal and beautiful wife Jackie, adorned in her rose dress, came into his viewfinder, he focused his camera and captured a silent 8mm color motion picture sequence of President John F. Kennedy's motorcade as it passed through Dealey Plaza in Dallas, Texas.

The historic *Zapruder* footage of the assassination of JFK, while not the only film of the shooting, has been described as being the most complete, giving a relatively clear view from a somewhat elevated position on the side from which the president's fatal head wound is visible. The footage became an important piece of evidence before the Warren Commission hearings and all subsequent investigations of the assassination. It is one of the most studied pieces of film in history, with some particular footage of the final shot helping to spawn theories of whether Lee Harvey Oswald was the lone assassin. [109]

What would they be telling us about the JFK assassination if there were a thousand *Zapruder* films being shot in Dallas on that fateful day instead of just one or two? I wondered about that. Then, I came to this conclusion. They'd be telling us the same thing. They would still be telling us and selling us the same lies.

The big difference between that dark November day in Dallas in 1963 and that sunny summer day in a rural Pennsylvania field in 2024, and two separate assassination attempts on two generational political figures - is all the technology that's available today. Today, because everyone is armed with a smartphone, we have a good shot at seeing what happened and why it really happened –this most recent assassination attempt of a presidential candidate that came within centimeters of changing world history.

Back then, the loner named Lee Harvey Oswald settled into his perch on the sixth floor of the Texas School Book Depository to take his loaded rifle and shoot and kill John F. Kennedy as his motorcade made its way through the Dallas streets. There were only a few people who literally bumped into and spotted Oswald at the scene of the crime, even though he worked in the building. And no one actually saw him in the window from the street and pointed up and said, "Look, he's got a gun."

They did in Butler. Many people saw that a figure, later identified as Thomas Mathew Crooks, was on the roof of the building, a mere 140 yards from where the president was speaking, and believed he had a gun. Some of these MAGA folks warned cops, Secret Service agents, and anyone willing to listen that there was a suspicious person in the area and he had a gun.

What did the Secret Service do with that information?

Apparently not much, and worst they didn't share it with other local authorities charged that day with providing enhanced protection of President Trump.

Didn't they share the information because they couldn't? Or perhaps didn't share the information because they didn't want the information shared?

In today's day of networking and connectivity via secured channels and various technological options that make communicating with each other easier than it has ever been in world history — they want you to think that they couldn't get on the same page frequency and coordinate some kind of plan to keep the president from being shot at in tiny Butler, Pennsylvania. Hell, this was Mayberry, and had it not been for some curious local cops who happened on the suspect, rushing him to take his shots, it's more than likely President Trump would have been killed. This is not meant to be a pejorative- but someone like *Barney Fife* saved the president's life on that day. *And thank God for Barney Fife.*

That this happened at all makes perfect sense to those in the deep state, deeper swamp, and anyone buried so deep with their head and heart in the bullshit of perpetuating the Anti-Trump narrative. They, this they – a cabal of evil-doers, as Bush used to say had tried everything else to get Trump. Why not bullets? And Why not now, just before he would be nominated at his RNC convention? It would surely throw the whole country into chaos, and if there is one thing that those who run the deep state and have their hands on the puppet strings love, it is chaos.

Here's where the plan fell apart. Trump lived. The shooter missed. And chaos ensued not from the loyal and calm Trump supporters who gathered there that day representing all those who had come to these rallies for years. The chaos came to those—*THE THEY-* who had organized this foolproof operation by standing down and failing to recognize the imminent threat to President Trump.

With the missed shots came the need for the cover-up and the blame game.

We didn't see the shooter. The slope was too dangerous for us to put a shooter on the roof. We didn't have a meeting with local police to devise a communication plan of who's on first and who can cover all of our security detail. The Counter Snipers didn't know if Crooks was a good guy or bad guy. We didn't have the technology to run our own drones before and during the event, but the 20-year-old kid did. But we, the FBI and Secret Service, did not have that level of sophistication or budget. And finally, we didn't think we needed men on that building because it was outside the perimeter, and we had the buildings secured from the inside. Finally, yes we saw some suspicious guy earlier, but we lost sight of him. Well, until we saw someone, one of our sharp shooters, shot him just after the shots were fired at the president. No, we didn't think to warn the president's people or delay the event....because, well, we had a communication breakdown.

That's what THEY, in a nutshell, want you, me, and WE, THE AMERICAN PEOPLE, to believe.

But this isn't Dallas of 1963.

Nor was it a parade or motorcade route through a big canyon of skyscrapers with many windows providing many perches and opportunities for those who wanted Trump dead to plant a slew of patsies with those dangerous AR Rifles that the left hate so much, but not as much as they hate President Trump and those who attend his rallies.

This was an open field, with but a few prominent places that Barney Fife types could figure out were dangerous for the former president. Yet they dropped the ball, and information was not conveyed. They, with they being the operative word, apparently didn't want the information to be shared with counter-snipers and those who could take out the said shooter before he got multiple shots away at the president.

Only two conclusions can be drawn by their actions and inactions. Was it negligence and dereliction of duty, or was it worse? A planned operation to take out the former and potentially future president of the United States.

That's up to you, me, and the American people to answer. But don't expect any help or clear communication from your government. It's been over 60 years, and we still don't have clear answers as to what happened in Dallas on November 22, 1963.

Some people still believe Oswald acted alone. Others blame the CIA, President Johnson, The mob, or combinations of all three. Many people wanted Kennedy dead for various reasons. And many people want Trump dead for many reasons.

And in the end, it's not so much who pulled the trigger, but more so who ordered the trigger pulled or looked away as it was pulled that matters most. Today, just I still have my doubts about Oswald acting alone, I also have my suspicions about the narrative and the people who are writing or pushing it today. The reason is obvious to us all and why it feels eerily similar to that dark day in Dallas. We have all seen the movie play out before.

In today's movie, they let the president take the stage while knowing that they had lost track of a *suspicious character*. Secondly, they let the kid into the perimeter and on the roof in the first place. Even worse, they failed to notice him in broad daylight on an open roof, a mere football field and a half from the president, until it was almost too late. Newly released footage shows how grotesquely negligent they were, as we see the gunmen scurrying across the rooftop, hunting for a better position just minutes before taking his shots at Trump.

Spotted on the roof by various MAGA supporters doing the job of the Secret Service, they provided eyewitness accounts and many smartphone points of view that were not available back at the time when Abraham Zapruder was capturing those horrific yet historical images of JFK being slain in Dallas.

The young man who wanted to kill Trump, as it turns out, was curious about that dark day in Dallas when Kennedy was killed. A day he probably saw differently than most of us. To him, that day was homework. It provided a goal and pathway to infamy. A chance to join a truly deplorable list and be mentioned in the same chapters of history as *Booth* and *Oswald*, nobodies who became household names and part of history for killing a president. To get the job done. The kid needed a plan so the kid did his research in preparation for what he hoped would be a kill shot. Crooks even sought the answer to how far the distance it was from Oswald to Kennedy on a Google search on his phone.

That distance from Oswald to Kennedy was about 265 feet.

The distance from Crooks to President Trump was about 390 feet.

The distance from JFK to DJT was getting closer and clearer, even if the answers to how they happened were not.

His plan was plausible, and with the lack of security provided to the president, it was probable that it could be pulled off. He had been practicing at the same facility, ironically right next to gunmen whose job it was to protect people like Trump, members of Homeland Security who trained police officers.

While seeming far-fetched, surprisingly, to some whose job it was to visualize and predict where potential threats were coming from, it was not a shot in the dark or too conspiracy to think they missed detecting him on purpose.

How else do you let the kid get as far as he did and eight shots off?

It's no secret now, but Crooks, in his attempt to join a contemptible list of losers, was more prepared for the day than was the highly trained Secret Service agency. And because of that he would be allowed to walk the field. He was even able to fly drones to get a better outlook. And then, on that Saturday, in the early evening, in a small Pennsylvania town, he would be ready to make history and add his name to a list of sick, sad, and evil individuals, and in his twisted mind, attempt to make America great again by killing Donald Trump.

Only thing is... he missed. Thank God. The loner and the sick, demented loser failed. And now we are left with only spin. The blame game is on steroids, with still hardly anyone losing their job for this grotesque dereliction of duty. Sure, the inept head of Secret Service quit. But did she quit because she failed to protect the president or because she didn't get the job done of eliminating him?

Many will have you believe that it was negligence, a lack of communication, and a comedy of errors by the Keystone cops that led to a tragic day in which, sadly, a former fireman named Corey Comperatore lost his life, and a former president named Trump nearly lost his.

That Crooks attended target practice around three to six times per month in 2024, and on one of these visits – May 23, 2024 – the range was also used by the Department of Homeland Security for "police training" is an interesting story.[110]

But what should really be the focus is how and why the communication broke down.

Newly released body camera footage shows the moment when police first confronted the gunman. An officer is seen being hoisted onto the roof, encountering the shooter, and then falling back.

"*This close, bro!*" *the officer yells.* "*Dude, he turned around on me. He's straight up!*" The video shows Butler County officers taking up heavy arms and race toward the building. "*This building. He's on top of this building,*" *an officer calls out.* "*He's got a bookbag. He's got mad s---, AR, laying down.*" As officers stream toward the building, other officers are seen offering a boost to the rooftop. "Next, next, next," an officer says in an apparent attempt to quickly get more officers into position. By then, though, Crooks is dead. "One in custody. AGR building south. Rooftop," an officer is overheard saying.

Later, in the calmer aftermath, the officers questioned how a gunman was able to access a rooftop firing position fewer than 400 feet from the podium where Trump had been speaking.

"I told them, post f------ guys over here," one officer is heard saying. "Why were we not on the roof?"[111]

And that is what appears to be the smoking gun.

Once again, an officer much earlier in the preparation for the rally told the Secret Service this:

"*I told them, post f------ guys over here,*" *one officer is heard saying.* "*Why were we not on the roof?*"

Why wasn't someone on the roof?

When you try to answer that question, think of a much larger dereliction of duty that has happened every day at our southern border for nearly four years. Why isn't the border secure? You can almost hear a voice echoing, "I told you guys to put some guys there at the border and, oh yeah, finish the wall."

Because what happened on July 13th either happened because the people who are paid to protect the president are inept and sloppy, or they are sinister and part of a deep state operation to kill him. The same reasoning can be applied to the Biden-Harris administration in regard to defending the southern border from an onslaught of illegal aliens invading America. Either they are inept and incompetent in dealing with the border, or it was part of their sinister master plan.

A negligent or intentional act. Whether at the southern border or on a rooftop in rural Pennsylvania. As the questions swirl around the near assassination of President Trump, the conspiracy theories and conspiracy theorists will be savaged by the press and by those who want the story to just go away. Yet they forget that some of us, whether we voted for, loved, or hated Jack Kennedy, are still awaiting answers to that crime of the last century that changed America forever.

They are answers owed to the American people, and if they are not revealed, as the Washington Post proclaims, then *"Democracy Dies in Darkness."*

Finally, the American people deserve answers to what happened on that day when a presidential candidate came to a town called Butler. And it doesn't matter whether you love Trump and *are Super MAGA* or you despise the man. It's every American's right to know the truth of what happened that day.

Because the skies are darkening across the republic as both the truth and lies collide over a field in rural middle America, and suddenly, the distance from JFK to DJT seems hauntingly close.

I was born in Dearborn Michigan

Dearborn, Michigan. My birthplace. It's the hometown of Henry Ford. The Ford Motor Company. Democrat congresswoman Rashida Tlaib and me.

I was delivered to this world via mom's good genes, stick-to-it-ness, and TLC in the early 1960s to a hospital called Dearborn Medical Center, which is no longer there. That's not shocking. Many things have changed in my birthplace over the many decades since and all over the country. I guess, in many ways, Dearborn was like many mid-western towns back in the day, filled with its share of white picket fences, white families, and, I must say, regrettably, its share of white racists.

Dearborn is the home of one of Michigan's most famous and polarizing mayors- a man named Orville Hubbard, who served as the mayor of Dearborn, Michigan, from 1942 to 1978, an effective administrator who served 15 consecutive terms while being nationally known as an outspoken segregationist who sought to keep Dearborn free of the perceived social and political ills of neighboring Detroit. A biographer described him as a "personal symbol of suburban America's resistance to racial integration."

In 1956, Hubbard received national publicity after telling an Alabama newspaper that he favored "complete segregation" of the races. For many years, Hubbard was unabashed in his comments about segregation. He once told a reporter from the *Montgomery Advertiser*: "They can't get in here. We watch it. Every time we hear of a Negro moving—for instance, we had one last year—in a response quicker than to a fire. That's generally known. It's known among our own people, and it's known among the Negroes here."

"I favor segregation," he told *The New York Times* in 1968. With integration, Hubbard said, "You wind up with a mongrel race. "Hubbard's racial views were not limited to African Americans. He was known to complain that "the Jews own this country," that the Irish "are even more corrupt than the Dagos," and as Middle Easterners began moving into Dearborn, that "the Syrians are even worse than the niggers."

Hubbard was an equal-opportunity hater and bigot. After the civil rights prosecution by the federal government and investigations by the Michigan Civil Rights Commission, Hubbard was more cautious in his public comments. In an interview with *The Detroit News* in the early 1970s, Hubbard claimed: "I don't keep the niggers out of Dearborn. I don't keep anybody out of Dearborn. I haven't done anything to encourage 'em. I don't do anything to discourage 'em." [112]

Needless to say, Orville Hubbard was a virulent racist and an abhorrent segregationist, and his views on race had no place at any time in America.

In a picture postcard of America and of towns like my birthplace of Dearborn, Michigan, I'd always hoped that it would look more like *Bedford Falls than Pottersville,* fictitious towns used to paint a picture of what is and what can be in Frank Capra's 1946 classic - *It's a Wonderful Life.*"

Bedford Falls, a town of the family hardware store, inclusive, where people knew your name, middle America, the best part of America, where good people are welcoming and judge you not by the color of your skin or creed but by the content of your character. Bedford Falls, a kind place made up of good characters and a town with character. A town where everyone is welcome.

Pottersville. A dark place made up of people who lack character, where you're judged by your bank account or the color of your skin, filled with people who only care what you can do for them to help them get ahead. An uncaring town run by the power-hungry and a place lacking a moral compass that dooms both the town and its people.

But heck, those places were made up and in the movies. My hometown of Dearborn was real, and I had a lifetime of real experiences there.

As I grew up and heard of Hubbard and his ways it made me cringe and left me feeling sad and angry. While I grew up not too far away in South Redford Township, many of my fondest memories of growing up involved Dearborn, Michigan.

As a teenager, I would go to the *Fairlane Town Center* and spend endless hours there with my friends. Later, when I went to college at the nearby University of Michigan – Dearborn campus, I put my new driver's license to good use, discovering the best cheeseburger in the world at Miller's Bar in Michigan. When I got my first real job at Maritz Communications Company, I worked in the Ren Cen in Downtown Detroit, where I helped create marketing materials for our client, you guessed it – The Ford Motor Company. Often, I'd visit many Ford engineering and marketing offices in Dearborn, Michigan. The greatest of these was the glass house, *The World Headquarters of Ford Motor Company. On* many occasions, I'd visit the Office of General Council, OGC, to get my work scripts approved. It was historic and a little daunting. The glass house was also a place where my first cousin worked as a personal waiter for The Deuce, Henry Ford II. I dated one of my greatest girlfriends ever, and she lived in Dearborn and married a great lady from Dearborn Heights. We loved to go to a place called La Shish, my favorite Arabic restaurant, which is no longer there. But there are many other Arabic restaurants that have taken its place.

Still, just as Hubbard's Dearborn was obviously far from a utopia and more of a dystopia, the Dearborn that I grew up with is unrecognizable today.

In many ways a shell of itself, the Dearborn of my youth is gone, for the good and bad. Sure, two of my favorite places on earth, The Henry Ford Museum and Greenfield Village Museums, two world-class attractions, are thankfully still there and give a glimpse into America's rich past.

But that brings me to today's Dearborn. How is Dearborn perceived, and what is this town really like today? Is it more *Bedford Falls or Pottersville*?

Today, Dearborn is home to the largest Arab population in the world outside the Middle East. New waves of immigration came from the Middle East in the late 20th century, Muslims and Christians
from Lebanon, Palestine, Syria, Iraq, and Yemen. Dearborn has the largest Muslim population in the United States per capita and the largest mosque in North America.[113]

Recently, Dearborn found itself on the editorial pages of the Wall Street Journal when an op-ed called it "America's Jihad Capital." The op-ed suggested that Dearborn's residents — including Muslim faith leaders and politicians — support Hamas and the Iran-backed group Hezbollah. Security measures were ramped up because the article was perceived to be "extremely inflammatory and, upon it being published, we received many calls from faith leaders across the community who no longer felt safe, according to "Dearborn Mayor Abdullah Hammoud," who was elected Dearborn's first Arab American mayor in 2021.

The op-ed suggested that Dearborn's residents — including Muslim faith leaders and politicians — support Hamas and the Iran-backed group Hezbollah. Dearborn is home to about 110,000 people, with a sizable population of Muslims and Arab Americans. In a statement, Stalinsky said in part that his "article is not political — it is about national security" and decried what he said are "anti-US and pro-jihad sermons and marches" in the city.

Michigan State Sen. Mallory McMorrow, the Democratic majority whip, wrote on X that the headline was *"not only irresponsible, it's downright dangerous." "Michigan is a diverse, beautiful place where hate, bigotry, racism, and demonization have no place."*[114]

And that is definitely true here today as it was in the days of Hubbard's Dearborn.

Yet, congresswoman Rashid Tlaib recently still made inflammatory remarks and is facing backlash from some of her fellow Democrats, including in her home state of Michigan, over her recent remarks about Palestinians amid the ongoing war between Israel and Hamas.

Tlaib, who is a Palestinian American and one of just three Muslim members of Congress, wrote: *"From the river to the sea is an aspirational call for freedom, human rights, and peaceful coexistence, not death, destruction, or hate. My work and advocacy is always centered in justice and dignity for all people no matter faith or ethnicity."*

Michigan Senate President Pro Tem Jeremy Moss suggested Tlaib's tweet was insensitive to Jewish people: *"This is not how Jews view the phrase 'from the river to the sea.' This is not how Hamas views the phrase 'from the river to the sea,'"* he wrote on X. *"Hamas uses it as a rallying cry,"* he added. *"And they don't simply want to displace Jews in Israel. They want Jews dead."*[115]

The genocide of Jews. Blacks not allowed in your town. Racism. Segregation. Evil policies and philosophies have no place in any neighborhood or hometown, albeit in Dearborn or Tel Aviv. I was born in Dearborn, Michigan. And while I still haven't found my Bedford Falls yet, I'm still looking for that place. A place where neighbors know each other, like each other, and tolerate each other even if they don't always agree with each other. I'm hopeful I can find that place and that all of America can. But if I don't find that place, I can still visit Greenfield Village soon because, after all, it is in Dearborn, Michigan, and sometimes it truly does take a village.

Project Much? Who are the real weirdos?

So you're the normal ones. Good to know.

Glad that's all cleared up. Well, I guess that fits right in with your George Orwell narrative -with definitions being the opposite, like in *1984*, where *"War is Peace," "Freedom is*

Slavery," "Ignorance is Strength," *and now* "Weird is Normal."

It reminded me of the projectionist, beautifully captured in the Italian film *Cinema Paradiso*.

In the old days – a man in the dark sitting in the projection booth was responsible for making sure the movies played in the old movie house, for the patrons who plunked down their hard-earned money to see a story- actually many stories, the film projectionist was essential and responsible for changing the narrative, the story and keeping the folks coming back for more. Week after week and year after year.

And while changing those reels is a thing of the past – today, they have many projectionists in many cities all across America changing the reel in real-time –as they project not many stories, but one story and one message all across the land – and that is to - *GET TRUMP*.

With enough plot turns to dizzy the most cynical of movie producers, these projectionists project not films but their twisted beliefs onto a man named Trump.

And the strange thing is, what they project onto to Trump and all of us, is what lives in them.

Many of these projectionists live in the power centers of Washington DC, New York, Hollywood, and, of course, on campuses all across America.

Operation Mockingbird is an alleged large-scale program of the United States Central Intelligence Agency that began in the early years of the Cold War and attempted to manipulate domestic American news media organizations for propaganda purposes. According to author Deborah Davis, Operation Mockingbird recruited leading American journalists into a propaganda network and influenced the operations of front groups.[116]

In 1948, Frank Wisner was appointed director of the Office of Special Projects. Soon afterward, it was renamed the Office of Policy Coordination (OPC). This became the espionage and counter-intelligence branch of the Central Intelligence Agency. Wisner was told to create an organization that concentrated on "*propaganda, economic warfare; preventive direct action, including sabotage, anti-sabotage, demolition and evacuation measures; subversion against hostile states, including assistance to underground resistance groups, and support of indigenous anti-Communist elements in threatened countries of the free world.* "Wisner established Mockingbird, a program to influence the domestic American media, and recruited Philip Graham (*Washington Post*) to run the project within the industry. Graham himself recruited others who had worked for military intelligence during the war. According to Deborah Davis, the author of *Katharine the Great* (1979): "By the early 1950s, *Wisner 'owned' respected members of the New York Times, Newsweek, CBS and other communications vehicles.*" [117]

Today, the impact of that once clandestine operation can be seen and heard on newscasts all across America as they seem to be singing off the same song sheet or reading off the same teleprompter.

Recently, you've seen them embrace the Democrat Dynamic duo as *"Joyful"* or *"Happy Warriors"* and the man from Minnesota as being *"Cuddly"* or simply *"The Coach."*

But the new buzzword they're all parroting on demand and command is really weird.

No, seriously, that's the word - *WEIRD*.

You see it echoed in unison on national and local newscasts by the purveyors of propaganda speaking like robots in unison: *"Donald Trump and JD Vance are weird...This Vance guy is as weird as Trump...and their policies are just plain Weird."*

But you know what? Think *Ministry of Truth* as in Orwell's *1984* masterpiece and you'll get it.

They're the WEIRD ones...but they insist that Trump and Vance are the Weird ones.

A classic case of projection. Brought to you by a really weird guy – Timothy Walz.

Hell, the W in his name probably stands for *Weird* or *Winston*.

As they try to brand Trump and Vance as being weird, let's look at some of the weird things the guy from Minnesota, whose already been branded as *Tampon Tim*, has done, like insisting that tampons should be made available in boys' bathrooms. Now that's really weird.

But there are other beauties from this weirdo.

He literally stood by and watched as his city of Minneapolis burned during the summer of love in 2020.

It was 6:29 P.M. on the last Wednesday in May 2020 when Minneapolis Mayor Jacob Frey phoned Minnesota Governor Tim Walz. Riots had erupted the day before over the police killing of George Floyd, and the city was overwhelmed. Frey pleaded with Walz to call in the National Guard. Less than three hours later, the city made a written request to Walz's office for 600 guardsmen to help quell the chaos that was engulfing the Twin Cities. Rioters were burning buildings. They were shooting at police officers and attacking them with Molotov cocktails, fireworks, bricks, and bottles filled with cement. At least three people died during the riots. Faced with one of the most serious public emergencies in Minnesota history, Walz froze. "He did not say yes," Frey said of his request to Walz. "He said he would consider it."

The far-left governor did not agree to call in the Guard until late the next day, according to a blistering postmortem, the *Review of Lawlessness and Government Responses to Minnesota's 2020 Riots*, released in October 2020 by the Minnesota Senate. Instead of sending in the 600 guardsmen that Minneapolis had requested, Walz sent in only 100 late that Thursday. The Guard wasn't fully mobilized until Saturday, four days after the first building burned, according to the senate review. Walz expected the riots to die down organically, a mistake he eventually owned up to. "I will take responsibility for underestimating the wanton destruction and the sheer size of this crowd," a frustrated Walz acknowledged days after the rioting began. He falsely suggested at one point that the overwhelming majority of the violence, as much as 80 percent, was being committed by outsiders — anarchists, white supremacists, even drug cartels — who'd descended on the city to sew chaos. It wasn't true. He engaged in finger-pointing, blaming Frey and St. Paul mayor Melvin Carter for not doing enough to protect their cities, calling their response an "abject failure," according to a report in the *Star Tribune* newspaper.

He blamed the mayors for not wanting the National Guard to be deployed and waffled on whether deploying the Guard was a smart move, considering that the riots had been prompted by police violence against a black man.

Now, four years after those riots caused over $500 million in property damage in Minnesota, Kamala Harris selected the 60-year-old Walz to be her running mate in a November faceoff with former president Donald Trump. For many, the 2020 riots, which began in Minnesota but expanded across much of the country, was their first exposure to Walz, a former teacher and congressman, who apparently projects Midwest dad vibes.[118]

Dad vibes? Really? That's weird, but perhaps not as weird as his wife's take on the fires and riots. She **actually seemed a little excited by it all.** *"I could smell the burning tires. That was a very real thing, and I kept the windows open as long as I could because I felt like that was such a touchstone of what was happening,"* Gwen Walz said. [119]

Perhaps this "I love the smell of napalm in the morning," moment was no apocalypse now to her and maybe even smelled like victory. She is, after all, the wife of Tim Walz and has had a front-row seat to how he sees the world that even included a *weird snitch policy* that encouraged fellow Minnesotans to turn in their neighbors if they broke the Draconian COVID-19 protocols.

Walz military record which has been called into question, not for his service, but his weird tendency to inflate his level of service.

What's really weird is that this was Harris's first shot to show that she was ready for prime time. She is not. She had other safer and smarter picks to choose from, like Mark Kelly, the Astronaut from Arizona, or Governor Shapiro from Pennsylvania, both of whom may have helped her in true battleground states. Yes, that would have been the smart move, but as she has proven time and time again, she's not that smart. She is, however, weird and aware. Kamala knew that picking Shapiro, a Jew, was an unspoken sin in a party controlled by the far left.

And that's not only weird, that's, let me see, it smells not of tires burning on warm Minnesota night but of racism and anti-Semitism. The same things these weirdos call many of us and our "cult leader," Donald Trump.

Weird. That's what they call the guy from Mar-a-Lago and the Hillbilly from the Hills who are pro family, pro America and pro G-d, two weirdos who offer these policies: *Protect the border. Help America become energy independent. Make America's neighborhoods safer. Build a strong economy with no inflation and better jobs. Create a world more secure and less war crazy.*

What's their plan? Oh, they don't have one. That's weird.

After the lady who would save our democracy from the evil force that was Donald Trump, she has been in hiding from doing any interviews at all, even from a press that fawns over her and has made her out to be the female second coming of, no silly, not of Jesus, someone really big - Obama. So they paint her, excuse me, draw her as almost a mystical figure, part Mother Theresa, part Rosa Parks, and Part Margaret Thatcher, and place her on their magazine covers because it's about time, while they make Donald Trump out to be the *Orange creature from The Mar-a-Lago Lagoon.* But we see through their weird narrative.

A narrative where she was installed as the presumptive Democrat nominee for President without garnering one single vote. Not bad for a failed and flighty prosecutor who sat by and watched as Joe Biden faded before our eyes while she ensured us that Joe was just fine. And she should know; she was, after all, the last person in the room with Joe as he made and implemented all his glorious policies to help America and Americans build back better.

How they anointed her a page out of the history books. More from the medieval times, or at least the days of England that a guy name Willie Shakes wrote about. While this was not Hamlet, there was something definitely rotten in Denmark or at the home of the fading King named Joe of Biden.

Call it what you want, a soft coup or perhaps a gentle nudge from Nancy with The Pillow guy standing over Joe's bed warning him to sign the letter? Whatever. Come up with your own weird scenario because these guys are weird. Weird personalities. Weird Policies. Weird for America.

How weird?

Well so weird that now they're trying to tell the public out there that they're drawing bigger crowds than Trump, even going so far as to add a crowd of people via AI into a shot of Kamala disembarking a plane to an empty tarmac.

Pretty weird, right? Makes you wonder what other weird stuff they'll come up with on Election Day. But don't worry. They're not the weird ones. They're the normal ones.

You know, how I know? I just saw it echoed on 37 different newscasts.

And somewhere, a man named Orwell is shaking his head and saying, "See, I told you so."

Does Anyone Remember a Patriot Named Ashli Babbitt?

"They just shot a girl who was trying to go inside the Capitol."

"They think she's dead."

The young woman who broke that news startled and jarred me. It slapped me in the face. Woke me up to the fact that suddenly, everything that was happening today in DC was even more real. With that I slowly lowered my video camera that I had pointed in the direction of the capitol and the uprising and protests that were going on there.

The young woman kept talking as I looked down at my phone, which was on its last legs.

"Yeah, I guess some cop shot her through the door."

"I was inside and made it into Pelosi's office," she added. *"I didn't see it happen or anything."*

"Are you sure she's dead?" I asked as if I could make a difference in the outcome of the answer.

"Yeah, she's dead. That's what I heard."

"It's all over social media," she said as I looked at my dead phone.

Of course, it would be all over social media. It wouldn't be until later that day that some of the media's spoon-fed narrative would come into focus.

423

It's amazing how much I saw by being there. And it's also amazing how much I missed on that day. The story that the legacy media would fill in for me later when I got back to Florida.

What I saw that day were thousands upon thousands of peaceful protesters in all hues, shapes, and sizes, all wearing their finest MAGA-ware. Most of what I saw was peaceful. I did, however, see fellow patriots sprayed with tear gas and shot with rubber bullets to the point where I got close enough that it affected my breathing. I also was in the center of a large group of MAGA nation who would yell USA, USA, and break into patriotic songs while shouting a potpourri of expletives in the direction of Biden, Pelosi, and Pence. Yet I wasn't anywhere close to where the girl, who would later be identified as Ashli Babbitt, got shot. She is still the only person who died on that day that was a direct result of the protest of January 6th.

But that's not how those on the left and the media see this day. They have twisted what happened on January 6th into a narrative that they often bill as a day when *"the worst civil uprising since the Civil War"* took place?

If this was close to the Civil War- then Ken Burns did a hell of a job making the Civil War look gruesome. Because this wasn't even close to the time when Abraham Lincoln saved the nation.

Most often they forget to mention one detail that is not minor in detail. In fact, it should be the lead, but it's often buried in the story. The reason being it will lend sympathies to those who espouse to the MAGA creed, including one Donald J. Trump.

What and who they fail to mention is the one and only person who was killed on that day as a result of what *some people call a riot, others call a peaceful protest that got out of hand, and finally others call an insurrection,* by those who run fast and loose with definitions that would make George Orwell blush. While it is true that some MAGA folks acted violently and out of character and should be punished to the fullest extent of the law, it is also true that the vast majority, as in 99.9% of those attending the J-6 day "Stop The Steal" rally acted like loyal, God-fearing and law-abiding patriots.

Her name is Ashli Babbitt. Sadly, That's what they leave out of the story. Ashli Babbitt was killed on that day by a Capitol Police officer who many feel overreacted. Still, no mention of her name in the famed Salem Witch Trail, pardon me, J-6 Select Committee, that Donald Trump correctly calls the UNSELECT COMMITTEE, perhaps for their bias and selective memory. They hardly mention her name during their long and drawn out proceedings?

A new video released in 2024 shows a clearer picture of the shooting death of Air Force veteran Ashli Babbitt by a Capitol Police officer. "J6: A True Timeline" shows the moment Babbitt attempted to enter the House speaker's lobby and was shot by Lt. Michael Byrd in the neck or shoulder.

"She's dead, she's dead," a protester cried out. "They just killed a girl," yelled another.

Drawn from official video, police body cameras, surveillance film, and the videos of those at the Capitol, the new timeline tries to put into focus the chaos of the day and include some of the context left out of media summations and the report released by the House Jan. 6 investigation. It highlights the aggressiveness of both sides and especially shows examples of a handful of police forcefully holding back the crowds who attempted to protest the election of Joe Biden as president. A video shows officers shooting rubber balls and chemicals into crowds. The video shows Babbitt followed by a journalist with her camera running approach the barricaded speaker's lobby. There were three officers there to meet her. Within seconds, there were other people behind Babbitt. The video then shifts to the House chamber, and a single gunshot can be heard. The timeline goes back to the lobby, where protesters are smashing the glass doors. At one point from the left and inside the lobby, a gun appears.

"There's a gun, there's a gun," a protester shouted. As Babbitt is pushed inside the chamber, Byrd is shown pulling the trigger. Babbitt is hit and falls back, laying on a Trump campaign flag she was using as a cape. Officers coming up from the first floor urge the crowd to "back up" as Babbitt is cared for.

"She's dead, she's dead, she's dead," one person screamed as three officers carried Babbitt down the steps.

The Justice Department investigated the shooting, deciding not to pursue charges against Byrd and reported this:

"The investigation further determined that Ms. Babbitt was among a mob of people that entered the Capitol building and gained access to a hallway outside 'Speaker's Lobby,' which leads to the Chamber of the U.S. House of Representatives. At the time, the USCP was evacuating Members from the Chamber, which the mob was trying to enter from multiple doorways. USCP officers used furniture to barricade a set of glass doors separating the hallway and Speaker's Lobby to try and stop the mob from entering the Speaker's Lobby and the Chamber, and three officers positioned themselves between the doors and the mob. Members of the mob attempted to break through the doors by striking them and breaking the glass with their hands, flagpoles, helmets, and other objects. Eventually, the three USCP officers positioned outside the doors were forced to evacuate. As members of the mob continued to strike the glass doors, Ms. Babbitt attempted to climb through one of the doors where glass was broken out. An officer inside the Speaker's Lobby fired one round from his service pistol, striking Ms. Babbitt in the left shoulder, causing her to fall back from the doorway and onto the floor. A USCP emergency response team, which had begun making its way into the hallway to try and subdue the mob, administered aid to Ms. Babbitt, who was transported to Washington Hospital Center, where she succumbed to her injuries." [120]

In that short report they mention the word *MOB* six or seven times, and appropriately so, because the Washington elites known as the J-6 Select Committee conduct the people's business on the Hill like a real deep state underworld mob. Like gangsters, they apparently found this was an open and shut case about a slain patriot that they never want to talk about even while they talk about J-6 and till we are red, white and blue in the face.

Her name was *Ashli Babbitt*. She was a Trump supporter. She was an American War Veteran.

And she died on this cold day in Washington DC, January 6, 2021.

But they won't tell you that. They won't even mention her name.

Her name was Ashli Babbitt.

It's a Conspiracy World After All (Sung to it's a small world)

At this point, I believe pretty much all the conspiracy theories over anything that the legacy media and most of my government tell me. Why wouldn't I?

Especially after all the lies regarding pretty much anything that they've told all of us.

- Russian Collusion that claimed Trump was a Russian spy and asset before, during and after the 2016 election
- 51 spies Claiming Hunter Biden laptop as Disinformation by Russians just before 2020 election- The Real October Surprise
- Covid-19 lies on effectiveness and dangerous side effects of vaccine
- Covid-19 lies on the effectiveness of masks, social distancing and lockdowns
- Covid-19 Lies about effectiveness of *Ivermectin* and *Hydroxychloroquine* drugs in fighting Covid-19
- The lies and double standards that were unleashed as LAWFARE on President Trump resulting in four indictments, one conviction while costing him time and money a creating the greatest example of election interference in the history of the United States.
- Cover-up on the deteriorating condition of Joe Biden throughout his entire administration
- Cover-up of the Butler Assassination attempt on Trump unfolding before our eyes
- Lies about Kamala Harris's record denying she was border czar etc,
- Lies that Kamala Harris is telling that she's now pro-cop, not against fracking and suddenly realizes there is a problem at the southern border and *what can be, unburdened by what has been*

What can be unburdened by what has been?

Maybe it means *we can now be truthful* as we sort through the maze of amazing lies told to us by these so-called leaders and media sources and finally feel unburdened by what has been.

In other words – seek to break away from the nonsensical and destructive lies of the past and live in the truth while gaining our freedom.

Yeah, she may have a point.

As one looks at these people who trade in lies the way a dealer in Turkish Bazar trades in rugs, nonchalantly, casually, and as if it is their second nature, it's a wonder we believe them about anything.

I'm reminded of the lesson in Aesop's Fables and the boy who cried wolf. The danger there is – there were so many lies or exaggerations that the boy told that when he actually told the truth about the danger of the real wolf- no one believed him.

That's where we are today. And it's also why I am more apt to dive deeply and more readily into deep conspiracy theories.

I've become illuminated to some degree by the Illuminati. It is not only a captivating story of power and control but also plausible. Regarding the Fed Reserve and the west and central banking systems – An evil and powerful way that the Fed becomes the loan shark to *We the People*. In this scenario, we pay a *VIG* or *the juice* to the banks on loans with heavy interest rates. Most bookies are kinder and more forgiving than these gangsters. And the conspiracy theory gets really interesting when you throw in the Titanic connection with The Fed Reserve.

The conspiracy theory links the Rothschilds, the sinking of the Titanic, and the creation of the Federal Reserve. It features three men and the Titanic, named Benjamin Guggenheim, Isa Strauss (actual name Isidor Straus), and John Jacob Astor, three wealthy men who died on the Titanic and each "opposed new Federal Reserve Bank." The Titanic's sinking happened in 1912, and the opening of the Federal Reserve happened in 1913. We get the hint - their opposition to the Fed and their deaths were somehow linked? A further conspiracy suggests that J.P. Morgan, the plutocrat financier who set up the investment bank that still bears his name, arranged to have the men board the ship and then sink it. Morgan did have a hand in the creation of the Federal Reserve, and it owned the International Mercantile Marine, which owned the White Star Line, which owned the Titanic. That's pretty much where the evidence ends. [121]

But it's not the end of conspiracy theories.

Regarding the moon landing, I still think that we went there, but I'm starting to have my doubts. I've often wondered why we haven't gone back more recently. I want to believe that we went to the moon because I watched the landing with my parents, and I was always inspired by that JFK speech in which he almost willed our nation to land there by the end of the decade. He would not live to see the mission. Whether 9/11 was inspired or encouraged by inside help by our government, I know that's dark, but it's also possible, regarding the Covid-19 fiasco, that has lessened my belief and confidence to almost the same amount of danger of dying from the original virus- of way less than one percent. Yes, I have one percent confidence in their stories and their lies disguised as truths.

The JFK thing has always bothered me and still does. Many people wanted Jack dead. Just as many want Trump dead today. And many of the same usual suspects are still around and hide in the shadows, hoping for just that. That they let that kid on the roof less than 400 feet from the president is not a series of miscommunication and f-ups; it's an intentional attempt to take down most likely the next president of the United States and the only man that truly stands between them and their boatload of lies that they feed the American people. You don't have to be suspect of the single bullet conspiracy theory nut then, or be a "why the hell didn't they see the kid on the pitched roof tin hatter" now, to know deep in your gut "that something really wrong and intentionally planned happened both in *Dallas and Butler*." Hopefully, someday, the real truth sans conspiracies will be exposed in the light of day where most everyone can see them.

Anyway, that's what I'm hoping for: that the darkest theories out there don't turn out to be true.

But is a *"Conspiracy world after all."* And just like that song *"Small World,"* once a conspiracy theory gets into your head, you can't get it out. Over time, sure it will fade away, just like the Disney song, depending on whether it's just another conspiracy theory or it turns out to be true.

"It's a Small World"
It's a world of laughter,
A world of tears.
It's a world of hopes,
And a world of fears.
There's so much that we share,
That it's time we're aware,
It's a small world after all.

MAGA Man - A Once Banned Twitter Refuge Becomes X Factor Breaking Internet

Leave it to Elon Musk and Donald Trump to literally blow up the internet just by sitting down and talking. That's something Kamala Harris can't and won't ever do. Sit down and have a substantive conversation off the cuff with anybody as the cameras roll.

That Trump and Musk had the audacity to sit down and have a conversation with no safety net or draconian rules in place is something that drives all those on the left to be triggered, clutching their pearls and speed-dialing their therapists. Trump is many things to many people and he is also *the most transparent president ever.* That's something he seldom gets credit for, especially when compared to those who served as president and those who want to become president. The contrast is startling. Trump makes himself available day or night and will walk into an often hostile media environment and field unscripted questions sans the use of notes or handlers. When compared to Biden, who they hid because he was unable to speak extemporaneously, if at all, or Kamala, who seems to be allergic to a press conference or sit-down interview, Trump is an open book.

And yes, sometimes that works against him, as the press will take a rant and rave that he makes at a rally out of context, harping on it instead of the vast amount of time he stayed on script and talked about policy issues and did it in an entertaining way. That moment at the Butler rally saved his life. Trump going off script and calling for the immigration slide was a man in his element. Comfortable in his own skin —even if sometimes his supporters are not.

I'm reminded of Silicon Valley giant Peter Thiel's quote, "The Media always take Trump literally but never take him seriously... and a lot of the voters who vote for Trump take Trump seriously and not literally."

No, he doesn't think he's better-looking than Kamala. Trump is just jazzing the audience. But there is a method to his madness. He thinks his wife is better-looking than Kamala. This is Trump's way of making a point as he references a Time cover portrait suited for an icon and natural beauty like "Sophia Loren." In drawing attention to the fawning drawing of Kamala, he's illustrating the contrast between coverage and double standards. Without saying it, he's reminding people that Time mocked Donald as an ugly, melting, animated, cartoonish monster, not the *"handsome better looking than Kamala figure that he is."* Hell, for those playing this celebrity game of Thrones magazine cover wars...don't be surprised if his "I'm better looking than Kamala comment" wasn't said to remind people that Vogue put Hillary, Jill Biden, and Michelle Obama on the cover of Vogue, but would have no part in putting the beautiful Melania on their cover of Vogue.

Trump is once again transparent with a purpose, playing 5-D chess, and those of us who get him and take him seriously and not literally know that. Speaking seriously and literally. The current legacy media had no problem - not taking seriously the fact that the President of the United States was banned from Twitter, literally believing he deserved his persona non grata status as his First Amendment **rights were trampled on.**

Seriously, the left literally and figuratively loved it. Knowing that Trump was banned, at the same time terrorists worldwide were left to enjoy their First Amendment rights probably gave them a tingle. That all changed when Elon Musk bought Twitter, cleaned house and rectified many of the ills that were plaguing the social media platform.

John Daniel Davidson of the Federalist shared an article titled *"The Twitter Files Reveal an Existential Threat"* in *Imprimus*, the monthly publication from Hillsdale College.

Elon Musk's takeover of Twitter...and the subsequent reporting on the Twitter Files by journalists Matt Taibbi, Bari Weiss, and a handful of others ... is one of the most important news stories of our time. The Twitter Files story encompasses, and to a large extent connects, every major political scandal of the Trump-Biden era. Put simply, the Twitter Files reveal an unholy alliance between Big Tech and the deep state designed to throttle free speech and maintain an official narrative through censorship and propaganda. This should not just disturb us, it should also prod us to action in defense of the First Amendment, free and fair elections, and indeed our country. [122]

As the two titans sat and talked uninterrupted for over two hours, I smiled, grateful for the vision of those who saw into the future as they formed a country. I couldn't help but think of their intentions of taking the idea of America - seriously and not literally. Our forefathers knew what the public square meant and as they debated, knew it was meant for everyone.

A place we thought Twitter was until it wasn't. The public square. A place saved by a patriot named Elon Musk, who came along just in time to tear down the curtain and expose the thought police tyrants who both seriously and literally wanted to monitor all of our free speech.

That was what I thought as I tried frustratingly to join the conversation that both those in the social media universe and the deep state surely didn't want to take place.

After a delay of about 40 minutes, Elon Musk came on and told the worldwide audience that X had been hacked but that the show would go on. And it did for over two hours. A conversation between two of the most important, famous, and influential people in the world. A wide ranging conversation, free flowing with ideas to be discussed, agreed upon or not, a talk between two guys largely about the future of this place called America. A place where the public square was resurrected on this very special night.

Musk set up the interview by saying we are going to have a conversation and get to know what Donald Trump is like in a conversation. *"It's hard to catch a vibe about someone if you just don't hear them talk in a normal way. When there is an adversarial interview – no one is themselves…and this is aimed at independent open-minded voters who are just trying to make up their mind."*

Musk, who recently made up his mind and was throwing his full support behind Trump, started the conversation where many of us would have had the chance to sit down one-on-one with the former president of the United States.

Musk spoke of The Butler rally and how the president almost lost his life. *"If we could start off with the assassination attempt which was an incredible thing. Your actions after the assassination attempt were inspiring. Instead of shying away from things, instead of ducking down, you were pumping your fist in the air and saying - Fight, Fight, Fight! The President of The United States represents America, and I think that is America. That is strength **under fire**.* [123]

Under Fire describes what the two men would face from the legacy media as they reviewed the two men's conversation, sentence by sentence, with many dismissing it as "softball questions" and a "conversation by two white, rich guys." Kamala Harris went so far as to mock the fact that Musk and Trump failed at being able to pull off live streaming without a hitch. They miss the point entirely. Both Trump and Musk enter the Arena that Teddy Roosevelt spoke about and do not hide from the spotlight. That Trump went there into friendly confines is no different than him going into hostile environments which he does often. Harris, on the other hand, goes nowhere and speaks to no one —for one simple reason. She is not qualified, not to give a two-hour presser, not to hold a friendly two-hour conversation discussing an array of ideas, and certainly not be able to handle the job of being president of the United States.

Elon Musk…the rocket man and electric car builder, and Donald J. Trump, the real estate tycoon, former and possibly future president of the United States. Just a couple of guys who happen to be white and rich. One from Queens, New York, and one from South Africa. Just a couple of guys who love America sitting down and talking - having a conversation. They have many things in common – but it's mostly this – they drive those on the left crazy. Oh, and one other thing. They are despised and hated by those who once used to sing both their praises. My how things have changed in America.

Some in the press took the opportunity at the White House Press conference to raise the danger of the two men sitting down and talking.

"I think that misinformation on Twitter is not just a campaign issue. It's a — you know, it's an America issue. What role does the White House or the president have in sort of stopping that or stopping the spread of that or sort of inter- — intervening in that? Some of that was about campaign misinformation, but, you know, it's a wider thing, right?" [124]

Sure, it's a wider thing. That's how we got here in the first place. Because social media companies like Twitter and others put their thumbs on the scales when it came to weighing in on being fair and balanced in regard to the arguments made and protected under our First Amendment, a Patriot named Musk had to step in and fight, fight, fight so that he and guys like Donald Trump could just sit down and have a conversation free from censorship in the public square.

The Emperor's New Pant Suit

They had all been on this big stage before. The big names with the big speeches wearing big fancy clothes designed by big names. The Clintons. The One, who was supposed to be the One after the One named Obama, forever lacking charm with her signature cackle and screech speech that had the ability to suck the air out of any room. The other. A polished politician now much older, but not quite as old as Donald Trump, he made sure he let everyone know that he was now less handsome, less commanding, but still no less a liar. The Clintons took the stage and did their best, showering praise on the unimpressive Kamala while heaving bombs in the direction of a man named Donald, who at one time they admired and now they had come to despise. Being beaten by an outsider and a smarter, more effective opponent does that to some people.

The Obamas were there too. The once hopeful couple had aged, but not as much as their words. Their rhetoric was now more pointed and angrier. They both could still deliver the words and the speech fine, but there was something missing.

The magic. And, of course, the charm. And that other important element that they supposedly introduced to all of America. The hope. It was gone, for they had truly changed. America had hoped that they would be different and not like the typical politicians who dealt with the issues of the day in traditional and dirty ways. They had all hoped that they would be, above all that, purveyors of promises, graceful keepers of the flame and the American dream, who truly saw America not as "red states or blue states but as the United States." That myth and charade had, after all, died years ago. The power couple from Chicago, and that's what they were, who had professed to speak to and for the people, were now speaking down to a good portion of the people who watched their speeches at home all over those *red, white, and blue states*. No, not to the people in this setting. They still were taking communion with these two high priests and hanging on each and every one of their sacred words.

Strangely, Kamala Harris was not in the venue when the Obamas spoke but instead had been shuffled off to Milwaukee to host an event for supporters there. Perhaps it was part of the deal that they had arranged. Part of the coup. An attempt to not hurt old Joe's feelings any more than they had to by being in the same hall with Barack Obama, who everyone knew was one of the chief architects of the plan to swap out Joe for Kamala. Dare I say to anyone normal watching, not in the hall but at home. It came off as being a little bit *Weird*. No not quite Trump or Vance Weird, but you get the drift. Those in the hall ate up all the words, perhaps because they were all still on a high. A high that some of them no doubt had from getting a free abortion or vasectomy or seeing to it that someone worthy or in need was getting these free services that the DNC was promoting as a perk to supporters of their "joyous" platform. The end result. They hung on every word from each of the Obamas as they smiled and looked at each other and reminisced a bit about the first time they "saw their faces." Yet, as they cheered and showered them with applause in the auditorium, something was different. You could feel it. They spoke all the right words, but as they were saying them, they seemed different because they were different. No longer charming and magical. And they knew it. Worse yet, the people felt it too. Perhaps it was because they had become part of the establishment, the elites that they so often railed against.

In this scene and at this moment they appeared angry. Petty. Hypocritical. *The Audacity of Hope?* Hogwash. Michelle Obama actually spoke about her parents not trusting people who made a lot of money.

Michelle Obama, the former First Lady (FLOTUS), worth more than $70 million, advised Americans against "*taking more than they need.*" Obama's speech, which was partly a tribute to her mother, Mary Robinson. "*She and my father didn't aspire to be wealthy,*" she said of her mother. "*In fact, they were suspicious of folks who took more than they needed. They understood that it wasn't enough for their kids to thrive if everyone else around us was drowning.*"[125]

Drowning? And that's precisely what many Americans listening and watching at home were doing. Drowning. Drowning in debt. Drowning with Inflation and job losses. Their American dreams drowning in doubt with no hope on the horizon.

The convention was filled with empty promises and many lies that offered little if any hope delivered from purveyors of broken dreams from people whose masks had slipped off. People like Oprah Winfrey. My how she had changed or had she? Oprah, who once seemingly brought much of the nation together in the afternoons in living rooms and kitchens all over America with the art of conversation, had soured. Gone was the joy. One of her guests on the show, and a one-time friend was a man named Donald J. Trump. The Donald had caught Oprah's fancy to the point that she once waxed on philosophically, if not in pure fantasy, about forming a team and running, not TV shows, but the whole show as President and Vice-President.

The Trump campaign shared a private handwritten letter Winfrey sent to Trump in January 2000. She penned the note in response to an excerpt Trump had sent her from his book *The America We Deserve* in which he wrote that she would be his "first choice for vice president."

Oprah's letter to President Trump: pic.
Twitter.com/QY1kYifPJS

— Trump War Room (@TrumpWarRoom) <u>August 22, 2024</u>

"Donald—I reviewed the book excerpt. I have to tell you, your comments made me a little weepy," Winfrey's letter reads. "It's one thing to try and live a life of integrity—still another to have people like yourself notice. Thank you." At the bottom of the letter, Winfrey added:

"Too bad we're not running for office. What A TEAM!"[126]

As evidenced by her appearance at the 2024 DNC, something had changed in their relationship. Who and what had changed? Was it The Donald or Oprah? You be the judge as you examine Oprah's words of unity to the congregation. *"Decency and respect are on the ballot in 2024,"* she said to rapturous applause. *"And just plain common sense—common sense tells you that Kamala Harris and Tim Walz can give us decency and respect."* Winfrey also encouraged voters to *"choose loyalty to the Constitution over loyalty to any individual,"* and invoked a Harris campaign slogan by adding: *"Let us choose the sweet promise of tomorrow over the bitter return to yesterday… We're not going back." "Let us choose joy because that's the best of America,"* Winfrey said in closing. *"But more than anything else, let us choose freedom. Why? Because that's the best of America. We're all Americans, and together, let's all choose Kamala Harris!"*

And that was the whole point of the evening setting up Kamala Harris for her prime time speech that would introduce her to the nation. A woman who got no votes for president in the 2024 primary and who had dropped out of the 2020 campaign because she was so unpopular and had her and her record destroyed at a debate by Tulsi Gabbard, only to be rewarded as the VP pick for seemingly intimating that Joe Biden was a racist at the same debate. Oh, the Joy of it all. I can hear Beethoven playing in the background.

As she made her way to her moment, adorned in her dark blue pantsuit. What? She wasn't going to wear red, the color of some Jezebel. Blue was the color of her pantsuit, and she tried to fill it in and the moment with a plethora of *thank yous* for the frantic crowd. When she did get started, there was actually some hope that she had changed. That she was not as mean or not as big a liar in covering up her tracks as an ineffective and destructive Senator and Vice-President, who took part in the biggest LIE IN THE HISTORY OF AMERICA for four years, and that was this:

"Joe Biden was fine and above doing the job as President," said the woman who was supposedly the last person in the room with Joe as he fumbled through each and every major policy decision, both foreign and domestic, that impacted all Americans and America. She was there in the room with him and stood beside him and was okay with the disastrous pullout from Afghanistan, in which, tragically, 13 marines were lost, many Americans were left behind, and billions of dollars of Defense equipment were left behind to be used by the Taliban. Think about that for a minute.

I will not go over her 37-minute lie-infested acceptance speech. There is no joy in that. And no lie is bigger than the one told about *JOE BEING OK TO RUN THE COUNTRY*. I will take issue with one of the lies that was a doozy, the one where she went on about January 6th an event she equated to 9/11 and Pearl Harbor in seriousness and destruction to our country.

"Consider — consider not only the chaos and calamity when he was in office, but also the gravity of what has happened since he lost the last election. Donald Trump tried to throw away your votes. When he failed, he sent an armed mob to the U.S. Capitol, where they assaulted law enforcement officers. When politicians in his own party begged him to call off the mob and send help, he did the opposite — he fanned the flames. And now, for an entirely different set of crimes, he was found guilty of fraud by a jury of everyday Americans, and separately — and separately found liable for committing sexual abuse. And consider, consider what he intends to do if we give him power again. Consider his explicit intent to set free violent extremists who assaulted those law enforcement officers at the Capitol." [127]

Being there on January 6th, that was simply not true. And most Americans know it. I went there to protest a fixed election that was rigged. The coup that took place then happened on Election Day, something similar to what they ironically were doing to one of their own – a fading and aging old man from Delaware named Joe. Elder Abuse and Lies.

There in DC, I stood peacefully with fellow patriots to protest an election that was not lost but stolen. I was equipped with the only weapon I have ever really used – common sense, and my words in my book GET Trump, that I dedicated myself to writing and telling the story of this remarkable man, patriot, and president who was there standing in the way of all those who barely saw us and when they did, they would trample over our God Given constitutional rights.

I've seen too many of their lies to take them as truths. They are fake, fake, fake…and Trump will fight, fight, fight… for not only what is right for America and all Americans, but he will fight for the truth.

As I listened to Michelle Obama wax on about the times we were living in, I smiled at the irony of her words.

"Something wonderfully magical is in the air," she said to the delegates and guests crowded into Chicago's United Center. *"A familiar feeling that's been buried too deep for far too long. It's the contagious power of hope."*

"Hope is making a comeback." **(125)**

She was right. Hope was making a comeback. But it does not emanate from this arena filled to the brim with lies, vapid platitudes, and broken promises. Hope was making a comeback in fields, arenas, assembly lines, grocery stores, schools, spots at the border, where suffering Americans were counting the days until Election Day and a time when they could vote for a man named Donald Trump who could once again take office and fix an ailing nation with his dose of hope and elbow grease.

JFK, RFK & John, John smiling down from above in MAGA Hats?

Has anybody here seen my old friend John?
Can you tell me where he's gone?
He freed a lot of people.
But it seems the good die young
But I just looked around and he's gone [128]

My family always got the Kennedys. Back in the 1960's we lived in a two family flat with our cousins downstairs and with us upstairs on a street called Kentucky in the city of Detroit. It was a home filled with spirited family gatherings and conversations, snowball fights, tossing of footballs and baseballs, beautiful Christmas mornings, and all the stuff that makes great family memories. It suppose it was like Hyannis Port with the Kennedys but without all the pomp and circumstance.

When JFK was killed, I was only a little kid, so my memories are in the retelling, yet the sadness that my family felt when our young president was taken from us was something I will always remember. The melancholy was reflected in my mom and dad's eyes and Uncle Danny and Aunt Becca's, evident even years after the assassinations as they spoke about Jack and his unfulfilled promise. A similar feeling was echoed as the nation lost Martin Luther King Jr. and Bobby Kennedy in the tumultuous and tragic year of 1968. That year, our Detroit Tigers won the World Series and helped our torn city heal from the riots of 1967. Back then, my two first cousins, Gus and Paul, along with their sister Cookie, would spoil me and my sister. They were good times. Family times. Times that have faded now into cherished memories.

On one of my most recent trips back home, I visited my cousin Paul, who sadly was on his deathbed fighting cancer in a hospital in Detroit. I apologized for not spending as much time and losing touch over the years. As we hugged and cried and said our goodbyes, but before I could go, he whispered to me, *"Trump has got to win to save America...Sorry, I didn't get to finish your book."* It stunned me. Through tears, I nodded my head and remembered a time not so long ago when I handed him my GET TRUMP book at his brother and my cousin's home – in secret, far away from the ridicule of his anti-Trump sentiments.

I thought about that a lot as I thought of what Robert F. Kennedy Jr. was going through in making it public that he supported Donald J. Trump for president. I knew a little bit of what he must have been going through. Only his task was multiplied by a thousand times.

Strangely, my paths would cross with Cheryl Hines and Rory Kennedy, Bobby Kennedy's wife and sister, respectively.

I interviewed them both at the Sarasota Film Festival, and the experience was delightful. I admired both women's talents, and they were gracious and generous with their time. That's what I thought of when I heard that RFK Jr. announced he was going to support Trump. That and my two cousins who loved each other but didn't see eye to eye politically.

Here was a Kennedy, a man whose family was the gold standard and brand of the Democrat party for years, endorsing the hated and evil orange man named Trump. Many intimated that he was not in his right mind. Questions were raised. Was he okay? Was he in his right mind? What had changed?

Well, the thing is, it wasn't Bobby Jr. that changed. It was the Democrat party that changed. The party of his father and his uncle are unrecognizable. They had changed drastically. And Bobby Kennedy Jr. was calling them out on it.

Before Biden dropped out of the race, he told CNN's Erin Burnett Out-front that President Joe Biden is a greater threat to democracy than former President Donald Trump, citing his effort to *"censor political speech"* and undermine the First Amendment.

"I can make the argument that President Biden is the much worse threat to democracy, and the reason for that is President Biden is the first candidate in history – the first president in history that has used the federal agencies to censor political speech, so to censor his opponent." [129]

After Biden dropped out, his focus turned to Kamala Harris. *"My uncle and my father both relished debate. They prided themselves on their capacity to go toe to toe with any opponent and the battle over ideas,"* Kennedy said. *"They would be astonished to learn of a Democratic Party presidential nominee who, like Vice President Harris, has not appeared in a single interview or an unscripted encounter with voters for 35 days."*

One of the main reasons Kennedy said he endorsed Trump was because he believed the former president would quickly end the Russia-Ukraine War.

Still, the news was met with a harsh rebuke from some of his own family. *"We want an America filled with hope and bound together by a shared vision of a brighter future, a future defined by individual freedom, economic promise, and national pride. We believe in*

Harris and Walz," Kathleen Kennedy Townsend, Courtney Kennedy, Kerry Kennedy, Chris Kennedy, and Rory Kennedy said in a statement. *"Our brother Bobby's decision to endorse Trump today is a betrayal of the values that our father and our family hold most dear. It is a sad ending to a sad story."*[130]

And the Kennedy story has always been filled with its share of sadness. But the sad story of which they speak is of a party that has shifted away from the values and the people the Kennedys always looked out for, the forgotten men and women in America who had no connections and lobbyists looking out for them- you know the kind of people you find at a Trump rally. MAGA people. And while this twist and turn in the story is obviously hard for some of Bobby's family to take – for some others who made the brand what it is, not so much. Sadly, John Jr., a friend of The Donald, isn't here to opine – but he always thought a lot of the man named Trump. Still Bobby Junior acknowledged his decision to endorse Trump had caused tension with his family. He is married to actor Cheryl Hines, who wrote on X that she deeply respects her husband's decision to drop out but did not address the Trump endorsement. *"This decision is agonizing for me because of the difficulties it causes my wife and my children and my friends,"* Kennedy said. *"But I have the certainty that this is what I'm meant to do. And that certainty gives me internal peace, even in storms."*

Storms have plagued this country and have led the ship that is America to go off course, something that both the kid from Queens and the boy raised around Camelot recognized. *"We are both in this to do what's right for the country,"* Trump said, later commending Kennedy for having *"raised critical issues that have been too long ignored in this country."*

With Kennedy standing nearby, Trump invoked his slain uncle and father, John F. Kennedy and Robert F. Kennedy, saying he knows *"that they are looking down right now and they are very, very proud."* Trump said that if he wins this fall, he will establish a new independent presidential commission on assassination attempts that will release all remaining documents related to John F. Kennedy's assassination.

Kennedy cast their alliance as "a unity party," an arrangement that would *"allow us to disagree publicly and privately and seriously."* [131]

"We talked about Abraham Lincoln's team of rivals. That arrangement would allow us to disagree publicly and privately and fiercely, if need be, on issues over which we differ and also work together on the existential issues upon which we are in concordance. I was a ferocious critic of many of the policies during his first administration, and there are still issues and approaches upon which we continue to have very serious differences."

But we are aligned with each other on other key issues, like ending of forever wars, ending the childhood disease epidemics, securing the border, protecting freedom of speech, unraveling the corporate capture of our regulatory agencies, and getting the U.S. intelligence agencies out of the business of propagandizing and censoring and surveilling Americans and interfering with our elections. Following my first discussion with President Trump, I tried unsuccessfully to open similar discussions with Vice President Harris. Vice President Harris declined to meet or even to speak with me." [132]

Sadly, even if some of his family doesn't get him, Thank God Bobby Jr. gets what was once important to the Democrat party that once got America and didn't try to get Americans with Draconian laws of censorship while trampling on their constitutional rights. And somewhere because of that, his cousin John, his uncle Jack, and his father Bobby are smiling as he imparts the wisdom and love they had for this country.

That Bobby Jr gets Trump and doesn't want to get Trump drives those on the left nuts. That he left the Democrat party does not promote some self-reflection to those closest to him, and the party is sad. Sadly, they can't see that the party of their youth has changed. Robert F Kennedy rightfully claims that he didn't abandon the Democrat Party but that the Democrat Party abandoned him. No this is truly not his father's or his Uncle's Democrat party anymore. Nor is it former Hawaii congresswoman Tulsi Gabbard's, as evidenced by her departure from the Democrat party and her recent endorsement of Donald J. Trump.

"This [current] administration has us facing multiple wars on multiple fronts in regions around the world, and closer to the brink of

nuclear war than we ever have been before," Gabbard said. "This is one of the main reasons why I am committed to doing all that I can to send President Trump back to the White House, where he can once again serve us as our commander in chief."[133]

While RFK Jr. states that he has many points of disagreement with the often brash businessman from Queens turned President, he cites the common ground that they share as his hope for building a better, healthier America that does not infringe on our First Amendment rights or plunge us into endless wars.

We are reminded of something his Uncle Jack said:

"So, let us not be blind to our differences--but let us also direct attention to our common interests and to the means by which those differences can be resolved. And if we cannot end now our differences, at least we can help make the world safe for diversity. For, in the final analysis, our most basic common link is that we all inhabit this small planet. We all breathe the same air. We all cherish our children's future. And we are all mortal."[34]

Yes, somewhere, his uncle, father, and cousin are smiling. And it wouldn't be too surprising if they were wearing MAGA red while rooting for Bobby Jr. to cross the aisle and fight, fight, fight to make America free and healthy and help make the Democrat party great again.

Has anybody here seen my old friend Bobby?
Can you tell me where he's gone?
I thought I saw him walkin'
Up over the hill
With Abraham, Martin and John (**128**)

Going Back to Butler...because that's what Leaders do

The scene of the crime. The battlefield. Leaders often return to the sight of a battle. It was not all that surprising that he should return to the place where his life nearly ended. That was perhaps the most Trump-like thing to do. It's what makes him unconventional as both a politician and a man. Unpredictable. Bold. Brave. Humbled by it all. And yes a little pissed off that the shooter interrupted his speech. On his Elon

Musk interview, he joked that upon his return to Butler, he would take the stage and say something like, "*Where was I when I was so rudely interrupted?*"

Again, so Trump. Making light of a dark situation. And let's face it, this man has had to face his share of dark situations. That's where the humor comes in. It helps him cope. It helps him live to fight another day. And that is what he was given…a chance to live to fight another day… as the bullet narrowly missed taking the president's life.

He takes nothing for granted. Not his voters. Not his country. Not his life.

That's why he's going back to Butler and why he's coming back to the White House.

It's part or the plan. The divine plan? Perhaps. More than likely, one designed to help save the republic with the help of a lot of patriots and angels. And one man, a leader who would never go away because he had a job yet to finish, and he knew the way.

Much like Abe, who came before him and shared a history with a Pennsylvania town named Gettysburg, this president will forever be connected with another Pennsylvania town named Butler.

And from all indications it is a place that the president will revisit for one reason more than any other – he owes the good people there the rest of his speech.

He will return there because he must. His return there to honor Corey's memory. And he will return there because that's what leaders do. They return to the battlefield, knowing that there are still days left to fight, fight, fight, and the fight runs through this small Pennsylvania town,

A place called Butler. A President named Trump.

The place where the movement almost died. And also the place where the movement rose again.

A place and time in history that will be remembered like Gettysburg because of a man and leader who always brought an honest fight to the battlefield to save the republic.

Get Trump...Get America...We the People Get Trump

If he has said it once, he has said it thousands of times, *"They're not coming after me...I'm just in the way. They're coming after you."*

Yes, on that, Donald J. Trump was always 100% right.

Sure, they were out to Get Trump, they were out to Get America, but mostly, they were out to Get You ...Me and all of us forgotten men, women, and children in America.

That's why he ran the first time. And why he ran the second time. And why he ran again for the third time. He didn't do it for himself. He did it for his country and for all of us, in truly a heroic move that was well George Washington-like.

They have been so wrong about this man, yet it doesn't surprise me because they have been just as wrong about America...and about you and me. All of us. And the sad but eye-opening thing is they don't care.

The Assassination attempt of President Trump brought it all home. It showed how much hate there was out there, but it also revealed how much love was out there as well. And it revealed one other thing that most honest people would admit about this man named Trump whether they loved him or hated him.

One thing that no one could ever say was that Trump was not a force of nature. In many ways a supernatural force. Who gets up after being shot at and pumps his fist? Fight, fight, fight? The man named Donald J. Trump. In doing so, he revealed what is at the heart of this Lion of a leader. Courage. It is the one virtue you can't fake, fake, fake. Where his opponent would cower from shots in the form of questions from the press, this man has stood up and taken every shot they have fired at him. Only now, they're using real bullets. Still, it doesn't matter, not really, not to him and not to MAGA nation. They know why he fights and why he can't stop fighting. Ever since he came down the escalator and got in the race, it was not to satisfy his ego but to save his country and make it great again. Proving not only how brave he was but how hard he would fight for the MAGA nation and for everyone in America. He rose like one of his buildings, reaching up toward the heavens, knowing that presidents don't hide in basements from the press or on the floor of the podium at a rally even after bullets whizzed by his head.

He knew that he must get up. The man named Trump has always known that fighters always get up. That's what they do. And that's what Donald J. Trump is. A fighter. For the American people. For their dreams, freedoms, and their liberty.

Upon seeing this man named Trump rise to his feet with fists pumping, the world's richest man, Elon Musk, a man who knew a little bit about reaching for the heavens himself, was so moved and inspired by his actions that he certainly had no regrets about recently throwing his hat into the MAGA ring and proudly endorsing him for President.

Elon Musk, a wickedly smart and wise man, had seen enough of the train wreck that was America. It made him both sad and angry. This man born in South Africa who had chosen to make America his new adopted home was worried about America and the direction it was heading. So he got busy trying to make a difference. His first real shot he fired into the fight was buying what he would say at a bloated evaluation and price, a social media platform called TWITTER that he believed suppressed free speech and the First Amendment rights of many Americans, including the former president of the United States. The thought sickened him - so he bought Twitter and changed its name to X. There he went through the slow, necessary, and painstaking process of cleaning up the mess in the hopes of making it a place and form more akin to a fair public square, where everyone, including even a banned POTUS, could go and speak his mind freely. It's not something he really wanted to do, but something he needed and was compelled to do for the greater good. He knew one other thing: that America was about dreamers and doers, people like himself and this man named Trump. Men who built tall skyscrapers or sent rockets in the same heavenly direction. Both men knew America was always about launching your dreams and it was always about getting up and fighting for them, no matter what.

Even if it meant getting up from a stage in a small Pennsylvania town after you have been shot at. Getting up and fighting for the people and his country. It's something that comes naturally to a man named Trump. Because you can't fake freedom or courage. Trump has said that he really shouldn't be here and that it was by fortune or fate that the bullet missed, and he was blessed with another chance to get up and continue fighting for America.

Because he was saved he still has a chance to save America.

At 6:11 pm on July 13, 2024, a bullet came within *earshot* of ending the life of Donald J. Trump and changing everything in America. Thankfully, it was not meant to be. Donald Trump miraculously would live to fight another day and, God willing, many more days.

In Ephesians 6:11 of King James Version, it says, *"Put on the whole armour of God that ye may be able to stand against the wiles of the devil.*[135]

The devil. The Lord. Two forces fighting each other for an eternity. But for what? For our souls. In the struggle of good vs evil, the devil's gun is always loaded. But it's no match for a man who stands tall and is equipped with the right armour and the courage of a Lion.

Good versus Evil. That's what this election is really about. They have shown us what they believe and where the priorities are and it's time to believe them. They take the side of the criminals over the victims, empathize with illegal aliens over American citizens, and oppressively rule rather than serve the people with grace and liberty.

There is only one man that continues to stand up for us. The outsider named Trump. The man who keeps getting up time after time, no matter how many times he's hit. Just a few questions before you vote. How many times have you been knocked down? How many times have you gotten up? How many times have you wanted to quit but didn't? Think of how many times Trump has been knocked down only to get up and do what?

Yes…fight, fight, fight…for you, for me and for America.

Trump's always said, "*They're not coming after me*, they're coming after you – I'm just standing in their way."

Standing in their way, taking fake allegations, fake impeachments, fake indictments, fake convictions, and real bullets.

Taking their best shots and getting back up to answer the bell. Who do you trust to get up and fight for America and forgotten Americans? Donald J. Trump a real proven fighter or Kamala Harris a fake, untested candidate who dodges questions and then laughs it off.

You cannot be a serious person if you vote for her just because she's a woman. There will be a time when all of America will proudly vote for a woman. I can't wait for that day to come when I can cast my vote proudly and make a little history while doing so, but that time is not now. This woman must not and cannot be the next president of the United States, not because she is a woman, but because she's not qualified.

Deep down, anyone who is fair and serious knows that. It has nothing to do with race or gender. There is only one *person in the arena who is ready to do the job, and he deserves y1our vote, not because he is a man but because he is the best and most qualified person to run the country.*

Donald Trump has a record, and it's a good one at making America great once, and he will do it again if we afford him the chance. Kamala Harris also has a record as part of the Biden administration. It has led to a failing economy with soaring inflation, a world on fire with multiple wars, a border invaded by millions of illegal aliens, and 13 dead soldiers in a shameful withdrawal from Afghanistan, one of America's endless wars that ended badly. Nothing Kamala has had her hand in or handed to her has turned out great. She's been on the job for nearly four years. On her watch, America has failed. She must not be given another chance to continue to take us down this dead-end road.

Each election is billed as the most important ever. This time, it's true. There is no hype. The stakes have never been higher in our republic's history. Our foundation has always been about securing our freedom and liberty. It is in our DNA.

It is something that makes Americans and America unique. Our constitution stubbornly protects us against enemies, foreign and domestic. And when we are blessed to have a leader, a real leader, someone who truly works for the people's best interest, then our union has not only a chance to survive but thrive.

The first time Trump won, he shocked the establishment. They didn't see it coming. In cleaning the swamp and exposing the deep state during his term, he made a lot of enemies while endearing himself to many of the American people. When Trump ran again in 2020, a plan, actually a *plandemic was* hatched to help oust him out of office. Stealing the election was complex, but not below their evil and sinister minds. A plan that installed a puppet in his place, creating nearly four years of suffering for most Americans who were not insiders connected to the deep state.

It set up the comeback for the man from Mar-a-Lago and the kid from Queens to give it one more run. He had to. Not for ego. Not for spite. Not for revenge. But for one reason. America meant too much to him. He could not give up. He had to get up one more time and fight for America. One more time to fight for this land and idea envisioned by great, brave men who created a country at a time of chaos with principles that still guide us today. The man named Donald Trump had to do it because he knew he was the only one standing in the way of those who wanted to destroy America, those who wanted to get Trump, get you, get me, and get America.

Strong, resilient, and without fear, the outsider was ready once again to make America great again. Once again, the bell was about to ring; the fighter was ready to fight for the thing he loved most. America. And the good news? The millions of forgotten men, women, and fighters for the American dream, who had heard the bell ringing all across the land, gathered here in his corner to stand behind and with their fighter and fight, fight, fight for the America that they know and loved and for an America that they knew was once great and would be again.

Epilogue: Not So Great Debate Awakens Nation As to what's at stake

As George Washington said, "*If freedom of speech is taken away, then dumb and silent we may be led, like sheep to the slaughter.*" Freedom of speech has been a basic freedom of our country since founded hundreds of years ago. It is the *God given right* to us express our thoughts, opinions, and beliefs as we choose.

On a recent night in America in the city of Philadelphia of all places, America's press chose to take sides in a presidential debate between two candidates running for the highest office in the land, and the most important job in the world. On this historic and shameful night, the press felt it was their job to do the unconscionable. Had Jefferson, Franklin, or Hamilton been on the stage on this night, they may have challenged the two scoundrels to a duel for their grotesque abuse of power, for slandering them, and for not doing their job. And that job is simply this. Be there as the "fourth estate" watchdog to check the government for the people, not just for some people but all the people. Not just for Kamala Harris and her supporters but also for Donald Trump and his people. You have but one job. Ask tough, fair questions to both candidates and then stay the hell out of the way. Don't put your finger on the scale to add weight to one argument or take it off to lessen the effect of another point.

On this night, they will be remembered for their obscene and intentional interference in a presidential debate. America's press, on a stage in a place called Philadelphia where 236 years ago, the Constitution was ratified by great men who often didn't see eye to eye. The actions of ABC's "debate moderators" David Muir and Linsey Davis will live in infamy. And serve as an abortion of the first amendment. A rape of one candidate's right to free speech. And finally provided startling good old-fashioned election interference that threatens to marginalize millions of American voters. But worse than all that, they have added even more doubt to the whole voting process – because of their blatant disregard for the Constitutional rights of one candidate running for office while playing favorites with the other candidate. Shameful. Sinful. Unforgivable. Actions that cause distrust in the system that our founding fathers birthed, cherished and put safeguards in place to protect. On this night in Philadelphia, it would not surprise anyone if the Liberty Bell didn't develop another crack or two. And it would not be shocking or far-fetched to believe the statue of Ben Franklin at his National Memorial could be seen cussing.

And I wouldn't blame Trump for cussing under his breath as he watched the trap set for him take shape on debate night in the city of brotherly love. As the former and hopefully future president debated his opponent, it was not only Donald J. Trump's inalienable rights that were interfered with, but also those same rights of - *We the People*.

That they did it at all - is no great surprise. That it was brazenly executed was a slight shock. But the fact that it was done in the matter it was done is both a bold and criminal act. And how we react will determine if we allow ourselves to be led, like sheep, *to the slaughter*.

Pre-debate, I wondered and scratched my head when I caught a shot of Kamala walking confidently with the potential first gentleman as a member of the press shouted to her a rare question, *"Are you ready for the upcoming debate?"* She kept walking, but it was in the way that she answered that told me all I needed to know. With great confidence and, dare I say, an air of cockiness, she looked back and answered, *"I'm ready."* It was the fact that she said anything at all that alarmed me. This woman who can barely answer any question without turning it into a word salad extravaganza, her cockiness, made me flashback to a time leading up to the 2020 election as I watched Biden sit in circles as horns honked from a few supporters while Trump packed stadiums. His arrogance and self-assurance were evident- even saying the quiet part out loud, "We have put together the most extensive and inclusive VOTER FRAUD organization" in the *history of American politics."*

"I'm ready." Words spoken by a woman who hardly ever looks ready for anything. Definitely not any random questions.

As I watched the Debate unfold, I thought of that Biden smirk and Kamala's cocky response.

Then it hit me. Sure, she was ready. And so too were the two moderators – one a fellow Sorority Sister of Kamala Harris and the other a man who made up a team of network news readers and propagandists who *gave Kamala 100 % favorable coverage and Trump 93 percent negative coverage.*

In Franklin's world, the intention of the founders for a scene and stage like this was simple. Two members of an impartial press were chosen to ensure that America and the American people were getting the news straight in a debate that would help choose the next president of the United States. But that charade of fairness and impartiality was over quickly and came crashing down with a thud - as the words that Franklin and his fellow brethren of great minds who painstakingly and with great care created these documents as a map for us to be a republic…if we could keep it.

On this night I had my doubts as I watched with anguish as a plethora of Kamala's lies went un-fact checked. Sadly, that is not a surprise. She served a platter of lies to the American people – leftover lies…the BLOODBATH LIE…THE PROJECT 2025 LIE…THE J-6 LIES, and finally, the CHARLOTTESVILLE LIE that got her boss to run. All Lies. All DEBUNKED by everyone everywhere. But not on this night. They would let it all go and with it they burned down the first amendment rights of a man named Donald J. Trump to speak the truth freely and without interference on a debate stage –that was more like a boxing ring.

And at the end, that was okay with The Donald; this was, after all, Philadelphia, so he channeled his inner ROCKY and did what he and the Rock did best. Fight. Fight. Fight.

All the while, he bit his tongue and seethed, and who could blame him if he looked mad at times as they fact-checked him the way the NAZIS interrogated JEWS in NAZI Germany. Muir …cockily and absurdly fact-checking Trump even to the point of questioning that he detected no sarcasm in one of TRUMP's responses about accepting the results of the 2020 election.

Still, the fighter that was Trump fought on against the lies slung by a vapid and empty suit named Kamala and the partial moderators.

The record will show that Trump was fact-checked a number of times, and with each case, there is more than enough evidence that Trump was right and, in essence, telling the truth in each instance. Especially in regards to abortions being carried out in the ninth month and beyond, as evidenced by the ghoulish actions of the former Governor of Virginia Northam, a practice the current Vice President Tim Walz has embraced in his state of Minnesota. Finally, the lies of crime being down are fudged numbers, not including FBI stats of California and New York, regarding the cats and dogs and geese being eaten by Haitians – time will tell, something Trump said on the debate stage. At the time of this writing, there have been reports made by some citizens that some of these heinous acts actually took place. Once again – we will have to wait to see if Trump was right again like he was about the Russian Collusion being a lie, *Hydroxychloroquine and Ivermectin* working to battle Covid-19, and Hunter's laptop being real and not some disinformation that 51 clowns and experts on the payroll of the deep state claimed was Russian interference.

And while they fact-checked even TRUMP's sarcasm- they were not the least bit curious as Harris lied early and often. For that reason, I invite everyone to fact-check Harris and a number of big, fat, juicy lies she told with a straight face. And not once was she fact-checked. Maybe that doesn't bother you, but perhaps you should at least be a little curious about the big lies she told on this night.

- Charlottesville - *Good People on Both Sides* - *DEBUNKED BIGLY*
- 2025 Project - Trump has his own platform. It's called MAGA; America First, Agenda 47 This is a *STUPID ASS LIE.*
- Blood bath was him not calling for violence but referring to what would happen to auto industry if EV vehicles were mandated *LIAR-LIAR PANTS ON FIRE*

- J-6 – Trump never sent or called for armed assault on capitol –instead asked supporters to Peacefully and Patriotically protest *BIG ASS LIE*

There were so many more, but the one that got me was the one she told about Trump rallies being boring, with many people leaving exhausted. That's simply not true. They are a phenomenon. Well-attended "love fests" that she wishes she could hope to draw in terms of attendance and energy. What's really sad is that the candidate, who is a candidate to play a KAREN or a MEAN GIRL in a HOLLYWOOD Production, had a chance to be civil. It would have earned her points, too, if she said something like this. *"Mr. President, let me just say on behalf of all Americans we are glad you are okay and our sympathies for Corey, who was heroic American who loved coming to your rallies and he was sadly and tragically taken on that day as he died a hero."*

Could you imagine if she said that? She was the only one who had the chance to say it. Instead, she was petty and mean. And Trump did something so many of his detractors fault him for not doing: he was, for the most part, a gentleman, taking the high road while Kamala did what does best –take the low road in her hungry quest for power.

What would Jack Kennedy do – had he been at a debate with an opponent who had faced bullets? Jack would have said something charming and sincere and won the day with his kindness and wit. Not with a sharp tongue filled with rehearsed hateful rhetoric.

Sure, Trump was mad. Who could blame him?

The truth will come out, and apparently, it is already starting to rear its beautiful and stubborn head thanks to a whistleblower at ABC – who is on record as saying that Kamala was given similar questions to the ones asked on debate night. But that was not all; in the agreement, allegedly, she would not be fact-checked or asked certain questions, while Trump would be fact-checked.

And there, ladies and gentlemen, you have it. A headline I don't ever want to see:

THE DEBATE: IT WAS RIGGED!

And I know that's not news to some of you voters in red, white, or even blue America. But it's a frightening, sad, and infuriating truth about the America that we live in today. And I know, I don't even have to look, but that Franklin statue in Philadelphia is cussing like a boxer who lost a fight on a bad fixed split decision.

But fret not. The fight is not lost, nor is it over - because our fighter is still standing and fighting for us and the truth.

On this night all those trying for years to massage Trump into the perfect candidate, with perfect debating skills and answers, a perfect temperament —the perfect gentleman and president got a more reserved Trump. Yet they still don't get it or him. On this night- yes, he was more presidential. Less volatile. Harris the mean girl. See you got your wish. Trump, for the most part, was gentlemanly. That he looked angry- shouldn't he be? Aren't you angry?

For the journalists and candidate Harris, this was a performance. Nothing they did on that stage rose to the heights of anything that resembled good old-fashioned reportage or resembled anything that would *prevent any of us from being led to the slaughter*. These two FAKE Journalists who make up FAKE NEWS opened the gate to the slaughterhouse, took the sheers in their hands, and tried to slaughter Donald Trump and all of us on debate night.

Forget about the dogs and cats for a moment – being eaten or not by Haitian illegal immigrants, they are trying to eat and get us. Sorry if you don't get that- but that's a metaphor. They hate Trump, and they hate us. Yes, they think we are *Deplorables*. And that's why a man named Bobby Kennedy Jr, a man named Elon Musk, and a woman named Tulsi Gabbard left the Democrat party that was once led by giants named Jack and Bobby. They were men who saw the real people and fought for them and their Constitutional rights. And yes, they even took a bullet for them.

I tried to imagine a man like JFK and RFK sitting ringside at this debate. They would have been infuriated at the unfairness of this debacle and surely be ashamed of the press. The press. Now, a punchline in a bad joke. No longer the first line of defense for our Constitutional rights.

And with a stacked deck, we all lose. When the press participates and has a rooting interest- the press is dead. Sadly, just like one of those dogs and cats killed in Ohio. What? That's farfetched. What's more likely? Finding a free and fair press in America today or discovering a Haitian who ate a dog or cat in Ohio?

Yes, we have to be able to laugh. Especially when the facts of how far we have sunk is almost too hard to report.

In the days that followed the debate, as the hardest working candidate in the history of American politics was taking a little time to hit a golf ball on a course, he built that bears his name in West Palm Beach, Florida- another lunatic was ready to take another shot at him. Once again, Trump dodged another bullet. But was this just another mulligan? The last Mulligan? I think not. They will try again. And the reason is not hard to figure out. Within hours of the second Trump Assassination attempt, the vitriol was being shot in his direction, not from sickos hiding behind the anonymity of their laptops or cell phones, but out in public, a former first lady named Clinton spewed hatred —even instructing the media to stay focused on a narrative that paints Trump as being dangerous and a threat to Democracy.

What do you think happens when that HATE is repeated and repeated and repeated 24 hours a day, seven days a week on news outlets, in halls of government, on college campuses, purveyed and packaged by Hollywood, and served up even at church coffee hours?

Bullets are fired by wacko nut jobs who think it's a good idea to rid the world of an evil and man named Trump. Evil acts are justified and America becomes a place that I am neither proud of nor recognize. An idea and place created by great people who founded it fought for it, and made it the symbol of a place where dreams come true. In today's America, the dreams for many have turned into dystopian nightmares. Surely today's America is no Capra movie. And the furthest thing from Bedford Falls. That's an America that Trump wants to return to and make great again for all Americans.

And when I heard the news in a poll that some 20% or so of Americans said that *it would be a good thing if Donald Trump was assassinated,* I was at first saddened and angered. But I was not shocked. I have seen the hatred directed and shot at him for years. And I've felt it directed at me and many of us in MAGA nation who have faced our own shots. *We the people* who see this man for what he truly is. A great American. A great President. A great fighter. Fighting for the forgotten men and women in America. A man that men like Washington, Lincoln, Jefferson, Franklin, and the Kennedy brothers would have admired for doing the one thing that none of those who hate him could ever do.

And that's fighting authentically with every ounce of energy - even to the death for a country and people he loves that much. Yes, the ghost of Patrick Henry is alive and still fighting in the person of Donald J. Trump. That's why they hate him so much and want to *get Trump*. And that's why we love him so much and why we the People…Get Trump. *Lambs led to slaughter? Not as long as a man named Donald J. Trump is standing in the way and fighting for all of us.*

Afterword: A Cry for Transparency & Fair Elections

Something Bobby Kennedy said about his Dad and Uncle really got to me. He spoke about how they would be outraged if a candidate failed to give press conferences and shunned debates on the way to applying for the job of President. Going forward, we must not let that happen again. For some candidates like Donald J. Trump, it's easy - he makes himself accessible. He is transparent. He goes into hostile environments and asks questions. Just like JFK and RFK did.

Moving forward, we should have two mandatory press conferences per month in July toward Election Day, where each major candidate fields an array of unscripted questions.

Further, this debate nonsense must stop. Here's an idea.

Three Presidential Debates.

One on Domestic Policy. One on Foreign Policy. One Town Hall on both Foreign and Domestic.

One Vice-Presidential Debate.

One debate where all four candidates sit down and have an unscripted chat.

Share the spotlight Media wise:

One debate on Social Media – X, Facebook, Rumble, Etc. in July.
One Debate hosted by Fox and CNN in August.
One Debate hosted by Newsmax, MSNBC & NBC in September.
One Debate hosted by ABC and CBS in October.
One Debate hosted by an array of all media in October.

Finally, One National Election Day, where everyone in America votes, and one limited early voting period. Only allow mail in ballots for absentee and military. Paper ballots and Picture IDs are needed to vote.

More free speech and fairer elections are the remedy to what ails us.

The result will be a more transparent campaign season and trusted result on Election Day and that's good for our country and We the People.

Acknowledgements and One very special number

For mom and dad who always loved America and taught me how to love it. And for all my family, friends and unsung patriots out there who battled and fought a little longer to help make America great, brighter, and hopeful for all Americans. A special thank you to my Aunt Antonia who taught me to love and respect the power of words.

These numbers add up. At least for me. 316. A number that may save us all. John 3:16 is, of course a very important verse in the bible: *"For God so loved the world that he gave his one and only Son, that whoever believes in him shall not perish but have eternal life."* As I handed in the original manuscript of this book to the publisher –the page count was *316*. And when I visited Palm Beach, I passed by Mar-a-Lago; I wondered and checked my GPS to see how far it was from Donald J. Trump's home to my home in Sarasota. The number miraculously was - you guessed it- *316*. Just a hunch, but I'm hoping and praying that number 316 is one we see on Election Night for President Trump.

A special thank you to my Aunt Antonia who taught me to love and respect the power of words

Front and Back Cover Design by Adam J. Batko

[1] [Conservative lawmakers unleash on CNN initially downplaying Trump assassination attempt | Fox News](#)*

[2] [https://washingtonstand.com/news/election-interference-google-scrubs-trump-assassination-attempt-from-autocomplete-result](#)**

[3] [HHRG-118-FD00-20230720-SD011.pdf (congress.gov)](#)

[4] Michael Charles, author of *Save America Now, Rules for Conservatives, and the Birth Famine* has some thoughts of who won the election in 2020.

[5] [It's Official: The Election Was Secure | Brennan Center for Justice](#)

[6] [Read: Former President Donald Trump's January 6 speech | CNN Politics](#)

[7] [George Gershwin – Let's Call the Whole Thing Off Lyrics | Genius Lyrics](#)

[8] [History of Richmond, Virginia - Wikipedia](#)

[9] [Talking Heads – Life During Wartime Lyrics | Genius Lyrics](#)

[10] [Lewis's trilemma - Wikipedia](#)

[11] Lee Strobel, The Case for Faith: A Journalist Investigates the Toughest Objections to Christianity

[12] Lee Strobel, The Case for a Creator: A Journalist Investigates Scientific Evidence That Points Toward God

[13] [Sean Penn Doubles Down on Mandatory Vaccination on Set and in Theaters (variety.com)](#)

[14] [Howard Stern Is Woke, Tells Off Critics: I Am Anti-Trump, Pro-Vaccine (variety.com)](#)

[15] [Gene Simmons rips anti-vaxxers: 'If you're willing to walk among us unvaccinated, you are an enemy' (thehill.com)](#)

[16] [Jimmy Kimmel jokes hospitals shouldn't treat patients who used ivermectin for COVID-19 treatment - CBS News](#)

[17] [The Vax-Scene - The Box Set - YouTube](#)

[18] Biden Officials Pressed Trans Medical Group to Change Guidelines for Minors, Court Filings Show - The New York Times (nytimes.com)

[19] You Can't Take It with You (film) - Wikiquote

[20] MSNBC's Joy Reid says Black people will look 'real weird' not voting for Kamala Harris (nypost.com)

[21] Academy Museum Backers Baffled by Lack of Jewish Representation (rollingstone.com)

[22] Opinion | When Representation Forgets to Include the Jews - The New York Times (nytimes.com)

[23] Eisenhower's farewell address - Wikipedia

[24] Jill Biden pitches the benefits of age on the campaign trail | CNN Politics

[25] Behar admits she holds back criticism of Biden, Maher tells her that's how 'you lose all credibility' (msn.com)

[26] End NYC's migrant crime crisis with sanctuary city law vote (nypost.com)

[27] Trump jokes he's been indicted 'more than Al Capone' at Iowa rally (youtube.com)

[28] FLASHBACK: Biden Tells Migrants To 'Surge to the Border' (freebeacon.com) (28)

[29] Remarks by President Biden on Supporting Ukraine, Defending Democratic Values, and Taking Action to Address Global Challenges | Vilnius, Lithuania | The White House

[30] Trump in victory speech: 'The forgotten men and women of our country will be forgotten no longer' | The Week

[31] Remarks by President Trump at the 2020 United States Military Academy at West Point Graduation Ceremony – The White House (archives.gov)

[32] Bruce Springsteen – Born in the U.S.A. Lyrics | Genius Lyrics

[33] Behar admits she holds back criticism of Biden, Maher tells her that's how 'you lose all credibility' | Fox News

[34] The Story Behind One of the Greatest Theme Songs in the History of Broadcasting - The Rush Limbaugh Show

35 Fact Check: Has Bill Gates Advised Eating Crickets to 'Stay Healthy'? - Newsweek

36 Answers to your questions about transgender people, gender identity, and gender expression (apa.org)

37 Queer - Wikipedia (37

38 What is Intersex? | Definition of Intersexual (plannedparenthood.org)

39 Asexuality – Parenting Rainbow Kids

40 Six ways to be an ally to asexual people (stonewall.org.uk)

41 Obama: I'd Be Fine with a Third Term If There Was Someone Who Would've Been a Stand-In with an Ear Piece :: Grabien News / Dec 1, 2020 / By Joseph Diaz

42 Jill Biden tells The View voters will 'choose good over evil' in 2024 and claims it's Trump who 'can't put a sentence together' | Daily Mail Online

43 Takeaways from special counsel's report into Biden's handling of classified documents | CNN Politics

44 Jill Biden supports Joe after debate: 'You did such a great job' (usatoday.com)

45 Biden says he is 'first black woman to serve with a black president' in latest gaffe (nypost.com)

46 Opinion | George Clooney: I Love Joe Biden. But We Need a New Nominee. - The New York Times (nytimes.com)

47 Being There (1979) - Quotes - IMDb

48 The full text of Biden's letter on exiting the presidential election race | US Election 2024 News | Al Jazeera

49 Why Biden finally called it quits in 'withdrawal by a thousand cuts' (nypost.com)

50 Kamala Harris defends Biden's intelligence when pressed on mental sharpness: 'He is extraordinarily smart' | Fox News

51 Report on Biden's memory is wrong, White House says | Reuters

52 Kamala Harris spent months shooting down concerns over Biden's mental competency | Fox News

53 Biden's mental sharpness and physical health doubted, Post-ABC poll shows - The Washington Post

54 https://youtu.be/lEFt-rD8gro?si=jitle4i_aEtr29lP

55 White House Calls Biden Videos 'Fake', Sparking Republican Outrage - Newsweek

56 Quote by Harry Truman: "Show me a man that gets rich by being a politic..." (goodreads.com)

57 Al Gore's Doomsday Clock Expires & Climate Change Fanatics Are Wrong Again | National Review

58 Border Crisis: Bill Clinton Says 'There Is a Limit' to How Many Migrants U.S. Can Take | National Review

59 1995 State of the Union Address - Wikipedia

60 Address to the Nation on Immigration Reform | The American Presidency Project (ucsb.edu)

61 Obama Leaves Behind a Mixed Legacy on Immigration (nbcnews.com)

62 How Trump will stop the invasion at our southern border (thehill.com)

63 FLASHBACK: Biden Tells Migrants To 'Surge to the Border' (freebeacon.com)

64 Trump met with Laken Riley's family backstage before Georgia rally | Fox News

65 Biden Regrets Calling an Undocumented Immigrant 'an Illegal' - The New York Times (nytimes.com)

66 Trump blasts Biden over Laken Riley's death | AP News

67 Immigration officials ordered to not use 'alien' - The Washington Post

68 SimplyBible.com https://www.simplybible.com › f75c-pques-pilates-que...

69 1984 Quotes: The 30 Best & Most Important Lines From 1984 (fourminutebooks.com)

70 "They're not after me, they're after you, and I just happen to be standing in the way." -Trump (youtube.com)

71 Joy Reid says she'd vote for a comatose Joe Biden (thehill.com)

72 Whoopi Goldberg Says She'd Vote for Biden Even If He 'Pooped His Pants' - Newsweek

73 Corey Comperatore ID'd as Trump rally shooting victim (nypost.com)

74 Melania Trump issues first statement after assassination attempt against husband (msnbc.com)

75 Former AG Barr: Dems need to stop with 'existential threat' rhetoric about Trump | Fox News

76 https://sashastone.substack.com/p/the-lawfare-made-me-a-trump-supporter?

77 Tucker Carlson Republican National Convention | Rev

78 Kai Trump defends grandfather, Donald Trump in RNC speech (usatoday.com)

79 Whoopi Goldberg Speaks On Kai Trump's RNC Speech (theroot.com)

80 The View's Joy Behar sparks furious backlash after branding Donald Trump a 'narcissist' and questioning his Christian faith in wake of assassination attempt: 'She should be fired' | Daily Mail Online

81 Joy Reid questions Trump's injuries, suggests it could have been 'glass' that hit former president | Fox News

82 A Minute by Minute Account of the Shooting at Donald Trump's Rally | Chicago News | WTTW

83 Sound of Freedom | Rotten Tomatoes

84 'Sound of Freedom': Box Office Triumph for QAnon Believers (rollingstone.com)

85 Judgment at Nuremberg (1961) - Spencer Tracy as Chief Judge Dan Haywood - IMDb

86 HHRG-118-JU01-Wstate-RodasT-20230426.pdf (house.gov)

87 50 million people worldwide in modern slavery | International Labour Organization (ilo.org)

88 Actor Jim Caviezel proclaims Trump 'the new Moses' after visiting him at Bedminster | The Independent (the-independent.com)

89 Abortion | Gallup Historical Trends

90 Dave Chappelle's Pro-Life Perspective | National Review

⁹¹ JD Vance defends 'childless cat ladies' comment after backlash (bbc.com)

⁹² Bill Maher: Being Pro-Choice Is Being 'Okay' with Murder | National Review

⁹³ Over 63 million abortions have occurred in the US since Roe v. Wade decision in 1973 | Fox News

⁹⁴ HHRG-115-JU10-Wstate-ParkerS-20171101-SD001.pdf (congress.gov)

⁹⁵ https://www.independent.co.uk/news/world/americas/us-politics/trump-afghanistan-us-service-members-b1916928.html

⁹⁶ From Benjamin Franklin to Benjamin Vaughan, 14 March 1785 (archives.gov)

⁹⁷ Here's what 'insurrection,' 'coup' and 'sedition' mean | CNN Politics

⁹⁸ Jan. 6 Capitol riot: Hundreds of convictions, but major mystery is unsolved | AP News

⁹⁹ Capitol rioter awaiting sentencing dies by suicide, coroner says (nbcnews.com)

¹⁰⁰ Aunt of January 6 defendant who died by suicide speaks to Congress (youtube.com)

¹⁰¹ Commentary: The Suicide of a January 6 Defendant; 'They Broke Him' - Tennessee Star

Harvard University - Wikipedia

¹⁰² Joe Scarborough: 'F-You' If You Don't Believe This Is The Best Biden Ever (newsbusters.org)

¹⁰³ Who Is Corey Comperatore? Trump Rally Victim Killed Identified - Newsweek

¹⁰⁴ 'Our people matter most': Marco Rubio pays tribute to firefighter Corey Comperatore | Pittsburgh Post-Gazett

¹⁰⁵ Trump honoring slain retired firefighter Corey Comperatore by bringing his helmet, jacket onstage for RNC 2024 speech ((nypost.com)

¹⁰⁶ Kamala Harris Tells NBC's Lester Holt 'We've Been To The Border.' He Responds: 'You Haven't' (forbes.com)

¹⁰⁷ Tim Walz previews Trump border wall attack: 'I'll invest in the 30-foot-ladder factory' (nypost.com)

[108] Kamala Harris' views on key issues over the years - WHYY

[109] Zapruder film - Wikipedia

[110] Records show lengths would-be Trump assassin went to prepare | Fox News

[111] Suspected Trump rally shooter visited gun range dozens of times, senator says, as new footage emerges - ABC News (go.com)

[112] Orville L. Hubbard - Wikipedia

[113] Dearborn Historical Museum (thedhm.org)

[114] Dearborn mayor blasts WSJ op-ed calling city 'Jihad Capital' (nbcnews.com)

[115] Democrats criticize Rep. Rashida Tlaib for her pro-Palestinian comments (nbcnews.com)

[116] Operation Mockingbird - Wikipedia

[117] Operation Mockingbird (spartacus-educational.com)

[118] When the Twin Cities Burned, Tim Walz Dithered | National Review

[119] Tim Walz's Wife Said She Wanted To Smell Fires Of The 2020 BLM Riots In Minnesota Because It Was A 'Touchstone' Moment (msn.com)

[120] https://www.washingtonexaminer.com/news/washington-secrets/2710404/shes-dead-shes-dead-jan-6-video-has-new-angle-on-ashli-babbitt-shooting/?

[121] Conspiracy Theory Says Rothschilds, Fed Proponents Sank Titanic - Business Insider

[122] The Twitter Files Reveal an Existential Threat - Imprimis (hillsdale.edu)

[123] President Trump's Interview with Elon Musk on X (youtube.com)

[124] https://www.whitehouse.gov/briefing-room/press-briefings/2024/08/12/press-briefing-by-press-secretary-karine-jean-pierre-67

[125] 'My Parents Taught Me Not To Trust Wealthy People': Michelle Obama, Worth $70M, Slammed For Hypocrisy | IBTimes UK

467

[126] Trump Campaign Trolls Oprah With Her Private Letter to 'Donald' (thedailybeast.com)

[127] Kamala Harris's 2024 DNC Speech: Full Transcript - The New York Times (nytimes.com)*** (127)

[128] Lyrics for Abraham, Martin and John by Dion - Songfacts

[129] RFK Jr. argues that Biden is a bigger threat to democracy than Trump | CNN Politics

[130] RFK Jr. says he's 'suspending' campaign; endorses Trump (newsnationnow.com)

[131] RFK Jr. suspends his presidential bid, backs Donald Trump | AP News

[133] Tulsi Gabbard endorses Donald Trump in 2024 presidential race (thehill.com)

[134] Quote by John F. Kennedy: "So, let us not be blind to our differences--but..." (goodreads.com)

[135] Ephesians 6:11 KJV - Put on the whole armour of God, that ye - Bible Gateway